JAPAN'S NEW REGIONAL REALITY

CONTEMPORARY ASIA IN THE WORLD
David C. Kang and Victor D. Cha, Editors

This series aims to address a gap in the public-policy and scholarly discussion of Asia. It seeks to promote books and studies that are on the cutting edge of their disciplines or promote multidisciplinary or interdisciplinary research but are also accessible to a wider readership. The editors seek to showcase the best scholarly and public-policy arguments on Asia from any field, including politics, history, economics, and cultural studies.

For a complete list of books in the series, see page 321.

Japan's New Regional Reality

GEOECONOMIC STRATEGY IN THE ASIA-PACIFIC

Saori N. Katada

片田さおり

Columbia University Press

New York

Columbia University Press
Publishers Since 1893
New York   Chichester, West Sussex
cup.columbia.edu
Copyright © 2020 Columbia University Press
All rights reserved

Library of Congress Cataloging-in-Publication Data
Names: Katada, Saori N., author.
Title: Japan's new regional reality : geoeconomic strategy in the Asia-Pacific /
Saori N. Katada.
Description: New York : Columbia University Press, [2020] | Includes bibliographical
references and index.
Identifiers: LCCN 2019047405 (print) | LCCN 2019047406 (ebook) | ISBN 9780231190725
(cloth) | ISBN 9780231190732 (paperback) | ISBN 9780231549080 (ebook)
Subjects: LCSH: Regional economics—Japan. | Geopolitics—Japan. | Japan—Foreign
economic relation—Pacific Area. | Pacific Area—Foreign economic relations—Japan. |
Japan—Economic policy—1989– | Pacific Area—Economic conditions.
Classification: LCC HF1602.15.P3 K38 2020 (print) | LCC HF1602.15.P3 (ebook) |
DDC 337.520182/3—dc23
LC record available at https://lccn.loc.gov/2019047405
LC ebook record available at https://lccn.loc.gov/2019047406

Columbia University Press books are printed on permanent and durable acid-free paper.
Printed in the United States of America

Cover image: © Planet Observer/UIG/Bridgeman Images
Cover design: Chang Jae Lee

Contents

List of Figures and Tables   vii
List of Japanese Terms   ix
Acknowledgments   xi
List of Acronyms   xiii

Introduction   1
I   Japan's Regional Geoeconomic Strategy   10
II   Foreign Economic Policy, Domestic Institutions,
and Regional Governance   30
III   Geoeconomics of the Asia-Pacific   45
IV   Transformation in the Japanese Political Economy   66
V   Trade and Investment: A Gradual Path   86
VI   Money and Finance: An Uneven Path   119
VII   Development and Foreign Aid: A Hybrid Path   150
Conclusion   183

Notes   197
Bibliography   263
Index   297

Figures and Tables

Figures

0.1.   GDP of Major Regions and Countries, 1990–2018   4

3.1.   Share of World GDP: United States, China, and Japan, 1960–2018   54

3.2.   Regional GDP and Changing Shares of Japan and China, 1989–2018   59

3.3.   Japan's Export Destinations, 1994–2018   60

3.4.   Growth of Intraregional Trade in Asia, 1985–2018   61

4.1.   Balance Between Private and Public Sectors, 1980–2018   76

4.2.   Keidanren Political Contributions to the LDP and DPJ, 1991–2017   80

4.3.   Outward FDI Flows from Japan by Region, 1985–2017   81

4.4.   Share of Japanese Firms with Overseas Operations and Overseas-to-Total Production Ratio, 1987–2018   82

5.1.   Increase in Bilateral and Regional FTAs, 1958–2018   88

6.1.   Dollar-Yen Exchange Rate, 1980–2019   126

6.2.   Reporting Banks' Foreign Claims in Asia: Japan and Other Advanced Countries, 1984–2018   136

6.3.   Samurai Bond Issuances, 1990–2018   143

7.1.   Total ODA by All Donors to All Recipients, 1995–2017   153

7.2.   Tied, Partially Untied, and Untied Aid, 1979–2017   161

7.3.   Public Opinion Polls on Foreign Aid, 1989–2018   167

Tables

1.1.   Stylized Summary of Japan's Regional Economic Strategy in the Twenty-First Century   24

3.1.   Chronology of Major Economic Events, 1990–2019   46

5.1.   Japan's EPA Partners: Status and Trade Shares as of 2018   95

5.2.   FTA Utilization for Exports in 2014   105

6.1.   Currency Denominations of Japan's Foreign Trade by Region, 1980s and 1990s   127

7.1.   Top Ten ODA Donors, 1985–2002   159

Japanese Terms

amakudari	descending from heaven; government officials obtaining jobs in the private sector or public corporations after retirement
futsū no kuni	normal nation
gaiatsu	foreign pressure
gosō sendan hōshiki	convoy system
gyōsei shidō	administrative guidance
habatsu	Liberal Democratic Party faction
kantei gaikō	Prime Minister's Office diplomacy
Keidanren	Japan Business Federation
keiretsu	business conglomerate
keizai kyōryoku	economic cooperation
kokka kōmuin rinri hō	National Ethics Law for Central Government Public Servants
kūdōka	hollowing out
naiatsu	internal pressure
sanmi ittai	development trinity approach
shingi-kai	advisory (or deliberation) councils
tatewari gyōsei	vertical administration or compartmentalization
tokushu-hōjin	special public corporation

yen-daka	yen appreciation or strong yen
yonshō taisei	four-ministry system
zaimukan	vice minister of international affairs at the Ministry of Finance
zaisei tōyushi	fiscal loan investment program
zoku	Liberal Democratic Party policy tribe

Acknowledgments

I have observed and analyzed Japan and its foreign policy from many vantage points as a scholar, teacher, and Japanese national living outside the country. Now is an exciting time, with Japan facing a new regional reality in the Asia-Pacific as China rises and the U.S. commitment continues to slip. The Japanese government must see a vast opening and step up its regional engagement so that it can keep the regional economic order intact. This is the new challenge that has given rise to Japan's geoeconomic strategy.

When a book project takes as long as this one has taken, the debts the author incurs accumulate so much that there is no way either to repay all of them or to cover everyone in a few pages of acknowledgment. Nonetheless, I would first like to thank all the mentors who have guided me on this project and others over many years. I am especially grateful to Laurie Brand, Jerry Cohen, Ellen Frost, Masahiro Kawai, Tim McKeown, T. J. Pempel, Barbara Stallings, and Shu Urata.

It is probably impossible to list all the brilliant and dedicated scholars, researchers, government officials, journalists, and experts from international organizations, businesses, and NGOs who have given their valuable time to share their insights with me. In particular, I am grateful to Izumi Ohno, Jun'ichi Sugawara, and Akihiko Tamura, who have always been my go-to people when I have questions on Japanese foreign economic policy.

During the writing stage, many of my academic colleagues were kind enough to read my manuscript at various points. In a manuscript review workshop hosted by the Center for International Studies in 2016, discussants Miles Kahler and William Grimes gave me valuable comments. I also thank all the workshop participants for their critiques. As I worked to revise the manuscript, several more people generously provided insightful suggestions; I thank in particular Mireya Solís and Gene Park. Not only are they generous scholars who spent hours reading the manuscript, they are also both my dear coauthors, who make my usually solitary scholar's life much more enjoyable. In addition, I am grateful for the advice of Hyoung-kyu Chey, Jacques Hymans, and Harukata Takenaka, each of whom read some of the chapters. I also benefited greatly from the thorough and constructive suggestions from the two anonymous reviewers at Columbia University Press. I thank the press's editor, Caelyn Cobb, and the series editors, Dave Kang and Victor Cha.

I would not have been able to complete this project if it were not for my intelligent, diligent, and conscientious research assistants. In particularly, Gabrielle (Gabi) Cheung helped me meet the final submission deadline with her amazing research skills and work ethic. I also thank Jun Ishida, Esther Kwon, Alex Yu-Ting Lin, Alex Melnik, Meredith Shaw, Chad Walker, Scott Wilbur, Kirby Wong, and Mingmin Yang. I am grateful for the help of the students in IR412 (Applied Data Science for IR) in 2017 who, guided by Benjamin Graham, helped with the figures and charts.

I would like to thank the School of International Relations at University of Southern California for giving me an academic home for all these years. This book has benefited from generous external funding from the National Endowment for Humanities Fellowship for Advanced Social Science Research on Japan and the Japan-US Friendship Commission. I am grateful as well for fellowship support from the East West Center in Washington, D.C., the Japan Foundation, and the East Asia Institute.

Finally, I feel so lucky to have a wonderful and supportive family: my husband of thirty years, Satoshi, and our beloved daughter, Kay. Our dinner-table discussions always cheer me up and give me energy to think and write about the world.

Acronyms

ABF	Asian Bond Fund
ABMI	Asian Bond Market Initiative
ABO	Asian Bonds Online
ACU	Asian currency unit
ADB	Asian Development Bank
AIIB	Asian Infrastructure Investment Bank
AMF	Asian Monetary Fund
AMRO	ASEAN+3 Macroeconomic Research Office
AMU	Asian monetary unit
APEC	Asia-Pacific Economic Cooperation
ASEAN	Association of Southeast Asian Nations
ASEAN+3	Association of Southeast Asian Nations + China, Japan, and South Korea
BIS	Bank for International Settlements
BITs	bilateral investment treaties
BOJ	Bank of Japan
BRI	Belt-and-Road Initiative
BRICS	Brazil, Russia, India, China, and South Africa
CEFP	Council on Economic and Fiscal Policy

CEP	comprehensive economic partnership
CEPEA	Comprehensive Economic Partnership for East Asia
CGIF	Credit Guarantee Investment Facility
CJK FTA	China-Japan-Korea free trade agreement
CME	coordinated market economy
CMI	Chiang Mai Initiative
CMIM	Chiang Mai Initiative Multilateralization
CPE	comparative political economy
CPTPP	Comprehensive and Progressive Agreement for the Trans-Pacific Partnership
DAC	Development Assistance Committee
DPJ	Democratic Party of Japan
EHP	Early Harvest Program
EMEAP	Executives' Meeting of East Asia-Pacific Central Banks
EPAs	economic partnership agreements
EPC	engineering, procurement, and construction
ERPD	Economic Review and Policy Dialogue
EVSL	Early Voluntary Sectoral Liberalization
FDI	foreign direct investment
FILP	Fiscal Investment Loan Program
FSA	Financial Services Agency
FSF	Financial Stability Forum
FTAAP	Free Trade Area of the Asia Pacific
FTAs	free trade agreements
GATS	General Agreement on Trade in Services
GATT	General Agreement on Tariffs and Trade
GCC	Gulf Cooperation Council
GDP	gross domestic product
G20	Group of 20
ICCLC	International Civil and Commercial Law Center
IFB	International Finance Bureau
IIAs	international investment agreements
IMF	International Monetary Fund

IPE	international political economy
IPR	intellectual property rights
ISDS	investor-state dispute settlement
JA	Japan agricultural cooperatives
JACEAP	Japan-ASEAN Comprehensive Economic Partnership Agreement
JBIC	Japan Bank for International Cooperation
JETRO	Japan External Trade Organization
JICA	Japan International Cooperation Agency
JOCV	Japan Overseas Cooperation Volunteers
LDP	Liberal Democratic Party
LME	liberal market economy
MAFF	Ministry of Agriculture, Forestry, and Fisheries
MAI	Multilateral Agreement on Investment
MDB	multilateral development bank
MDGs	Millennium Development Goals
METI	Ministry of Economy, Trade, and Industry
MITI	Ministry of International Trade and Industry
MMM	mixed-member majoritarian
MOF	Ministry of Finance
MOFA	Ministry of Foreign Affairs
NAFTA	North American Free Trade Agreement
NDB	New Development Bank
NEXI	Nippon Export and Investment Insurance
NGO	nongovernmental organization
NPL	nonperforming loan
ODA	official development assistance
OECD	Organisation for Economic Co-operation and Development
OECF	Overseas Economic Cooperation Fund
OEP	open economy politics
OREI	Office of Regional Economic Integration
PAFTAD	Pacific Trade and Development Conference
PBEC	Pacific Basin Economic Council
PECC	Pacific Economic Cooperation Council

PFM	prospective founding member
PPP	public-private partnership
PTAs	preferential trade agreements
RCEP	Regional Comprehensive Economic Partnership
RCI	regional cooperation and integration
REMU	Regional Economic Monitoring Unit
RMB	renminbi
RTAs	regional trade agreements
SDGs	sustainable development goals
SDRs	Special Drawing Rights
SMEs	small and medium enterprises
SNTV	single nontransferable vote system
SOEs	state-owned enterprises
STEP	special terms of economic partnership
TPA	trade promotion authority
TPP	Trans-Pacific Partnership
TRIMs	Agreement on Trade-Related Investment Measures
TRIPs	Agreement on Trade-Related Aspects of Intellectual Property Rights
UNDP	United Nations Development Program
WTO	World Trade Organization

JAPAN'S NEW REGIONAL REALITY

Introduction

"Japan is back," proclaimed Prime Minister Shinzō Abe in a speech in Washington, D.C., in February 2013, as he promised a more active Japan in the realms of economic and foreign policy. The Japan that has returned, however, is not the same Japan that used to engage in trade conflicts with the United States twenty-odd years ago, and this new Japan influences the Asia-Pacific region in ways that are quite different from the past. In this book I argue that the Japanese government has, for the two decades since the 1990s, shifted its regional geoeconomic strategy from one based on neomercantilism (promoting the country's industries) to a more liberal one that aims to set rules and establish institutions for the region's public good.

The new realities of both regional and domestic dynamics have motivated this shift. Regionally, the rise of China and the growing economic conflict between the United States and China in the twenty-first century have created an economic environment where Japan can gain more regional influence by siding with the United States in support of a U.S.-led liberal regional order in Asia. Domestically, the country's political economy has been transformed, particularly with the increased distance between the Japanese government and globalized businesses since the bubble economy burst in the early 1990s. The changes in the leading political parties, the administrative and economic reforms, and the globalization of Japanese businesses all represent powerful elements of this transformation. These are also signs that the nature of the Japanese state has changed: although the country still pursues economic growth, its big businesses are now globalized and no longer rely on the government's direct support to operate competitively. What today's Japanese globalized businesses would welcome, rather, are measures that help to "level the playing field," such as economic rules protective of property rights and open access to global markets and business opportunities, as well as stable legal, political, and financial environments in which to operate.

To sustain its relevance in the economic realm, the Japanese government has shifted its regional strategy in support of these necessities and toward obtaining a strategic upper hand against its rival, China, as the leader in regional economic governance. In turn, these strategies have led Japan to become much more supportive of U.S.-led neoliberal policies, as evidenced by the Japanese government's decision to join the Trans-Pacific Partnership (TPP) negotiations in 2013. As this strategy is implemented, however, domestic politics and institutional structures have influenced policy making differently in various economic issue areas. Japan's transformational path is an example of how institutions and their path dependence heavily influence the state's adjustment to the external challenges.

Geoeconomics of the Asia-Pacific

Geoeconomics examines the use of economic instruments by governments in pursuit of national goals as they cultivate economic and political advantages in economic growth, competitiveness, and sustainability.[1] There has been a revival in geoeconomics as a way to understand international relations as China's economic and political challenges become major concerns for the status quo powers of the United States and its allies. Couched in this line of investigation, this study examines Japan's regional geoeconomic strategy and focuses on the shifts that have taken place since the mid-1990s. As elaborated in chapter 1, a country's regional geoeconomic strategy determines its strategic direction in pursuit of national goals and establishes the framework in which concrete foreign economic policy decision making takes place.

The politico-economic conditions surrounding Japan and the Asia-Pacific have dramatically changed in the quarter-century since the early

1990s. After being hailed as a miracle economy and feared for the dominance of its currency around the world, Japan began to stagnate after its economic bubble burst. Despite multiple efforts to stimulate the economy, including the round of Abenomics from 2013 through 2019 (the time of this writing), however, the country has yet to revive a sufficient level of economic growth—the primary objective of this massive policy stimulus. Meanwhile, the changing dynamics between the United States and China have dominated the geopolitical and geoeconomic landscape of the Asia-Pacific. The U.S. presence in Asia in both military and economic realms remains significant even after the end of the Cold War, but the ebb and flow of U.S. commitment to the region has raised concerns among its traditional allies, such as Japan.[2] At the same time, other important events such as the War on Terror and the global financial crisis (2008–2009) have vastly undermined the U.S. economic presence in the region. Nonetheless, as observed in the International Monetary Fund's (IMF) influence at the time of the Asian financial crisis (1997–1998) and China's accession to the World Trade Organization (WTO) in 2001, the influence of U.S.-led multilateral institutions continued to loom large in the region. Most recently and despite this dominance, there are signs of the United States pulling back again. After the U.S. rebalancing strategy under the Barack Obama administration failed to gain traction and achieve economic leadership, incoming president Donald Trump pulled the United States out of the now-defunct, region-wide free trade and investment agreement known as the TPP.

A striking feature of the region during this period has been the dynamic growth of many Asian economies, particularly that of China. Despite a temporary shock from the Asian financial crisis in the late 1990s, the region's economic growth and dynamic transformation continued (figure 0.1). China's entry into the WTO spurred its economic growth, and the country's confidence continued to grow after the global financial crisis in the late 2000s. By 2010 China had overtaken Japan as the world's second largest economy (and hence the largest economy in Asia) in terms of nominal gross domestic product (GDP) (chapter 3). China also began to "go global" in the twenty-first century.[3] With a massive accumulation of foreign exchange reserves and increasing excess capacity, China has begun to invest outward and extend loans and currency swaps to countries around the world.[4] Now one can easily see China's swelling presence in the region, from infrastructure investment and economic cooperation to regional institution building.

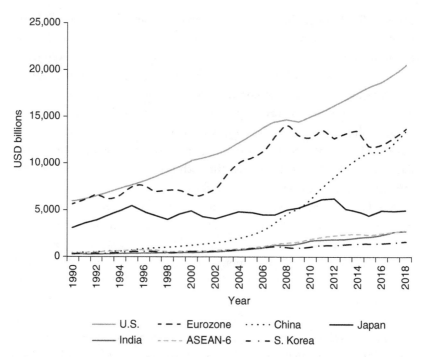

Figure 0.1 GDP of Major Regions and Countries, 1990–2018. ASEAN-6 includes Indonesia, Malaysia, the Philippines, Singapore, Thailand, and Vietnam.
Source: IMF, "World Economic Outlook: GDP, Current Prices, Billions of U.S. Dollars," https://www.imf.org/external/datamapper/NGDPD@WEO/OEMDC/ADVEC/WEOWORLD.

Furthermore, China's aggressive stance when dealing with regional maritime disputes, most notably in the South and East China Seas, has distressed many countries in the region, including Japan.

It was in this domestic and regional context that the Japanese government began to adopt a new, more liberal regional geoeconomic strategy. The intent was to gain advantages in Asia's regional economic competition in the midst of expanding Chinese influence and the increasingly precarious commitment from the United States. The region's growth and stability are vital for Japan's long-term prosperity and security, and thus the government strives to maintain its influence in the region while engaging (with the hope of prevailing over) China. To this end, Japan's regional geoeconomic strategy has been an essential component of regional economic integration and development in East Asia.

Japan's State-Led Liberal Strategy and Its Implementation

Geoeconomic dynamics have imposed external pressure on the Japanese government to adopt what I call a "state-led liberal strategy." As will be discussed extensively in chapter 1, this strategy aims for a high level of economic rule setting in the region. The government has also become increasingly interested in formal rules and regional institution building in all economic issue areas, ranging from trade to investment to financial affairs. Such a strategy is the best way for Japan, with its relatively large economy (second in the world until 2010, and third largest after the United States and China since then), to take advantage of its current position, both geographically and economically, in the face of the U.S.-China rivalry. Japan can use its strategy to shift the balance between the two great powers and can also cast the deciding vote to shape the regional economic order.

At the same time, this strategy is the inevitable outcome of Japan's economic maturity. As will be discussed in chapter 1, Japan continues to pursue economic growth, but in recent decades the country has had to look to the nearby regional economy in search of profitable investment opportunities and new manufacturing bases. The Japanese government, therefore, pursues the regional geoeconomic strategy in order to establish advantageous conditions for Japanese business operations in East Asia. In the process, it has had to face the challenges of a "disembedded" state, as Japanese businesses are no longer under the direct guidance of the state, and economic resources at the government's disposal are limited. Furthermore, the fragmented structure of the bureaucracy, which lacks the glue previously provided by businesses, has made it difficult for the government to pursue coherent policies under this new liberal economic strategy.

As such, Japanese foreign economic policy is moving into uncharted territory. While Japan is arguably a unique case, it is also a harbinger of what's to come for many more interventionist states in the region and beyond. On the one hand, not many countries have Japan's economic size, which allows it to single-handedly influence the system, and none of the larger countries that have adopted a developmentalist strategy have achieved the level of economic maturity that Japan has. Additionally, Japan faces rapid demographic aging and holds a precarious but influential position between the United States and China. No other country seems to operate under these same conditions. On the other hand, Japan is the forerunner of what is possibly in the works for many so-called developmental states that have achieved high levels of economic development. From South Korea to Taiwan to Indonesia to China, the importance of economic growth continues to agonize political leaders and government elites. As these countries reach their economic plateau where marginal return on investment stagnates, their governments are plagued with the problem of excess savings and capacity, which must be utilized effectively in order to secure further economic growth. Some of the worrisome signs are already visible in China's Belt-and-Road Initiative (BRI), as the Chinese leadership is in a tremendous rush to broaden the country's economic reach to expand external markets and investment sites for growth. So far China has taken a mercantilist approach in most areas, but there are signs that the country, in the long run, would also be interested in its own version of "liberal world order" to open other markets once it is at the top of the global economic pecking order. Meanwhile, all states that outgrow developmentalism will experience its persistence in the forms of institutional rigidity, vested interests, and developmental norms.

Book Outline

Chapter 1 lays out the main argument of this book. It first defines the concept of regional geoeconomic strategy. After reviewing the discussion on Japan's foreign policy characteristics in both historical and comparative terms, the chapter analyzes the shift of the Japanese government's regional geoeconomic strategy from one that is bilateral, informal, and based on embedded mercantilism to one that is based on a regional and formal approach and on global and liberal standards.

Chapter 2 discusses foreign economic policy, with particular interest in the systemic and domestic divide in comparative and international political economy. Debates over the transition of a developmental state as well as the variety of capitalism are important parts of the literature on this discussion. The chapter concludes with a discussion on the source of Japan's new state-led liberal regional strategy.

Chapter 3 focuses on the changing geoeconomic environment in the Asia-Pacific, with an emphasis on the rivalry between the United States and China following the global financial crisis. This rivalry has become critically important in the backdrop of Japan's regional strategy. As the Japanese economy struggles and loses importance within the region, Japan has ironically gained a strategic advantage given the precarious power balance between China and the United States.

Chapter 4 is dedicated to Japan's economic transformation. It first considers the triangle of legislators, bureaucracy, and big businesses and then turns to government-business relations. It is important to point out that the nature of these relationships has shifted over time and has undermined the neomercantilist connection between the two components.

In chapters 5 through 7, I analyze three economic issue areas of the Japanese government's regional geoeconomic strategy. Chapter 5 focuses on trade and investment. Under the stagnant progress in liberalization and rule setting through the WTO and other multilateral efforts, the number of preferential trade agreements and bilateral investment treaties has multiplied in the past quarter-century. The Japanese government's approach to regional trade started in 1989 with establishment of Asia-Pacific Economic Cooperation (APEC), although its policy toward APEC included many of the old-style principles of economic governance, such as a visible reluctance to engage in formal agreements and an animus toward aggressive liberalization. As APEC's liberalization process stalled in 1997–1998 and the region was hit by the Asian financial crisis, the Japanese government began to turn to free trade agreements (FTAs). The government's motivation, choice of early FTA partners, and participation in negotiations for a trilateral investment agreement with China and South Korea all indicate a gradual shift in Japan's trade and investment strategy toward formalization and liberal rule-based arrangements. The competition to establish region-wide FTAs, which began in the late 2000s, continues to this day. The chapter examines the TPP negotiations, of which the Japanese government became the twelfth and last negotiating party to join in July 2013. With the basic agreement concluded in October 2015, the TPP would have been the rule-setter for the region's trade and investment relations. After President Trump withdrew the United States from the agreement in 2017, the Japanese government managed to push forward with regional trade and investment rulemaking through the conclusion of the TPP-11.

On the topic of regional monetary and financial affairs, the subject of chapter 6, the Asian financial crisis unquestionably had the strongest impact in shaping Japan's regional strategy. Until then, the government's regional efforts were very limited and half-hearted, and there was little interest in institution building in Asia. This political atmosphere completely shifted in the aftermath of the Asian financial crisis as the Japanese government took an active lead in proposing an Asian Monetary Fund (which did not materialize) and then in supporting the Chiang Mai Initiative (CMI). The latter has led to a well-defined institution with the ASEAN+3 membership and establishment of the ASEAN+3 Macroeconomic Research Office (AMRO), which serves as its research headquarters. Meanwhile, other monetary and financial efforts progressed, though more informally. The Asian Bond Fund—supported by the Executives' Meeting of East Asia-Pacific Central Banks (EMEAP) and technical assistance led by the Japanese government—has helped to expand bond markets in Asia tenfold in fifteen years. After many attempts across five years beginning in 1999 to increase the use of the Japanese yen gained little support from Japanese businesses, the government finally gave up. This dynamic of Japan's difficulties in managing the market continues as China tries to expand the use of its currency—the renminbi (RMB)—in the region. The lack of business interest in Japan fueled the Japanese government's reluctance to support Chinese government efforts.

Chapter 7 analyzes the Japanese government's regional strategy in foreign aid and developmental support. The institutions to extend foreign aid have long been in place for Japan, and bilateral arrangements continue to dominate in this area, with the exception of Japan's active engagement with the Asian Development Bank. Japan's traditional "economic cooperation" symbolized the mercantilist nature of Japanese aid. While Japan operated as an aid superpower in the 1990s under changing global development norms, the government was pressured to untie its aid procurement from its domestic sources and divert resources from economic infrastructure to the social sector. As the Japanese aid budget was gradually reduced in the 2000s, the government produced a sharper articulation of the country's development and foreign aid objectives, including human security and legal system development in Asia. Meanwhile, private-sector involvement in Japanese developmental assistance has continued, with a different structure. Recently the public-private partnership, instead of tied aid, has become the dominant modality, but the Japanese government has generally had a difficult time expanding that modality. The BRI and Asian Infrastructure Investment Bank (AIIB) initiatives proposed under Chinese leadership introduced other challenges to Japan's regional strategy from 2013. With the participation of fifty-seven founding members around the world, the

AIIB was inaugurated in January 2016, but neither Japan nor the United States has joined. Japan continues to use liberal policy diffusion to its advantage, concomitantly, as it strengthens national financial instruments for Japanese businesses to gain advantage against the spread of BRI projects, a sign of a possible reverse course.

The conclusion wraps up the study with an overview of the pattern of Japan's new regional geoeconomic strategy in three issue areas and a discussion of implications for state-led liberal strategy to diffuse high standards and rules. The contrast of three issue areas provides insights into the importance of domestic institutions. The book concludes by speculating on the impact of Japan's new regional geoeconomic strategy on economic regionalism and regional governance in the Asia-Pacific.

CHAPTER I

Japan's Regional Geoeconomic Strategy

How do we characterize Japan's foreign economic relations and the evolution of its geoeconomic strategy? How does the change of such strategy over time affect the regional economic order in the Asia-Pacific? This chapter places the shift in Japan's regional economic strategy in historical and comparative context.

Economic relations with Asia have long been an important foreign policy consideration for the Japanese government. The U.S. presence in the region throughout the postwar period and Japan's economic dominance there since the 1980s became the basis of Japan's old-style regional geoeconomic strategy, which relied on bilateral ties and capitalized on a mercantilist approach. Such a strategy, however, has given way to a new, state-led, liberal strategy since the late 1990s. This new strategy is characterized by a region-wide orientation with emphasis on formal rules and global standards. The Japanese government has pursued this strategy in all three areas of economic engagement with Asia covered in this study: trade and investment, money and finance, and development and foreign aid. However, the paths that the government has taken to implement the strategy in respective issue areas have varied widely.

This chapter starts with a definition of the concept of regional geoeconomic strategy and discusses the elements that constitute such a strategy. After examining the main characterization of Japan's past regional geoeconomic strategy and in contrast to that of a similarly positioned state, Germany, the next section discusses the new strategy taken by the Japanese government in the twenty-first century as China's power has risen. I argue that Japan's domestic politico-economic transformation presents sufficient conditions for the government to move from the old-style strategy to the new one.

Regional Geoeconomic Strategy

Defining Regional Geoeconomic Strategy

Regional geoeconomic strategy refers to the foreign policy track that a government pursues in the region with a particular set of national goals ranging from the promotion of economic benefits to the maintenance of stability and the enhancement of its influence. Although such a strategy of geoeconomics bears an unmistakably realist tone, economic issues inevitably include multiple transnational ties and participation of many subnational actors in the form of complex interdependence with many actors involved.[1] Despite the relatively coherent strategic direction that has emerged since the late 1990s, the implementation and policies associated with specific issue areas, such as trade, finance, and development, could diverge from the prototype. What is nonetheless common among national and subnational actors is their desire and demand to maintain (and enhance) their respective influence in the region for economic prosperity and stability.

For the Japanese government, the motivations arise not only from narrow material interests but also from domestic political imperatives and the pursuit of influence and leadership. As will be discussed in chapter 3, the Japanese state has gradually "disembedded" or "decoupled" from big businesses as the economy transformed from a catch-up to an advanced one, thus weakening the mercantilist drive of the government. At the same time, the country's search for sources of economic growth continues. Such disembedding makes some geoeconomic strategy difficult to implement as the government loses guidance and control over big businesses' behavior. Given such conditions, three theoretical considerations are especially important in specifying what constitutes a regional geoeconomic strategy.

First, a regional geoeconomic strategy is undertaken by a government in pursuit of national interests and goals. Hence such strategies would be considered part of economic statecraft, with both negative (sanctions and penalties) and positive (support and incentives), as well as defensive and offensive, foreign policy instruments.[2] To protect a country's national interests broadly defined, it is important for governments—particularly those of large countries that have power to influence the system—to support a certain regional order or regional economic governance structure as a public good.[3] Japan's relatively large economic size, especially within the regional economy, leads us to recognize that the "small country" assumption does not apply to Japan. That is, Japan is a large nation that has power to affect and change the system, either deliberately or inadvertently. Regionalism and regional institution building therefore become options for large powers in their regional geoeconomic strategy.[4]

Second, having a regional geoeconomic strategy means that the government utilizes it to manage its geopolitical and geoeconomic challenges, where tensions exist in terms of the struggle to capture relative gains or to prevail in rule-setting competitions.[5] Even though the liberal international economic order supported by the United States since World War II is still a lasting feature of global economic governance, the emergence of new powers such as Japan, China, and other BRICS economies through the course of post–Cold War history makes such geoeconomic challenges more prevalent.[6] This regional strategy could, however, come with various instruments derived not only from the government's direct actions deploying financial resources such as foreign aid or economic sanctions but also from diffuse sources of influence ranging from economic norms and rule setting in the promotion of certain economic models. Moreover, as this study will elaborate in subsequent chapters, the ways that the government can deploy these strategies vary in different issue areas, depending on the particular contours of governmental institutions and government-business relations.

Finally, the statist approach to regionalism in East Asia follows the intergovernmentalism described in European integration analysis, where much of the regional geoeconomic strategy in cooperating and forming regional institutions (i.e., regionalism) is led by top-down government actions.[7] This study focuses on the executive branch of the government, including the prime minister and the Cabinet Office, and ministers and top bureaucrats from the main foreign policy ministries, such as the Ministry of Foreign Affairs (MOFA), the Ministry of Economy, Trade, and Industry (METI), and the Ministry of Finance (MOF), and to a lesser extent governmental special agencies, such as the Japan International Cooperation Agency (JICA). Some actions might involve legislation or ratification, such as FTAs, while most are predominantly influenced by an executive logic rather than a legislative or electoral one.

Despite the overwhelmingly top-down tendency, regional geoeconomic strategy as defined in this study treats "domestic preferences" seriously, as does Andrew Moravcsik.[8] Foreign economic policies and strategies are often embedded in national economic imperatives, whether the strategies have liberalist or mercantilist tendencies seen in "embedded liberalism" or "embedded mercantilism."[9] Domestic political and economic dynamics are often the key in defining governments' preferences and interests in engaging in active (or inactive) foreign policy.[10] Overall, the way in which domestic economic interests are aggregated and channeled to and within the government greatly influences regional geoeconomic strategies. When it comes to the implementation of such regional strategy and the paths that policies develop, Japan's policy-making institutions and government-business relations have become critical in determining the choice of policies as well as their relative effectiveness.

In sum, an analysis of regional geoeconomic strategy provides revealing insights into the positioning of the major actors working to shape regional political economy and governance. The changes in Japan's regional geoeconomic strategy have influenced major transformations and configuration of East Asia's regional economic order since the mid-1990s.

Japanese Foreign Policy Characterization Since 1945

A vast amount of scholarly work has been produced on Japanese foreign policy and its relations with Asia and the world, particularly since the rise of the Japanese economy from the 1970s. From the time of "Japan as Number One" to "cool Japan," scholars, journalists, and experts have captured many aspects of Japanese foreign policy characteristics.[11] Focusing on Japan's pacifist constitution and ambivalence toward its security role, particularly after the end of the Cold War, Japan's foreign policy was based on antimilitarist culture and resorted to "checkbook diplomacy."[12] Having thrived economically under the Yoshida Doctrine as the government focused on economic recovery and growth while relying on the U.S. security umbrella, Japan managed to achieve enormous economic success by the 1980s.[13]

At the pinnacle of Japan's power, the reactiveness of its foreign policy to foreign pressure (*gaiatsu*) was an enigma. Calling Japan a "reactive state,"

Kent E. Calder explains how Japan reacted, though erratically, to foreign pressure in its policy making because of (1) the geopolitical environment and its dependence on the United States, which supported Japan's economic rise, and (2) Japan's own fragmented domestic foreign policy decision-making structure.[14] On the other hand, some scholars saw Japan as a much more pragmatic and strategic foreign policy actor during this period, pointing to its economic successes and focusing on how effectively the Japanese government controlled the economy.[15] Others examined Japan's technological and economic powers and labeled its strategy as "mercantile realism" and "embedded mercantilism."[16] As the Japanese economy stagnated and the animated debate outside of Japan regarding the nature of Japanese foreign policy subsided, new syntheses emerged. David Arase calls Japan an "active state" as it engaged in the war on terror, and Thomas Berger, Mike Mochizuki, and Jitsuo Tsuchiyama title their collective assessment of Japan *Adaptive State*, emphasizing a liberal consensus among the Japanese elite and public on its mission in the world.[17]

Although they are not within the scope of this book, these have been recurrent debates over the direction and priorities of the country's foreign policy within Japan since the beginning of its modern era starting with the Meiji Restoration of 1867, after the arrival of the Black Ship a dozen years earlier.[18] More than a century later, as the Cold War drew to a close, the central debate focused on whether Japan should engage the world as a normal nation (*futsū no kuni*) and build increased global presence in the security field or remain a unique civilian power under the peace constitution.[19] An alternative and predictive approach in the context of Japan's precarious relations with the world is for the country to engage in foreign policy as a middle power.[20]

Over the course of modern history, Japanese foreign policy has adjusted to external environment, and the policies have reflected the domestic institution. As will be discussed in chapter 2, the nexus of external and internal dynamics defines Japan's strategy and its implementation.

Japanese Foreign Policy in Comparative Perspective

How do the tenets of Japanese foreign policy fit in comparison with those of other countries? Scholars often compare Japan and Germany because of the two countries' defeat in World War II; comparative constraints arising from their history of aggression, militarism, and totalitarianism; and their respective postwar economic success.[21] Particularly relevant to this study is the work that focuses on Japan and Germany in the context of their respective regions, Asia and Europe. Under postwar U.S. hegemony, both Asia and Europe were porous regions penetrated by U.S. power.[22] What was strikingly different between them, nonetheless, was the region-wide configuration of security and economy for Western Europe under the Cold War and the stark bilateralism of the hub-and-spoke alliance system for Asia, with the United States as its hub.[23] West Germany began its return to the global community by embedding itself into the American-supported "European project" and by creating strong ties with its longtime regional rival, France. Meanwhile, Japan was detached from China during the Cold War (at least until the late 1970s), while the United States promoted Japan's economic connection to Southeast Asia.[24] Owing to the regional configuration shaped largely by the Cold War, regional integration in East Asia was significantly delayed.

In terms of positioning among major powers within the region, it has been evident for the past several decades that Japan has possessed a potential characteristic of a pivotal (or pivot) state. Geopolitically, such a state is one "that could not only determine the fate of its region but also affect international stability."[25] In the context of policy diffusion, a pivotal state holds both high capability and credibility, which could trigger competitive forces that intensify cascading effects of diffusion.[26] In the twenty-first century, as U.S. hegemonic power in several regions has waned and overlapping spheres of interest have increased, pivot states hold the key to regional stability and norm building.[27] As will be discussed later in this chapter and in chapter 3, Japan has long occupied an important position in East Asia, but its function as a pivotal state in the economic realm heightened in the first two decades of the twenty-first century owing to the rise of China. Positioned between the two great powers of the United States and China and still possessing a large economy, Japan's regional geoeconomic strategy is bound to have measurable influence on regional economic prosperity, stability, and order.

Finally, it is essential for this study to build on the important existing literature on domestic sources of foreign economic policy as it examines Japan's foreign policy characteristics. Democracy and domestic institutions are relevant for foreign economic policy making as they structure the execution, norms, and political foundation.[28] The welfare states of Europe, for example, have implemented foreign policy based on their social welfare norms.[29] Meanwhile, economic imperatives and government-business interaction have also shaped foreign policy. In that sense, Japan shares neo-mercantilist characteristics with European late developers Russia and Germany.[30] Beyond that, one can argue that Japanese industrialization and its geoeconomic strategies have been the model that others have followed. Since the 1930s Japanese geoeconomic strategists saw the country's regional economic expansion in the form of a "flying geese pattern" where gradual technology diffusion takes place based on product cycle.[31] In the process of economic exchanges, explicit learning has taken place among the late-developing nations of Asia to emulate Japan's industrial success.[32] Consequently, an interdependent pattern of foreign economic strategy has emerged among East Asian governments.

The next section focuses on the transformation of the Japanese regional geoeconomic strategy during the quarter-century from the time when Japan was the rising dominant economic power in the 1980s and early 1990s (old style) to the time after the Japanese government's presence, especially in relative terms, contracted in the late 1990s (new style).

The Old-Style Japanese Regional Geoeconomic Strategy

Collaboration between the government and private business sectors of all kinds has been a central feature of Japan's expansion of its global reach in trade and investment since the 1970s. As Japan's regional production network through foreign direct investment (FDI) expanded in Asia, so too did the involvement of the government's "visible handshake" in support of such private efforts.[33] This took the form of foreign investment insurance, administrative guidance, foreign aid, and public funding, conducted through bilateral channels with each Asian country.[34] When questioned in the mid-1990s about why Japan, which then was considered the overwhelmingly dominant economic power in East Asia and was expected to become possibly the next global economic hegemon, resorted to a "bilateral, informal, and interventionist" approach to its foreign economic policy, particularly in Southeast Asia, Peter Cowhey named three suggestive factors:

First, informal diplomacy favors Japan over the rest of the world. Backed by the largest stock of foreign investment, the largest foreign aid flows, major trade flows, and the proximity of being the closest economic superpower, Japan does better than its rivals in the triad by playing by informal rules. Second, there is no set of formal rules that could be written to advance Japanese interests that would neither significantly assist U.S. and European interests more (e.g. stronger defenses of intellectual property) nor articulate a standard of conduct that might seem an overt challenge to Atlantic sentiments. Third, Japanese politics and economics make informal bilateral policies feasible and desirable. They have created the traditions of informal government intervention without extensive formal rules at home and industrial groups that are experienced in building their businesses on developing long standing relationships, not contracts and rules.[35]

Cowhey's three factors are a succinct characterization of Japan's old-style regional geoeconomic strategy. In the early 1990s, at the height of Japan's economic power, the characteristics of the government's regional strategy boiled down to these three vital elements: *bilateralism, informal rules and relations,* and *embedded mercantilism.* These three elements, respectively, constitute the structure, mode of engagement, and underlying values under which the government and its affiliated public institutions dealt with Japan's interaction with Asia.

Bilateralism. The concept of bilateralism has often been invoked in the context of security relations in the Asia-Pacific, where the United States has long deployed a hub-and-spoke system of bilateral alliances with specific partners, including Japan.[36] Thus the experts often cite this concept to describe U.S.-Japan relations. According to T. J. Pempel, bilateralism "means that two countries . . . cede particular privileges to one another that they do not give to other countries."[37] Bilateralism was also the chief modus operandi for the Japanese government to manage relations with its East Asian neighbors. The government had a constant desire, throughout its modern history, to lead the region collectively. But Japan's attempts at regionalism, from the disastrous Greater Co-Prosperity Sphere in the 1930s to the little-noticed Minister Conference for the Economic Development of Southeast Asia of the 1960s, did not succeed, owing to the obstacles of its own war legacy and the Cold War.[38] In addition, the United States was often reluctant to support such multilateral regional efforts.[39] Hence the Japanese government's relationships with the countries in East Asia have historically developed through bilateral channels led, first, by the war reparation efforts of the mid-1950s and, later, by trade and foreign aid activities and the bilateral diplomacy often represented through the Ministry of Foreign Affairs.[40]

Japan was also deeply involved in economic bilateralism with the United States. Japan's heavy trade, capital, and technology dependence on the United States throughout the postwar period, along with its trade surplus with the United States since the mid-1960s, repeatedly pulled the two countries into bilateral trade conflicts and negotiations.[41] These interactions created constant bilateral pressure on Japan to liberalize its economy through "results-oriented" remedies pursued by the U.S. government to correct trade imbalances through trade negotiations and financial liberalization talks.[42] The impressive increase in Japan's outward foreign direct investment since the second half of the 1980s was, in part, an outgrowth of a massive trade surplus, sudden appreciation of the yen after the Plaza Accord of 1985, as well as gradual domestic production cost increases and financial liberalization.[43]

Informal rules and relations. The Japanese government's preference for and strategy of using informal rules and relations during this period reflected first and foremost a general resistance in the region to resorting to legalistic agreements, which was visible in the context of Asia-Pacific Economic Cooperation (see chapter 5).[44] Asia overall is known for having no regional court for regional dispute settlements and for following the "Asian way" of informality and consensus.[45] Formal rules were often (and still are in some cases) seen as the imposition of Western values and a tool of the dominant powers to interfere in and control the internal affairs of Asian countries and compromise their sovereignty.[46] Until the late 1990s the Japanese government rarely utilized a formal or legalistic approach to regional economic matters.[47] During this time the government often emphasized its sensitivities to a developing Asia, protective of its independence and sovereignty norms, as Japan reestablished its relations with the region and avoided formal or legalistic measures. By doing so, Japan saw a definite advantage in resorting to informal rules as it had by far the largest economy in the region and thus its power could largely determine the terms of these negotiations.

The government also refrained from efforts to institutionalize regional arrangements, which would have been a way to construct formal relations.[48] During the late 1980s and into the 1990s, when various regions around the world underwent the "third wave of regionalism," East Asia and the Asia-Pacific saw very little institution building.[49] Some efforts in setting up Asia-Pacific and inclusive (or "open regionalism") institutions emerged in the early 1990s under APEC and the ASEAN Regional Forum, but (as will be discussed in later chapters) it was only in the aftermath of the Asian financial crisis that some exclusively East Asian institutions emerged.[50]

Embedded mercantilism. Pempel coined the term "embedded mercantilism" following the corresponding logic of John Gerard Ruggie, who introduced the concept of "embedded liberalism," where post–World War II free trade liberalism was embedded in the social purpose of a stable economy and compensation for the losers of economic liberalization.[51] For Japan and many East Asian developing economies, the pursuit of a mercantilist export-promotion strategy was embedded in the countries' social contracts to compensate for their nonexporting and weak, uncompetitive sectors.[52] For the export sector and, later, the large national firms investing abroad, the mercantilist government supported their efforts in overseas ventures by providing financial guarantees, subsidies, and even administrative guidance extended internationally.[53]

Those economies, with Japan as the forerunner, have gone through a "catch-up" economic development process with the interventionist state taking a central role in resource mobilization and industrialization strategy.[54] As part of Japan's economic outreach to the Asian region, intranetwork cooperation among the government and businesses established the strategy of "Asia in Japan's embrace."[55] The Japanese government pursued "economic cooperation" under the trinity approach in the region, in which foreign aid provided funding and technical expertise for much-needed physical infrastructure and manufacturing know-how.[56] This approach allowed the government not only to contribute to the recipient countries' economic development but also to profit Japanese businesses both directly (by procurement and contracts) and indirectly (by creating better economic and political environments for Japanese business operations).[57]

Japan's regional economic strategy prior to the mid-1990s was thus based on its path-dependent bilateral institutional preference, which pursued economic growth for Japan by capitalizing on its overwhelming economic power, especially in comparison to other regional players (including China), and utilizing its government-business network on a regional scale.

Japan's State-Led Liberal Regional Strategy

General Characteristics

Japan's new regional geoeconomic strategy was motivated by external pressures of China's challenge and was shaped by the Japanese government's urge to gain advantage in regional geoeconomic competition to secure the sources of its economic growth. In contrast to the three components of the old-style strategy (bilateralism, informal rules, and embedded mercantilism), the new, state-led, liberal regional strategy is characterized by regionalism as its structure, formal rules and institution building as its mode of engagement, and the promotion of liberal global standards as the underlying values. This new strategy is "state-led" in the sense that it encompasses the initiatives taken by the government in a top-down manner. It is "liberal" not necessarily because it aims to pursue economic neoliberalism or free-market fundamentalism but because the strategy aims to nurture the functioning of free market. The strategy is implemented occasionally through policies to liberalize the economy but more often by nurturing rules and institutions that would support the smooth functioning of the liberal market.[58]

Regionalism. In most cases, the term "regionalism" refers to a policy-guided approach to regional integration that reflects and shapes the strategies of the governments and other actors in the region, while "regionalization" is the natural process in which economic and social activities connect countries into a relatively coherent geographic region.[59] As mentioned previously, during the "third wave of regionalism" of the late 1980s and early 1990s, East Asia was viewed as a region with a high level of regionalization without much regionalism.[60] The rise of regionalism, nonetheless, arrived in East Asia following the Asian financial crisis, in which many diverse regional constructs emerged in various issue areas such as the environment, drug control, trade, and finance.[61]

Following the neofunctionalist "bottom-up" theory of regional integration, some have suggested that "politics has (or might have) caught up with markets" in the region's trade and investment integration.[62]

Meanwhile, others, most notably John Ravenhill, argue that trade regionalism emerged principally through intergovernmental collaboration following the Asian financial crisis; thus it has emerged from a "top-down" process.[63] In the area of financial regionalism, the shock of the financial crisis helped the regional governments collaborate more closely as they identified the International Monetary Fund (IMF) and global financial institutions, which attacked the region, as extraregional "others."[64]

As the Japanese government began to cooperate with other Asian governments through the regionalism (not regionalization) process, the question of membership became problematic. The notion of "region" is inherently a fluid construct, and for Japan it is excruciatingly so.[65] As a country deeply dependent on the United States, Japan sees U.S. inclusion (in the form of "Asia-Pacific") and exclusion (in the form of "East Asia") as a major challenge. The emergence of regionalism, nonetheless, began to demand a clearer definition of membership even for Japan.[66] Under this challenge, the Japanese government has demonstrated an eclectic preference for membership in its state-led liberal regional strategy; it mostly prioritizes the Asia-Pacific but occasionally prefers East Asia. This reveals Japan's diverse domestic and strategic positions, as will be discussed in the following chapters.

Formal rules and institution building. Associated with the rise of regionalism as part of Japan's new geoeconomic strategy, the adoption of formal rules and institution building has become a centerpiece of its regional approach since the dawn of the twenty-first century. Formal rules and formal institutions provide structure for governance that can reduce transaction costs and increase transparency at the expense of flexibility.[67] Hence the trade-off between hard (legalistic, binding, and enforceable) and formal rules versus soft (nonbinding and nonenforceable) and informal rules comes from the flexibility that the latter provide versus the precise obligations and enforcement of the former.[68] Formal rules and institutions are often preferred by the players that want to lock in the status quo, while a shifting power balance makes it more difficult or less likely for formal institutions to emerge.[69] Despite some progress in installing formal rules, East Asia, particularly in comparison to other regions, houses regional institutions that are thin and shallow. The level of delegation is low, and sovereign pooling of collective decision making among governments is not in place.[70]

In this context, the Japanese government has shifted its regional geoeconomic strategy from informal to formal.[71] This shift is quite evident in both trade and investment, as well as monetary and financial relations. After relying primarily on the global/multilateral approach to trade liberalization and rulemaking, the government has since 2000 turned to preferential trade agreements, first bilaterally and later with multiple members, such as the Japan-ASEAN Comprehensive Economic Partnership Agreement (JACEAP) and the TPP. These are highly formal and institutionalized strategies in the area of trade. In finance, slightly loose but still rule-based regional cooperation began in the form of the Chiang Mai Initiative for a regional emergency funding arrangement. Some of the politically sensitive rules, such as conditionality for the loans at the time of balance-of-payments crises, are, however, to be borrowed from the IMF through a so-called IMF-link to avoid sovereignty-damaging conflicts in the region (see chapter 6).

Promotion of global standards. A striking feature of Japan's state-led liberal regional strategy has been its promotion of liberal, global, and high standards. Japan has consistently been a supporter of the rule-based multilateral institutions of the General Agreement on Tariffs and Trade (GATT) and the World Trade Organization, as well as international financial institutions such as the IMF and the World Bank. Nonetheless, it has occasionally challenged some of the standards promoted by these institutions as being too intrusive or based on the double standards of advanced Western economies.[72]

There is still inherent tension in the Japanese government's adoption of and adherence to the global standard. On the one hand, the government has been an advocate of a "high" standard as seen in its promotion of the Singapore issues at the WTO negotiations in the second half of the 1990s.[73] On the other hand, the promotion of these liberal standards contrasts with even Japan's own position throughout the U.S.-Japan trade conflict or Japan's criticism of the IMF at the time of the Asian financial crisis. Furthermore, many of these standards still represent fairly high bars for a large part of Japan's domestic sector, which represents the inefficient (and protected) half of the country's dual economy. Agriculture is the most prominent example for Japan, but noncompetitive industries concentrated among small and medium enterprises (SMEs) are also included.

These facts notwithstanding, as Japan continues to be a large creditor nation—still a provider of foreign investment, emergency funding, and foreign aid—its strategic position particularly vis-à-vis a developing Asia can be considered that of the enforcer of contracts and rules in order to protect its economic interests and financial resources.[74] Common liberal norms such as the rule of law, human rights, and democracy, which Japan either resisted or was reluctant to fully embrace even into the 1990s, have become an important piece of Japan's values-oriented diplomacy in the region.[75]

These three characteristics of Japan's state-led liberal regional strategy have emerged gradually. These tenets and general tendencies have actually manifested differently across the three economic issue areas of trade/investment (chapter 5), monetary/finance relations (chapter 6), and foreign aid/development (chapter 7). Suffice it to note, however, that these tendencies contrast starkly with the old strategy the Japanese government adopted during the 1980s.

Varying Paths of Policy Implementation

Despite the rise of a coherent new approach, the actual implementation of the state-led liberal strategy has been complex. The concrete achievements of this strategy in various economic issue areas covered in this book, from trade to finance to foreign aid, are not uniform. As a brief summary, table 1.1 breaks down the level of implementation into three basic aspects of Japan's new regional geoeconomic strategy. Although the Japanese government has launched various policies in line with the new geoeconomic strategy, there is visible unevenness in structure (from bilateral to multilateral), engagement (informal versus formal), as well as underlying values (from embedded mercantilism to liberal global standard).

Furthermore, the paths that the government has taken to move from the old-style regional engagement to the new in each issue area vary. First, some strategies have taken more time to materialize than others. Compared to the state-led strategy in financial areas, where the Asian financial crisis kicked off many actions right away, the implementation of trade and investment strategy starting with small FTAs took more than a decade to reach its full form with the TPP negotiation. Second, some actions, such as the pursuit of the TPP, embody a coherent strategy as a package to address liberal trade and investment order in East Asia, while Japan's policies in other areas were not quite coherent. In the areas of both finance and development, the paths were either uneven or mixed. Particularly in the area of infrastructural development, we observe some reversals of the liberal strategy toward mercantilist behavior. In the area of finance, some parts of the

TABLE 1.1

Stylized Summary of Japan's Regional Economic Strategy in the Twenty-First Century

	Trade and Investment	Money and Finance	Development and Foreign Aid
Structure (bilateral versus regional)	(M) Moving from bilateralism to regionalism	(H) Clear regional membership	(L) Largely maintaining bilateralism
Engagement (informal versus formal rules)	(H) Formal agreements with binding obligations	(M) Formal institutions in some areas but informal in others	(M) Bilateral dialogues through country programs
Underlying values (embedded mercantilism versus liberal global standard)	(H) Increasingly liberal especially through the TPP	(M) Following liberal norms with modifications	(M) Liberal and value-based engagement of businesses, rule of law

Note: Evaluation: Low (L), medium (M), and high (H) relevance in the new strategic direction.

strategy, such as the emergency funding mechanism of the Chiang Mai Initiative, have achieved significant success while others, such as currency initiatives, did not take off.

Questions and the Argument

This study poses two layered questions related to Japan's regional geoeconomic strategy and its implementation. The upper layer is about the broader feature of transformation in the Japanese government's geoeconomic strategy in the Asia-Pacific. How and why has the government shifted its strategy from the old style to the new since the latter half of the 1990s? The lower layer focuses on the implementation of the state-led liberal regional strategy across different issues areas. How was the strategy implemented, and what has shaped the respective and particular path in each issue area? In response to these questions, the basic argument of this study is that the new strategy has come about as a deliberate geoeconomic response to the changing regional economic landscape and Japan's relative position in it, while domestic institutional constraints have heavily defined the implementation of this strategy. Hence, as will be discussed in chapter 2, this project takes the external-internal nexus seriously as a central premise of understanding foreign policy formation.

In the broad scope, the shift from Japan's old-style strategy to the new one over the course of the 1990s into the first two decades of the twenty-first century has come about as a way for the government to respond to the changing geoeconomic environment in the Asia-Pacific. One can identify multiple sources that have motivated the government to shift its regional geoeconomic strategy during this period. At the global level, uncertainty associated with multilateral trade liberalization rounds via the GATT (Uruguay Round, 1986–1994) and the WTO (Doha Round, 2001–2015) stimulated the emergence of preferential trade agreements, from the North American Free Trade Agreement (NAFTA) to the TPP, as alternatives or possible hedges. The WTO is not the only multilateral institution that has experienced a challenge from regional or bilateral arrangements. During the Asian financial crisis many Asian leaders saw the IMF as the agent of a Wall Street–led power play that undermined Asia's economic success, a concern that led to regional financial cooperation and institution building.[76] By the early 2000s the Asia-Pacific gradually became active in both regional free trade negotiations and regional financial cooperation. Furthermore, as we will see in chapter 3, the rise of China and the tension associated with the rise of the "Beijing Consensus" or state capitalism have led to concerns that China might disrupt the global liberal economic order guided by the United States since the 1940s.[77] The global financial crisis in the late 2000s heightened China's challenges to, and doubts about, the U.S.-led economic order even more.

Through these processes, the international economic order under U.S. auspices, which sustained and supported Japan's economic rise for more than fifty years, has slowly transformed and is showing signs of fatigue. The Japanese government needed policy measures to respond to these new realities. At the same time, the growth of the Chinese economy particularly since the late 1990s began to redefine the geoeconomic landscape of East Asia. The changes have motivated the Japanese government to come up with a geoeconomic strategy as a way to reconfigure the regional economic environment in Japan's favor. Ironically, there is a parallel between the U.S.-Japan conflict in the 1970s and 1980s when the United States demanded economic liberalization, high standards, and neoliberal rules for "fair" trade against Japan. In the first two decades of the twenty-first century, Japan is in a position to assert similar conditions against China and, to a lesser extent, other emerging economies to protect Japan's economic advantages as an advanced economy and a major investor in the region. The challenge is particularly urgent in East Asia, where private Japanese firms have culti-vated supply chains and production networks in the past few decades.[78]

Moreover, as a slowly declining country (at least in a relative sense) in the region, which still maintains a significant level of economic presence, Japan has the pressing task of installing institutions, rules, and standards in its favor. As Joseph Grieco analyzed in the 1990s, a declining power has an urgency to build institutions to lock in its current advantage, while a rapidly rising power would resist such urgent institutionalization in a region, as time is on its side.[79] Here the Japanese government, par-ticularly in the aftermath of the Asian financial crisis, began to capitalize on rulemaking and regional institution building to lock these institutions in place.

In short, Japan's state-led liberal strategy is, on the one hand, a way for the government to cope with the changes in regional and global economic realities as Japan's economy itself has stagnated. On the other hand, it is a strategy to capitalize on Japan's pivotal role in the region under U.S.-China competition. Its ultimate goal is to shape the regional economic envi-ronment under liberal rules for the regional market that would most favorably accommodate Japanese firms and their activities and enhance Japan's influence in the region.

When it comes to implementation of the strategy, the institutional setup, actors, and path dependence influence the policy outcome. As discussed previously, many governmental actors are involved in Japan's foreign pol-icy making. The configuration of these governmental actors and their rela-tion to the market and private business actors involved determine policy making. As will be explored in chapters 5 through 7, business actors push for certain policy in some cases while opposing them in others. In many cases, furthermore, their involvement is minimal or nonexistent.

The ways in which each issue area involves governmental actors and businesses influence the paths. As will be demonstrated in chapters 5 through 7, the more streamlined the policy-making environment with a small number of bureaucratic actors involved (as the case of finance), the easier it is to coordinate to reach an agreed path. By contrast, coordination among many ministries, seen in trade, leads to more coordination time and a slower and more timid start. It is also easier to push forward issues that have limited direct or immediate costs to the market and private business actors, while the Japanese government cannot usually rely on Japanese market actors to support its strategy wholeheartedly.

Alternative Explanations

Globalization and External Pressures

Like every other country in the world, Japan has experienced globalization pressures. In addition, the success of the Japanese economy as well as its developmentalist strategy over the course of the 1950s to 1980s exposed Japan to stark foreign pressure to liberalize and reform its economy. It is also evident that the Japanese government has often used *gaiatsu* to reform the economy.[80] One could argue that these pressures have fundamentally changed Japanese foreign economic strategy and policies. Nevertheless, as the immediate trigger of Japan's policy shift, the gradual globalization pressure is quite diffuse. In addition, the government's geoeconomic strategy shifted much more clearly in the twenty-first century, long after the U.S. pressure to change Japan waned.

Instead of coercive pressure such as that seen in the U.S.-Japan trade conflicts, another type of external influence comes as the forces of emulation. Instead of strategically responding to the changing geoeconomic environment, the Japanese government might have actively emulated the United States or Europe as their respective regions began their regional integration through standardizing rules in trade and finance, a trend that intensified from the 1990s. Although the overall regionalism trend during this period undoubtedly motivated the government to become more proactive in its regional engagement (see chapter 2), the fact that Japan still follows the liberal tactics, particularly in the aftermath of the global financial crisis and the euro crisis from the late 2000s to the early 2010s, introduces a contradictory piece of evidence against this thesis. Why should Japan emulate models of formal rules and a high level of regional institution building that were placed under a skeptical light in the 2010s?

Functional Determinants and Other Regional Players' Interests

Particularly focusing on the lower layer of this study's argument, namely, uneven implementation, one can argue that the level of success in implementing the new regional strategy for Japan depends not on the country's domestic institutional factors but on other factors that shape regionalism. Regional institution building contains multiple levels of difficulty and sophistication, and the way in which a government has to compromise on sovereignty depends on the issue areas. As Bela Balassa outlined in his "roadmap" to regional integration, free trade agreements would impose much lower costs to sovereignty than the establishment of a common market or regional monetary union.[81] Phillip Lipscy emphasizes that interstate bargaining defines particular institutional structures.[82] Some regional initiatives succeed not because of Japan's strategy but because of growing support from other governments. A clear example of this alternative explanation is the Chiang Mai Initiative and how its success came mainly from the fact that the Chinese government came onboard.

Although acknowledging both of these alternative factors is critical in understanding how economic regionalism in East Asia is shaped, this study focuses mainly on the Japanese government's strategies and policies. The outcome (or the success) of regional institution building is discussed in some cases, but the eclectic structure of East Asia's regionalism itself is not what this study aims to analyze.

Narrow Economic Interests

What is the ultimate goal of the Japanese government's regional strategy? The proponents of geoeconomics suggest that a government engages geoeconomic strategies by using the country's economic power to achieve its foreign policy goals.[83] This study also argues that the government ultimately seeks to achieve the country's foreign policy goals with the new regional strategy. Others would argue, however, that Japan might be simply pursuing its material interests by establishing economic rules and standards in the region that would benefit not only Japanese firms but more specifically the elite managers who manage the regional production network.[84]

It is undoubtedly important for Japan to pursue its economic interests in the region, and in a way, the definition of its foreign policy goals includes such narrow economic interests. Nonetheless, this study argues that the Japanese government's new strategy goes beyond a government pursuing mercantilist interests. Japan's initiatives to build regional institutions and establish rules correspond, rather, to supplying regional public goods and competing for influence. The government would argue that such order and governance building in East Asia would be beneficial to all the economies in the region as well as being advantageous for Japan.

At the dawn of the twenty-first century, the Japanese government shifted its regional geoeconomic strategy in the Asia-Pacific from bilaterally focused informal engagement with mercantilist values to one that engages the region collectively under formal rules in pursuit of global standards. Geoeconomics of the region has driven this broad shift in strategy, while there have been distinct paths to implement the strategy based on issue areas largely defined by the underlying policy institutions.

CHAPTER II

Foreign Economic Policy, Domestic Institutions, and Regional Governance

T he Japanese government's regional geoeconomic strategy shifted by the early twenty-first century from an old-style bilateral, informal, and mercantilist approach to a state-led liberal strategy where the government engages in region-wide rule- and institution-building initiatives capitalizing on global standards. What motivated the government to shift its strategy? How has it gone about translating the strategy into policies? We need to examine both the systemic level of the regional and global geoeconomic environment as well as the domestic institutional and political context to answer these questions.

The challenge of "levels of analysis" in international relations has long been a theme of foreign policy analysis. This study examines both the strategy (a general direction of foreign economic policy) and policies (concrete choices of instrument to carry out the strategy) with the state as the agent to implement them. This way, we can connect how the region's geoeconomic environment determines the general geoeconomic strategy, while the implementation of such a strategy through policy instruments can vary in different issue areas. As foreign policy straddles the systemic-domestic nexus, this approach provides some insights that bridge the two levels.

This chapter starts with a discussion of the analytical challenges arising from divides between comparative political economy (CPE) and international political economy (IPE) as well as systemic versus domestic-level analysis. After laying out where the project fits in these debates, the next section focuses on the literature on the developmental state and varieties of capitalism and how this study is placed in these two clusters of debate. The final section examines the sources of Japan's state-led liberal strategy in the context of disembedding businesses from the state.

Bridging the Comparative and International Political Economy

Foreign Economic Policy in the CPE-IPE Divide

Two levels of analysis in political economy—international and domestic—have posed challenges and offered insights for scholars examining a state's economic policies. Foreign policy resides at the nexus of these two levels. There have been multiple scholarly efforts to bridge the gap between the two levels. The seminal work by Peter J. Katzenstein and his team asserted the importance of domestic structure as the critical factor in determining foreign policy responses.[1] The collection organized by G. John Ikenberry, David A. Lake, and Michael Mastanduno examined U.S. foreign policy "after hegemony" and emphasized the importance of the role of the state.[2] Robert D. Putnam proposed the framework of a two-level game to analyze the entangled dynamics of diplomacy between the international and domestic levels.[3] More recently, the debate between open economy politics (OEP) and its critics has revealed the importance of both levels in achieving unbiased analysis.[4]

The challenge imposed by the gap has also led to a divide between CPE and IPE approaches. The shortage of dialogue between the two led Nicola Phillips to argue that "neither IPE nor CPE in isolation seems capable of pushing forward a fully satisfactory set of debates that take due account of both the nature of contemporary states and the structural context in which they are rooted."[5] This book aims to tackle this challenge and bridge the two levels by focusing on the role of the state, consisting of political leaders and bureaucracy, which is exposed to strategic challenges in bargaining and managing regional and global relations while being constrained and influenced by domestic politics and institutions.[6]

Systemic-Domestic Nexus of Regional Geoeconomic Strategy

The emergence of Japan's state-led liberal strategy in the twenty-first century addresses the fundamental debate in IPE over the complex interaction between international systems and domestic politics.[7] On the one hand, models that privilege external forces are often applied to explain how regional and international systems influence a state's policy, an approach best known as the "second image reversed."[8] Extending further, Thomas Oatley asserts the importance of systemic effects in foreign economic policy making.[9] My study contributes to explaining how, in general, Japan's state-led liberal regional strategy has been motivated by systemic considerations such as the rise of China and diffusion of liberal economic norms. Outside forces impose costs on Japanese actors, leading them to follow, in most cases, global "norms" or "standards." As discussed in chapter 1, the theory of Japan as a "reactive state" is a well-established understanding of Japanese foreign policy making and economic reform, where *gaiatsu* was effective and/or useful in changing Japan's behavior.[10] Some of these foreign pressures are structural, such as the pressure of financial globalization, while others are relational, for example, in the form of U.S.-Japan trade conflicts.[11]

On the other hand, the domestic politics model represented by the OEP paradigm, emphasizing internal political dynamics and institutions as the main sources of a country's foreign policy and strategy, has dominated recent IPE literature.[12] Here, domestic politics and institutions are critical components of policy making, leading to inside-out propositions of state behavior. According to this inside-out perspective, changes in Japan's strategy come from within through shifting domestic coalitions and economic, political, or institutional foundations. Japan's prolonged economic slowdown since the 1990s as well as its demographic decline obviously exemplify these major changes. Institutional changes, most prominently electoral reform, imposed pressure to change Japan's political economy as well. Frances McCall Rosenbluth and Michael F. Thies argue that the electoral reform of 1994 that introduced heavier representation of single-member districts in the Lower House has shifted Japanese economic policy toward a more liberal direction.[13] In examining the trade policy making of Japan and Thailand, Megumi Naoi argues that legislators have promoted trade liberalization by giving out side payments, while Amy Catalinac argues that new electoral incentives in Japan have moved politicians to focus more on the country's security policy.[14] In addition, as will be considered in chapter 4, multiple economic and administrative reforms have been put in place in response to a series of grave economic and political crises slowly brewing in Japan in the more than twenty years since the mid-1990s.[15]

Japan is not merely a passive norm-taker: it has also proposed an economic model based on its developmental experiences.[16] To add complexity, for a relatively large country like Japan, not only does the system affect the country's policy choices, but these choices in turn most likely affect the system, thereby creating a feedback loop.[17]

Global Economic Governance Challenges and Japan's Strategic Response

The Japanese government's motivation to pursue a state-led liberal strategy emerged under the particular systemic dynamics of recent decades. There are three major channels that have applied pressure on the Japanese economy and the government to liberalize and conform to the "global standard," all of which have guided Japan's broad policy shifts. The first channel is conventional globalization pressure. Although the Japanese economy had largely resisted foreign pressure toward full-blown economic liberalization during its growth era of the 1950s to 1980s, Japanese businesses and economic actors, with some exceptions such as the agricultural sector, have recently become much more receptive to liberalization. In this context, the government became equipped to "reregulate" the economy with more market-shaping rules in response to liberalization and regulatory reforms.[18] Moreover, many of Japan's competitive firms are fully integrated into global and regional production networks. Japanese businesses that have incrementally "gone global" in the past several decades have become willing agents for transmitting liberalization forces with demands of investment protection and intellectual property rights through the establishment of rules, rather than the direct guidance of the government and neomercantilist protections, which could cause a backlash and retaliation from other governments.

The second channel has been the weakening and stagnation of multilateralism in global economic governance and the associated rise of economic regionalism. In particular, owing to the "preferential" and exclusionary nature of free trade agreements, such dynamics have incurred a "domino effect" of FTAs through the pressure of trade and investment diversion or political pressure.[19] Meanwhile, regional configurations such as the regional emergency funding mechanism of the Chiang Mai Initiative or regional trade agreements (RTAs) could be construed as defensive ventures to create regional buffers against global pressures or as an insurance policy.[20]

The third channel comes in the form of policy diffusion.[21] Along with China's economic rise, competition has become a major force behind policy diffusion in the realm of preferential trade liberalization through FTAs.[22] During the period covered in this study, particularly in the twenty-first century, the competitive pressure on policy diffusion has intensified in the Asia-Pacific, as two major powers, the United States and China, began to clash in shaping regional economic governance. On the one hand, the liberal commercial model of the United States has insisted on transparent rules (which benefit the "status quo" economic powers), while the rising Chinese economic power, on the other hand, has been skeptical of that model. The Chinese have viewed the liberal commercial model as a measure that would inhibit "catch-up" strategies among emerging economies and thus kick away the economic growth ladder.[23]

Each of these three channels has shaped Japan's new regional geoeconomic strategy. The Japanese government has obtained policy knowledge and experience regarding how to shape liberal markets for the past several decades. With the waning power of worldwide liberal economic governance and order, the region has become an important stage for economic rulemaking and the country's prosperity. As discussed below, with Japan's economic maturity, the lack of domestic investment opportunities, and an aging and declining population, Japanese big businesses have started to focus more on East Asian economic development and growth, expanding into this area in the past several decades. In this context, the Japanese government can use the country's relatively large size and liberal economic strategy to shape the regional economic order as a pivotal state (discussed in chapter 1) in the Asia-Pacific, which can in turn influence global economic governance. This geoeconomic strategy has therefore become fundamental for Japan.

Developmental State and Variety of Capitalism Debates

External pressures in various forms, from globalization and economic liberalization to policy diffusion, as well as the government's reaction to these pressures frequently interact with domestic politico-economic institutions to shape policies. In East Asia the developmental state and its associated institutions feature prominently in the scholarly work to explain the rapid growth of these economies. The adaptation of developmental state institutions to economic globalization and to the state's own economic maturity have become important factors in understanding such interaction. Hence an active debate over the utility and endurance of the developmental state model has emerged.[24] The debate over the Japanese economic and political system since the late 1980s evolved largely in this context.[25]

Developmentalism is seen among late developers and late industrializers. These economies are in need of "catching up" to early industrializers by jump-starting the process of industrialization and economic growth. To overcome the systemic disadvantages of late industrializers, states tend to become the core architects of the catch-up process as they engage in active industrial policies of resource mobilization and planning.[26] To accelerate the process of industrial upscaling often led by the industrial policies pursued by governments, these economies mobilize domestic (and sometimes also foreign) savings and stably channel cheap capital to rising industries by employing financial repression through banks. Governments provide plenty of incentives for domestic industries to upgrade through support of research and development and preferential access to capital and technology. In addition, these governments usually secure competitive foreign exchange rates (undervalued currency) and provide subsidies for domestic firms so that the country's exports have a price advantage abroad. Concurrently, these governments often engage in protectionist policies against imports not only to nurture nascent domestic industries but also to establish a high-price domestic market from which national industries can profit and expand internationally, even at a loss.

Japan has pursued a similar version of this stylized catch-up strategy since the Meiji Restoration and the "Rich Country, Strong Army" state of the late 1800s; South Korea and Taiwan did so in the 1960s and 1970s, and China has arguably done so since the 1980s. As a foundation of East Asia's economic success from the 1950s to the 1990s, scholars have highlighted close government-business relations as a critical institutional feature that has long allowed governments, particularly the bureaucracy, to take the lead in industrial policy and planning in Japan, South Korea, and Taiwan.[27] According to Peter B. Evans, these states managed to enjoy favorable conditions for a successful developmental state as the state itself enjoyed "embedded autonomy."[28] These state-society relations came in the form of relative insulation of bureaucratic elites from societal and business pressures that allowed them to avoid private rent seeking or political gridlock while embedding bureaucratic institutions into close relationships with business groups through consultation and cooperation to achieve effective policy implementation.

By late 1990s and particularly in the aftermath of the Asian financial crisis, many pundits started to question the continued viability of the developmental state model.[29] Especially for Japan, but even for the advanced economies of South Korea and Taiwan, the debates regarding "the death of the developmental state" have emerged largely from two sources.[30] The first cluster of the debate is couched in the broader question of the retreat of the state. Such a retreat under globalization had become an increasingly important question in the late twentieth century, where the end of the Cold War, pressures of financial liberalization, and a series of economic crises cast shadows of doubt on the effectiveness of the state in managing the pressures and impacts of economic globalization.[31] In particular, the Asian financial crisis inflicted a major blow on those who have long argued in support of the effectiveness of government intervention in economic development, including that for East Asian governments, as the neoliberal camp ran an intellectual and ideological victory lap over the failure of East Asia's economic model.[32] On the ground, some states, like South Korea, argues Thomas Kalinowski, used their last developmental state instruments to facilitate the country's economic recovery after the crisis, but the economic liberalization measures and market reforms implemented through the strong hand of the state ultimately led to the final demise of the developmental state model.[33] Although the Asian economies recovered relatively quickly from the devastating crisis, those economies that relied more heavily on the International Monetary Fund's rescue packages, such as Thailand, Indonesia, and South Korea, were exposed to increased liberalization and reform pressures in the aftermath of the crisis.[34]

The second source of the developmental state's demise emerged from the very economic successes of these economies along with the expanding global reach of their businesses. It could be argued that once economic success allows a country to join the group of advanced economies, the country should unwind and move away from economic developmentalism as a mature economy.[35] This is because most mature economies eventually experience a fundamental problem where they become "less able to generate enough profitable investment opportunities to absorb domestic savings."[36] The problem is particularly acute for developmental states that have long mobilized capital in support of industrial policy and economic growth.[37] Such countries house high levels of technology and high-skilled labor but, in general, are now at a competitive disadvantage in manufacturing standardized products owing to rising labor costs. Many of these mature economies would at least try to move from a manufacturing to a service economy. At the same time, these economies also start to invest heavily abroad for higher returns and/or experience a large influx of migrant workers attracted to the higher wages in these mature economies that will serve to meet the demographic challenges that typically plague more advanced economies.[38]

The jury is still out on the "death of the developmental state" thesis, however, and the debate was revived in the second decade of the twenty-first century. In the aftermath of the global financial crisis, the world under the discredited "Washington Consensus" searches for an alternative paradigm of global economic governance as well as solid sources of economic growth.[39] Relatedly, China's continued rise has focused the world's attention on "developmentalism with Chinese characteristics," and China's global reach has had a normative impact on developmental strategy.[40] One can also observe the diffusion of developmentalism in general and the developmental state model in particular as political leaders strive to survive in emerging and developing countries from Latin America to Africa.[41]

There are two main clusters of arguments among proponents of the enduring nature of the developmental state model. The first is the durability of a "developmental mindset" among elites of East Asian economies that creates the consensus on development strategy and shapes policies.[42] Richard Stubbs also argues that the relevance of developmental states persists because the ideas once brought immense success to such societies, and institutional path dependence such as internal policy networks die hard.[43] Examining the reemergence of financial activism and emphasis on balanced growth, South Korea has demonstrated that such a mindset persists well into the twenty-first century.[44] Others also joined the debate by examining the continued role of the developmental mindset in policy making in East Asia, from entrepreneurial financing to energy policies.[45] The second push-back against the demise of the developmental state thesis takes on a variety of forms but commonly focuses on the inconsistent retreat of developmentalism and the erratic path of said retreat. Such variation can emerge in sectoral differences where some strategic sectors continue to be supported by strong state guidance and covered by state-owned enterprises.[46] A "zig-zagging path" is also observed, where several East Asian governments have taken up different levels of control over their countries' respective economic policies depending on the leading parties' political and ideological leanings.[47]

Japan's state-led liberal strategy in this study relates closely to the developmental state debates. First, has Japan kept its developmental state characteristics into the 1990s, or did it shed such a mindset by that time? Second, how has graduating from developmentalism affected Japan? Third, focusing on East Asia, how has the ongoing developmentalism in the region affected Japan's geoeconomic strategy in the region?

The other important cluster of scholarly work is on the varieties of capitalism. Focusing mostly on Western advanced economies, this CPE analysis categorizes advanced economies into two types of models: One is the liberal market economy (LME) model with free-market system, "where the equilibrium outcomes of firm behavior are usually given by demand and supply condition of competitive market." The other is the coordinated market economy (CME) model, where firms and other actors strategically interact to produce results. Institutional settings including financial systems (stock market–based versus bank-based), legal systems (formal contracts versus informal relations), employment protection (low versus high), as well as innovation style (rapid versus incremental development) contrast these two models.[48] Countries such as the United States and United Kingdom as well as Commonwealth countries like Australia and New Zealand belong to the LME group, while Germany, France, Japan, and most Nordic countries are CMEs.

Japanese business practices and economic management fall squarely into the CME model, which also includes higher leverage of public influence over the private sector and the strong state.[49] Some scholars argue that Japan, paired with Germany, houses a "nonliberal capitalism" where hierarchical and organizational coordination is valued and the trust in free-market laissez faire is low.[50]

With the focus on market reforms, Steven K. Vogel nonetheless criticizes the tendency in the scholarship to dichotomize government versus market as well as regulation versus competition. Even in the economies considered very liberal, he says, the government must play a leading role in market design, while when a country goes through deregulation and liberalization, there are more rules to "craft markets." In the case of Japan, the domestic market reform since the 1990s from regulated market to "free market" has produced only incremental changes.[51] This has been due to strong complementarity among multiple aspects of the country's economic system.

In sum, these debates are far from over and continue to be one of the most important discussions regarding international and comparative political economy. Nonetheless, the significant transformation of the state's role in countries' external economic engagement is the focus of this study, and Japan's economic transformation is an important starting point in examining the systemic-domestic nexus.

Sources of Japan's State-Led Liberal Strategy

Disembedding Businesses

This study connects the domestic politico-economic evolution of Japan's postbubble economy with its regional geoeconomic strategy in the Asia-Pacific. The old-style regional geoeconomic strategy seen most prominently in the 1980s was founded on the developmental model that the Japanese government and Japanese businesses had followed throughout the modernization-cum-industrialization process over the 150 years since the Meiji Restoration. In recent years the government has nurtured its business activities and overseas ventures by managing an external environment favorable to Japan's exports and investments.[52] It is debatable as to when Japan stopped following the developmental state model; it remains that the ultimate national goal of economic growth based on government-business cooperation has long unified the objectives and strategies of all the relevant governmental ministries. The "all Japan" strategy of combining foreign aid, investment, and trade overseas was dubbed as the "development trinity" (*sanmi ittai*) approach.[53] After almost a century of implementing economic developmentalism, the Japanese economy had in many ways caught up with the advanced economies of Europe and the United States by the end of the 1970s.[54] Japan has also accrued a sizable trade surplus since the late 1960s (with the exception of the oil crisis years of the 1970s), and by the early 1990s the country had grown to become the largest creditor country in the world. The new liberal regional geoeconomic strategy is therefore couched in the phasing out of Japan's developmentalism.

In this study I argue that Japan's economic maturity created the disembedding of big businesses from state-led mercantilism and has had profound influence on Japan's geoeconomic strategy as well as the implementation of the economic policies associated with this strategy. By designating Japan as an advanced capitalist economy, we can characterize two aspects of the country's economic structure—each epitomizes postdevelopmentalism but at the same time continued importance of the government's institutions and leadership role. On the one hand, Japan is a postdevelopmental country, as evidenced in several ways. First, as discussed by Robert Wade, the Japanese economy suffers from a shortage of profitable investment opportunities.[55] The investment to gross domestic product ratio for Japan has fallen from 42 percent in 1970 to below 20 percent, particularly in 2009–2010 after the global financial crisis. Second, the Japanese economy has gone through multitudes of economic liberalization, economic reforms, and regulatory reforms. Despite frustrating doubts on the Japanese economy's ability to move toward a liberal and open economy, scholars have identified important changes in Japanese business strategy and corporate governance.[56] Third, as will be discussed more extensively in chapter 4, the "disembedding" of Japan's government-business relationship has proceeded quite seriously. As large private businesses exited overseas to circumvent the government's regulatory and administrative control, the government has lost its means to control the behavior of the private sector.[57]

As businesses have expanded and labor costs have gone up, Japanese competitive businesses from Toyota to Sony began to implement a global production strategy via investing overseas.[58] This trend became prominent for Japan starting in the latter half of the 1980s.[59] As Dennis Tachiki identifies, through their recent foreign direct investment initiatives, East Asian firms have engaged in a global production network where different stages of production are spread across national borders, which contrasts quite starkly with the earlier generation of FDI.[60]

As global value chains develop rapidly where many components of manufacturing production are compartmentalized and located all around the world, these firms have been engaging in "strategic coupling" with global firms as part of regional and global production networks.[61] These trends associated with major firms "going global" have had critical impacts on the "embedded autonomy" of the state-business dynamics described earlier. As large East Asian firms' operations become global and competitive, they "graduate" "from the tutelage of the developmental state."[62] Such large firms then have many options for sources of funding, technology acquisition, and market access as they begin to operate globally, causing the states to gradually lose their ability to shape these firms' behavior.[63] Hence the very success of developmentalism in nurturing competitive national businesses allows firms to become independent of the government. As a result, "disembedded autonomy" becomes a distinguishing feature for Japan and advanced economies in Asia.[64]

Of course, there are variations in the level of state-business connections, and we see occasions when the private sector collaborates with (or at least apparently supports) the government's actions. Some sectors such as finance are more prone to stronger connection to the government. Nonetheless, the government does have little power in guiding Japanese businesses to do what they do not have an interest in doing, or what they see as being associated with high costs or high risk. These trends of decoupling occurred against the backdrop of the fastest and largest demographic decline, heavily burdened by the high costs of care for the aged, and vast public debt that restricts financial resources available for the Japanese government. Chapter 4 further explores the power balance between the resource-strapped Japanese government and big businesses.

On the other hand, the government is still stuck with assisting declining or uncompetitive businesses, and it continues to be in charge of economic growth and redistribution. Furthermore, the stickiness of institutions and relationships nurtured under Japan's developmentalism era has become the primary source of resistance against economic reforms and has imposed continued economic problems for Japan during the "lost" two decades since the early 1990s.[65] Other sticky mechanisms, such as social compensation that externalizes the costs and internalizes the benefits or the political power of the elites, have slowed the pace of change.[66] Faced with the more rapid economic drive by China and lingering developmental mindset among East Asian economies, Japanese government officials and political leaders— supported by these sticky institutions—began to shift the country's regional engagement with the goal of reviving its economic growth.

In short, Japan's state-led liberal geoeconomic strategy for the region emerges as the focal point of foreign economic policy. Japan needs profitable investment sites overseas to grow—sites where Japanese businesses can effectively compete and receive protection under the rule of law. Hence the government has adopted a state-led liberal strategy as "marketcraft" to establish and maintain rules and institutions of economic engagement in the region.[67] This has been an important step under the regional geoeconomic environment in competition with China, as discussed in chapter 1, as Japan is also in support of maintaining a U.S.-led liberal economic order in the region. Japan's position in managing China's economic rise shapes the country's overall strategy. Globally competitive businesses headquartered in Japan generally welcome such efforts taken up by the government as they worry about their trade relations and the security of large amounts of invested assets in the region.

Uneven Paths

Nonetheless, in practice, concrete policy choices are still affected by political interests and dominant institutional setting in different sectors or issue areas. Most strikingly, as will be discussed in chapter 4, a highly fragmented structure of the state apparatus that implements Japan's regional geoeconomic strategy influences policy making and, subsequently, policy effectiveness. On the bureaucratic side, Japan's vertical administration or compartmentalization (*tatewari gyōsei*) has been a long-discussed feature, and different ministerial (or even bureau) priorities have often been pursued.[68] During the rapid-growth era of the 1950s to 1970s, the ministries worked closely together in support of a coherent national goal in pursuit of economic catch-up and growth, and Japan's business interests and extensive personal network among elites functioned as glue. After the economic crisis hit Japan in the 1990s, political leaders made significant efforts to place more power into the hands of elected politicians in order to gain an upper hand in policy making and centralize the administrative process. Prime Minister Ryūtaro Hashimoto's administrative reform initiatives since the late 1990s deliberately affected institutions where the power of the prime minister was strengthened (see chapter 4). Yet elected officials' control over ministerial power still falls short.[69] There were some noticeable efforts by strong prime ministers such as Junichirō Koizumi (2001–2006) and Shinzō Abe (2012–present), who were helped by public opinion and the media to control the economic ministries. But the institutional and political path dependence, informational advantage, and high level of human capital of these ministries and their officials have made it very difficult for politicians to fully prevail over the ministries' preferences. Nonetheless, the power of the prime minister's office has gradually dominated, as demonstrated in the case of the TPP negotiations under Prime Minister Abe in 2013. Recently installed institutional innovations have enabled the government to overcome such bureaucratic fragmentation, paving the way for the smooth implementation of Japan's state-led liberal strategy.

Chapters 5 through 7 will demonstrate that the fluctuation of the government's implementation of Japan's new state-led liberal strategy derives largely from the institutional setup in different issue areas and Japan's businesses involvement in implementation of the strategy. In the areas of trade and investment (chapter 5), although rulemaking through free trade agreements, including the TPP, has become the key feature of the state-led liberal strategy, the country-specific interests of large Japanese firms operating in the region and the dominance of Ministry of Foreign Affairs' diplomatic channels have slowed the process of establishing a region-wide trade agreement. In addition, the lowest common denominator among all the participating ministries guided the relatively shallow level of trade and investment liberalization through the FTAs. In the areas of finance and monetary policy (chapter 6), the dominance of the Ministry of Finance in guiding regional cooperation allowed Japan's regional strategy to become more coherent. But the rulemaking aimed at generating regional monetary and financial arrangements has been limited, even in the case of yen internationalization, because of little interest and support from Japan's private financial sector. In the areas of development and foreign aid (chapter 7), the existing structure of bilateral foreign aid has dominated even in the current new phase, but rulemaking is gaining prominence in the approach to development.

During the first two decades of the twenty-first century, the Japanese government shifted its regional economic strategy in support of formalization of rules and regional institutions with promotion of liberal and global standards. The impetus toward such a strategy is the competitive geoeconomics under the rise of China, which has made the Japanese government lean on the side of liberal rule setting in East Asia. Japan's domestic political and institutional transformation since the mid-1990s has also reinforced such a strategic choice. As the economy matured, the government's direct role in guiding big businesses dwindled over time. Instead, establishing the "level playing field" for Japan in Asia has become an imperative for the Japanese government.[70]

CHAPTER III

Geoeconomics of the Asia-Pacific

The shift in Japan's geoeconomic strategy took place over the course of twenty-five years, from the late 1990s into the first two decades of the twenty-first century, when East Asia underwent dramatic economic development and major political transformations. This period has been defined by the rapid rise of China in contrast to the slow decline of Japan, and the U.S. struggles to remain engaged with the region. Prior to this time, the Cold War and the preponderance of the U.S. economic presence shaped Japan's relationship with the Asia-Pacific, as Japan's rapidly expanding economy grew increasingly important to the Asian region. Since then, the dynamics between China and the United States have largely shaped the contours of Japan's geoeconomic strategy in the region. As outlined in the chronology in table 3.1, two major economic shocks also defined and redefined the region's economic priorities during this time. The first was the Asian financial crisis (1997–1998). Despite a vast shock, both economic and psychological, the crisis was relatively short-lived as the region recovered quite swiftly. Nonetheless, the crisis became an important prompt for changes in terms of both the region's economic priorities and governance. Second, the global financial crisis (2008–2009) cast doubt on the neoliberal economic order preached by the United States, and triggered the Chinese government to become increasingly proactive in matters regarding regional and global economic governance. Ultimately,

TABLE 3.1
Chronology of Major Events, 1990–2019

Year	Global and Regional Events	Events in Japan and Economic Partnership Agreements
1990	Malaysian prime minister Mahathir bin Mohamad proposes creating East Asian Economic Caucus (Dec.).	
1991	EMEAP established (Feb.). Helsinki Disciplines agree on tied aid for export promotion (Dec.).	Failure of Tōhō Sōgo Bank and onset of banking crisis (July).
1992	Treaty of Maastricht signed in European Union (Feb.).	Japan's first ODA Charter adopted (June).
1993	World Bank's "East Asian Miracle" report published (Sep.). First APEC Summit held on Blake Island, Washington (Nov.).	Lower House election leads to loss of LDP majority (July).
1994	NAFTA enacted (Jan.). Uruguay Round culminated (Apr.). Bogor Declaration announced at APEC Summit in Bogor, Indonesia (Nov.). Mexican peso crisis begins (Dec.).	Electoral reform law enacted (Jan.). Japan Investment Council established (July).
1995	WTO established (Jan.).	Jūsen loan companies collapse (Feb.). Settlement reached on U.S.-Japan disputes over automotive trade (June). APEC Summit held in Osaka (Nov.).
1996	G7 Summit held in Lyon, France (June).	Ryūtaro Hashimoto elected as prime minister (Jan.).

Year	Global and Regional Events	Events in Japan and Economic Partnership Agreements
1997	First G8 Summit, including Russia, held (June). Asian financial crisis begins (July). Hong Kong reverts to Chinese sovereignty (July). APEC EVSL gradually collapses (Nov.).	Consumption tax hiked from 3 percent to 5 percent (Apr.). Bank of Japan Law revised (June). Proposal to create Asian Monetary Fund issued (Sep.).
1998	Summit meeting held in Beijing between President Bill Clinton and President Jiang Zemin (Oct.).	Bank of Japan given de jure independence and Big Bang enacted (Apr.). New Miyazawa Initiative begins (Oct.). Long-Term Credit Bank of Japan (Oct.) and Nippon Credit Bank (Dec.) nationalized.
1999	Euro formally established (Jan.). China's "Going Global" strategy launched (Mar.). ASEAN+3 (Japan, China, and Korea) start top-level meetings (Nov.).	Yen Internationalization Initiative begins (Apr.).
2000	Chiang Mai Initiative established (May). Millennium Development Goals (2000–2015) announced at UN Millennium Summit (Sep.).	G8 Summit held in Okinawa (Aug.).
2001	September 11 attacks occur (Sep.). WTO Doha Round starts (Nov.). China formally enters WTO (Dec.).	Administrative reform law enacted (Jan.). Junichirō Koizumi appointed as prime minister (Apr., in power until 2006).

(continued)

TABLE 3.1
Chronology of Major Events, 1990–2019 (*continued*)

Year	Global and Regional Events	Events in Japan and Economic Partnership Agreements
2002	Monterrey Consensus on foreign aid adopted (Mar.).	Japan-Singapore EPA enters into force (Nov.).
2003	U.S.-led invasion of Iraq begins (Mar.).	Invest Japan Office established (May).
2004	Korea-Chile FTA signed and enters into force (Apr.). APEC Summit held in Santiago, Chile (Nov.).	
2005	ERPD process integrated into CMI (Nov.).	Japan-Mexico EPA enters into force (Apr.).
2006	P4 among New Zealand (May), Singapore (May), Brunei (July), and Chile (Nov.) enters into force. ADB adopts Regional Cooperation and Integration Strategy (July).	Japan-Malaysia EPA enters into force (July).
2007	Korea-United States FTA signed (June). Subprime mortgage crisis emerges (July).	Japan-Chile EPA enters into force (Sep.).
2008	Lehman Brothers collapses at height of global financial crisis (Sep.) First G20 Summit held in Washington, D.C. (Nov.)	New JICA established (Oct.). ASEAN-Japan Comprehensive EPA (Dec.) and Japan-Philippines EPA (Dec.) enter into force.

Year	Global and Regional Events	Events in Japan and Economic Partnership Agreements
2009	Barack Obama inaugurated as U.S. president (Jan.)	DPJ wins election, ending longtime LDP rule (Aug.). Japan-Thailand EPA (June) and Japan–Switzerland EPA (Sep.) enter into force.
2010	Chiang Mai Initiative Multilateralization launched (Mar.). Seoul Development Consensus for Shared Growth announced at G20 Summit in Seoul, South Korea (Nov.).	Prime Minister Kan expresses interest in participating in TPP negotiations (Oct.). APEC Summit held in Yokohama, Japan (Nov.).
2011	AMRO established in Singapore (Apr.). Secretary of State Hillary R. Clinton launches U.S. rebalance policy at APEC Summit in Hawaii (Nov.)	Great East Japan earthquake, tsunami, and Fukushima nuclear meltdown occur (Mar.). Japan-India EPA enters into force (Aug.).
2012	ECB announces offer of support to eurozone countries afflicted by sovereign debt crisis (Sep.). UN Conference on Sustainable Development held in Rio de Janeiro, Brazil (June).	Japan-Peru EPA enters into force (Mar.). Three of the Senkaku/Diaoyu Islands nationalized (Sep.). LDP regains majority in Lower House election; Shinzō Abe elected prime minister (Dec.).
2013	President Xi Jinping announces BRI launch (Sep.)	Prime Minister Abe announces Japan's participation in TPP negotiations (Mar.), followed by formal participation (July).

(*continued*)

TABLE 3.1
Chronology of Major Events, 1990–2019 (*continued*)

Year	Global and Regional Events	Events in Japan and Economic Partnership Agreements
2014	FTAAP endorsed at APEC Summit in Beijing (Nov.).	Japan–Australia EPA enters into force (July).
2015	Completion of application to (Mar.) and inauguration of AIIB (June). BRICS New Development Bank launched (July). UN adopts 2030 Agenda for Sustainable Development (Sep.). Agreement reached on TPP-12 (Oct.).	Prime Minister Abe announces "Partnership for Quality Investment" (May).
2016	AIIB officially launched (Jan.). TPP-12 agreement signed (Feb.). AMRO established as an international organization (Feb.). G20 Summit held in Hangzhou, China (Sep.).	G7 Summit held in Ise-Shima, Japan (May). Japan–Mongolia EPA enters into force (June). Legislative ratification of TPP-12 completed in Upper and Lower Houses (Dec.).
2017	President Donald Trump inaugurated and United States withdraws from TPP (Jan.). First BRI summit held in Beijing (May). U.S. announces vision of a "Free and Open Indo-Pacific" at APEC Summit in Da Nang, Vietnam (Nov.).	Bilateral swap agreements with Southeast Asian countries renewed (Apr.).
2018	U.S.–China trade war begins (Jan.). CPTPP agreement consolidated (Jan.), signed (Mar.), and entered into force (Dec.).	Japan–EU EPA signed (Jul.).

Year	Global and Regional Events	Events in Japan and Economic Partnership Agreements
2019	Second BRI Summit held in Beijing (Apr.).	Japan–EU EPA enters into force (Feb.). First round of talks on U.S.-Japan trade agreement held in Washington, D.C. (Apr.). G20 Summit held in Osaka, Japan (June).

Sources: ADB; AIIB; Bloomberg; Cabinet Office; Ministry of Economy, Trade and Industry of Japan; Ministry of Foreign Affairs of Japan; Ministry of Foreign Affairs and Trade of New Zealand; OECD; Prime Minister's Office; United Nations; White House; World Trade Organization.

despite the continued influence of the United States in the region and the efforts of President Barack Obama's administration to rebalance to Asia, the relative weight of the U.S. economy, in terms of both trade and investment and ideological prominence, has weakened visibly since the global financial crisis.

East Asia has long been a vital region for Japan. Indeed, as discussed in the introduction, in the face of long-term economic stagnation accompanied by a declining population in recent years, the economically vibrant region, which includes a rapidly growing China, has become even more important for Japan's economic survival. Under these circumstances, the triangular dynamics among the United States, China, and Japan provide an important setting for explaining how a new state-led regional geoeconomic strategy has emerged, and why the Japanese government is keen on employing such a strategy in the Asia-Pacific.

This chapter contextualizes Japanese state-led liberal strategy in regional geoeconomics of the twenty-first century first by examining the shift in the regional economic balance from the end of the World War II. The chapter then turns to the rise of China and the challenges it has introduced to the regional economic order based on the liberal economic model. Finally, it examines Japan's changing position in the regional economic evolution before concluding with some notes on how this environment closely connects to the origin of Japan's new geoeconomic strategy.

Japan in the Shifting Balance in the Asia-Pacific

How did Japan's economic position shift over time? For more than fifty years from the end of World War II, the U.S.-Japan relationship has been the cornerstone of Japan's regional strategy in the Asia-Pacific, from the restoration of Japan's economic ties with Southeast Asia through the end of the Cold War.[1] Indeed, a strong bilateral security alliance consistently reinforced close economic ties between the two countries. However, Japan's export-led growth strategy also gave rise to a series of trade tensions and bilateral trade talks with the United States, from the first U.S.-Japan Textile Negotiations of the mid-1950s to the Structural Impediment Initiative Talks between 1989 and 1990. Nonetheless, by the mid-1990s, after the automobile parts trade dispute, the bilateral trade conflict between these two countries had largely quieted down.[2] On the investment front, in the aftermath of the Plaza Accord (1985), the Japanese yen underwent significant appreciation. Bolstered by well-crafted industrial strategies, Japan quickly directed its outward foreign direct investment toward both the United States and Southeast Asia. Throughout these changes, Japan's economic and security dependence on the United States continued to serve as the lynchpin of the country's foreign policy. Meanwhile, there appeared to be no calculation by the U.S. administrations during the time regarding the U.S.-China-Japan triangle as to how to integrate Japan's role in formulating U.S. policy toward China.[3]

Until about that time, the Japanese government had not considered China an economic competitor in the Asia-Pacific. In fact, it was important for the Japanese government during this time to promote China's engagement in the regional and global economy as the country began to open up its economy to the outside world. The Japanese government's actions in the aftermath of the Tiananmen Square Incident of 1989 clearly demonstrated this commitment. As the rest of the G7 governments imposed severe business sanctions against the Chinese government, Japan worked to soften this stance among the Western powers by becoming the first country to lift economic sanctions against China, claiming that it would be more dangerous to isolate China in a time of crisis.[4] Several years later, nonetheless, China's aggressive military posture and nuclear testing raised concerns in Japan of its potential power projection. At that point, Japan's relationship with China was also influenced by the dynamics of the

U.S.-Japan-China triangle. In 1998, when President Bill Clinton (1992–2000) flew to Beijing for a summit meeting with President Jiang Zemin, his nine-day stay in China without making a stop in Tokyo raised major concerns of "Japan passing" amid the country's economic stagnation.

Since the decade of the "War on Terror" for the United States in the 2000s, Asia has been relatively neglected in terms of U.S. foreign policy and overall resources allocated to the region.[5] Meanwhile, China's economic reach extended beyond its borders as the country began to engage in a "going global" strategy after the Asian financial crisis.[6] By the early 2010s there was a clear increase in tensions between the United States and China owing to China's massive trade surplus with the United States. In particular, China's heightened presence in the global economy after the global financial crisis introduced an added level of complexity to the region's already complicated dynamics. Correspondingly, Japan's position between the two major trading partners began to change as well. On the one hand, in 2008 China overtook the United States as Japan's largest trading partner, and with increased direct investment in China, Japanese firms began to manufacture many of their products there. Furthermore, investment from around the region had transformed China into a "Factory Asia."[7] On the other hand, the U.S. government began to look to Japan as an important supporter of its continued regional presence. From the Nye-Armitage Report of 2000 to the crystallization of Obama's rebalance strategy to Asia in 2011, Japan has figured prominently in the U.S. Pacific strategy.

Rise of China and Challenges to the Global and Regional Economic Order

Thanks to two decades of rapid economic growth, China became the second-largest economy in the world in 2010, overtaking Japan. In the mid-2010s, as the Chinese economy continued to grow, though at a more moderate rate than before, there were increased concerns that China might "eclipse" the United States in the near future.[8] Although this topic is beyond the scope of this study, debates over the consequences of China's rise and its implications for the dominant position of the United States in the global order in the areas of both economics and security continued well into the 2010s. To contextualize Japan's regional geoeconomic strategy, I highlight three essential aspects of China's economic rise during this period: The first is the timing and magnitude of China's economic growth and expansion compared to that of the United States and Japan. The second focuses on the nature of the challenge that China's economic expansion poses for the United States, and how it clashes with U.S. dominance in the global economy. Third, both China's rise and the country's dissatisfaction with global economic governance translate into China contesting the existing regional and global economic order, particularly in the aftermath of the global financial crisis.

The economic balance among the United States, Japan, and China underwent significant shifts with the rapid economic growth of the two Asian economies: the Japanese from the 1950s to the 1980s and the Chinese from the 1980s through the 2010s (figure 3.1). Based on the market exchange rate, the U.S. economy continues to be the largest economy in the world. The size of the Japanese economy came closest to that of the United States around the early 1990s, partly helped by the strong yen, but has since stagnated. Meanwhile, the Chinese economy grew very rapidly

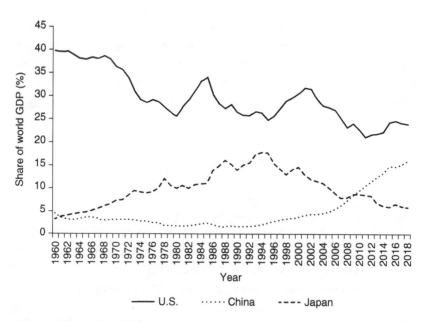

Figure 3.1 Share of World GDP: United States, China, and Japan, 1960–2018.
Source: World Bank, "GDP (Current US$)," https://data.worldbank.org/indicator/NY.GDP.MKTP.CD.

in the twenty-first century as it caught up to Japan in 2010, and it continues to inch up.[9] Of course, with a large population of 1.4 billion (as of December 2018), China's gross domestic product per capita still ranks among the upper-middle-income level of developing countries according to the World Bank's categorization, while both the United States and Japan belong to the upper-income group.

The nature of the challenge introduced by China's explosive growth comes in the form of a sharp contrast and ideological battle between China's economic model and the prevailing "Western" norms and perspectives governing economic development. China has followed the "socialist market economy" model since its modernization reform and has adopted Deng Xiaoping's Open Door Policy starting in 1978. Many elements of China's economic development strategy during this time have taken after the developmentalist state model.[10] China's strong state-centralism in the economy, which Ian Bremmer calls "state capitalism," has appeared to enjoy many advantages in the world under the liberal economic order.[11] The primary engine of China's rapid growth is large-scale export promotion supported partially by the country's state-owned enterprises (SOEs) and judiciously controlled capital accounts, which allow the government to carefully manage financial inflows and outflows. As the Chinese economy rose and began to clash with the "Washington Consensus" model of free-market capitalism prevailing in the global economy, some began to dub China's economic strategy the "Beijing Consensus."[12]

It is not in the scope of this book to elaborate on the details of this clash, but examples are abundant. In the realm of currency competition, the Chinese leadership has resisted U.S. pressures to revalue China's currency and to liberalize capital accounts, in turn criticizing the dominant role of the U.S. dollar in the global economy and the U.S. government's irresponsible macroeconomic management. There has also been substantial progress made toward enhancing the use of the Chinese currency, the renminbi, internationally.[13] In the area of trade, China has pushed for free-trade agreements based on "Asia-only" membership and on varying degrees of speed and levels of economic liberalization. Meanwhile, the United States has pursued a much higher standard in trade liberalization and rule setting in the Asia-Pacific, first through its bilateral trade agreements with Singapore, Australia, and South Korea and later through TPP, which includes restrictions on SOEs. Since 2018 the United States and China have been in the middle of a trade war. President Trump claims that China is employing unfair trade practices against the United States as it "steals technology" and dumps cheap goods produced with massive state subsidies, ultimately causing and worsening a massive trade imbalance between the two countries in China's favor.

China's contention against the U.S.-led liberal order of global economic governance has led to many more instances of systemic repercussions outside of the U.S.-China power balance.[14] By the 2010s China's challenges to global governance had taken on the form of dissatisfaction against the slow accommodation of China's rising power, as the United States and the West (including Japan) continue to dominate the global economic governance structure.

Above all, the global financial crisis immensely affected the way in which China began to contest the system of economic governance. This massive economic crisis, second only to the Great Depression of 1929–late 1930s in the magnitude of overall damage to the global economy, emanated from the United States. That country's subprime mortgage crisis emerged in 2007 through bad mortgage loans packaged into a variety of financial products such as mortgage-backed securities and collateralized debt obligations. When one of the largest investment banks, Lehman Brothers, collapsed under the weight of the bad loans in September 2008, it triggered a massive downturn in stock markets, an unprecedented credit crunch, and deleveraging not only in the United States and Europe but around the world.[15] The global crisis, at the end of the day, created an estimated $6 to $14 trillion worth in stock market and output losses.[16] Many governments stepped in with massive fiscal stimulus packages and bailouts in order to save their economies. Not only is the magnitude of the crisis an important page in the recent history of the globalized economy, but it is also vital in multiple ways for reshaping the power dynamics within the global economic order.

First, the crisis originated in the United States and affected Europe most severely. This was in stark contrast to the major financial crises of recent decades that had emerged from developing regions such as Latin America (1982, 1994, 1998, and 2001), Asia (1997), and Russia (1998). The global financial crisis has cast profound doubt on the appropriateness of the neoliberal economic model promoted mainly by the advanced economies and international financial institutions in the past three decades supporting economic globalization, particularly through financial liberalization, deregulation, and privatization. Hence the crisis discredited neoliberalism and the Washington Consensus.[17] In addition, emerging economies complained of a double standard when governments of the advanced countries were able to engage in massive fiscal stimulus programs to speed up the recovery of their own economies, a policy that was not permitted during other financial crises prior to this one.

Furthermore, an extensive rethinking of economic growth strategies and international economic governance took place during and in the aftermath of the crisis, which prompted efforts to improve financial regulations and promote sustainable growth. Most prominently, the exclusive club of global economic governance shifted to the newly created Group of 20 (G20) heads-of-state summitry that included many emerging market economies.[18] The old Group of 7 (the United States, the United Kingdom, France, Germany, Japan, Canada, and Italy) continues to exist, but in the aftermath of the crisis the G20 seems to have become an important forum for economic governance.

Second, many of the emerging market economies recovered much more quickly and robustly from the crisis partly because they were not as severely affected by the so-called toxic financial assets.[19] These governments were also able to implement fiscal and financial stimulus packages to boost their economies, which were most heavily affected by the export downturn, as exemplified by China.[20] China's speedy recovery from the global financial crisis has quickened the shift in the global economic power balance, placing the country at the forefront of postcrisis economic recovery despite concerns over its economic governance.

Third, these dynamics have also imposed added challenges to global economic governance because they affect and are affected by the challenges of worldwide multilateral institutions of trade (World Trade Organization), macroeconomics (International Monetary Fund), and development finance (World Bank). The WTO, the highly anticipated multilateral trade institution that succeeded the GATT in 1995, became ineffective as a trade liberalization forum after a dozen years of Doha Round negotiations failed to yield any agreement. The round first entered into negotiations in November 2001 in hopes of making further progress toward worldwide trade liberalization in many difficult areas, such as agriculture, services, and investment. Meanwhile, preferential free trade agreements with exclusive memberships proliferated not only among industrialized countries but throughout the world (see figure 5.1).[21] As will be discussed in chapter 5,

Asia is no exception; despite a slow start, Asia's mostly bilateral FTAs multiplied rapidly into the 2000s.

The financial crises led to criticism against Bretton Woods institutions such as the IMF and the World Bank. At the time of the global financial crisis, the ideological legitimacy and policy credibility of these institutions, which were widely perceived as a way to promote neoliberal reforms throughout the developing world, came under attack. While the IMF addressed the major economic crises in Europe and elsewhere under the global crisis, it was also simultaneously responding to the criticisms of the newly empowered governments of various emerging market economies, such as China, Russia, India, Brazil, and South Africa (often grouped as the BRICS).[22] These governments have begun vocally demanding that the IMF undergo reform to more readily reflect their voices in its decision-making processes.[23] A decade earlier, severe criticism in the aftermath of the Asian financial crisis had already prompted some reforms at the IMF, such as a lowering of conditionality for its bridge-funding mechanism.[24] The IMF furthermore undertook some rethinking and came down in favor of greater capital controls and exercising more caution towards excessive financial liberalization.[25] Nonetheless, these changes did not satisfy the emerging powers, which were collectively determined to make relevant changes in the institution.[26]

Regional Economic Dynamics and Japan

Despite the slowdown in Japan's economy for more than two decades, the twenty-first century has been the century of Asia's dominance—now led by China—which continues to resonate throughout the world due to both a quantitative rise and a qualitative shift of the region's economies.[27] In fact, in spite of some setbacks after the Asian financial crisis, the majority of the economies in the region have seen continued economic growth (quantitative rise) in the past two decades. The overall GDP growth of the East Asian economies has been sustained by the double-digit GDP growth of China, as illustrated in figure 3.1. Many Southeast Asian economies, too, have experienced rapid economic development during the past several decades to become middle- to upper-middle-income economies and are now aiming to become high-income countries within the next ten years.[28]

During the period from the late 1980s to the second decade of the twenty-first century, the economic weight of the two large regional powers, Japan and China, within East Asia clearly altered. As demonstrated in figure 3.2, over the course of these thirty years, the combined economic weight of both countries accounted for around 75 percent of the regional GDP of East Asia (i.e., Northeast and Southeast Asia combined). What has been transformed is the balance between the two in favor of China at the expense of Japan. Hence Japan's relations with the region in the twenty-five years between 1990 and the mid-2010s have changed from the "leader of the pack" of the hierarchical flying-geese pattern to the position of one of the region's leaders among peers.[29] Meanwhile, as noted previously, the rivalry between the United States and China in the economic governance of the region intensifies, and Japan has come to occupy a strategic position with which it can tip the power balance toward either country. Such a pivotal state function is crucial in guiding the direction of the regional economic order in Asia.

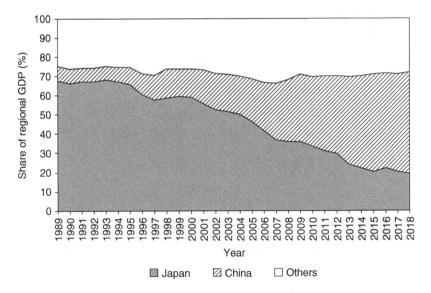

Figure 3.2 Regional GDP and Changing Shares of Japan and China, 1989–2018. The World Bank's category "East Asia and the Pacific" is used as the denominator in relevant calculations.
Source: World Bank, "GDP (Current US$)," https://data.worldbank.org/indicator/NY .GDP.MKTP.CD.

Meanwhile, Japan's trade dependence on East Asia (both Northeast and Southeast) has noticeably increased at the expense of its exports to the United States (figure 3.3). A large part of Japan's exports within the region constitute intrafirm trade to support the supply chain of Japanese industries, where Japanese firms export parts to produce manufactured products in Asia, increasingly in China. Significant quantities of final products are still exported to advanced economies outside of the region, such as the United States and Europe.[30] This regional production network has also contributed to the integration of trade within the region in the twenty-first century (figure 3.4).[31]

East Asian economies, with their focus on manufacturing production, have also transformed qualitatively during the past quarter-century. The Asian financial crisis was an important catalyst for the developing Asian region in terms of putting in place much-needed reforms, capacity building, and building increasingly protective buffers against future crises for these economies.[32] Some reforms also spilled over into political and social

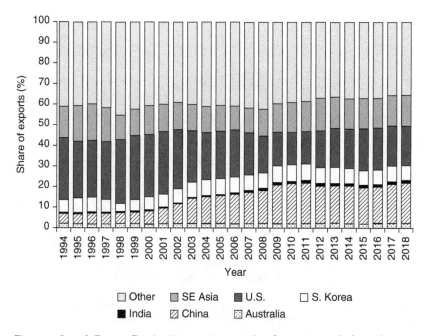

Figure 3.3 Japan's Export Destinations, 1994–2018. Southeast Asia includes Indonesia, Malaysia, the Philippines, Singapore, Thailand, and Vietnam.
Source: IMF, "Direction of Trade Statistics (DOTS)," http://data.imf.org.

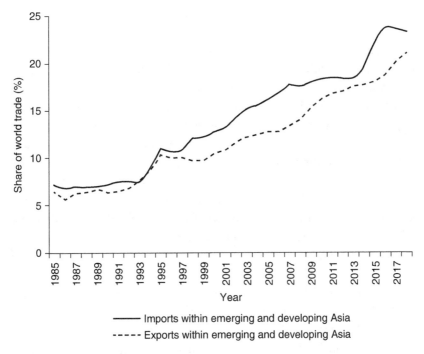

Figure 3.4 Growth of Intraregional Trade in Asia, 1985–2018. The denominators used in calculations are the world's total imports (CIF) and total exports (FOB), respectively. The IMF's category "emerging and developing Asia" includes China, ASEAN countries, South Asian countries, and Pacific Island nations.
Source: IMF, "Direction of Trade Statistics (DOTS)," http://data.imf.org.

spheres, which in turn led to deeper democratization for many of Southeast Asia's former soft-authoritarian states, and such economic growth has enhanced the middle class.[33] Nevertheless, it was premature to conclude that all of Asia's countries successfully transformed into fully open economies and liberal democracies following the Western model. This is because the economic reforms that took place in the aftermath of the Asian financial crisis have produced mixed results in terms of changing economic governance for most Asian countries, including China.[34] Governments' roles in their economies remain dominant as they still rely on their "performance legitimacy" by providing economic growth through trade and investments, with some governments relying on particular government procurement rules (Malaysia) or large state-owned enterprises (China and Vietnam).[35]

With some exceptions, such as Singapore, economic liberalization is yet to be complete in the financial sector, with prudential banking regulations followed only on a surface level in the form of mock compliance.[36] Partly to protect their vulnerable financial sector, the same Asian economies led by China have accumulated massive foreign exchange reserves since the Asian financial crisis under (mostly) managed floating exchange rate regimes.[37] The large foreign exchange reserves not only work to shield their economies against future currency crises but also have emerged as these governments continue to pursue export-promotion through depressed exchange rates.[38]

The risk-averting financial and fiscal management styles of these Asian governments have ironically saved them from the major detrimental impact of the global financial crisis in the late 2000s. Most of the Asian economies, including Japan and South Korea, whose financial institutions are the most liberalized and global in the region, were not heavily affected by the toxic financial assets of mortgage-backed securities. This was because the banks were slow in recovering from their own domestic financial crises of the late 1990s and were exceedingly cautious about their business practices.[39] Unlike during the Asian financial crisis, the Asian governments were free and able to stimulate their economies via fiscal measures, as prominently represented by the massive $586 billion (RMB 4 trillion) stimulus package doled out by the Chinese government in November 2008. As such, and despite a dramatic cut in consumption in the United States and Europe and declining exports from Asia to these regions, East Asian economies bounced back quite quickly from the crisis, along with the emerging economies of Latin America as well as India.[40] As discussed earlier, the economic model based on neoliberal principles was at least temporarily discredited around the world as the United States struggled to regain its economic foothold and Europe was further hit by its sovereign debt and euro crisis starting with Greece in 2010.[41]

Geoeconomic Environment Since 2013

The year 2013 was quite an important one for geoeconmic developments in the Asia-Pacific, on two accounts. First, large economic initiatives such as the Trans-Pacific Partnership and the Belt-and-Road Initiative along with the Asian Infrastructure Investment Bank emerged in full shape in

2013. Although negotiations for the TPP had already started prior to 2013, Japan's admission as the twelfth and the last member of the TPP in July made the TPP larger and much more formidable in the region. Second, 2013 was the year when both Japan and China saw the rise of strong political leadership: Prime Minister Shinzō Abe and President Xi Jinping. Since then, both have managed to push their countries' respective economic agendas forward. As discussed earlier, a change came in the aftermath of the global financial crisis, when the collapse of the global economy and doubts on the liberal economic order under U.S. leadership became real concerns for world leaders. Emerging market economies, particularly China, on the contrary, continued to grow, while international institutions ranging from the IMF to the WTO faced reform challenges and stagnation.

After a few years of searching for a desperately needed "breakthrough" for American commercial policy, then-president George W. Bush began engaging in the TPP in 2008. During this time the United States faced the subprime mortgage crisis and the economy was facing recession, and efforts to engage in free trade agreement negotiations in the previous few years had failed to bear fruit.[42] American businesses were also desperately looking for opportunities in Asia, whose economies recovered much more quickly and robustly from the global financial crisis than the United States or Europe had. By 2011 the TPP had become the economic pillar of the Obama administration's foreign policy toward Asia, dubbed the "pivot" or "rebalance." At the Asia-Pacific Economic Cooperation summit in Hawaii, Secretary of State Hillary Clinton made a famous speech in which she referred to the TPP: "We are also making progress on the Trans-Pacific Partnership (TPP), which will bring together economies from across the Pacific—developed and developing alike—into a single trading community. Our goal is to create not just more growth, but better growth. We believe trade agreements need to include strong protections for workers, the environment, intellectual property, and innovation."[43]

It is beyond the scope of this book to examine the multitude of objectives that encompass the U.S. rebalance strategy.[44] Suffice it to note that some experts in both the United States and China suspected that the rebalance was actually targeted at China, and they perceived the TPP to be an economic containment strategy against the rising regional power.[45] It is evident, however, that an important part of the TPP challenge is to produce an unquestionable success in establishing robust trade and investment rules and to pave the way for an expansion of TPP membership throughout the region.[46] That way, negative externalities such as trade and investment diversion accruing to China from its exclusion in this grouping might motivate its government to join TPP later on, after the first twelve countries establish these "high-standard" rules.[47] The U.S. government was adamant on enlisting Japan as a key country among the TPP negotiating members. On the one hand, since Japan enjoys significant economic weight in the region, its participation in the TPP has become, geoeconomically, highly important in the U.S. pursuit of achieving these goals and in shaping the regional commercial order (see chapter 5).[48] On the other hand, by having parallel bilateral tariff negotiations, the U.S. government could pressure Japan on further market opening—particularly in the area of agriculture, which the Japanese government has long resisted.

Concomitantly, China has adhered to a "win-win" strategy through trade and outward investment, as China stands to gain economically and strategically. Akin to Japan in the postwar period, infrastructure investment has, in the recent past, guided China's economic growth and development. From a business perspective, the Belt-and-Road Initiative and the Asian Infrastructure Investment Bank funding of infrastructure projects aimed at providing more business opportunities for Chinese companies in the region. From a geostrategic perspective, the BRI and AIIB will surmount the TPP's suspected China-containment tactics by effectively connecting China to Asia, the Middle East, Europe, and Africa. As will be discussed more in chapter 7, the BRI, with its proposed $1 trillion funding, has aimed to cover the infrastructure investment gap in Asia in support of economic connectivity in the region. The last two BRI summits have attracted significant interest from leaders around the world, including those from beyond Asia, while the United States and Japan have shown more distance. At the same time, China's increasing economic presence in small developing countries has begun to evoke concerns.[49] In response to concerns of increasing debt to China among these economies, President Xi emphasized debt sustainability as an important consideration during the BRI summit in April 2019.

Additionally, the new multilateral development banks (MDBs) such as the AIIB and the New Development Bank (NDB) established by the BRICS challenge the dominant influence of the incumbent powers such as the United States and Europe (and to a lesser extent Japan) over development funding, norms, and policies. By establishing an "outside option" and a true alternative to the IMF or the World Bank, the Chinese government is now in a position to defy the "liberal economic order" and "Washington Consensus" preached by the United States and these Bretton Woods institutions.[50]

Furthermore, from 2016 forward, the gradual rise of populism around the North Atlantic translated into electoral victories of several populist leaders. In particular, the election of Donald Trump in November 2016 once again shifted geoeconomic dynamics. Keeping his campaign promise, President Trump, with "America First" economic priorities and disdain for multilateral institutions, withdrew from the TPP soon after his inauguration. The United States has also created a countercoalition against China and enticed Japan through a U.S.-Japan bilateral trade agreement. In late 2017 the Trump administration formulated a "Free and Open Indo-Pacific" strategy to counter Chinese initiatives in the region. This strategy pursues the geostrategic goals of containing China's ability to dominate Asia and bolstering partnerships with major democratic countries like Australia, India, and Japan. Since 2018 the administration has engaged in a trade war with China, imposing tariffs on Chinese products to balance the U.S. trade deficit with the country.

In the quarter-century from the late 1990s through the first two decades of the twenty-first century, the balance of economic power in the Asia-Pacific shifted from U.S. dominance, where Japan was the major economic challenger, to economic competition between the United States and China. This competition has become particularly intense and systemic since the global financial crisis. China's rise has emerged as a new challenge as well as a new opportunity for Japan, as this phenomenon sets the stage for Japan's state-led liberal strategy in the region. On the one hand, Japan has struggled to maintain a solid foothold in the region as its relative importance declined. The traditional bilaterally based and hierarchic style of Japanese regional relations is no longer an effective means of influence under rising levels of development in the region. On the other hand, Japan's position between these two rival great powers has provided it with a rare strategic opportunity. Japan's strong economic connections to both the United States and China as well as Southeast Asia have placed the country in a unique position of influence and power, which provides Japan a space to move strategically in the field of regional rule setting and institution building.

CHAPTER IV

Transformation in the Japanese Political Economy

T he shift in regional economic power balance among three major powers—the United States, China, and Japan—during the two decades of the 1990s and 2000s gave a strong impetus for Japan's new geoeconomic strategy to focus more on the region, with global standard-setting as a tool to promote Japan's presence. Meanwhile, Japan's domestic politico-economic structure underwent visible transformation during the same time. This has contributed to reinforcing the direction of the new Japanese regional geoeconomic strategy of the twenty-first century and shaped the paths of its implementation, as the domestic economic policy-making structure determines the priorities and instruments available to the government.

In other words, the old regional strategy of bilateralism, informalism, and heavy government involvement in Japan's regional economy and expansion was dependent on the country's domestic structure of the "iron triangle," "Japan Inc.," or the "alliance capitalism" that had dominated Japan's political economy since the 1950s.[1] Under this system, the close ties among Liberal Democratic Party (LDP) politicians, the economic bureaucracy, and big business helped extend Japan's economic reach both within Asia and far beyond the country's immediate sphere of influence.[2] A good example of the old practice was the prevalence of request-base foreign aid (chapter 7), where Japanese businesses could become brokers of the government's foreign aid projects that would ultimately benefit these very companies involved in the recipient government's requests. In what is often called the "development trinity" of foreign aid, investment, and trade, the Japanese government held the central position in guiding the country's regional economic strategy.

Conversely, once the political distance between the LDP, the bureaucracy, and big business widened owing to economic reforms and changing political norms, those informal arrangements became increasingly difficult to assemble for the sake of Japan's economic outreach in Asia. Furthermore, Japan's large private corporations outgrew the government's guidance— gradually through the 1970s and 1980s for the manufacturing sector and abruptly in the 1990s for the financial sector after the country's financial crisis. Many of these firms now operate in Asia independently and usually in competition with one another. All these changes have made it difficult for the government to maintain close government-business collaboration, the degree of which differs depending on the issue area (chapters 5, 6, and 7).

This chapter focuses on two interrelated aspects of domestic politico-economic institutions: The first is the relationship among the three major actors in economic policy making: political parties, the economic bureaucracy, and influential large businesses. Throughout the transition years of the 1990s into the early 2000s, the longstanding close ties among these three entities significantly loosened. The second aspect is the power balance between the government and big business. Known as the "convoy system" in finance or as dominance of administrative guidance (*gyōsei shidō*), the power of the state over businesses was one of the dominant theories about Japan.[3] As ties between businesses and the government loosened, however, the state's direct influence over private firms steadily declined. Therefore the government must find new ways to stay relevant and govern in the face of globalized businesses in a regional economic order constantly in flux.

Changes in Politics and Governance Institutions in Japan

The political environment that permitted close ties and active collaboration among politicians, the bureaucracy, and big business in Japan throughout the high-growth era and into the bubble economy of the 1980s phased out in the 1990s based on the country's economic maturity, dwindling economic and political resources, and shifting electoral and party politics.[4]

One major feature of this transformation is the loosening of the institutional connection between the government entities and businesses. These institutional changes have contributed to the fluctuation of the government's role in policy making.

Politicians, Bureaucrats, and Businesses

Many factors have contributed to the loosening of the connection among politicians, the economic bureaucracy, and big businesses in Japan over the course of the 1990s into the 2000s. One of the most revealing empirical studies is by a team of scholars led by Michio Muramatsu and Ikuo Kume, who conducted surveys on legislators, bureaucrats, and industry associates in three different time periods at about ten-year intervals.[5] Through the vast amount of survey data collected and analyzed, several structural shifts in Japan's economic governance among these three actors became clear. First, the regularity and frequency of contacts between the government (both legislators and bureaucrats) and industry associations visibly decreased in the 2000s. Second, the bureaucrats' assessment regarding ministries' contacts with these associations has changed from predominantly positive and productive to negative and detrimental, and the purpose of contacts has shifted from pursuing cooperation to obtaining information. Finally, bureaucrats have become increasingly wary of catering to certain business interests. From the industry associations' side, overall trust in both legislators and bureaucrats in securing positive responses on policy formulation or change has sharply declined as well.[6]

Regarding the shifting dynamic between legislators and bureaucrats, there has been a slight decrease in frequency of contact, especially from bureaucrats to politicians. A more prominent shift in the relationship between these two groups, however, can be found in their perceptions of each other. Essentially, perceived policy influence has moved away from the bureaucrats into the hands of politicians in all important policy issue areas, ranging from security to economic policy to political reform. The perceived powers in national policy making of the prime minister and other ministers appointed primarily from elected members of the Diet have also visibly increased at the expense of higher-ranking bureaucrats. It is important to note, nonetheless, that the LDP's dominant influence over bureaucrats has declined with the change in government that took place in

1993–1994. This change has led the bureaucracy to become more politically neutral in recent years.[7]

Finally, regarding the relationship between legislators and bureaucrats, it is helpful to understand how political elites measured their successes in influencing policy making. Muramatsu argues that there are four configurations in the game of legislature-bureaucracy cooperation: legislative domination, bureaucratic domination, positive sum, and negative sum.[8] Through the three surveys taken of bureaucrats, it was found that the positive sum understanding of legislature-bureaucracy cooperation that dominated in the first two periods (late 1970s and late 1980s) had receded to the third rank in the early 2000s, below legislative domination (first ranked) and negative sum (second ranked). This indicates the collapse of the alliance between the legislature and the bureaucracy in leading the country and signals the increased influence of other nonstate actors in this area. Furthermore, although the amount of time bureaucrats spent meeting with officials from other ministries did not change drastically from the 1980s to 2000s, there was a visible decrease in the amount of time each bureaucrat spent coordinating policies with other ministries over the course of the study.

Shifting Political Institutions

How and why has this distance among the three main actors emerged? Muramatsu argues that this phenomenon can be attributed to three major events affecting Japan since the late 1980s: first, the end of the Cold War and the associated acceleration of globalization; second, the political turmoil and interruption of the LDP's long rule (changes in the governing party) in 1993 and 2009; and third, the government's fiscal constraints due to Japan's enduring economic stagnation.[9] Following Muramatsu's lead, I highlight four interrelated changes discussed in the literature: instability in the ruling government; the 1994 electoral reform; administrative reforms legislated under Prime Minister Ryūtaro Hashimoto (1996–1998) and utilized by Prime Minister Junichirō Koizumi (2001–2006); and the gradual distancing of politics and business due to various political and bureaucratic scandals.

The first and most obvious shift since the early 1990s came out of instability in the ruling party in government. Despite political challenges from a mostly labor-supported "left" by the Japan Socialist Party, the LDP maintained majority party status for thirty-eight years after its inception in 1955. It lost power in August 1993 owing to the splintering of Ichirō Ozawa and fifty-plus LDP members who formed new parties. The LDP came back into power under a coalition agreement with the Socialist Party within a year, but several major changes, including a transformative law that introduced a new electoral system and a bureaucracy that grew more distant from the LDP, also exerted major influence during this time. These institutional changes, combined with protracted economic stagnation, continuously put pressure on the LDP, whose rural electoral base was aging fast and decreasing in number. When Prime Minister Koizumi came into office with the pledge to shake up the LDP, he enacted several major reforms that removed the protection and privileges enjoyed by the LDP's traditional constituents, mostly in weak and uncompetitive business sectors or in the rural agriculture sector. Consequently, the LDP experienced backlash from former staunch LDP supporters from these areas. The global financial crisis and the combined ineffectiveness of Koizumi's three succeeding prime ministers (in three years) in the late 2000s sealed the LDP's fate, as seen in the Democratic Party of Japan's (DPJ) landslide victory in the Lower House elections in August 2009.

The DPJ's rule, however, ended up lasting for a mere three years and three months. Ruling the country for the first time after more than fifty years of LDP dominance and experiencing several major disasters, some invited and others beyond its control, the DPJ lost massively against the LDP in the December 2012 Lower House election.[10] During its three years in power, the DPJ was plagued by the party's own internal discord under a divided Diet, where the Upper House was dominated by the LDP since 2011, and could not achieve its promised goals and objectives.[11] Although the DPJ tried to control the bureaucracy, it completely failed to implement any changes to that effect. Also, many policy failures emerged from a lack of cooperation between the DPJ and the bureaucrats.[12] The revived LDP rule under Prime Minister Shinzō Abe began in December 2012 following the DPJ's defeat. With strong electoral victories by the LDP, Abe's administration is expected to last much longer than several previous administrations. This expectation of stability has affected the country's economic policy, from monetary policy to Japan's commitment to the TPP. Furthermore, a multiyear period of political stability has allowed some of the old Japanese network politics to return.

The second element of change is the electoral reform of 1994, a topic of intense discussion among scholars of Japanese domestic politics. This reform changed Japan's Lower House (House of Representatives) electoral system from a single nontransferable vote (SNTV) system to a mixed-member majoritarian (MMM) system dominated by single-member districts.[13] The major motivations behind the electoral reform were to reduce the corruption and money politics associated with the personal vote strategy on the part of (mostly) LDP members and to encourage broader policy debates so as to appeal to the interests of the median voter.[14] The expected consequence of the electoral reform, particularly within the LDP, was the reduction of factional (*habatsu*) and special-interest policy tribe (*zoku*) politics that characterized the SNTV system.[15] Frances McCall Rosenbluth and Michael F. Thies argue that this new electoral system reduced the influence of special-interest groups and "introduced a neoliberal policy bias" in domestic economic policy that would ultimately lead to an increase in income inequality and social insecurity.[16] The neoliberal inclination of the new electoral system would also be enhanced by the reduced role of the *zoku* members of the Diet, as special-interest groups lost one more channel through which they could previously influence policy making.

There are continued debates on the connection between the electoral reform and administrative reform.[17] Nonetheless, the changes that Prime Minister Hashimoto put in place and Prime Minister Koizumi effectively used are elements that make up the third key change in Japan's politico-economic institutions. With the return of the LDP as the majority party (from June 1994 in coalition and since November 1996 on its own), a series of administrative and economic reforms were enacted under the Hashimoto cabinet. Indeed, administrative reforms were desperately needed in Japan in the face of a dramatically changing society and an economy constrained by increasingly tight fiscal conditions. Corruption scandals and criticism over an economy mishandled by the ministries also led to pressure to reform. Furthermore, the main objective of Hashimoto's reform was to establish strong political control over the bureaucracy by his party through streamlining the bureaucratic structure and consolidating the government's policy-making power in the Cabinet Secretariat.[18]

Among the ministries heavily involved in coordinating foreign economic policies, the Ministry of Foreign Affairs was the only one to remain untouched by the administrative reforms. The Economic Planning Agency was absorbed into the Cabinet Office. The "mighty" Ministry of

International Trade and Industry managed to escape a major reform, with the exception of a slight name change to the Ministry of Economy, Trade, and Industry and the creation of the Nippon Export and Investment Insurance (NEXI), which split from MITI to provide trade insurance separately. The Ministry of Finance went through measurable restructuring: first, the financial supervisory function (the former Banking and Securities Bureaus) were split from the MOF to become a separate agency (first the Financial Supervisory Agency in 1998 and later with the new title of Financial Services Agency, or FSA, in 2000) governed by the Cabinet Office.[19] Additionally, the revision of the Bank of Japan Law in 1997 gave the Bank of Japan (BOJ) more independence from the MOF starting in April 1998. Despite other financial functions moving to the FSA as a consequence of the MOF reform, the International Bureau (formerly the International Finance Bureau), which dealt with foreign exchange rate policies and economic cooperation (including international financial institutions and multilateral development banks), remained under the MOF. Finally, the Ministry of Agriculture, Forestry, and Fisheries (MAFF) had a portion of its environment-related division move to the newly upgraded "Ministry" of the Environment but largely remained intact.

These changes came into effect in January 2001 under an extremely unpopular prime minister, Yoshirō Mori (with a single-digit approval rating for his cabinet by early 2001). It was the popular Koizumi (with cabinet approval rate fluctuating from 79 percent during his honeymoon period to 34 percent at its lowest),[20] however, who utilized the new system effectively as he stayed in office for over five years from April 2001 to September 2006. This new administrative configuration has consolidated policy-making power in the hands of the Cabinet Office under the prime minister. Koizumi was also able to move much of his reformist agenda forward with the help of the Council on Economic and Fiscal Policy (CEFP) established under the Cabinet Office to decide important policy matters and to coordinate and accommodate each of the ministries' diverse interests.[21] Koizumi used the new government structure when he checked off many of the items on his reform agenda, which included the privatization of Japan's postal service; solving the nonperforming loan (NPL) problem through banking reform; tax and pension reforms; special public corporation (*tokushu-hōjin*) reform; and fiscal restructuring. The Koizumi administration was quite effective in concentrating power in the hands of the prime minister's office and fending off other LDP politicians trying to gut the reforms, while Koizumi was simultaneously uninterested in controlling the bureaucracy and micromanaging the reform process to take away bureaucratic control over the details.[22] His reforms were met with the dichotomous perceptions of the glass half empty with limited success versus the glass half full and largely successful.[23] There also remained continuing sectionalism among the ministries, which shaped the ways in which the government could implement its regional strategy in different issues areas.[24] Nonetheless, Koizumi's leadership and relative centralization of power translated into a fresh take on some areas of Japanese foreign policy, including a major shift in favor of free trade agreements (chapter 5) and support for the East Asia Summit.[25]

The fourth element of institutional change is the distance that has developed between the economic ministries and big businesses, though this change is much less prevalent with small businesses. Such distance emerged through several channels. One was the pressure to improve the professional ethics of public officials. The combined effects of economic malaise and scandals among economic bureaucrats in the latter half of the 1990s shattered the long-held view (or myth) about the integrity of incorruptible public officials in the civil service. After a series of scandals attributed to prominent MOF officials in 1998, the National Ethics Law for Central Government Public Servants (*kokka kōmuin rinri hō*) was passed in 2000, which prohibited civil servants from socializing with individuals belonging to the private firms they regulated. Public officials who received or accepted paid dinners and gifts would be penalized. This was an attempt to eliminate the cozy relationship between government bureaucrats and private firms, which had often led to corruption, collusion, and unethical conduct by civil servants. It also aimed at reestablishing the public trust and respect in government and the civil service. Notwithstanding, the scandals and the installment of the ethics law led to a dramatic rise in information costs, as these changes made it extremely difficult for the economic ministries to acquire "frank views" from their respective industries.[26] From the business side, the strict ethics law and code also began to hinder "information gathering and exchange of opinions between the public administration and private corporations."[27]

The second channel emerged through the declining role of and intense scrutiny over the *shingi-kai* (advisory council) system.[28] Hailed as a major channel that "provide[s] big businesses with one of the major formal means of access to governmental decision-making,"[29] these legally sanctioned consultation bodies (article 8 of the National Administration Organization

Act) were often utilized by ministries such as the MITI and MAFF with large and influential interest groups.[30] The change in the structure of *shingi-kai* came in 1999 in the context of the Hashimoto's administrative reform, where 211 council meetings were reduced to 105. The economic ministries in particular saw a major drop in the number of councils: METI, from 32 in 1996 to 7 in 2006; MAFF, from 22 in 1996 to 6 in 2006; and MOF, from 18 in 1996 to 4 in 2006, with an additional 6 for the FSA.[31] Furthermore, to secure transparency and to avoid any appearance of collusion among special-interest groups and the ministries, the 1999 reform also mandated the publication of all minutes from council meetings.[32]

The third channel that distanced government and business relations came from the major reform of the Fiscal Investment and Loan Program (FILP) in 2001. As a way for the Japanese government to "spend without taxation," the FILP was considered to be "a powerful weapon of industrial strategy."[33] Even at the time of the 2001 reform, from the total amount of ¥598 trillion ($6 trillion) in FILP, 28 percent was directed toward private-sector finance through governmental financial institutions such as the Japan Development Bank and Japan Export Import Bank.[34] These institutions previously channeled savings and insurance funds from the Postal Savings and Postal Life Insurance to policy-guided private use.[35] The reform also abolished any obligation on the part of the Postal Service to transfer its deposits to the MOF's Trust Fund and instead created a system of FILP bonds to attract funding from the market, which placed the Postal Bank under obligation to absorb a large portion of those bonds.

The fourth channel, whose phase-out does not yet seem conclusive, is the pressure against the *amakudari* (descending from heaven) practice in which government officials assume high-level positions in private corporations after leaving their government positions. The *amakudari* system has long consolidated the government-industry connection. Once considered a typical feature of the "iron triangle," the practice has since come under attack, as it came to be perceived as a form of obvious collusion between the government and special-interest groups. By the late 1990s the ministries began to refrain from placing their officials in private corporations, and the revision of the National Public Service Act in 2007 made it illegal for public officials to acquire a position within two years of departure from public office at an entity related to the official's previous domain.[36] The revised law also installed a government-run center that streamlined the job-matching process into one channel, effectively prohibiting public officials or offices to act as intermediaries for job searching or for approaching outside institutions with the intention of seeking a position.[37] These reforms, however, have experienced pushback not only from the ministries but also from the opposition parties, and many opaque *amakudari* practices continue to persist.[38] Nevertheless, it is clear that the "descending" process has become intensely scrutinized and is much more difficult to pull off today compared to previous years.

In sum, both political party dynamics and various stages of administrative reform, along with the scandals that result from the traditionally close relationship between the Japanese government and businesses, have created a significant distance and uncertainty in the government-business relationship. Businesses and special-interest groups can still strategically pick between the politicians and bureaucrats as their primary target for lobbying.[39] The obstacles, however, seem to have grown substantially since the mid-1990s. By creating more arm's-length institutions surrounding economic policy making, this new domestic politico-economic configuration ultimately sets the stage for the transformation of Japanese regional geoeconomic strategy and shapes the distinct paths for its implementation in multiple issue areas.

The Power Balance Between the Government and Big Business

The expected influence of the Japanese government in leading domestic economic strategy by guiding the private business sector has long waned, as the power balance of and relations between the government and big business shifted over the course of past several decades. On the one hand, the government's ability to shape economic strategy has weakened vis-à-vis Japan's large and successful manufacturing firms. Although it is a crude measure, the sum of private corporations' profits began to outstrip that of government revenue in the 2000s, as Japanese corporations grew larger relative to stagnant government revenue (figure 4.1). In addition, owing to a massive and enduring fiscal commitment to medical care and social security for the aging population under a weak economy, the government's ballooning public debt has served as a major fiscal resource constraint. On the other hand, many of Japan's major industries have since begun to operate globally without the constraints of the "high cost" structure of the

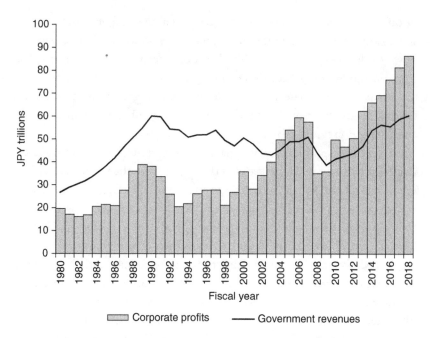

Figure 4.1 Balance Between Private and Public Sectors, 1980–2018. Corporate profits refer to Japanese corporations' ordinary profits (*keijō rieki*).

Source: Ministry of Finance, "Tax and Stamp Revenues," various years, https://www.mof.go.jp/english/tax_policy/taxes_and_stamp_revenues/index.htm; Ministry of Finance, "Monthly Statistics (*Zaisei kinyū tōkei geppō*)," various years, https://www.mof.go.jp/pri/publication/zaikin_geppo; Ministry of Finance, "Financial Statements Statistics of Corporations by Industry," various years, https://www.mof.go.jp/english/pri/reference/ssc/results_index.htm.

Japanese economy.[40] Along with the gradual loosening of close ties and the fragmenting of LDP-bureaucratic collaboration in the government, the power balance between the two most important actors in Japan's economic strategy, government and big business, was transformed from one of close and symbiotic relationship to a more arm's-length cooperation in the 1990s and well into the 2000s.

Financial Reforms

Liberalizing the Japanese market has been on the global agenda for decades, and the U.S. government actively engaged in the pursuit of this goal, as seen in the Structural Impediment Initiative (SII) talks of the late 1980s.[41] The U.S. government has also pressed for liberalization of Japan's finances since the mid-1980s.[42] Although the Japanese government took some steps in the 1980s, serious reforms came about in the 1990s forward.[43] As Japan's economic bubble burst in the early 1990s and its economic stagnation continued, the Japanese government needed to formulate ways to revive economic growth. Although Japan's slow growth had already started in the first quarter of 1991, a stark realization of the fundamental economic challenges in Japan surfaced only in 1995 along with the financial crisis, when a group of large housing loan companies, the Jūsen, collapsed under the weight of massive NPL problems. Concomitantly, some smaller banks began to fail. As discussed more in depth in the following section, much of the blame was placed on the close-knit system of financial management and the financial bureaucracy, which presided over the now failing system.[44] A large economic downturn followed in 1997 after an untimely increase in the consumption tax from 3 to 5 percent in April of that year and subsequent collapses of several prominent financial institutions, including the Hokkaido Takushoku Bank and Yamaichi Securities, in the fall.[45] The "financial mess" led Japan to suffer from the so-called Japan Premium, a risk premium of over 0.6 percent charged on offshore loans to Japanese banks, compared to similar banks from other advanced economies, for more than a year (November 1997–March 1999).[46]

The Japanese government planned (1996) and enacted (1998) legislation for the country's "Financial Big Bang" to reform Japan's domestic financial governance structure, with the end goal of establishing a "free, fair, and global" financial market (chapter 6). Such a move emerged from combined pressure of dealing with the NPLs and implementing economic reform, along with the pressure of an aging population that relies on its savings to support itself.[47] Legislators revised securities, banking, and insurance laws in 1998, which lowered or eliminated the barriers to entry among banks, security firms, and long-term credit banks. In addition, holding companies were now permitted, allowing major corporations to house different types of financial businesses under a single headquarters.[48] With some delay in the early 2000s, the barriers between the three primary types of insurance businesses (life, nonlife, and other) were lifted. Finally, a partial lifting of the freeze on the payoff system (deposit protection) kicked in during 2002, with its complete lifting occurring in 2005. Along with market liberalization, transparent rules following the "global standard" were to be installed in the financial markets. All these measures demonstrate the political acknowledgment that Japan's post–World War II "convoy system" (*gosō sendan hōshiki*) in finance ceased to guide Japan's financial system.[49]

Economic Reforms and Keidanren's Commitment

The economic and financial crisis and slow growth also motivated Japanese economic elites to call for a series of economic reforms. Efforts toward liberal reforms and restructuring in Japan's corporate governance during this time were expansive and not within the scope of this study. It is important to note that the reforms moved very slowly and produced mixed results.[50] The protected sectors opposed them and the bureaucracy resisted letting go of control, but also politicians and businesses themselves preferred à la carte and gradual liberal reforms to a set of reforms that would transform Japan into a full-blown liberal economy. Nonetheless, some visible changes in the economic system and corporate governance took shape during this time. Examples include the following:

- Thirteen city banks that presided, respectively, as main banks over their horizontal *keiretsu* (business conglomerates) were merged into three megabanks (Mizuho, Tokyo-Mitsubishi-UFJ, Sumitomo-Mitsui) and a smaller Risona bank.[51] These megabanks conducted universal banking, as the regulatory barrier for entry into the securities market was also lowered.
- After the resolution of the NPL problem, the banks closely complied with the Basel II capital adequacy ratio, and Japanese corporations started to adopt international financial reporting standards for accounting.
- Cross-shareholding among the *keiretsu* firms declined from 18.5 percent of the total stock in 1987 to 7.6 percent in 2003.[52]
- Foreign investors began to expand their ownership of companies in Japan from less than 5 percent in the late 1980s to above 25 percent in the mid-2000s.[53]
- Labor market flexibility increased, though there was still a commitment to lifetime employment for core workers. Companies accelerated the externalization of labor (through the creation of nonregular workers)

through the revision of the Labor Standards Laws and Worker Dispatching Act.[54]

Not all attempts made by the government were successful in reforming the Japanese economy, but the trend of reforms has continued in the areas of corporate ownership, the *keiretsu* system (both horizontal and vertical), labor relations, finance and accounting, price competition, and the general bureaucratic relationship with the government. Whether Japanese corporations and economic governance have fundamentally transformed as a result of these moves has been fairly controversial, with some arguing a major shift and others claiming that most elements of both entities have largely remained the same.[55]

On the government front, the public debt accrued in Japan multiplied throughout the 1990s and continued to grow well into the 2000s. By the early 2010s roughly half of the Japanese government's revenues came from borrowing by issuing Japanese Government Bonds, while a quarter of these revenues were used to pay for the interest and principal on its large public debt. Private contributions to the political parties also declined, particularly from the major peak association of the big businesses, Keidanren (figure 4.2). The fluctuation among the parties and administrative reform played a major role in this change, and the reduction has become increasingly obvious since the mid-1990s.[56]

Manufacturing Sector Exits

Another prominent development in the Japanese economy over the course of these two "lost" decades has been the increase in the outflow of foreign direct investment. By the 1980s the early phase of the phenomenon with a measurable FDI outflow from Japanese manufacturing firms investing abroad either to reduce their production costs to be more competitive or to circumvent protectionist backlash (particularly in the United States) had already begun. This was especially apparent in the aftermath of the dramatic appreciation of the yen following the Plaza Accord in 1985.[57] Scholars have debated whether the increased outward FDI from Japan was a genuine effort on the part of the government to follow through with the product life-cycle in the flying-geese model or a part of private firms' exit

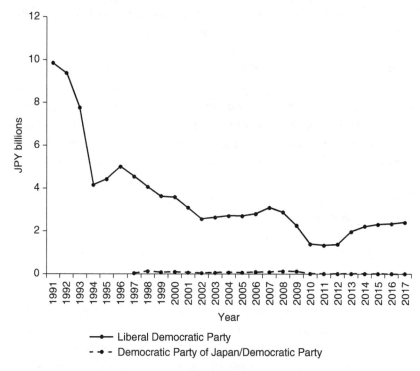

Figure 4.2 Keidanren Political Contributions to the LDP and DPJ, 1991–2017. Contributions made to the LDP are recorded under *Ippan Zaitan Hōjin Kokumin Seiji Kyōkai*. Those made to the Democratic Party of Japan (1997–2015) and Democratic Party (2016–2017) are recorded under *Kokumin Kaikaku Kyōgikai* from 1997 to 2010, under *Minshutō* from 2011 to 2015, and under *Minshintō* from 2016 to 2017.

Source: Ministry of Internal Affairs and Communications, "Summary of Political Funds Balance Reports" (*Seiji shikin shūshi hōkokusho no yōshi*)," various years, http://www.soumu.go.jp/senkyo/seiji_s/data_seiji/index.html.

strategy when faced with unwelcome economic regulations and unfavorable business conditions in Japan.[58] Another viewpoint comes from within the context of regionalization in Asia and sees the increased outward FDI as a way for the Japanese elite to utilize their network to preserve their power and influence against the forces of globalization.[59] The Japanese government also provided support and public credit during this period, essentially acting as a conduit for many distressed manufacturing sectors seeking international expansion in order to survive.[60]

Japan's outward FDI for manufacturing production, which started in the late 1980s, intensified in the 2000s. With outward FDI on the rise and

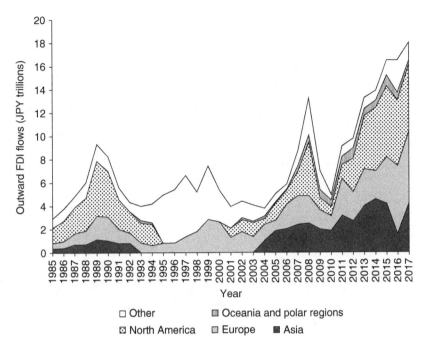

Figure 4.3 Outward FDI Flows from Japan by Region, 1985–2017.
Source: OECD, "FDI Flows by Partner Country, 1985–2013 (FDI Statistics According to Benchmark Definition 3rd Edition)" and "Outward FDI Statistics by Partner Country, 2014–2017 (FDI Statistics According to Benchmark Definition 4th Edition)," available at https://stats.oecd.org/index.aspx?DataSetCode=FDI_FLOW_PARTNER.

establishment of the global value chain of manufacturing, the foreign production share for much of Japan's overseas manufacturing expanded noticeably from the mid-1990s after a massive *yen-daka* (yen appreciation or strong yen) episode of 1995 into the first decade of the twenty-first century. The destination for these funds gradually shifted from mostly North America and Europe to include Southeast Asia and, most notably, China (figure 4.3).

With these FDI outflows, the ratio of firms that produce overseas has increased steadily since the late 1980s and reached 67 percent of all manufacturing firms producing abroad by the late 2000s (figure 4.4). This ratio continues to increase. In the processing-type industries in the manufacturing sector, one finds the highest ratio (above 80 percent) of overseas production. Correspondingly, the ratio of overseas production to the total production by these manufacturing industries has also gone up, from around

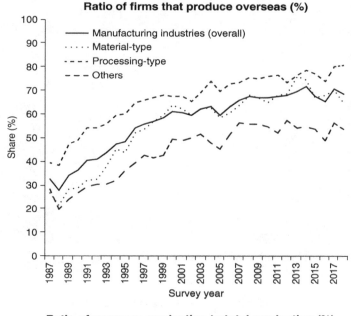

Ratio of firms that produce overseas (%)

— Manufacturing industries (overall)
····· Material-type
---- Processing-type
-- Others

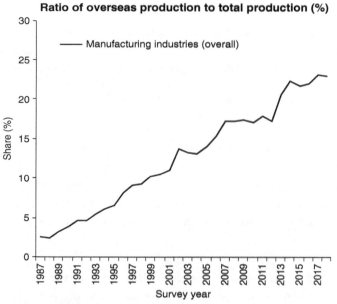

Ratio of overseas production to total production (%)

— Manufacturing industries (overall)

Figure 4.4 Share of Japanese Firms with Overseas Operations and Overseas-to-Total Production Ratio, 1987–2018. The sample covers firms that are listed in the first and second sections of the Tokyo and Nagoya Stock Exchanges.
Source: Cabinet Office, "Surveys of Corporate Behavior," https://www.esri.cao.go.jp /jp/stat/ank/menu_ank.html.

3 percent in 1987 to above 20 percent after 2012. From the perspective of Japan's global exports, Japanese overseas production surpassed the amount of Japanese firms' exports from their domestic production in Japan in 1999.[61] On the industry base, 36 percent of transport equipment and 21 percent of electronic machines were produced abroad by 2004, up from 17.1 percent and 14.4 percent, respectively, ten years earlier.[62] Furthermore, owing to increased overseas production, it has been difficult for Japan to accrue a trade surplus even under the favorable conditions of a cheap yen invited by Abenomics in the early 2010s.[63]

There are three major implications for Japan's political economy after domestic firms' globalized production. First, and most often discussed in Japan, are the concerns over the so-called hollowing out (*kūdōka*) of industries and jobs in Japan as production gradually moves overseas.[64] After a few waves of FDI outflows (usually following the *yen-daka* episodes), anxieties over hollowing out have started to intensify.[65] Concerns about hollowing out are also amplified by the decrease in employment in the manufacturing industry.[66] Thus, in the aftermath of the massive *yen-daka* following the global financial crisis, METI's next White Paper on International Economy and Trade focused on and analyzed the effects of FDI outflows. Though the ministry came to an inconclusive verdict on the effects of hollowing out, concerns over the outflows' negative impact on Japan's domestic production were brought to the forefront when the recession in Japan continued on.[67]

Concomitantly, starting in the mid-1990s the Japanese government began to promote inward investment into Japan, and in 1994 it established the Japan Investment Council, chaired by the prime minister, in pursuit of this goal. Under Prime Minister Koizumi in 2003, a section called the Invest Japan Office was established within the Japan External Trade Organization (JETRO). Moving forward, although inward FDI to Japan is still very small compared to either the amount of Japan's own outward FDI or to the inward FDI of other advanced economies, there was nonetheless a visible uptick in inward FDI into Japan between 1995, when FDI made up roughly 0.63 percent of GDP, and in 2005, at 2.21 percent of GDP.[68] This was partly because foreign investors stepped in to fill the financial vacuum that opened up after many Japanese banks stopped financing, as the banks themselves focused on settling their own NPL problems.[69]

The second implication is the importance of the supply chain. Japan's manufacturing FDI has tended to expand its overseas operations through the creation of "regional production networks."[70] Given the high level of dependence between suppliers and subcontractors and their parent company, smaller firms are often pressured to follow parent companies abroad.[71] Nonetheless, with fragmentation and modularization of manufacturing production, the vertical intraindustry trade across investment sites has connected locations where Japanese firms are currently invested.[72]

Finally, the business strategy of investing in multiple countries around the region has established diverse and differing interests among all corporations regarding the government's regional geoeconomic strategy, and such globalization of production has subsequently decreased the leverage that the government has historically held over corporations. As a result, what Hidetaka Yoshimatsu calls "Japan's mercantile economic dominance" in the region has waned. For example, despite the Japanese government's push to protect the country's dominance in technology, some tech firms have actually merged with their fiercest competitors that were previously stealing Japanese technology in the region with the intention of utilizing their competitor's edge in the market.[73] Meanwhile, auto manufacturing firms such as Toyota, Honda, and Mitsubishi, which began to localize production in Southeast Asia, have adopted a variety of strategies and rationales to effectively operate in the region. At the end of the day, none of these firms was interested in the regional economic integration scheme promoted by the Japanese government.[74]

In sum, Japan's economic environment has transformed. Not only have most big businesses cultivated overseas production bases, in many cases in Asia, but they have also become less attached to domestic concerns and the government's policy guidance. The ability of any entity, even Keidanren, to assemble a unified position has also declined. Mercantilist policy is difficult to conduct when firms have globalized extensively, which also blurred the importance of their nationality and undermined establishment of common interests.

Domestic economic, political, and institutional transformations prominent since the 1990s have redefined the foundation of Japan's regional geoeconomic strategy. Thanks to the country's economic maturity, liberalization, political instability, and the reform pressure of the 1990s, Japan's traditional economic governance structure of the iron triangle and convoy system has eroded. This was demonstrated by the distancing of and decreasing cohesion among big business, the bureaucracy, and political parties.

Most notable in this context is the separation between businesses and the government, which reduced the cooperation and information flows between the two. As successful and globalized Japanese businesses began to operate overseas, especially expanding their production network, the government's control and guidance over these businesses has weakened.

In the past, Japan's industrial policy and old-style regional geoeconomic strategy were underwritten by the centrality of the economic bureaucracy and its collaboration with businesses. With a relatively small size compared to the government and in need of its protection, businesses tended to have a common view on the government's foreign economic policies. Peak associations such as Keidanren along with stable party politics dominated by the LDP coordinated this relationship. This was the time when the Japanese government could largely guide and motivate businesses through public funding or the convoy system to channel finance. These conditions no longer held by the late 1990s.

These transformations have ultimately set the stage for the new regional geoeconomic strategy embraced by the Japanese government toward the East Asian region. This region is where many large Japanese businesses operate. Not only that, the government is in search of both economic growth and the role it can play in the changing domestic politico-economic environment. In addition to the geoeconomic challenges associated with the rise of China (discussed in chapter 3), Japan's domestic political changes have established the foundation for the new regional strategy. In this context, the slow and sticky pace of institutional transformation and reforms has shaped the different paths of implementation of the state-led liberal strategy in three economic issues areas, as will be discussed in the following three chapters.

CHAPTER V

Trade and Investment

A Gradual Path

Within the general shift in Japan's regional geoeconomic strategy, the Japanese government has altered its regional trade and investment strategy (hereafter "regional trade strategy") from one led by specific business interests through informal economic regionalization without many formal agreements to a new strategy with full engagement with free trade agreements.[1] The FTA engagement started bilaterally characterizing the early round of Japan's regional trade strategy in the early 2000s, which has given way in the 2010s to the negotiation of multimember or region-wide FTAs, such as the trilateral agreement among China, Japan, and South Korea; the Trans-Pacific Partnership; and the Regional Comprehensive Economic Partnership.

Although these FTAs are couched in terms of "trade," the agreements launched by the Japanese government since the early 2000s primarily cover investment agreements. The government has established an explicit connection between trade and investment in its state-led liberal regional geoeconomic strategy where Japan's economic partnership agreements (EPAs) include an investment chapter.[2] Japan launched these EPA negotiations starting in the late 1990s, not only in support of trade liberalization but also for investment liberalization and the protection of Japanese investments in partner countries.

The broad framework of the Japanese government's regional trade and investment strategy tilted toward liberalization through formal trade agreements during the period of the late 1990s into the early 2000s as the country grappled with global and regional economic challenges. These included the stalling of the World Trade Organization's multilateral trade rounds, the rise of China, and proliferation of FTAs by others toward preferential trade liberalization. Meanwhile, the implementation of this new trade strategy taken by the Japanese government was slow and uneven, particularly in the early stages of this shift, influenced heavily by institutional setup and domestic politics of Japan's trade policy making.

This chapter first discusses what has motivated Japan's regional trade strategy by sketching out the global trends in trade and investment governance, which also include the FTA strategies of the United States and China. The following section covers the previous history of Japan's regional trade strategy from the U.S.-Japan bilateral trade conflicts to the Asia-Pacific Economic Cooperation process. The third section discusses the evolution of Japan's bilateral FTA strategies in East Asia from the early 2000s and the move to more multilateral and regional expansion since then. The fourth section examines the source of the Japanese government's choices for early FTA partners by demonstrating how domestic politics and institutional path dependence guided the slow and gradual implementation of its state-led regional trade strategy. The fifth section examines trade and investment rulemaking that is the hallmark of the Japanese government's new liberal trade strategy applied to the China-Japan-Korea trilateral investment agreement signed in May 2012. The chapter concludes with a discussion of how Japan's participation in the TPP and its leadership in successfully completing the Comprehensive and Progressive Agreement for the Trans-Pacific Partnership (CPTPP) negotiation highlight the most advanced features of Japan's state-led liberal strategy.

Evolution of Global Trade and Investment Governance and Japan's Strategic Response

Post–World War II dominance of trade multilateralism faced the rise of regional and bilateral trade and investment arrangements from the early 1990s into the mid-2010s.[3] This "third wave of regionalism" came about as both Europe (via the European Single Market in effect in January 1993) and the United States (via the North American Free Trade Agreement in effect from January 1994) turned to regional partners for preferential trade and investment relationships.[4] Difficulties during the Uruguay Round (1986–1994) of the General Agreement on Tariffs and Trade partially contributed to the rise of the advanced economies' regional turn in the early 1990s. Nonetheless, the Uruguay Round was completed successfully, producing agreements on several trade provisions, such as the Agreement on Trade-Related Aspects of Intellectual Property Rights (TRIPs), the Agreement on Trade-Related Investment Measures (TRIMs), and the General Agreement on Trade in Services (GATS), along with the establishment of the WTO with robust dispute settlement understanding.[5] Despite these developments, bilateral and minilateral preferential trade agreements increased in number throughout the 1990s and beyond, as the WTO's new Doha Development Round, launched in 2001, stalled (figure 5.1).

In the area of investment, a push for multilateral investment agreements took the form of both the pursuance of the so-called Singapore issues in the context of the WTO and the Organisation for Economic Co-operation and Development's (OECD) negotiation of the Multilateral Agreement on Investment (MAI) (1995–1998), but neither of these efforts materialized.[6] Meanwhile, the number of international investment agreements (IIAs), including bilateral investment treaties, as well as most of the exclusive FTAs

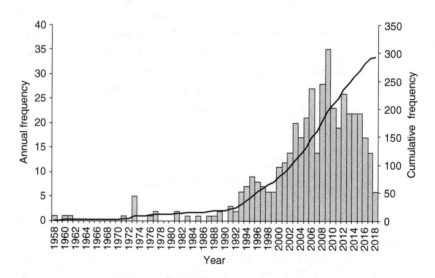

Figure 5.1 Increase in Bilateral and Regional FTAs, 1958–2018.
Source: WTO Secretariat, "Regional Trade Agreements Database," http://rtais.wto
.org/UI/PublicMaintainRTAHome.aspx.

that included investment chapters, had exploded to over 3,300 by mid-2017.[7]

In the Asia-Pacific the enactment of the North American Free Trade Agreement among the United States, Canada, and Mexico in 1994 was a shocking event for East Asian exporters that had long and heavily relied on the U.S. market. After NAFTA came into effect, the U.S. government pursued "competitive liberalization" through bilateral FTAs and a push for a high-standard and rule-based trade system as well as trade liberalization without exclusions or exemptions.[8] In this context, the George W. Bush administration (2001–2009) negotiated and signed bilateral FTAs with Asia-Pacific partners, including Singapore (signed in May 2003), Australia (signed May 2004), and South Korea (signed June 2007). The U.S. government was at the same time eyeing the high-quality FTA among the four small countries of Singapore, Chile, New Zealand, and (later) Brunei in the Asia-Pacific, called the P-4 (otherwise known as Trans-Pacific Strategic Economic Partnership Agreement), which entered into force in 2006. In September 2008, coincidentally at the time when the U.S. economy was facing the collapse of Lehman Brothers and the height of the global financial crisis, the Bush administration began its negotiation on the TPP.

The FTA frenzy in East Asia and the Asia-Pacific finally took off in the early 2000s. Soon after successfully completing WTO accession in December 2001, China launched its FTA negotiations with Hong Kong and Macao, as well as with the Association of Southeast Asian Nations.[9] By the following year, China and the ASEAN leaders had signed the framework agreement that would lead to the ASEAN-China Free Trade Area by 2010. Over the next few years China and ASEAN released several agreements related to the free trade of goods and an agreement on a dispute settlement mechanism. China moved quickly with its Early Harvest Program (EHP) agreement on tariff liberalization beginning in January 2004.[10] China engaged in the FTA with ASEAN as a form of South-South cooperation where China "gives six and takes four" and allowed ASEAN to negotiate as a group. This approach by China contrasted with the bilateral FTA approach that Japan insisted on in the early phase of its FTA moves of the 2000s. The Chinese government saw this regional strategy as a way, in the future, to gain influence over global trade governance.[11] Although some argue that the agreement with ASEAN, whose text was a mere twenty-one pages long, was largely symbolic, it was enough to stir up the FTA competition with Japan.[12]

With both the United States and China implementing their respective FTA strategies by the first decade of the twenty-first century, Japan's old-style regional trade strategy underwent a recalibration. Facing challenges in pushing through trade and investment liberalization and rulemaking at the multilateral level, the Japanese government had to make a move to utilize EPAs as its foreign policy instruments to promote and install trade and investment rules and create an open economic environment at the regional level to support post–Asian crisis Japan's regional production network.[13] Here one can observe a shift from informal to formal institution building as well as the adoption of liberal trade rules. Nonetheless, the new state-led strategy started with bilateralism that later coexisted with the region-wide approach in its regional trade and investment strategy, making it a multilayered process.[14]

Old-Style Regional Trade and Investment Strategy: GATT/WTO to APEC

Japan's Trade Strategy Prior to the Late 1990s

To emphasize how significant a shift has taken place in Japan's regional trade strategy, we need to examine the past. First, the key dynamics for Japan were how U.S.-Japan relations dominated and how reluctant the Japanese government was in engaging in formal and regional rulemaking. From the end of World War II through the early 1990s, its commercial relations with the United States, which supported Japan's economic recovery and rapid economic growth in the context of the Cold War, dominated Japan's trade agenda and strategy. Japan continued its high export dependence on the U.S. market with a substantial bilateral trade surplus since the mid-1960s. During this time the Japanese government also encountered fierce pressure to curtail its exports to the U.S. market (via the Voluntary Export Restraints measure, for example) and expand its imports from the United States (via the Structural Impediment Initiative Talks, for example).[15] In parallel with negotiations to open trade regarding manufacturing products, a series of bilateral (U.S.-Japan) and multilateral market-opening measures targeted Japan's agricultural products, from beef and dairy products to oranges, other fruits, and peanuts from the mid-1970s through the GATT Uruguay Round, which concluded in 1994.[16] It was not until 1995, after the conclusion of the bilateral U.S.-Japan auto and auto parts negotiations, that the U.S. pressure to balance the trade deficit by liberalizing the Japanese market subsided.[17] Meanwhile, high tariffs on agricultural products such as rice, wheat, and dairy remained into the twenty-first century and created barriers for the Japanese government to engage in preferential trade liberalization, as discussed in the next section.

From the 1960s through the 1980s the Japanese government made limited efforts to establish regional frameworks to address broad economic issues, including trade around the Pacific. These were either loose, quasi-governmental arrangements, such as the Pacific Basin Economic Council (PBEC, 1967), Pacific Trade and Development Conference (PAFTAD, 1968), and Pacific Economic Cooperation Council (PECC, 1980), or proposals that fizzled out prematurely either at the proposal stage or without having much impact on regional economic governance, such as the Intra-Regional Trade Promotion Talks (1959), Organization for Asian Economic Cooperation (1962), Japan-Southeast Asia PTA (1967), Asian Lomé Convention (1975), and Japan-ASEAN Preferential Trade Arrangements (1977).[18]

From the 1970s to the turn of the century, when other governments around the world were establishing numerous FTAs and BITs, Japan had only nine BITs and no FTAs.[19] Such reluctance by the Japanese government to engage in formal agreements largely came from its staunch support of the multilateral and global trade arrangements through the GATT/WTO process.[20] Moreover, until the founding of APEC in 1989, regional arrangements were not welcomed by the extraregional hegemon, the United States.[21] There was also a tendency for the Japanese government to consider such arrangements unnecessary owing to various connections already established by the regional production network of major *keiretsu* corporations and increasing Japanese foreign investment since the mid-1980s.[22]

Asia-Pacific Economic Cooperation

The founding of APEC in 1989 was arguably the first major step where the Japanese government took a lead in its regional economic strategy. Building onto the low-profile or failed regionalist attempts discussed above, the Japanese government paved the way to APEC formation.[23] The

Japanese Ministry of International Trade and Industry moved behind the scenes prior to Australian Prime Minister Robert Hawke's official speech in South Korea in January 1989 to launch APEC. MITI not only negotiated internally in Japan to secure support for this arrangement but also approached the U.S. government for support.[24] The impetus behind MITI's initiative going back to 1986 came from its realization that the Japanese government needed a regional trade strategy as other advanced economies moved toward that direction.[25] In geoeconomic terms, in other words, "APEC was born out of fear" of the U.S. turning isolationist and the balkanization of the world economy.[26] As the Cold War ended, concerns over the sluggish progress of the Uruguay Round of the GATT emerged, not coincidentally along with the institutionalization of regional economic arrangements that began to solidify with the signing of the Single European Act (1986) and the U.S.-Canada Free Trade Agreement (1988).[27]

APEC was primarily a trade liberalization forum, and it started as an arrangement where the principle of "open regionalism" promoted nondiscriminatory trade opening around the world. But some APEC members, including Japan, also insisted that APEC maintain trade facilitation and technical cooperation as important pillars for the forum, as many Asian members required support in strengthening local institutions for their economic growth. Trade liberalization was to take place through a voluntary process of unilateral measures ("concerted unilateralism"), and all twenty-one APEC members had to resort to a consensus to set any major goals.[28] The position taken by the Japanese government in the APEC forum, particularly from the time when the Bill Clinton administration (1993–2001) began to engage with APEC seriously in 1993 through the collapse of liberalization negotiations in 1997, clearly illustrates that Japan's shift toward a new regional economic strategy of EPA/BIT had not yet taken place. The government was still reluctant to apply formal liberalization rules to the regional economy and tended to be in strong conflict with the governments that compelled the forum toward trade liberalization and rule setting.

The Japanese government pushed back against the U.S.-led strategy utilizing formal rules with an explicit timeline to liberalize trade and investment in the region through the time of the Bogor Declaration in 1994 and the Early Voluntary Sectoral Liberalization (EVSL) in 1997.[29] Japan was not willing to provide any substantial "down payment" in the form of unilateral trade liberalization on behalf of others. The first effort was for the government to emphasize trade facilitation and economic cooperation over economic liberalization as APEC moved forward. After pushing back on the "Action Plan" for a trade liberalization timeline, the government introduced the idea of the "Partnership for Progress" program to help developing members of APEC with their economic adjustment.[30]

Second, Japan suggested that the process of trade liberalization take the form of concerted unilateral action where the methods and pace of trade and investment liberalization would be left to the discretion of each member, and hence liberalization would proceed under voluntary action and not through any formal agreement, binding commitment, or specific timetable. To this end, it insisted on including "flexibility," particularly when it came to the completion dates and target levels of trade liberalization. Facing the pressure to swallow the package of nine sectors slated for trade liberalization in 1997 EVSL discussion, the government once again stressed the "voluntary" nature of this process and rejected liberalizing particularly two sectors, fishery and forestry products, and other products that were listed as the second tier.[31] Overall, "Japan succeeded in eviscerating virtually all traces of the type of liberalization program sought by the United States" at this stage.[32] With Japan's strong opposition and the onset of the Asian financial crisis in 1997, the EVSL was shelved at the APEC Summit in Kuala Lumpur in 1998, and since then APEC has ceased to function as the central forum of trade liberalization efforts in the Asia-Pacific.[33]

Despite the efforts the government put in place to establish this regional economic forum, the policy content and the Japanese attitude toward trade liberalization had not evolved much from the mode of "embedded mercantilism," when Japan resisted opening its markets despite U.S. pressure. Japan's position was largely derived from its strong antipathy to agricultural opening and to using APEC as a group to pressure its members toward trade liberalization. While the government was keen to support economic integration of the Asia-Pacific, it maintained its long-held position on trade liberalization: selective, gradual, and preferably unilateral.

Gradual Emergence of State-Led Liberal Strategy in
Trade and Investment

The shift in the Japanese government's regional economic strategy finally came about in the late 1990s as it began to negotiate bilateral economic partnership agreements with South Korea, Mexico, and Singapore. By 2000, when more than one hundred FTAs had come into effect around the world, including in North America and Europe, Japan was one of a handful of industrialized economies that had not concluded any preferential trade agreements. From then through the end of 2015, the Japanese government concluded fifteen FTAs (fourteen bilateral and one regional), all of which are still in effect (table 5.1) and cover about 23 percent of Japan's trade.[34] Japan's early efforts started as bilateral FTAs and then gradually expanded to cover Southeast Asia and other Pacific partners over the course of ten years. During this time Japan, China, and South Korea managed to conclude and sign a trilateral investment treaty in May 2012. Finally, in March 2013 the Japanese government decided, after more than three years of deliberation, to join the TPP negotiations. A trilateral FTA among Japan, China, and South Korea, as well as the broader RCEP, were still undergoing negotiation as of late 2019.

Bilateral to Regional EPAs

The initial trigger that changed the government's trade strategy from the multilateral WTO-only to bilateral and preferential trade agreements with specific partners emerged primarily from Japan's defensive reaction to the changing global commercial arrangements of the late 1990s.[35] By the late 1990s it was keenly felt that Japanese commercial policy was lagging behind that of other nations. At that point the government could not count on the WTO or APEC. The Asian financial crisis in 1997 also caused Japanese businesses to realize that Japan could not take the smooth operation of regional production networks across borders in East Asia for granted.[36] Despite such defensive strategic calculations, the implementation of this new strategy came in a piecemeal manner, starting from bilateral FTAs with a lower quality and only then multiplying into mega free trade arrangements such as the TPP and RCEP.

The concrete steps for the Japanese government to pursue bilateral FTAs came as the Commerce and Industry Minister Herminio Blanco of Mexico visited Japan in the summer of 1998 and invited the then chairman of the Japan External Trade Organization, Noboru Hatakeyama, to Mexico to discuss an FTA.[37] Closely following Mexico, Korea's Ministry of Trade proposed to Japan to engage in the joint study of a possible FTA between

TABLE 5.1

Japan's EPA Partners: Status and Trade Shares as of 2018

No.	Partners	Status (year)*	Share of total trade volume (%)**
1	Singapore	In force (2002)	2.23
2	Mexico	In force (2005)	1.21
3	Malaysia	In force (2006)	2.21
4	Chile	In force (2007)	0.62
5	Thailand	In force (2007)	3.86
6	Indonesia	In force (2008)	2.51
7	Brunei	In force (2008)	0.16
8	ASEAN	In force (2008)	15.25
9	Philippines	In force (2008)	1.46
10	Switzerland	In force (2009)	0.78
11	Vietnam	In force (2009)	2.53
12	India	In force (2011)	1.11
13	Peru	In force (2012)	0.21
14	Australia	In force (2015)	4.23
15	Mongolia	In force (2015)	0.04
16	TPP-12	Signed (2016)	30.10
17	TPP-11	Ratified (2018)	15.17
18	European Union	Signed (2018)	11.53
19	Colombia	Under negotiation (2015)	0.12
20	Japan-China-ROK	Under negotiation (2019)	27.06
21	RCEP	Under negotiation (2019)	48.00
22	Turkey	Under negotiation (2019)	0.27
23	Gulf Cooperation Council	Postponed/suspended (2007)	7.10
24	ROK	Postponed/suspended (2008)	5.69
25	Canada	Postponed/suspended (2014)	1.42

*For agreements under negotiation, postponement, or suspension, the year in parentheses refers to the date of the most recent round of negotiations, as of July 2019.

**This indicates Japan's trade volume with a particular partner as a share (%) of Japan's total trade volume in 2018.

Sources: Ministry of Foreign Affairs of Japan, "Economic Diplomacy," https://www.mofa.go.jp/policy/economy/fta/index.html; and Japan Customs, "Time Series Data," http://www.customs.go.jp/toukei/suii/html/time_e.htm.

the two countries.[38] At the end of the day, the Japanese government moved most quickly on its FTA with Singapore, whose then Prime Minister Goh Chok Tong, during his visit to Japan in December 1999, discussed it with Prime Minister Keizō Obuchi (July 1998–April 2000). Japan's first bilateral FTA, the Japan-Singapore Economic Partnership Agreement, came into effect on November 30, 2002, less than three years after the initial proposal.

After negotiating a difficult FTA due to agricultural market opening, Mexico became Japan's second FTA partner in 2004. Since then the Japanese government launched multiple bilateral negotiations with Malaysia, Thailand, and the Philippines in 2004 and with Indonesia in 2005, as well as a regional FTA with ASEAN in 2005, with Chile, Brunei, and the Gulf Cooperation Council (GCC) in 2006, and finally, with Vietnam, India, Australia, and Switzerland in 2007. Many of these negotiations were concluded relatively swiftly—in nine months with the Philippines and sixteen months with Malaysia.[39]

The FTA negotiation with South Korea, which METI originally considered making Japan's first FTA, did not proceed smoothly. Since the beginning of bilateral FTA negotiations in December 2003, both sides experienced difficulty and the negotiation stalled. From South Korea's perspective, the economic benefits from this FTA would fall disproportionately to the Japanese, and from Japan's viewpoint, there were starkly concerning agricultural issues, such as seaweed. Furthermore, the South Korean government began to prioritize its FTAs with the United States, Europe, and China over Japan following Korea's FTA Promotion Roadmap in 2003.[40] The Korean government began to aggressively engage in these FTA negotiations and concluded the one with the European Union (in effect since 2011) and one with the United States (signed in 2007; in effect since 2012). Korea's FTA activism placed further competitive pressure on the Japanese government in terms of not only its speed and decisiveness but also actual market access for certain products. As of 2014, 41 percent of South Korea's two-way trade was covered by FTAs that either have been signed or are in effect, while Japan's FTA coverage was only 23 percent (table 5.1). Some Japanese businesses felt direct pressure as a consequence of the European Union–Korea FTA, through which Japanese-made automobile exports were still subjected to a 10 percent tariff while Korean manufactures were exempt.

During this period of bilateral FTA frenzy, the Asia-Pacific region became known as an FTA "spaghetti bowl" or "noodle bowl" in which FTAs crisscrossed around the region and beyond without a coherent system of coordination among them.[41] Because of the rules of origin agreed on in each bilateral FTA, on many occasions the regional supply chains established by Japanese firms were not effectively supported by the bilateral FTAs.[42] Connecting the newly established bilateral FTAs between Japan and major ASEAN members into one overarching Japan–ASEAN agreement, however, proved to be difficult. Negotiations hit a snag in their first year in 2005 owing to a fundamental difference between Japan and the ASEAN members on an acceptable method of determining the level of FTA tariff concession. The Japanese government insisted on honoring the level reached through the respective bilateral FTAs, while the ASEAN members demanded the utilization of a common tariff; the two sides later reached agreement. The ASEAN–Japan Comprehensive Economic Partnership was finally signed in April 2008 and went into effect that December, which allowed the firms to use cumulative rules of origin and the expanded chapter on economic cooperation.[43] Consequently, ASEAN became the core of East Asian FTAs, where ASEAN as a unit concluded by the end of 2010 the so-called ASEAN+1 FTAs with all the major regional partners: Japan, South Korea, China, India, Australia, and New Zealand.[44]

The major powers in the region—China, Japan, and the United States—all had their own preferred schemes for region-wide FTAs, and their respective visions included different memberships, principles, and norms for economic integration.[45] The contrasting visions of multiple region-wide FTAs emerged in the mid-2000s. ASEAN+3, whose membership was reminiscent of the East Asian Economic Caucus proposed by Prime Minister Mahathir bin Mohamed of Malaysia in 1990 in the context of APEC, was the preferred arrangement for China as its government proposed to pursue a study of its feasibility between 2004 and 2006. Meanwhile, when it came to an East Asian FTA, the Japanese government preferred to include three major democracies in the wider region—Australia, New Zealand, and India—in the form of ASEAN+6, which houses the same membership as the early phase of the East Asian Summit (with its first meeting in December 2005). The Japanese METI proposed the establishment of the Comprehensive Economic Partnership for East Asia (CEPEA) in April 2006, whose idea was endorsed by the ASEAN+6 meeting in January 2007.[46] In addition to these two regional FTA proposals, the business supporters of APEC have, since November 2004, promoted the idea of an FTA among the twenty-one APEC members—the Free Trade Area of the Asia Pacific (FTAAP)—and officially proposed it in 2006 at the APEC Summit in

Vietnam as a long-term goal. This was also the preferred arrangement of the United States.

Competition among the three regional free trade schemes diminished as the United States joined the bandwagon in 2008 for the P-4 negotiations. The official TPP negotiation started in 2010 under the Barack Obama administration, and the TPP Agreement expanded to twelve members when Japan joined the negotiation in July 2013. At the time the TPP was agreed to (October 2015) and signed (February 2016) by the twelve member countries, it was a pathbreaking treaty covering 40 percent of global GDP and one-third of world trade.[47] The TPP was the trade and investment agreement that commanded the highest standards, in terms of both market access and rule setting, and its standards were far higher than those established previously by the WTO. Included in the thirty chapters of the agreement are rules covering e-commerce and high levels of intellectual property rights (IPR) protection, which effectively meet and address the challenges of twenty-first-century economies. Importantly for the region, as discussed in the next section, a number of TPP rules, such as those that cover state-owned enterprises and competition policy, were specifically designed to constrain China's commercial advantage.

The Japanese government's decision to participate in the TPP elevated Japan's influence in its regional trade strategy, as it became the pivotal state in the course of FTA diffusion in the Asia-Pacific.[48] Reacting to the TPP expanding its "high-standard rules" in Asia, the Chinese leadership compromised with the Japanese and agreed to the ASEAN+6 configuration of a regional free trade area in August 2011. This was then taken up by ASEAN members as the "ASEAN++" formula whereby all six of ASEAN's FTA partners were invited to join the RCEP negotiations.[49] In early 2017 the incoming U.S. president, Donald Trump, withdrew from the TPP. Prime Minister Abe nonetheless insisted on keeping the TPP alive with the remaining eleven members. In December 2018 the CPTPP, or TPP-11, came into effect.

These new directions in Japan's trade and investment policies in the Asia-Pacific since the late 1990s constitute a state-led liberal strategy. The first impetus for the Japanese government to adopt such a strategy, as discussed previously, was a defensive response to stalled trade multilateralism, the rise of exclusionary FTAs elsewhere, and China's trade approach in the region. Such competition triggered a mostly top-down cascade of competitive trade and investment strategies led by governments in pursuit of their geostrategic and geoeconomic advantage.[50] Although Japanese businesses occasionally demonstrated their interest in having preferential access to economies with which the Japanese government was negotiating FTAs, such a bottom-up business push did not dictate the government's priorities, as demonstrated in Japan's choice of FTA partners. If anything, the business groups have shown diffuse interest in establishing a good business environment, including trade and investment rules favorable to protection of their property rights and assets. Of course, such interest matched Japan's recent state-led regional trade and investment strategy.[51]

A broad trend by the Japanese government in support of regional, formal, and liberal trade strategy has existed since the late 1990s into the 2010s, but the path the government has taken to implement the strategy has been quite gradual. Some characteristics of the government's trade and investment policies illustrated in the next section nonetheless exemplify how the domestic economic and bureaucratic structure underpinning the country's free trade and investment influence the concrete choices and sequencing of these developments. From the initial FTA negotiations with Singapore in 2001, the Japanese government has cautiously expanded its bilateral FTA partners in the face of domestic opposition from the agricultural sector under a fragmented policy-making structure among four ministries with different perspectives on FTAs.

The Early Stage of State-Led Liberal Strategy in Trade and Investment

Choice of EPA Partner and Domestic Politics

Japan's choice of EPA partners and its gradual shift from smaller bilateral to larger multilateral EPAs reflect the forces that define the actual implementation of Japan's new trade strategy under political compromise as the government began to make the shift from its old-style regional trade strategy to the new one. In this early stage, APEC, defunct as a trade liberalization forum since the late 1990s, has become the shell or forum for many of the FTA negotiations. Out of fifteen FTA partners for Japan, only Switzerland (in effect since 2009), India (in effect since 2011), and Mongolia (in effect since 2015) are non-APEC members.[52] It is not a coincidence that all three Latin American partners—Mexico, Chile, and Peru—are members of APEC. Even more indicative, all three countries initiated their FTA negotiations with Japan when each hosted its respective APEC summit: Mexico in 2002, Chile in 2004, and Peru in 2008.[53] Beyond this priority, Japan, the second largest economy in the world until 2009 and the third largest since 2010 and thus with more market power relative to smaller economies, reflected several elements of institutional persistence from the past in its EPA partner choices.

The first domestic political factor that shaped the Japanese government's FTA partner choices at the initial stage clearly came from the lingering effects of "embedded mercantilism" in Japan, most prominently the opposition of the agricultural sector to trade liberalization. Despite the small size of the agricultural sector (about 1.1 percent of Japan's GDP in 2015), its political power and strong connections to the Ministry of Agriculture, Forestry, and Fisheries and the Liberal Democratic Party *zoku* (tribe) politicians cannot be easily dismissed.[54] There had long been a consensus that any agricultural market access concession allowed through FTAs should not jeopardize or influence the WTO negotiations. One can argue that the government's shift in trade strategy from "multilateralism only" to smaller, bilateral FTAs could be construed as swapping the gains (wider access to export markets) with control (ability to specify the terms of liberalization), with the protection of agriculture at the center.[55] In this sense, it is conceivable that the government chose to engage in FTAs in favor of small partners without much agricultural sector challenge instead of with larger partners. Therefore Singapore, which has virtually no agricultural sector, was Japan's ideal first FTA partner.

Facing staunch opposition by the agricultural sector, particularly after the Singapore agreement, the Japanese government balanced its liberalization needs and protection demands by effectively utilizing the ambiguity in article 24 of the GATT/WTO rules, which guides FTAs. The article states that "substantially all the trade" is to be liberalized through preferential trade agreements, and the conventional interpretation of this phrase is that each FTA should reach 90 percent in tariff elimination ratio, leaving plenty of room for carve-outs and exemptions for agricultural products from liberalization. With respect to Japan's FTAs with its other Southeast Asian partners apart from Singapore, the ratios of tariff elimination for Japan have hovered around 91.2 percent (Indonesia) and 97.7 percent (Brunei).[56] Most of the remaining tariff lines are from agricultural products where the elimination ratio is as low as 40 percent (Indonesia).[57]

In the case of Mexico, where the weight of foodstuff imports was 21.8 percent (1999–2004 average), much higher than any bilateral FTAs with Asia, the strong business interests in the FTA with Mexico were pitted against the agricultural opposition.[58] The smooth FTA negotiations after Mexico with several Southeast Asian economies from 2004 through 2007 are also attributable to the changes in the approach the MAFF and the agricultural opposition began to take after the struggle in the Mexican case. Instead of digging their heels in on the negotiation, the MAFF began to provide maximum concessions at the start of negotiation and connected Japan's (limited) agricultural opening with the technical cooperation in the area of farming and food production, and with the help of Japan's agricultural cooperatives.[59]

Nevertheless, the long gestation time for Japan's FTA with Australia as well as its long-term hesitation to engage in FTAs with major agricultural producers such as New Zealand, Canada, and the United States, let alone China, can be attributed to the agricultural issue. The FTA with Switzerland later on became an interesting case where the usually resistant MAFF was willing to engage in the bilateral negotiation as both are members of the G10 like-minded agricultural protectionist group in the WTO.[60] This was one way for the Japanese government to expose the economy to trade liberalization in a bite-size manner.

At the end of the day, these FTAs and globalization constituted an important part of the liberalization process in Japan. The option for LDP politicians in countering domestic protectionist interests, argues Megumi Naoi, was to provide side payments to legislators whose districts stand to lose from such gradual opening.[61] Implementation of the policy changes following the state-led liberal strategy has also been supported by the gradual modification of bureaucratic institutions.

Bureaucratic Fragmentation

The Japanese government's move to start with bilateral FTA partners was also dictated by a fragmented policy-making structure among four ministries with different perspectives on FTAs. As discussed in chapter 4, there was a long tradition of bureaucratic turf and sectionalism in Japan, and this high level of sectionalism was reflected in the way the government started to manage its free trade strategy.[62] The government conducted

EPA negotiations under the so-called *yonshō-taisei* (four-ministry system), consisting of METI, the Ministry of Foreign Affairs, the Ministry of Finance, and MAFF. All four ministries must be involved in EPA negotiations, because EPAs are comprehensive FTAs that not only liberalize trade through tariff reduction but also include chapters on investment, the movement of people, competition policy, government procurement, trade facilitation, and economic cooperation. As the Japanese government began to shift from WTO-only to FTAs, it became evident that FTA policy making was an important part of the country's regional geoeconomic strategy even during this early phase. Accordingly, each ministry separately set up a new bureaucratic structure to strengthen its respective capacity to engage in FTA negotiations.[63]

This administrative fragmentation arising from institutional path dependence eventually proved to be problematic, as the bureaucratic infrastructure lacked a centralized command structure to deal with new developments and each ministry looked out for its own ministerial interests. For example, METI would pursue trade liberalization through FTAs, while the main objective of MAFF was to protect Japan's agriculture by resisting agricultural liberalization. Between METI and MOFA, despite both promoting FTAs, their preferred channels were different. METI, in support of Japanese industries operating in East Asia, saw a region-wide FTA as most effective in supporting Japanese economic interests, while MOFA had a preference for bilateral arrangements.

The first consolidation of Japan's FTA strategy, then, came between 2003 and 2005 and was led by the reformer Prime Minister Koizumi, who effectively used a new administrative structure that gave more power to the Cabinet Office (chapter 4). The Koizumi administration used this new power to facilitate a cross-ministry mechanism to coordinate Japan's FTA policies. In December 2003 the Cabinet Office under Koizumi first institutionalized FTA-related meetings among the fourteen ministries at the directors-general level in attendance to facilitate interministerial coordination.[64] Furthermore, the Council of Ministers on the Promotion of Economic Partnership met several times in 2004 on Japan's FTA strategy and announced the "Basic Policy for the Promotion of Future Economic Partnership Agreements" (Basic FTA Policy) in December 2004.[65] This document codifies a broader (and WTO-plus) nature of Japan's FTAs that article 5 states includes "investment treat[ies], mutual recognition agreement[s] as well as efforts towards improvement of [the] investment environment" for Japan.

The policy implementation structure has become an important component of the Japanese government's state-led liberal strategy in the area of trade and investment. As discussed in the next section, in his second term Prime Minister Abe succeeded in entering into the TPP negotiation despite significant domestic opposition because the TPP Task Force established under the Cabinet Office assumed solid control over TPP-related policies.

Business Influences

In contrast to the path-dependent "embedded mercantilism" in protecting agriculture and the prevailing bureaucratic institutions, specific business interests have been a weak predictor of Japan's state-led trade strategy and its implementation. It is true that the Keidanren (Japan Business Federation), the most powerful and reputable peak business association, has demonstrated strong support of the government's "liberal" turn, including both domestic reform and its FTA strategy to establish open markets in the region with a high level of investment protection.[66] But when it comes to FTA policy formulation, the government has hardly responded to special business interests. This is evidenced by the choice and priorities of its FTA partners until the emergence of the TPP in the early 2010s.

The Japanese government did not start out negotiating FTAs with the countries that Japanese businesses most favored as FTA partners. In the 2000s it was widely reported that Japanese manufacturing companies found China by far the most desirable partner with which to establish an FTA, followed by the United States.[67] Not only are these two countries Japan's largest trading partners, but China's trade and investment barriers were also very concerning, especially for Japanese firms that operated in Asia. Meanwhile, most Japanese businesses seemed to be indifferent either to the Southeast Asian countries that the government was negotiating FTAs with in the mid-2000s (with the exception of Thailand) or to the FTAs in general. Some 13.5 percent of respondents answered that FTAs would have no impact on their businesses.[68] The business interests are reflected in the low GDP gains from trade liberalization with first-choice EPA partner countries. Most of the sixteen EPA partner countries (table 5.1) for Japan have produced negligible GDP gains, with the exception of Thailand (0.35 percent) and Australia (0.16 percent).[69]

There is a contrast in the motivations behind the intraregional and cross-regional FTAs concluded by the Japanese government in this early phase. Japan's second and fourth FTAs were with cross-regional partners with very small amounts of trade with Japan: Mexico (1.2 percent of Japan's total trade) and Chile (0.6 percent). For these two cases, however, the Japanese government was actually influenced by specific Japanese industries that were heavily exposed to potential losses in Mexico or Chile if the Japanese government did not engage in FTAs with them.[70] In the case of Mexico, strong business support came from a very small number of specific Japanese industrial sectors, such as the auto, home electronics, and trading companies that were (or were worried about) being excluded from the Mexican market and its government procurement. The concern stemmed from the Mexican government's policy of not extending procurement and tax exemption benefits if the home government does not have an FTA with Mexico.[71] In the case of Chile, the FTA between Chile and South Korea concluded in 2004 created a significant trade diversion effect (and worries of market loss) for Japanese automakers.[72] The strong bottom-up push by a small group of Japanese industries moved Prime Minister Koizumi to conclude Japan's second FTA with Mexico even at the expense of alienating farmers by labeling them a selfish national enemy and invoking "internal pressure" (*naiatsu*) on them.[73]

In contrast, Japanese business interests in most other FTA partners in Asia have not been uniformly strong. The limited trade opening interests of the Japanese firms are demonstrated by a relatively low FTA utilization rate. According to the Japan External Trade Organization's company survey of 2,995 firms both small and large, only between 16.7 (Philippines) and 32.6 (Thailand) percent of companies that export to these countries used FTA tariff benefits as of 2014, almost ten years after Japan's first FTA came into effect (table 5.2).[74] The low utilization rate of Asia's bilateral FTAs during this period also came from the added costs of multiple sets of rules of origin in the so-called noodle bowl, which was a large burden not only for relatively small firms but also for large firms.[75] Among Japanese businesses, there are inconsistent or competing interests in trade liberalization through FTAs in Asia. This is because some of the influential firms are already producing manufactured products in the region through foreign direct investment, as discussed in chapter 4. Hence they are indifferent or even against an FTA between Japan and the host government that would potentially increase competition from other firms that do not have investments in the host country.

TABLE 5.2
FTA Utilization for Exports in 2014

Countries	No. of firms*	In use (%)	Usage under evaluation (%)	Not in use (%)	No response (%)
Thailand	1,105	32.6	11.0	36.8	19.6
Indonesia	791	25.9	12.3	36.0	25.8
Malaysia	784	18.9	9.1	42.5	29.6
Vietnam	748	18.3	11.2	40.5	29.9
Philippines	580	16.7	11.0	37.9	34.3
India	559	18.1	11.6	35.8	34.5
Mexico	384	21.1	8.6	33.6	36.7
Chile	160	30.6	6.3	27.5	35.6
Switzerland	132	23.5	6.1	56.8	13.6
Peru	79	17.7	13.9	53.2	15.2
Other ASEAN countries	927	6.0	5.7	21.4	66.9
Australia	534	—	15.0	—	85.0

*Number of firms that exported to the countries on the list in 2014. Includes firms that did not respond to the survey.

Source: JETRO, "2014-nendo Nihon kigyō no kaizai jigyō tenkai ni kansuru ankēto chōsa," 43, https://www.jetro.go.jp/world/reports/2015/07001962.html.

It is true that the Keidanren regularly publishes calls for Japan's active FTA strategy every time an FTA hits a difficult phase.[76] Many of these policy recommendations, however, have been published not to lobby or pressure the government but rather to support the government's position and give more credibility to the government's strategy.[77] Although the general Japanese business posture has changed over time as Japan's FTA experience and partners have expanded, the bottom-up business pressure of FTAs was limited at least in the early stage of Japan's bilateral FTA efforts.[78]

In this generally limited business interest in support of the Japanese government's regional strategy, there is an important exception where the government's approach perfectly meets the interests of business. As elaborated in more detail in the next section, the encompassing nature of Japan's EPAs includes not only trade liberalization but also investment protection. This investment protection is of particular importance to Japanese businesses in countries where they have a high level of direct investment, such as Thailand and Malaysia. Not only does Japan have large FDI stock in these two countries through its overseas production going back to the late 1980s in auto manufacturing and home electronics, many of the parts are procured from Japan.[79] Moreover, since the Asian financial crisis of the late 1990s, these Japanese firms have started to import finished products from these countries back to Japan.[80] The importance of both the supply chains for these products and the protection of investments in those countries has motivated investment rule setting in the context of Japan's EPAs.

In sum, the pattern of FTA partner choice in the initial stage of Japan's regional trade strategy demonstrates some new steps mixed in with the path dependence of the old-style modality of the Japanese government's policy making. Although the government began to take a formal and institutionalized approach in its regional trade and investment strategy, the EPAs began bilaterally with small partners that would not face major opposition from the heavily protected agricultural sector. In contrast to extraregional FTAs, Japanese businesses, though welcoming the government's active trade strategy, were not the ultimate movers of the regional FTAs.

Rulemaking as Trade and Investment Strategy

WTO-Plus Rules

Diffusing Japan's preferred trade and investment rules is an important component of the state-led liberal trade strategy. By the mid-1990s, as the Japanese economy had entered its advanced industrial stage, the government was already pushing for the WTO's Singapore issues that include rules on investment, procurement, competition policy, and trade facilitation. As the WTO negotiations stagnated in the 2000s, bilateral and regional FTAs have become important forums for such rulemaking.

On the international front, the Japanese FTAs have been crafted so as not to undermine the country's bargaining position in the WTO. At the same time, the Japanese government has been conscious of using the FTAs to achieve agreements on so-called WTO-plus items. Particularly important for Japan from these WTO-plus commitments as the government negotiated with developing countries are trade in services, intellectual property rights, government procurement rules, investment protection, and the movement of professional people.[81] In addition, standards regarding e-commerce, the environment, and security were added to the list as the Japanese government learned these issues from negotiating FTAs with advanced countries such as Australia and Switzerland.[82]

As the government began to learn such FTA tactics, one can see early indications of how Japan's FTA content transformed and expanded the rules it preferred. This evolution is clear as one compares the first Japan–Singapore FTA (in effect since 2002) with that with Thailand (in effect since 2007) or the Philippines (in effect since 2008). The original Japan–Singapore FTA included a very low level of AFTA-rules-of-origin allowance (40 percent), which was expanded as Japan negotiated FTAs with Thailand and the Philippines. The government began to use a negative list for service liberalization compared to a positive one used with Singapore. Moreover, several important elements were added that allowed Japan to entice FTA partners in Southeast Asia, such as a chapter on the movement of people and economic cooperation. Finally, one of the important components of the FTAs with all the Southeast Asian economies (except for the first one with Singapore) is an "improvement of business environment" chapter as part of an effort by the Japanese government to cooperate with the partner governments to facilitate smooth business support. Some of these differences between Japan's first FTA and subsequent ones might arise from the fact that Singapore is a very small and advanced economy. But an analysis of the review that took place with Singapore in 2007 indicates that there was clearly some learning taking place between the time the Singapore FTA was negotiated (2000–2002), and its review in 2006 and 2007.[83]

Investment Rules and Trilateral Investment Treaty

The Japanese government has also demonstrated its strong interest in rule setting in investment. Its competitive dynamics were visible as Japan engaged in studies and discussions over trilateral free trade and investment agreements with China and South Korea, as each respectively established its own regional free trade strategies in the Asia-Pacific. In the late 1990s, as Korea's Kim Dae-Jung government proposed to study an FTA with Japan, it also proposed to work on their bilateral investment treaty.[84] Although the negotiation of this bilateral FTA stalled owing to multiple voices of opposition and general tension between the two countries, the two governments swiftly concluded their BIT in 2002 (in effect on January 1, 2003).[85] This was a pathbreaking BIT for Japan, as it was the first of the "new generation" of investment agreements that sought to discipline host governments in favor of investors by "liberalizing the admission of investment, improving the transparency of investment laws, and prohibiting performance requirements," which became the template of Japan's BITs that followed.[86]

This Japan-Korea BIT with liberal components followed the trend set by the United States and Canada in the late 1980s and by the failed Multilateral Agreement on Investment negotiated within the OECD context in the late 1990s. The Japanese government was a big supporter of the MAI, and it was also a leader in advocating for the WTO negotiations on investment rules for the Doha Round. But the former fell through in 1998 as it faced strong opposition against its overambitious investment liberalization goals, and the latter was dropped from the Doha agenda in 2003.[87] Thus it was important for Japan and South Korea to pursue this BIT because both countries wanted to establish "an important precedent in the economic rules, which Japan and South Korea hope to elevate to the regional standard to guide further integration of China into the regional economy."[88]

During this time, Japan maintained its old-style BIT with China that was signed in 1988, which did not include several important elements that Japanese businesses would have liked, ranging from intellectual property protection to pre-establishment national treatment to guarantees for transfers of funds. Particularly worrisome for Japanese businesses was the lack of enforcement, as the 1988 BIT did not include any effective dispute settlement mechanism.[89] As both the Chinese and Japanese governments began to see the benefits of investment protection as the major capital surplus countries, the renewal of the old BIT became imperative.

Beyond the bilateral engagements among the three countries, tripartite economic dialogue among China, Japan, and South Korea had already started as early as 1999 in the context of the newly emerged ASEAN+3 forum, where leaders from the three countries met and endorsed the concept of economic cooperation. By 2001 the trilateral FTA was proposed in the form of the Trilateral Joint Research Project that brought together think tanks of the three countries to conduct a study on the impact of the trilateral FTA if they were to eliminate all tariffs. But it took until 2010 and explicit demonstration of Japan's interests in the TPP before the three governments finally began to move to official negotiation of the trilateral FTA.[90] Meanwhile, the Japanese government officially proposed the China-Japan-Korea (CJK) Trilateral Investment Treaty in September 2004 with strong support from South Korea.[91] With reluctant China finally coming on board, the three governments officially began to negotiate the Trilateral Investment Treaty at the CJK leaders meeting in January 2007. After fourteen rounds of negotiation in five years, the treaty was signed in May 2012.[92]

As Gregory P. Corning argues, it was the Japanese and Korean governments that demanded the new generation of trilateral investment agreements with China, while the terms of the agreements strongly reflected China's preferences.[93] A *Nihon keizai shimbun* editorial complained that although some of the longstanding problems such as IPR protection and checks against mandatory technology transfers had been addressed, the CJK treaty still allowed China to treat pre-establishment foreign investment differently from home investment through an opaque permit process and remaining restrictions against foreign investment.[94]

In sum, the Japanese government's regional trade and investment strategy has been couched in its desire to establish liberal rules in the regional economy through trade and investment agreements. Shaping the regional economic governance has been one of a few ways in which Japan, whose businesses have largely become decoupled with the protection of the state, can play an important role. This is especially the case as rule-setting competition takes place under the rise of China and its economic influence.

The Ultimate Instrument of the State-Led Trade and Investment Strategy: TPP and CPTPP

TPP and Japan's Strategic Advantage in the Asia-Pacific Economy

The TPP was clearly a pathbreaking free trade agreement, and Japan's participation marked a departure from the relatively timid liberal turn in its trade strategy until then. Despite Japan's gradual transformation from its old-style trade and investment strategy toward its newer, more liberal strategy, discussed previously, the TPP was a radical step whose impacts on the Japanese economy, particularly in its most heavily protected agriculture sector, are significant. As if to prove this point, opposition to the TPP was quite widespread and intense in Japan.[95] If that was indeed the case, what motivated the Abe administration to insist on joining TPP negotiations in 2013, and how and why did the Japanese government manage to conclude the original TPP agreement and, later, lead TPP-11 even as the United States withdrew?

Above all, the prospective and large economic gains from the TPP were important for Japan. According to analysts, Japan could expect to gain the largest GDP growth among the twelve member countries at an additional 2 percent over the next ten years after the TPP conclusion. This would have been the result of not only tariff and nontariff reductions but also the vitalization of Japan's economy brought about by structural reforms (discussed in the next section).[96] For competitive Japanese businesses, the TPP was attractive because it would have opened up markets not only in the United States but also in other member countries whose markets were still heavily protected. Economic gains notwithstanding, the Abe administration was also motivated by vital strategic gains in the realm of geoeconomics of the Asia-Pacific that Japan could expect through participation in the TPP. In the background, as discussed in chapter 3, was the regional geoeconomic context with the rise of China and an ideological conflict between market capitalism and so-called state capitalism.[97] Such strategic gains for Japan come in two related forms.

The first strategic gain that the Japanese government expected to acquire from its commitment to the TPP came through Japan's pivotal state role to tip the balance in its favor amid great-power rivalry in the region. Under the Obama administration (2009–2016), the TPP was the pillar of the U.S. geoeconomic strategy in Asia. Whether the Obama administration intended to exclude and contain China is debatable, but it was, without a doubt, the priority of the United States to push rule-based trade and investment agreements in order to gain an upper hand in the region's dynamic economic environment. Many strategists, including Michael D. Swaine, went as far as to claim that U.S. strategists saw the "TPP not as an economic undertaking but primarily as an instrument of the US regional strategy, designed to contain China, strengthen its economic control in the region, and undermine (intra-Asia) regionalism."[98]

From the Chinese perspective, America's TPP initiative was alarming; its stringent liberalization and behind-the-border rules such as restrictions on the SOEs fundamentally challenged China's economic growth model. Furthermore, these rules would exclude China from joining the negotiations in the near future. The TPP also divided Asia between the "can-do" countries and the rest. The Chinese leadership would have very much preferred the ASEAN+ preferential trade arrangements whose proposals emerged in the mid-2000s, such as the East Asia Free Trade Area (ASEAN+3, including China, South Korea, and Japan) scheme promoted by China, or even the Comprehensive Economic Partnership Agreement (ASEAN+3 plus India, Australia, and New Zealand), which was proposed by Japan. As a roadmap to achieve the FTAAP based on the twenty-one APEC member countries, which both the United States in the late 2000s and China (since 2014) have promoted, it became crucial which model—the TPP or Asia-based modality—established itself first in the region to sets its path.[99] In this context, Japan, possessing advanced technology and abundant capital as the world's third largest economy, played an undeniably important role.

The second strategic gain for Japan arises from this regional great power competition. Here, the Japanese government can take advantage of its position as a pivotal state of diffusion in the region and beyond, allowing the country not only to disseminate certain rules and policies but also to leverage its position in shaping these rules.[100] This was a deliberate strategy. METI undoubtedly understood how, as part of the government's regional trade strategy, the TPP would strengthen Japan's position to leverage trade, as the competitive pressures of market access and rule setting would motivate potential FTA partners such as the European Union or China to become more actively engaged with Japan.[101] METI's strategy worked. China's concerns over being excluded from the regional trade regime as the region divided between TPP and non-TPP groups led China to shift its policy toward accommodating Japan's preferences. Since 2011 both countries have more actively engaged in the three-country FTA among China, Japan, and South Korea, as well as in making the CEPEA (ASEAN+6) the main platform of the regional trade liberalization forum now known as the RCEP.[102] As the TPP reached its basic agreement in October 2015, there was another acceleration in the China-Japan-Korea Free Trade Agreement and Japan-EU FTA negotiations, and several East Asian governments (including South Korea, Thailand, the Philippines, Taiwan, and Indonesia) began to show significant interest in joining the TPP.

Even within TPP negotiations, Japan's strategic leverage was evident. The role that the Japanese government played in these negotiations, which included twelve members with very diverse levels of economic development and state involvement in the economy, was critical to the success of the TPP. Japan was an intermediator between the advanced and Western members demanding liberalization and rules, on the one side, and developing countries with high protections and state involvement, on the other. Here, the Japanese government's long history as a "developmental state" played a large role. It was because of this prior experience that Japan was able to convince the developing members that there were possible paths toward economic liberalization.[103] In this way, the Japanese government was able to contribute significantly to shaping a new phase of trade governance in the region, even if the TPP did not originate from Japan. Consequently, Japan managed to get away with the most lenient and favorable terms regarding market access to politically sensitive agricultural items (i.e., the five sacred areas). The tariff liberalization in Japan's agricultural products under the TPP agreement was at 81 percent, far lower than that of the second lowest member, Canada, at 94 percent.[104]

A Long Road to TPP: Domestic Opposition and Institutional Changes

As demonstrated in this chapter, the geoeconomic context in the Asia-Pacific has essentially motivated the Japanese government's liberal regional geoeconomic strategy. Meanwhile, Japan's domestic policy-making framework has played a critical role in defining policy choice and implementation. This two-layered process applies to the Japanese government's success in pursuing the TPP and the CPTPP as well.

Because of its potential impact on the U.S. liberalization strategy in the Asia-Pacific, Japanese government officials demonstrated strong interest in the development of the P-4 agreement as early as 2008.[105] Such expert interests, however, did not expand into political or public spheres in Japan until October 1, 2010, when Prime Minister Naoto Kan announced, during his general policy speech before the 176th Extraordinary Session of the Diet, his interest in joining TPP negotiations:

> Further, at the 18th APEC Economic Leaders' Meeting, which I will chair, Japan will work together with the United States, the Republic of Korea, China, ASEAN countries, Australia, Russia, and other countries to build a better environment for shared growth and prosperity for the countries of the Asia-Pacific region. Economic partnership agreements (EPAs) and free trade agreements (FTAs) will be important bridges in this regard. As part of this, *we will look into participating in such negotiations as those for the Trans-Pacific Partnership agreement* and will aim to build a Free Trade Area of the Asia-Pacific. With a view toward making the East Asian Community a reality, I want to open our country to the outside world and move forward with concrete steps of negotiations as much as possible.[106]

This announcement was made in anticipation of the Yokohama APEC Summit scheduled for the following month; nonetheless, the revelation of Japan's intention to participate in the TPP negotiations then was considered to have been quite sudden and scarcely vetted.[107] Subsequently, the opposition to Japan's joining the TPP emerged immediately and forcefully. The most powerful domestic opposition came from the agricultural sector—farmers and the Japan Agricultural Cooperatives (JA)—which launched a massive opposition campaign sounding the alarm on the dangers the TPP posed not only to Japan's agriculture but also to its food safety and the Japanese people's traditional ways of life.[108] Other groups, such as the Japan Medical Association and the insurance sector, were also uncomfortable with Japan entering into the negotiations.[109] Even within Kan's own party, the Democratic Party of Japan, 114 Diet members in the group who were wary of the TPP congregated around former prime minister Yukio Hatoyama to discuss the possible negative effects of Japan's future as a member of this mega FTA.[110] From that point onward, joining the TPP negotiations proved to be remarkably difficult for Japan, partly due to the 3/11 triple disaster that hit the country in 2011, which took the government's attention away from the trade deal, ultimately dragging the TPP negotiation process out for another two and a half years.

During this period the majority party in the Diet changed from DPJ (September 2009–December 2012) to the LDP (December 2012–present).

With the LDP's electoral victory in December 2012, the Japanese government finally announced in March 2013 its official decision to join the TPP negotiations. Prime Minister Shinzō Abe and the LDP leadership at that time managed to join them after making an electoral campaign promise to protect the five sacred areas of farm products from full liberalization (rice, wheat, pork and beef meat products, dairy, and sugar). After obtaining approvals from all the TPP negotiating members, the Japanese government joined the negotiations beginning with the eighteenth round in Malaysia in July 2013. In tandem with the multilateral negotiation rounds, the government also began engaging in bilateral trade negotiations with the United States, focusing on bilaterally important issues including liberalization of the U.S. auto market and the Japanese insurance market.

The Abe administration implemented the TPP strategy by tackling several institutional requirements to secure the initiative's success. First, it secured Japanese businesses' support. As the government gradually lost its ability to directly influence the country's big businesses, it became increasingly vital for its policies to meet their needs. In this regard, most big businesses welcomed the government's decisive steps from the start. The Keidanren issued several statements from November 2010 through the conclusion of TPP negotiations (October 5, 2015) clarifying their supportive stance for the agreement, first urging the government to join the negotiations and then later, together with the other TPP members, urging their early and speedy conclusion.[111]

Many of Japan's globalized businesses stand to benefit from the TPP via a direct expansion of market access to the United States and other relatively closed markets such as Malaysia or Vietnam. This is important since the ratios of Japanese manufacturing companies' overseas production has risen steadily for the fifteen years between 2001 to 2014, from 10 percent in 2001 to close to 25 percent in 2014 (figure 4.4). Given the expected demographic decline and slow growth in domestic consumption, this trend will continue. The TPP is even more beneficial for Japanese big businesses compared to bilateral FTAs because its trade and investment rules cover larger areas beyond those of bilateral agreements facilitating the operation of supply chains, and these rules also protect businesses' proprietary technology and investment. Such supply-chain and intrafirm trade have given rise to a much stronger need for trade and investment rules protecting not only access to markets but also assets and intellectual property rights in the countries of production.[112] As the Japanese government proceeded with TPP negotiations, the rules of origin that accommodate supply-chain trade became vital,[113] so as to benefit Japan's production network in Asia. This demonstrates how institution building and rule setting have become important duties for economic ministries, as Japanese businesses began to accrue much higher profits abroad, particularly in Asia, and the Japanese government's direct role in guiding the private sector waned.

The second essential factor was Prime Minister Abe's tactical use of the TPP as a catalyst for Japan's renewed growth strategy, dubbed "Abenomics." As soon as Abe came into office in December 2012, his administration put in place the "three arrows" of Abenomics. The first arrow is conducting bold monetary policy, which has brought monetary growth (more money in the economy), a consistent rise in the Nikkei Stock Index, and steady yen depreciation that places Japan's exports at an advantage. The second arrow is the implementation of flexible fiscal policy, though this has clear limitations given Japan's large government debt. To achieve tangible results in the third arrow, structural reforms, the Japanese government created an artificial but useful *gaiatsu* through the TPP to facilitate politically difficult structural and regulatory changes. The Abe government also initiated agriculture reform in the context of the third arrow to keep the agricultural opposition to the TPP spearheaded by the Japanese Agricultural Cooperatives at bay.[114]

Finally, bureaucratic sectionalism was also overcome by Prime Minister Abe as he fortified his TPP negotiation team with a hundred-member TPP task force, headed by Akira Amari as the minister of state in charge of TPP negotiations. Among the task force members, thirty were tasked with dealing with domestic opposition and coordinating relevant issues among the LDP, the business community and the ministries, while the remaining seventy officials joined the TPP negotiation team from across several ministries.[115] As discussed previously, the Japanese government has managed its other FTA negotiations since the early 2000s through a four-ministry structure representing (usually conflicting) ministerial interests and preferences leading to slow and inefficient negotiations with the goal of catering to the lowest common denominator. By creating a centralized and top-down TPP task force under the Cabinet Office, Abe's team was able not only to speed up the policy-making process but to simultaneously minimize bureaucratic sectionalism.

After countless rounds of negotiation, the pace of TPP talks hastened in 2015, as U.S. lawmakers reluctantly endowed President Obama with the trade promotion authority (TPA) in June, and as the upcoming U.S. presidential election of 2016 loomed near. This finally led to a successful agreement in October 2015 and the signing by all twelve members in February 2016. But before ratification, the victory of anti-TPP candidate Donald Trump in the U.S. presidential election dashed any hopes of materializing the TPP. Making good on his election promise, as one of his first acts as president, Trump withdrew his country from the TPP in January 2017.

The Japanese government, nonetheless, insisted on keeping the TPP alive. To start, Japan became the first country to ratify the TPP agreement in December 2016.[116] Even after the U.S. withdrawal, the Japanese government continued by assuming the role of TPP-11's leader and staunchest advocate starting in spring 2017. The renewed negotiation processes were not easy, as some smaller countries such as Vietnam and Malaysia were unenthusiastic about the TPP without the large U.S. market, while other larger market economies like Canada insisted on more progressive rules and separate protections. Despite rocky negotiations, however, the eleven remaining members finally arrived at an agreement on the Comprehensive and Progressive Agreement for the Trans-Pacific Partnership and collectively signed it in March 2018. After six out of eleven members completed domestic ratification, the "TPP without the United States" came into effect on December 30, 2018.[117] Behind this success was the Abe administration's determination and actions. Tokyo organized and led almost all the TPP-11-related meetings from July 2017 through January 2018. To support these actions, Prime Minister Abe expanded TPP headquarters, and these Japanese TPP negotiators were quickly dispatched to other member countries for policy coordination discussion.[118]

There are several reasons why the Abe administration continued to commit to the CPTPP. On the one hand, Japan hopes to use it as a bulwark against the Trump administration's campaign for bilateral "America first" free trade agreements.[119] At the time of this writing, U.S.-Japanese bilateral trade talks have concluded, where the Japanese government insisted on the CPTPP as the benchmark for liberalization in agriculture. On the other hand, the CPTPP sets precedents against China. After proposing the

Free Trade Area of the Asia Pacific as the host of the 2014 APEC Summit, China has focused on the Regional Comprehensive Economic Partnership as a proper route to the FTAAP.[120] Japan's CPTPP commitment was a useful leverage for the Japanese government's FTA negotiation with the European Union, which was signed in July 2018 and came into effect in February 2019. Hence it has become even more crucial for Japan to use the higher standards and rules established by the TPP as a template for the region. In general, these formal rules and institutions can protect the region from falling prey to the power struggles between the two regional superpowers and also enhance an open trade environment. They can further improve Japan's credibility as a provider of regional public goods. Finally, such rule-based economic order supported by the Japanese government's commitment and new policy-making framework helps Japanese businesses expand their investment and market access in the growing region.

In sum, Japan's active participation in the TPP negotiations prior to the Trump era facilitated the U.S. objective of ensuring that rule-based trade and investment order prevail in the Asia-Pacific. The Japanese government was willing to put aside some important domestic opposition from losing sectors in Japan and push through the process.[121] Despite some difficulty with selective membership in the TPP, which does not cover all the economies of East Asia, Japan's move to participate in and successfully negotiate for the TPP is an extension of the regional trade and investment strategy the government has fostered over the past two decades. Even after the U.S. retreat, the Japanese government kept moving forward with this geo-economic strategy in trade and investment.

The Japanese government's regional trade and investment strategy in East Asia first developed in the post–Cold War era with the formation of APEC, where MITI moved actively behind the scenes. Since then, the Japanese strategy has shifted toward establishing formal trade and investment agreements, first bilaterally and then region-wide. In the early stage of Japan's state-led liberal strategy through FTA negotiations, the government selected smaller partners that would not incur high domestic adjustment or political costs and went with bilateral arrangements that satisfied the lowest common denominators among the four ministries involved in the negotiations. The motivation for bilateral and then regional FTAs emerged mostly from the government (top-down), as Japan competed to shape the trade and investment order in the region. The evolution of these new approaches demonstrates Japan's evolving domestic politics of trade, on the one hand, and the institutional path dependence of Japan's bureaucratic structure, on the other. Nonetheless, pressured by competition and moved by experience and accumulated FTA expertise, the government has been able to gradually take a more proactive stance toward larger and higher-standard FTAs in the 2010s.

The Japanese government has pursued formal arrangements where the rules of trade and investment were set through FTAs. This approach has led the government to engage in TPP negotiations from 2013. Furthermore, the earlier FTA negotiations have prepared the government to engage more actively in regional trade and investment strategies and to use such strategies not only to challenge the Chinese preponderance in the regional economy but also to clamp down on Japan's domestic resistance to liberal approaches. There is a continued feedback loop in institutional adjustment to the new strategy.

CHAPTER VI

Money and Finance

An Uneven Path

J apan became a commanding financial power in the 1980s, especially in the aftermath of the September 1985 Plaza Accord, as the value of the yen doubled against the U.S. dollar over the course of the next eighteen months. It was not until the Asian financial crisis of 1997–1998, however, that the Japanese government began to show its determination to apply actively its financial power and expertise to shape the regional monetary and financial order through regional cooperation and conscious promotion of the use of the yen.[1] These policy moves aimed at overcoming the region's financial vulnerability and overdependence on the U.S. dollar. During the next twenty years, the government would lead the way in regional financial institution building in three ways: by establishing the Chiang Mai Initiative of emergency funding mechanism; by nurturing the Asian Bond Market Initiative (ABMI) to increase bond issuance in the region; and by diversifying the use of currency away from the U.S. dollar monopoly to the use of the yen and possibly a regional currency in the future. The road for all these efforts has not been smooth, however. Particularly in the aftermath of the global financial crisis and the euro crisis of the early 2010s, China's active engagement in the regional and global monetary order—including the internationalization of the renminbi as well as increased financial presence—complicated Japan's regional strategy.

The Japanese economy, meanwhile, experienced prolonged deflation and stagnant growth after a series of domestic financial crises in the second half of the 1990s into the early 2000s, which led to a fundamental restructuring of government bodies such as the Ministry of Finance and the Bank of Japan that have governed financial and monetary matters. During this time Japanese legislators also mandated financial liberalization and reform by the name of "Big Bang," which aimed to revive Tokyo as the financial hub. From the late 1990s into the 2000s, bank mergers also consolidated three megabank groups.[2]

As of 2019, despite twenty years of tackling regional financial cooperation, the achievements of Japan's state-led liberal financial and monetary strategy (hereafter regional financial strategy) are uneven at best. Despite obvious interlinkage among these initiatives and a limited number of government players involved, which should facilitate coordination, distinct aspects of Japan's regional financial strategies have not progressed evenly nor merged smoothly. The CMI has had strong traction in institution building, although the effectiveness of this institution is yet to be tested, and the ABMI seems to have helped Asian countries' efforts in developing markets for direct finance. Meanwhile, none of the currency initiatives proposed thus far by the Japanese government has produced tangible results. This lackluster level of regional monetary achievement and financial strategy has derived from both regional factors, such as China's monetary strategies, and Japan's domestic political configuration in pursuit of formalized regional arrangements based on the global standard seen in the country's state-led liberal strategy. In the area of money and finance, the MOF's prominence and the Japanese financial sector's involvement influence the ways in which the government can pursue its regional strategy.

This chapter first reviews the evolution of global and regional financial and monetary governance, paying particular attention to the institutional or systemic power of the United States as the backdrop for the Japanese government's regional financial strategy. The second section discusses the rise of Japan's financial power from the 1980s into the early 1990s in the East Asian region, where the dollar standard dominated, and then considers the rise of Chinese financial power in the 2010s. After covering incentives toward financial regionalism in the aftermath of the Asian financial crisis in the third section, the chapter examines the achievements and failures of Japan's financial initiatives since the 2000s along with an explanation of the various degrees of progress in the three areas of regional financial strategy by focusing on regional and domestic factors. The final section focuses on the rise of the RMB and Japan's reaction, concluding with an analysis of the forces that have shaped Japan's new regional financial and monetary strategy.

U.S. Dominant Power and the Evolution of Global Financial and Monetary Governance

In the post–World War II global economy, no area seems to exhibit more disproportionately significant power of the United States than the area of global monetary and financial governance. For starters, the U.S. dollar has been the main and vastly dominant international key currency that permits the United States to have "exorbitant privilege" in pecuniary terms or in terms of its coercive power.[3] More recently, the market power of (mostly short-term) capital movements deployed by the U.S.-based hedge funds, institutional investors, and large investment banks can sink the balance of payments of midsize emerging market economies in an instant. The "market" of various kinds is heavily influenced by the U.S.-based "big three" credit rating agencies (Moody's, S&P, and Fitch Ratings) operating around Wall Street.[4] The U.S. government has the largest number of voting shares in both the IMF and the World Bank, which are enough to give the country the only official veto power in both institutions, and the latter has always been presided over by an American as its president.[5] Last but not least, a vast majority of the economists who fill both the public and private financial institutions are trained (mostly in economics and finance) in U.S.-based universities.[6]

Such U.S. dominance persisted into the 1990s under financial globalization. As famously characterized by John Williamson, the decade of the 1990s was heavily influenced by the "Washington Consensus" of neoliberal reforms and financial opening.[7] This was also the time when financial liberalization steps taken by the United States, the United Kingdom, and Japan opened up short-term cross-border capital movements that were long restricted under the Bretton Woods system.[8] This global trend influenced Asia, too. Despite economic developmentalism and the associated financial repression and bank domination, some Asian economies (with the notable exception of China) began to liberalize their capital accounts in the early 1990s to attract short-term foreign capital in addition to foreign direct investment.[9]

The currency crisis in Thailand in the summer of 1997 triggered a series of financial crises, collectively called the Asian financial crisis, that spread to both Southeast Asia (especially Indonesia) and Northeast Asia (especially South Korea). Not only did the crisis cause significant economic damage among the countries that were hit, it also became the major battlefield of ideas and policies over financial and monetary governance for East Asia. Controversies emerged over the causes of the crisis and the appropriate prescription for Asia's economic troubles.[10] Asian leaders saw the economic, social, and political calamity brought about not only by the crisis but also by the IMF's prescription for solving it, as the IMF demanded further economic liberalization, macroeconomic tightening, and fiscal austerity.[11] These developments made Asian governments yearn for regional financial institutions and a regional solution to the crisis.[12] Facing this massive crisis at both the global and regional levels, the Japanese government showed leadership. Globally, it pushed for the expansion of G7 (then becoming G8 including Russia in 1997) to include emerging economies in the form of G20 finance minister and central bank governor meetings for financial discussions.[13] This initiative corresponded to the ongoing efforts toward building the New International Financial Architecture.[14] Concomitantly, the Financial Stability Forum (FSF), housed in the Bank for International Settlements (BIS), was established among G7 members to facilitate the promotion of international financial stability. Regionally, the Japanese government's proposal to establish an Asia-only financial mechanism, to be named the Asian Monetary Fund (AMF), at the height of the crisis in 1997 stirred up the global financial community, with particular pushback from the United States and the IMF.[15] Although the AMF idea died quite quickly, the Japanese government continued to support regional financial initiatives.

Meanwhile, many of the Asian economies that experienced the crisis became prudent in financial reform and management and cautious in the face of financial liberalization, with large-scale "hoarding" of foreign exchange reserves.[16] For China, the Asian financial crisis was a catalyst in making the Chinese leadership engage in reform and embrace the marketization and good market governance leading its rush toward accession into the World Trade Organization in 2001.[17]

The triumph of the neoliberal paradigm did not last long, however. Geo-economics of money and finance dominated by the United States faced a big challenge during the global financial crisis of the late 2000s, which spread mostly to Europe and not so much to Asia.[18] The subprime mortgage crisis that rocked U.S. financial markets in 2007 culminated in the collapse of the Lehman Brothers on September 15, 2008, which led the United States into the biggest recession since the Great Depression of the 1930s.[19] To tackle the crisis, the G20 finance ministers' meeting was immediately upgraded to the G20 heads-of-state summit, which first met in November 2008 in Washington, D.C., with many emerging economies represented alongside the G7 leaders. The FSF was expanded to the Financial Stability Board to include all G20 members, and a multitude of financial issues from macroeconomic imbalances to sustainable growth were discussed in subsequent G20 summits.[20] As financial contributions and support were needed from emerging economies such as China and Brazil, the advanced economies quickly agreed to put in place the IMF quota reform, designed to give more voice to these economies.[21]

Correspondingly, the global financial crisis affected the financial power balance and global governance in several major ways. First, it cast major doubt on the health and reliability of the U.S. dollar and the international currency system dominated by dollars. The dollar's dominance in the global economy was already a concern at the time of the Asian financial crisis, as the East Asian economies had long faced a "double-mismatch" challenge, in which they had no viable alternatives but to borrow short term in dollars for local long-term projects.[22] As will be discussed, such concerns led to relatively short-lived efforts toward internationalization of the yen (1999–2004) and a regional currency arrangement called the Asian Currency Unit.[23] After the global financial crisis, such currency instability intensified China's move toward the internationalization of its own currency, the RMB, for hedging purposes, which had already started in the latter half of the 2000s.[24] It was not only its currency over which the United States lost credibility in the crisis; the overall "Washington Consensus" model, which was hyped as the right course of action at the time of the Asian crisis, was also severely discredited.[25]

This loss of credibility for the United States and its economic model in many ways translated into gains of confidence by the newly rising power, China. This shift was the second major impact of the global financial crisis. Having survived the crisis via a large stimulus package and experienced a V-shaped recovery, China became in 2010 the second largest economy in the world (GDP based on official exchange rates). Since then, China has moved forward with RMB internationalization efforts and expanded bilateral currency swap arrangements around the world. Collaborating with the BRICS members through summits and financial initiatives such as the establishment of the New Development Bank (NDB) in 2014, China gained increasing credibility as the champion of the developing world.[26] China has also raised concerns over what it sees as a double standard on the part of international financial institutions such as the IMF in treating "privileged" countries such as the United States in its surveillance.[27] The speed of RMB internationalization seems to have slowed in the aftermath of the stock market crash of summer 2015 and domestic political pushback against financial liberalization and reform in China. But the RMB promoters have continued to pursue their goal through such measures as the Belt-and-Road Initiative. Such moves have also been helped by the inclusion of the RMB in the IMF's currency unit, Special Drawing Rights, in October 2016.

The third impact of the global crisis came in the form of a significant challenge to regional financial cooperation and projects. The sovereign debt crisis in Europe (2009–2014), particularly the near default of the Greek government, has shaken the euro zone, which used to claim to be *the* "model" of successful economic regionalism.[28] In general, the Asian financial crisis presented centripetal forces for conversion, particularly between Japan and China, while the global financial crisis ten years later pulled these two major regional powers apart with its centrifugal forces, as China embarked on the ambitious regional monetary and financial project on its own.[29]

In sum, the two major financial crises have shaken the global and regional financial and monetary order since the late 1990s. Even though the U.S. dollar continues to be the currency standard in the Asia-Pacific, the Asian crisis enhanced the regional players' interest in regional financial cooperation. Meanwhile, the global crisis once again moved these major players apart, as the rise of China's financial power rearranged the region's financial landscape. As discussed in the next section, Japan's state-led financial strategy was shaped during these twenty years, while the Japanese economy suffered significant economic damage from both crises.

Exchange Rate Obsession and the Rise of Yen Power;
Japan's Old-Style Strategy

From the 1970s into the mid-1990s Japan became notorious (or admired) for its enormous trade surplus against the United States, which had allowed

Japan to accumulate its financial power and buy up premier properties around the world. During this time, Japan's old-style monetary and financial strategy nonetheless focused its energy on maintaining, often unsuccessfully, a stable yen–dollar exchange rate and depressed the value of the yen in favor of the country's powerful export interests. One can identify three characteristics of this old-style strategy pursued by the Japanese government during this period: *bilateral*, *informal*, and *embedded mercantilism*. First, the government was focused on U.S.-Japan monetary and financial relations and had no interest in cultivating the yen bloc in East Asia, despite concerns over "yen power" emerging around the world.[30] Second, most of Japan's economic expansion in the region was led by businesses, and there was no serious effort on the part of the government to formalize or institutionalize monetary and financial cooperation in the Asia-Pacific region until the Asian financial crisis. The Japanese monetary authority was happy to rely on the U.S. dollar as the informal currency framework for the region. Moreover, there was little effort by the government to institutionalize regional monetary and financial cooperation until the late 1990s. Finally, Japan's government-bank-firm relations typically seen in embedded mercantilism motivated Japan's financial sector to expand its credit in the region as it followed manufacturing companies.

Having thrived in a dollar-dominant world and relying on manufacturing exports and natural resource imports for its economic growth for several decades, Japan has developed a foreign exchange rate obsession centering on the dollar-yen exchange rate.[31] This obsession has been exacerbated not only by the volatile fluctuation of the yen's nominal exchange rate vis-à-vis the dollar since the 1973 end of the Bretton Woods system of the pegged exchange rate (figure 6.1) but also through various political and economic events. The Dollar-Yen Agreement (1984), Plaza Accord (1985), and series of trade and economic disputes with the U.S. government all forced Japanese companies and the government to adjust to an increasingly strengthening yen (with a few phases of exceptions).[32] Even the monetary policy of the BOJ, which allegedly unleashed the bubble economy of the late 1980s and its ultimate collapse in the early 1990s, has been attributed to the country's exchange rate obsession.[33]

Faced with U.S. protectionist pressures against Japan's massive trade surplus and the rising yen, the Japanese government stepped up the country's capital recycling program throughout the world in several ways: large purchases of U.S. treasury bills, the expansion of foreign aid and other official

Figure 6.1 Dollar-Yen Exchange Rate, 1980–2019.
Source: Bank of Japan, "Main Time-Series Statistics," http://www.statsearch.boj.or.jp
/index_en.html.

flows in support to debt-ridden countries around the world, and the encour-
agement of outward foreign direct investment.[34] As a result, various forms
of Japanese capital outflow to the rest of the world expanded dramatically.[35]
Despite such efforts, Japan could not reverse the *yen-daka* (strong yen) challenge until the late 1990s (figure 6.1).[36]

The power of the Japanese yen became most prominent by the second
half of the 1980s, as demonstrated by the fact that Japanese banks occupied
five to seven spots out of the top ten largest banks in the world.[37] This was
the time when the possibility of the Japanese government and businesses
in creating a "yen bloc" in Asia raised a concern.[38] A challenge to the dollar dominance in East Asia or a regional economic bloc was not part of
Japan's geoeconomic ambitions during this period, however. From the
1980s into the first half of the 1990s, the international use of the Japanese
yen gradually increased in East Asia for trade payments (as the mode of
payments), particularly with respect to Japan's imports from Southeast
Asia (table 6.1).[39] But as a store of value, it was not prominent, as the Japanese yen constituted only about 12 to 14 percent of the foreign exchange
reserves of Asian countries.[40] There were also several domestic obstacles
that prevented the yen from challenging the U.S. dollar as Japan's preferred

TABLE 6.1

Currency Denominations of Japan's Foreign Trade by Region, 1980s and 1990s

	1983		1986		1989		1992		1995	
	Yen	Other	Yen	Other	Yen	Other	Yen	Other	Yen	Other
Exports										
All regions	40.5	59.5	35.5	64.5	34.7	65.3	40.1	59.9	36.0	64.0
North America	14.0	86.0	17.3	82.7	16.4	83.6	16.6	83.4	17.0	83.0
Western Europe	51.0	49.0	51.2	48.8	42.2	57.8	40.3	59.7	34.9	65.1
Southeast Asia*	48.0	52.0	37.5	62.5	43.5	56.5	52.3	47.7	44.3	55.7
Imports										
All regions	3.0	97.0	9.7	90.3	14.1	85.9	17.0	83.0	22.7	77.3
North America	5.0	95.0	7.8	92.2	10.2	89.8	13.8	86.2	21.5	78.5
Western Europe	13.0	87.0	28.9	71.1	27.7	72.3	31.7	68.3	44.8	55.2
Southeast Asia*	2.0	98.0	9.2	90.8	19.5	80.5	23.8	76.2	26.2	73.8

*Includes Indonesia, Malaysia, Singapore, Thailand, Philippines, Brunei, Myanmar, Laos, Cambodia, Vietnam, South Korea, Taiwan, India, Pakistan, Sri Lanka, Maldives, Bangladesh, Afghanistan, Nepal, and Bhutan.

Sources: Ministry of Economy, Trade, and Industry, *Yushutsunyuū kessai tsūkadate dōkochōsa*; and Ministry of Finance, *En-no kokusaika suishin–kenkyūkai hōkokusho betten shiryō*, https://www.mof.go.jp/about_mof/councils/yen_internationalization/index.html.

currency in East Asia. These ranged from concerns over Japan's domestic macroeconomic stability to the protection of profits accrued by Japanese banks from currency-hedging businesses.[41] The division among elite bureaucrats is also an obstacle, as the former MOF official Haruhiko Kuroda notes that some interests on the part of "internationalists" in the ministry aimed to establish Tokyo as a global financial center with increased use of the yen globally, while others focused more on stability of the financial system and macroeconomic autonomy in Japan and opposed financial liberalization and increased use of the yen abroad.[42]

As the U.S. dollar provided the focal point of intra-Asian exchange rate stability, there was no imminent need for regional coordination or an institution for currency management, which led to regional currency management described as "cooperation without institutions."[43] Furthermore, there was very little development in the way of establishing formal regional institutions related to financial and currency arrangements during this period. The BOJ took the initiative in 1991 to establish the Executives' Meeting of East Asia-Pacific Central Banks (EMEAP), which was created to oversee monetary matters in the region.[44] These low-profile, deputy-level meetings among the central bankers have been held semiannually since 1991 to nurture relationships and exchange information.[45] Other exchanges among central bankers and financial ministers in the region have taken place in the context of Japan-ASEAN finance ministers meetings or the Asia-Pacific Economic Cooperation finance ministers meetings. Nonetheless, these arrangements have all remained mostly inconsequential when it comes to supporting financial integration or achieving policy coordination within the region.[46]

Finally, one can see the embedded mercantilism nature of Japan's old-style regional strategy not only in the way the MOF opted for policies in favor of protecting the domestic financial sector at the cost of stagnant yen internationalization but also in the way overseas financial businesses were supported by the government and closely linked to Japanese foreign direct investment. In a way, the Japanese government and businesses used the country's financial power to buy support for the global expansion of the Japanese production network.[47] As Japanese manufacturers began to "go global" in the late 1980s under the protectionist backlash and massive appreciation of the yen against the dollar, Japanese money followed. Particularly in East Asia, moves on the part of Japanese manufacturing firms to Southeast Asia came with the expansion of Japanese banks following their best customers.[48] Asia's increased regional production network was supported by each country's reliance on bank funding from Japan.

An Ambitious Start to State-Led Liberal Strategy: Regional Financial and Monetary Cooperation

Postcrisis Initiatives in Regional Financial and Monetary Cooperation

The two-year period of financial upheaval and uncertainty between 1997 and 1998 as Asia faced financial crisis delivered several direct and pressing catalysts that shifted the Japanese government's regional financial strategy from the old style to the new. Although defensive in origin, many regional financial initiatives at this initial stage corresponded to the state-led liberal strategy of regional institution building. Despite the miscarriage of the Asian Monetary Fund, the Japanese government pursued an ambitious regional financial strategy. Defying the country's own financial difficulties, the Japanese government moved forward partly to establish a regional framework to avoid future financial crises and partly to help reconnect the Japanese economy closer to East Asia as a way to revive Japanese financial power and take the lead in regional regulatory rule setting and institution building. Hence the Japanese government became heavily involved in new regional financial architecture building in East Asia, focusing on three major developments in regional financial and monetary affairs: (a) emergency funding and a liquidity mechanism under the CMI and the ASEAN+3 Macroeconomic Research Office (AMRO); (b) the ABMI and Asian Bond Fund (ABF); and (c) regional currency initiatives from the internationalization of the yen to the Asian currency unit discussion.

The target of the Japanese government's financial strategy was to shape regionalism efforts in this area by building institutions and establishing rules.[49] Therefore the three components of Japan's state-led financial strategy were all essential for Japan to install. The government considered all three components a package deal as it strove to strike a balance between buffering against financial globalization pressure experienced by East Asia and the region's need to maintain the regional financial markets open for Japanese businesses.[50] The Japanese government also pursued its own active financial liberalization during this time.

In the first decade after the Asian financial crisis (and before the global crisis), as the Chinese authorities somewhat selectively cooperated in response to Japan's lead, the Japanese government negotiated multiple agreements for regional financial and monetary cooperation. Some of these initiatives did not fully materialize even after a decade of effort, and others were opposed or later undermined by China's revitalized financial and monetary engagement, such as bilateral currency swaps and the internationalization of the RMB (discussed in the next section). Some efforts were more defensive and took a suspicious position against the trend of financial liberalization, while others were designed to promote further economic integration in the region by nurturing robust links among financial markets.[51]

The most institutionalized regional effort was the establishment of an emergency funding mechanism, the Chiang Mai Initiative, in May 2000. The CMI inherited the mandate of the AMF in terms of regional financial cooperation. In the context of ASEAN+3 (Japan, China, and South Korea) established at the time of the Asian financial crisis, this framework became the core of the region's emergency liquidity mechanism. The early phase of the CMI consisted of the expanded ASEAN Swap Agreement—a small regional currency swap facility that had existed among ASEAN members since 1977—and a web of bilateral currency swaps among the ASEAN+3 members. The CMI has two basic objectives: the first is to provide emergency liquidity during times of financial crisis such as the Asian financial crisis, and the second and longer-term goal is to enhance regional cooperation in terms of both currency stabilization and financial monitoring.

The second component of the financial strategy package for the Japanese government came in the form of Asian Bond Initiatives in the context of ASEAN+3 to support the development of alternative funding to bank lending for development. These initiatives provided a means of directly addressing regional needs for financial stability, a lesson that unmistakably came from the Asian financial crisis. The crisis revealed the financial vulnerability of East Asian economies, ranging from domestic financial weakness to perverse investment climates. More important, however, the "double mismatch problem" came about as East Asia borrowed short-term in dollars and invested in long-term assets denominated in the local currency.[52] This mismatch in length of maturity and choice of currency imposed more costs and risks on borrowers. In a region with a relatively high degree of savings, there was an emerging sense that "surplus savings from East Asia [flowing] out of the region to Western financial markets and then returning by way of loans to Asian borrowers . . . makes little economic sense."[53] In addition, the East Asian economies' heavy reliance on indirect financing through banks created intense financial vulnerabilities for many in terms of collusion, moral hazards created by bank financing, and inefficiencies due to a lack of alternative sources of funding.[54] Nurturing bond markets as a means of direct finance was seen as an effective solution. The bond market–related initiative that the Japanese government particularly supported was the Asian Bond Market Initiative, whose aims were twofold: to facilitate access to markets through a wider variety of issuers and to enhance market infrastructures to foster cross-border regional bond markets in Asia.[55]

Finally, among the three initiatives pursued by the Japanese government during this first phase, a set of currency initiatives were arguably the most crucial part of its regional financial and monetary strategy. While the depegging of the Thai baht in July 1997 was the immediate trigger of the Asian financial crisis, dollar-yen exchange rate volatility (especially depreciation of the Japanese yen to the U.S. dollar after spring 1995) had also put pressure on many Asian economies prior to the crisis. Many East Asian currencies became more unstable as these currencies, most of which had been pegged in one way or another to the U.S. dollar, were forced to float.[56] Having become highly dependent on their investments and trade with each other but also engaging in trade competition throughout the 1990s, East Asian governments were eager to see their exchange rates stabilize.[57] For Japan, too, the currency volatility, from significant depreciation of the yen in 1998 to sharp appreciation in 2001, imposed high levels of uncertainty.[58] Hence the Japanese government worked to implement new currency measures and foreign exchange stability in the region in a few formal ways.

One way was through the "internationalization of the yen," which entailed the increased use of the yen in East Asia, including pegging of Asian currencies to the yen.[59] With this initiative, the Japanese government overcame its long-held reluctance toward a wider use of the yen outside of Japan. In 1999, for the first time since efforts to use the yen for overseas exchanges started in 1980, the government adopted yen internationalization as its official policy.[60] The other strategy was to propose a regional monetary union. Here, a notable initiative in the form of the Asian currency unit was floated initially in late 2005 from the newly established Office of Regional Economic Integration (OREI) at the Asian Development Bank (ADB) under the leadership of its then director Masahiro Kawai and new ADB president Haruhiko Kuroda. The proposed ACU models itself after the European currency unit (ECU) that existed as the region's currency unit before the euro. This ECU constituted a unit of exchange based on the weighted average of the values (basket) of the relevant currencies.

Explaining the Sudden and Forceful Shift of Regional Financial and Monetary Strategy

The Japanese government had several and somewhat mixed motivations behind this shift in regional financial strategy. There were also some enabling factors that triggered the specific responses to the upheaval of the Asian financial crisis. From a geoeconomic standpoint, the government was compelled to respond defensively in two ways. First, it tried to contain the crisis. The government faced a stark realization of the dearth of regional networks among the financial policy makers around Asia.[61] Japan became the core member of the "Friends of Thailand," which assembled liquidity support for Thailand from July through August 1997. This group did not include the United States.[62] The MOF vice minister of international affairs at the time, Eisuke Sakakibara, swiftly announced the Asian Monetary Fund proposal in September 1997, a $100 billion regional emergency funding mechanism among the countries that participated in the Thai crisis rescue.[63] The Japanese government was also involved in extending bilateral financial support to Indonesia and South Korea, along with IMF packages assembled throughout the fall and winter between 1997 and 1998.[64] The second defensive response was against the attack by neoliberal forces that took the form of bashing against the Japanese (and later Asian) developmental model.[65] There was a history to this debate: the MOF challenged the World Bank's approach to development in the 1990s (chapter 7), emphasizing the importance of government-guided policies of a developmental state. The Japanese argued that the benefits of such an approach had been evident among the high-growth economies of East Asia, such as South Korea and Indonesia.[66]

This initiative was considered the first forceful attempt on the part of the Japanese government to establish an Asia-only financial framework defying the United States. American and European financial authorities immediately voiced their opposition to this initiative, claiming their concerns over increased moral hazards and possible authority competition of the AMF against the IMF. The AMF idea died quickly (by November of the same year) owing to such opposition. The Chinese were also reluctant to support the AMF.[67] Instead, the Manila Framework Group was set up to coordinate financial rescue efforts under the auspices of the IMF.

There were a few other economic motivations for Japan facing the Asian financial crisis. Above all was the high exposure that Japan had vis-à-vis the East Asian economies in crisis. After expanding its regional production networks since the late 1980s, Japan had significant economic and financial exposure in the region, which affected not only Japan's trade balances but also its financial sector performance (figures 3.3 and 6.2).[68] As the Thai crisis spread to the rest of Southeast Asia as well as South Korea, the shock was big for Japan.[69]

During the same period, Japanese banks were suffering from a slow-brewing nonperforming loan crisis in the aftermath of the bursting of the Japanese economic bubble in the early 1990s. This culminated in a full-blown financial crisis in 1997–1998 when several large banks, from the Hokkaido Takushoku Bank to the Long-Term Trust Bank, collapsed.[70] After several years of sluggish growth and being detrimentally affected by the untimely consumption tax rate increase in 1997, Japan's economy was pushed into recession and deflation by the crisis by 1998. Facing the domestic financial crisis, Japanese banks needed to exit from overexposure to the Asian economies. Such dual financial crises, domestic and regional, required the government's active involvement.

Simultaneous to these dual crises, the Japanese economy was undergoing systematic financial liberalization in order to revive the country's economy, with an ambition to place Tokyo at the financial center of the region, if not of the world. The "Big Bang" financial reform was legislated under Prime Minister Hashimoto in November 1996, about a year prior to the domestic financial calamity. As discussed in chapter 4, this reform was intended to enable Japan's financial markets to become "free, fair, and global." The reform aimed to make Japan's financial markets and institutions fundamentally market-oriented, with transparent and clear rules accepted as international standards (i.e., legal, accounting, and prudential), so that Tokyo could ultimately compete with the financial markets of New York, London, Hong Kong, and Singapore.[71] This move was also considered "a constructive way to steer attention away from the sorry past to a bright future."[72]

Coincidentally, the implementation of the Big Bang started in April 1998 with full liberalization of the foreign exchange market, which lifted all prior approval requirements and allowed nonfinancial institutions to deal directly with foreign exchange transactions. All other financial liberalization steps were completed in 2005. The government's desire to promote Tokyo as an international financial hub on par with New York and London could be facilitated if the use of the yen expanded beyond national borders, which motivated the yen internationalization discussion.[73] To promote the increased use of the yen, the Japanese government reduced its control over the country's finances to make Japan's short-term capital and money markets more attractive. These measures included a tax exemption withholding for nonresidents and foreign corporations that earned interest from Japanese government bonds, maturity diversification of government bonds, and the improvement of settlement systems to facilitate cross-border transactions. Of course, in the face of the Asian financial crisis, the increased use of the yen could also address the government's concerns about overdependence on the U.S. dollar.

The final piece of the puzzle and an important enabling factor behind the swift introduction of Japan's regional financial strategy in the aftermath of the crisis is the policy structure behind it. Unlike the areas of trade and investment or of foreign aid, the bureaucratic structure behind finance and monetary strategy has been dominated by the MOF, which has facilitated consensus building. At the same time, the breakup of the MOF right at the time of Asian financial crisis and de jure BOJ independence have had an impact on the effectiveness of the regional strategy in the following years.[74]

The main actor in regional financial cooperation under the MOF was the International Finance Bureau (IFB, *Kokusai Kinyū Kyoku* or *Kokkinkyoku*), which changed its title to International Bureau at the time of the administrative reform in 2001. Unlike some other functions, such as the Banking Bureau or Securities Bureau, that were removed from the MOF in 1998 to become a part of a newly established Financial Services Agency (chapter 4), the IFB remained in the MOF. Along with the MOF's vice minister for international affairs (*zaimukan*), it became the governmental focal point in response to the Asian financial crisis. As regional financial cooperation become more routinized and institutionalized, the MOF created the Regional Financial Cooperation Division under the International Bureau in July 2001 to oversee efforts related to such cooperation. In addition, the BOJ's International Bureau, including the newly established Center for Asian Financial Cooperation from 2005, conducted certain operations of regional financial cooperation. Furthermore, public financial institutions including the Japan Bank for International Cooperation (JBIC), Nippon Export and Investment Insurance (NEXI), and the Japan International Cooperation Agency (JICA) provided official financial support, guarantees, and technical assistance on monetary and financial matters.[75] The shock of the Asian financial crisis and antagonism against the IMF and global financial "mafia" also helped Japan to spearhead financial regionalism efforts during this decade.[76]

In sum, the Japanese government, led by the MOF, responded quite swiftly to developments through regional financial cooperation initiatives, which later shaped the steps the government would take in its foreign economic strategies toward Asia's regional financial architecture into the twenty-first century.

Uneven Path to Creating Japan-Led Regional Financial and Monetary Environment

Regional Financial Environment After the Global Financial Crisis

In the first several years following the Asian financial crisis and Japan's domestic financial crisis, the Japanese government implemented regional financial and monetary cooperation initiatives that were half defensive and half in line with its state-led liberal strategy. Behind this regional agenda was the fact that Japan was also interested in installing capacities and rules in the financial and monetary affairs of the region, and such motivation became particularly strong after the global financial crisis.

The global crisis posed mixed financial blessings for Japan. On the one hand, Japan's financial sector was relatively untouched by the "North Atlantic financial crisis" from 2007 to 2009, as very few Japanese banks and financial institutions were exposed to such toxic assets as mortgage-backed securities. When Lehman Brothers collapsed, the Nomura Group was able to acquire its Asian division for $225 million. As European and American investment banks withdrew from their lending businesses in Asia to cover their losses at home (called "deleveraging") in the aftermath of the crisis, Japanese megabanks expanded their lending to the region.[77] This trend of Japanese financial presence (figure 6.2) continued in the late 2010s as aggressive monetary easing depressed domestic lending rates. On the other hand, Japan's real economy was hit tremendously hard by the global financial crisis through shrinking exports exacerbated by intrafirm trade and the government's slow response to the crisis.[78] Furthermore, owing to the reluctance on the part of the BOJ to engage in the same level of aggressive monetary easing as its American and European counterparts practiced at the height of the crisis, the Japanese yen appreciated sharply against other currencies.[79]

On the geoeconomics front, the global financial crisis started a new chapter for East Asia's financial and monetary cooperation and the Japanese government's engagement in such efforts. As discussed previously, this

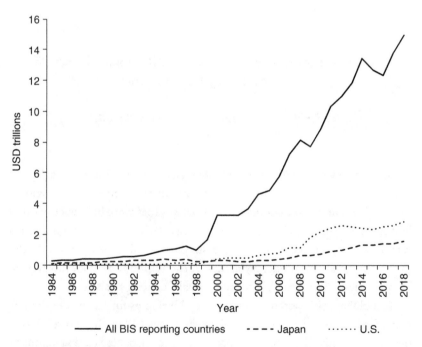

Figure 6.2 Reporting Banks' Foreign Claims in Asia: Japan and Other Advanced Countries, 1984–2018. Asia refers to ASEAN+3 countries.
Source: Bank for International Settlements, "Summary of Foreign Claims: Residence of Counterparty, by Nationality of Reporting Bank," https://stats.bis.org/statx/srs/table/b4.

crisis introduced a shifting power balance between the United States and China, discredited the most advanced regional monetary project, the euro zone, and changed the global financial governance structure, particularly with the introduction of the G20 summit. Emerging economies of Asia and beyond rebounded more quickly than the advanced economies, and the major emerging powers India, Russia, and Brazil also acquired a more effective voice in global financial governance.[80] In addition, the IMF had undergone reforms in balance-of-payments crisis management since the Asian financial crisis and introduced new financial instruments such as the flexible credit line and precautionary and liquidity line in the face of the global crisis. These changes made the IMF a "much less scary partner in managing crises."[81] Under this financial environment, Japan's state-led liberal financial strategy, which had emerged in the aftermath of the Asian financial crisis, took uneven paths both in terms of how each area has progressed and in terms of the reach each achieved in the three elements of the new strategy; *regionalism, formality or institutional building*, and the pursuit of *liberal and global standards*.

Successful Regional Institution Building: CMIM and AMRO

With the global financial crisis as a catalyst, as concerns of access among the Asian economies to dollar credit mounted, the multilateralization of the CMI, called the CMIM (Chiang Mai Initiative Multilateralization), came into effect on March 24, 2010. This upgraded structure consists of a self-managed "reserve pooling arrangement" among the member central banks with a pooled fund of US$120 billion.[82] This was a considerable achievement of regional institution building under Japanese and Chinese coleadership. Since the establishment of the CMI in 2000, its structure consisting of bilateral swaps was problematic. Not only was the funding access of a potential crisis country much smaller than the total CMI amount of over $80 billion (as of 2007), there were also concerns about incoherent (and behind-closed-doors) decision rules and conditions of activation for each bilateral swap line.[83] Hence so-called multilateralization (i.e., pooling), which was a process of pooling together these individual bilateral swap arrangements with the aim of creating a potentially much larger fund per use, had long been the agenda for the CMI. After the ASEAN+3 finance ministers meeting in 2004 put forward such a proposal to strengthen the

CMI through multilateralization, the monetary authorities of the member countries agreed to do so. At the finance ministers meeting in Kyoto in May 2007, members moved to establish "a self-managed reserve pooling arrangement governed by a single contractual agreement."[84] The proposal did not, however, materialize until the global financial crisis.

A major shock to the CMI at the time of the global crisis was that the governments of South Korea and Singapore turned to currency swap agreements offered by the U.S. Federal Reserve rather than to the CMI as they faced a temporary dollar crunch following the Lehman collapse in fall 2008.[85] The ASEAN+3 leaders finally accomplished establishment of the CMIM as the two major creditors in the group, China and Japan, agreed to share the same amount of capital contribution to the pooled reserve (at 32 percent each) while South Korea agreed to contribute 16 percent.[86] The CMIM also bound the participating central banks through commitment letters with the obligation to transfer funds once a particular country receives a green light for the currency swap.[87] Furthermore, the member governments agreed on a voting share and voting mechanism for policy issues and currency swap activation. Later in 2011 AMRO's advisory panel was set up to activate CMIM swaps.[88]

In terms of rule setting that aspires to meet the global standard, the CMIM presents an interesting picture. Originally, the CMI was established as a mechanism not only to protect Asia from the international financial crises but also to shield the region from brutal neoliberal reforms imposed by the IMF. For the viability of the CMI, particularly in the eyes of this new institution's creditor nations, mainly Japan and China, the influence of the IMF or its equivalent is essential in avoiding moral hazards and installing macroeconomic discipline among the borrowers. Since its start, the CMI contained the "IMF-link," a condition of the IMF agreement that set the activation level of CMI funding. This IMF-link started at 90 percent. This meant that a country in crisis had access to only 10 percent of the CMI funds without the IMF agreement in place. The level of the IMF-link remained a contentious issue throughout the CMI's history. Along with the accumulation of a spider web of bilateral swaps, such a high rate of IMF-link effectively made the CMI quite difficult to use. Although the ratio of the IMF-link requirement was gradually reduced from 90 percent to 70 percent and the agreement in 2012 revealed a plan to reduce the share to 60 percent in 2014, the latter has not materialized, as creditor nations have been reluctant.

Furthermore, such a link was necessary as the region lacked any financial monitoring or surveillance of its own. Despite the necessity, regional financial monitoring capacity developed slowly. Since May 2000 the region's financial ministries have met annually for peer review and policy dialogue on monetary and financial issues through the Economic Review and Policy Dialogue (ERPD). This ERPD process was integrated into the CMI in 2005, as the IMF-link was simultaneously reduced to 80 percent.[89] Nonetheless, even as the CMI expanded, pooled more swap agreements, and succeeded in getting a lower IMF-link, the ERPD mechanism has proven to be insufficient, lacking the rigor for the basis of financial commitments through the CMIM. This required the establishment of an independent regional surveillance organization, AMRO, which was fully endorsed by the ASEAN+3 finance ministers meeting in Hanoi in 2011.[90] It took another six months for the Japanese and Chinese governments to agree on the AMRO director, where the two governments agreed to split the first three-year term into the first year held by Chinese director Wei Benhua and the next two years by Japanese director Yōichi Nemoto. AMRO, which started out temporarily with status as a Singaporean think tank, finally became a full-fledged international organization in February 2016 after the ratification of all member governments.[91] As a way to strengthen its surveillance capacity and promote cooperation, AMRO signed a Memorandum of Understanding with the IMF in October 2017. Throughout this process, the Japanese government has been a solid supporter of AMRO's enhanced capacity, with the expectation that AMRO's financial surveillance and peer pressure would improve the macroeconomic and financial management of the member economies.[92]

Despite its improving modality and increasingly available resources, the CMI/CMIM has been neither activated nor called on since its establishment. In addition, several developments in regional finance and monetary affairs after the global financial crisis have undermined the utility and cohesion of this regional project. The major challenge came from the Chinese government as it began to extend bilateral currency swap agreements around the world as part of its RMB internationalization efforts (discussed later in the chapter). From December 2008 through October 2013, the People's Bank of China extended twenty-five bilateral currency swap agreements from South Korea to the European Union, which included five more Asian economies: Hong Kong (2009), Malaysia (2009), Indonesia (2009), Singapore (2010), and Thailand (2011).[93] The Japanese government began extending its own bilateral currency swap agreements under Prime Minister Abe's second term (December 2012–present) with Singapore, the Philippines, Indonesia, and Thailand.[94] In contrast to the Japanese government's proactive efforts in the bilateral currency swaps with these Southeast Asian countries, the two bilateral swaps between China and South Korea (in their own currencies) were allowed to lapse in 2013 and 2015, respectively, as the governments did not renew the original agreements signed under the CMI.[95]

Notwithstanding the rise of bilateral currency swap agreements, the CMIM has been part of the Japanese government's preferred regional financial strategies in the face of a rising China and continuing demands for funding access from Southeast Asian countries. By announcing Japan's support for making the CMIM even more usable by reducing the IMF-link to 60 percent, the government has put further pressure on China (which has not expanded its bilateral swap agreements since its 2015 stock market crash) to either compete with Japan bilaterally or come around to further support regional financial cooperation.[96]

Asia's Financial Integration Supported by ABMI

Bond market initiatives have been quite successful over the past twenty years since the Asian financial crisis, where the region's overall bond market expanded twenty-five-fold, from about $400 billion in 1997 to over $11 trillion in 2016.[97] Although the bulk of this increase was led by China's rapidly developing bond market, the trend has also contributed to increased regional financial integration.[98] Efforts to nurture the region's bond market continued into the twenty-first century, as the Japanese government has been keen to nurture legal and institutional environments that would sustain successful bond market development through technical solutions.

In the aftermath of the Asian financial crisis, the idea of the Asian bond market emerged first from Thailand in summer 2002. The creation of a bond market requires both issuers of bonds and investors willing to invest in them. The Thai initiative focused mainly on the investor side, as Prime Minister Thaksin Shinawatra proposed that the members of ASEAN+3 contribute 1 percent of each country's respective foreign exchange reserves to launch a regional fund to purchase Asian bonds. The leaders first discussed this idea at the East Asia Economic Summit in Kuala Lumpur in October 2002. The EMEAP adopted the idea to set up the ABF and formally announced it in June 2003. The central banks of eleven Asia–Pacific countries (including Australia and New Zealand) pledged $1 billion for the purchase of semisovereign and sovereign bonds from less advanced (i.e., not Japan, Australia, or New Zealand) countries in the region. The Asian Bond Fund's second phase (ABF2) launched in June 2005 and invested its funds in Asian local currencies issued by sovereign and quasi-sovereign issuers. These efforts were also made with an aim to facilitate investment in Asia's local bond markets.[99]

On the other hand, the Japanese government was much more interested in supporting bond issuers to develop regional and local bond markets in East Asia. As early as October 1998, with the New Miyazawa Initiative, the MOF was interested in supporting local bond market development in order to tap into local savings and avoid heavy reliance on foreign capital. Furthermore, such efforts could allow Japan to instill, without direct pressure, open financial order in the region, which had become fearful of financial opening following the Asian financial crisis. In December 2002 Japan officially proposed the idea of the ABMI at an ASEAN+3 meeting in Thailand, and the proposal was officially adopted in August 2003 at the ASEAN+3 finance ministers meeting.

One way that the Japanese government had been directly involved was to provide support to the local-currency bond issuance in East Asia during this time. The JBIC became the entity that started to issue local-currency bonds in countries like Thailand and China in 2004 in order to increase local market liquidity and to finance local infrastructure projects. These efforts were slow going, as the negotiation was stalled by "a combination of legal ambiguity and bureaucratic conservatism in the host countries."[100] Since then, the Japanese government continued to support the ABMI, especially utilizing facilities via public financial institutions such as JBIC, NEXI, and JICA. The JBIC has devised four functions: issuing local-currency bonds, extending additional credit guarantees to Japanese-affiliated overseas subsidiaries or Japanese companies invested in Asia, recertifying collateralized bond obligations, and guaranteeing credit for Samurai bond issuance.[101] Meanwhile, the NEXI applies Overseas United Loan Insurance for bond purchases to lower their risk. The JICA provides technical assistance mostly to strengthen the financial and macroeconomic capacities of ASEAN+3 governments.[102]

With Japan's full support, ABMI, in its first phase (2003–2008), focused on issues associated with developing infrastructure and technical capacity toward the objective. These include creating a new securitized debt instrument, a credit guarantee and investment mechanism, foreign exchange transactions and settlement issues, and rating systems, as well as two task forces, on technical assistance coordination and special support on ad hoc issues.[103] One tangible product of the first phase of the ABMI efforts was the establishment in 2004 of the Asia Bonds Online (ABO) website maintained by the Asian Development Bank, with funding support from the Japanese MOF. The ABO provides data and information on the bond markets of each ASEAN+3 member country and of the region for investors. The same section at the ADB also regularly publishes *Asian Bond Monitor*.[104]

The second phase of the ABMI (2008–2012) produced the "New Roadmap" after accumulating five years of expertise in developing local bond markets. As proposed by the Japanese government, the old working groups were restructured to four task forces.[105] Task Force (TF) 1 focuses on the promotion of bond issuance in local currencies through a Credit Guarantee Investment Facility (CGIF), established in 2010. The CGIF was set up with $700 million in funds to extend guarantees to local currency–denominated corporate bonds, whose credit rating might not attract investment without a guarantee.[106] TF2 works to increase demand for the local currency bonds using the ABO and expanding outreach to investors. TF3 promotes cross-border trading of bonds in the region through the standardization of market practices and harmonization of regulations. These efforts led to the establishment of the ASEAN+3 Bond Market Forum in September 2010 to foster the "standardization of market practices and harmonization of regulations relating to cross-border bond transactions in the region" through a common platform.[107] Finally, TF4 works to establish the Regional Settlement Intermediary (RSI) as a means of improving regional bond market infrastructure.[108] The third phase, known as the "New Roadmap Plus," began in 2012, with nine thematic emphases from the previous four task force items, including support for small and medium enterprises and for an infrastructure-funding scheme.

One could argue that the impact of these regional bond initiatives has only marginally contributed to the impressive expansion of local-currency bond markets in Asia. But it is certain that the regional financial architecture fundamentally changed from the time of the Asian financial crisis, when many economies in the region were faced with the challenge of

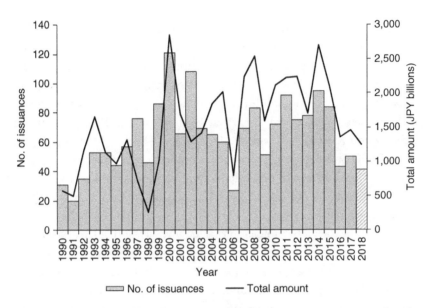

Figure 6.3 Samurai Bond Issuances, 1990–2018. Data for 2018 covers January to July only. *Source:* Ministry of Finance, "Monthly Statistics," https://www.mof.go.jp/pri/publica tion/zaikin_geppo/.

"double-mismatch" due to their overdependence on bank lending. Although the bond issuances of the past twenty years are locally based (and not Asian regional bonds), they have contributed to more efficient financial intermediation and integration of East Asia. The Japanese government has been active in nudging these governments away from their customary bank-based financial intermediation and from fear of financial restructuring through national and regional technical support, guarantees, and funding. What is more, the Japanese government has encouraged these economies to raise funds in Japan by extending JBIC guarantees to Samurai-bond issuances by Asian governments in Japan (figure 6.3).[109]

From State-Led to Market-Led? Yen Internationalization Efforts and Asian Currency

The financial turmoil and sharp downturn of the U.S. economy in the last years of the 2000s led to further concerns over East Asia's dollar dependence, and the onset of the global financial crisis kicked off another round of political pressure to curb such dollar dependence and hedge against the dollar's potential demise. Political heavyweights supported regional currency initiatives in Japan.[110] Similar calls also came from Chinese leaders. At the first G20 Summit in November 2008, President Hu Jintao insisted on the establishment of a "fair, just, inclusive, and orderly" international financial order.[111] Then-governor of the People's Bank of China Zhou Xiaochuan advocated for the use of Special Drawing Rights instead of U.S. dollars for international liquidity in spring 2009.[112] Nevertheless, Asia's moves to offset dollar dominance did not lead to regional institution building nor any new standard-setting achievement by the Japanese government.

By the time the global financial crisis hit, it was clear that Japan's attempts since 1999 to enhance yen internationalization were going nowhere.[113] Domestic resistance among important business entities against dedollarization led in large part to its failure. The difficulties Japanese businesses had in weaning themselves off dollar dependence came from several sources. First, foreign exchange transactions had developed into an important business not only for Japanese banks but also for the central sections of Japan's leading trading and manufacturing companies. Because those entities make substantial profits in currency trading, hedging, and arbitrage, they are at best lukewarm to the idea of the wider use of the yen.[114] Especially given the very sophisticated foreign currency hedging instruments that had been available to large Japanese companies over the years, there was only limited interest in shifting all transactions to the yen, which itself incurred a high one-time cost. Second, globalized businesses from Japan, the largest creditor in the world, had a high level of foreign investment in the dollar areas of the world. Third, exporting companies, which tend to price to the market and for customers (particularly in the United States), preferred to use the dollar.[115] In addition, these companies were concerned that the higher demand for the yen would lead to its appreciation. Finally, Japan's large natural resource import needs led those importing companies to rely on the dollar. Overall, despite all the steps taken by the Japanese government to set up an accommodating regulatory environment for regional and global use of the yen, the market players did not follow its lead.[116] Japan's businesses had their own logic for hanging on to the dollar.

An alternative solution against excessive dollar dependence and/or intraregional exchange rate volatility including the possible recurrence of competitive devaluation was to establish a regional monetary union. East Asia does not score too badly as a candidate for a common currency, according to the theory of an "Optimum Currency Area" (OCA), which specifies the conditions under which a group of countries could benefit from surrendering the exchange rate as an instrument of balance-of-payments adjustment in the process of creating a monetary union.[117] In tandem with and in the context of ASEAN+3, East Asia began to gradually entertain this possibility in the early 2000s.[118] To overcome any political hurdles, and with the aim of learning from the European experience, economists and policy makers in the region under the Japanese government's leadership conducted a joint study with the European Union (the so-called Kobe Research Group). They published a report in July 2002 recommending a monetary integration process as phase 1 by 2010; preparation for a single currency as phase 2 (by 2030); and the launching of a single currency as phase 3, which would start in 2030.[119] This led to the ACU proposal in 2005. While the ACU idea was picked up by ASEAN+3 at the finance ministers meeting in May 2006, the discussion on it as a usable currency ended then.

Instead of establishing regional coordination or a central institution, the region maintained its foreign exchange rate stability by unilateral policies among most of the East Asian monetary authorities to maintain a soft peg to the dollar, and the Chinese determination to keep its RMB-dollar rate stabilized. This kept East Asian currencies quite stable in terms of each other (and vis-à-vis the RMB and the U.S. dollar) in the 2000s.[120] In addition, the accumulation of massive foreign exchange reserves among East Asian central banks (particularly by the Chinese) provided stability for their exchange rates.[121] Furthermore, the euro crisis demonstrated the difficulty of developing monetary union and regional currency. In a low-key manner, nonetheless, Japan continued its efforts in this area. Several prominent Japanese economists at government-affiliated research institutions such as the Research Institute of Economic, Trade, and Industry (RIETI) and the Policy Research Institute have continued their policy advocacy regarding the importance and utility of a regional currency unit, referred to as the ACU or Asian monetary unit.[122] The concept is still being brought up as a way to consider the ACU as a surveillance indicator, but with the rise of the RMB, there has not been further discussion of bringing a regional currency to the main stage.

Factors Setting Apart the Three Components of Japan's Regional Financial Cooperation

For Japan's state-led strategy in the regional financial and monetary area, the genesis and impetus of the region's financial institutions emerged from outside pressure and East Asia's position in the global financial architecture. The evolution of its subset of institutions depended on domestic preferences and structures. Such political dynamics led certain areas of financial cooperation to proceed more smoothly, producing regional financial cooperation without coherence or coordination across important dimensions. Phillip Y. Lipscy argues that institutional changes via competition are less likely to occur when network effects and barriers to entry are both high.[123] According to his theory, CMI, a possible competitor to the IMF, would have experienced much more stringent network effects and higher barriers to entry. Although the Japanese government in collaboration with the Chinese government have taken explicit measures such as the IMF-link to lower the potential threat of CMI as an outside option to the IMF, the East Asian region has managed to establish this new institution while excluding the United States. Despite a high level of internationally nested constraints, the Japanese government has managed to push for the CMI to effectively make it into the most robust of any regional financial mechanisms that developed in the aftermath of the Asian financial crisis. In fact, institution building for the CMI was relatively easy for the Japanese government because the government did not have to rely on the domestic financial sector to shape it. In a way, Japan's support of the Asian Bond Market Initiative has also been part of the government's strategy to shape the regional financial architecture and install expertise, capacity, and high standards.

On the other hand, the regional currency initiative, including yen internationalization, has not seen the light of day as a regional institution. The foreign exchange arrangement reverted to the dollar-based soft peg as the Asian financial crisis shock subsided, despite efforts by the region's creditor governments to reduce the dominance of the U.S. dollar in the region. It was the domestically embedded preferences that swayed East Asian governments to continue their reliance on the dollar. Despite network effects of the dominant dollar that stands at the top of the "currency pyramid," the region has enough favorable conditions in place to insist on regional currency cooperation if the majority of the governments are on board.[124] Nonetheless, soft and informal arrangements with the U.S. dollar at the center have persisted, and the Japanese government could neither challenge the market nor convince its players, such as the megabanks, to follow its lead. The government could work to shape the regional financial and monetary environment, but that strategy achieves only limited success when it cannot incentivize the private sector to be behind such efforts.

RMB Internationalization and Japan's Responses

Despite a relatively cooperative relationship between Japan and China in the area of finance and money, geoeconomic clashes between the two began to intensify as the Chinese government's push to internationalize the RMB after the global financial crisis. Such a challenge introduced another twist to the Japanese government's state-led liberal strategy in monetary affairs. In addition to bilateral currency swap agreements that the People's Bank of China began expanding since late 2008 (discussed earlier), the Chinese government began to implement various measures to expand the international use of the RMB from offshore RMB deposits to RMB-denominated bond issuances in both Hong Kong and the mainland. Gradually but surely, China has also liberalized its capital accounts and allowed capital investment and smoother payment transactions. Although the jury is still out on whether the RMB will be a key international currency in the near future, it has become a significant alternative to the dollar at least in Asia and in cross-border trade and financial transactions, and likely in central bank reserves as well. Before its slowing from summer 2015, more than a quarter of China's total trade was settled in RMB, and RMB offshore financial markets grew rapidly, not only in Hong Kong but also in Singapore, Taipei, Tokyo, London, Paris, Frankfurt, Luxembourg, and New York.[125]

Despite its initial enthusiasm about RMB use, the Japanese government was not fully forthcoming in supporting the RMB internationalization effort after the global crisis. In the early days, the Japanese government showed support by setting up a Japan-China agreement on "Enhanced Cooperation for Financial Markets Development Between Japan and China" during the summit meeting between the two countries' leaders on December 25, 2011, which aimed to promote the use of the Japanese yen and RMB in cross-border transactions between the two countries.[126] At the time of this agreement, the BOJ also agreed to hold RMB sovereign debt as a component of its foreign exchange reserves and to issue RMB-denominated bonds by companies in Japan.[127] With this agreement, Japan became in June 2012 the first country besides the United States to engage in direct RMB currency exchange between the two countries at foreign exchange markets in Tokyo and Shanghai. Japanese banks began to engage in trade settlements between the yen and the RMB, but the overall amount of direct currency trading between the two countries has been limited.[128]

Nonetheless, such cooperation foundered for the next five years until 2018, as the Japanese government did not sign on to any of the four important initiatives that the Chinese government advanced to promote RMB internationalization. First, despite the thirty-plus bilateral swap arrangements that the Chinese monetary authority has extended around the world, Japan and China had not renewed the yen-RMB currency swap agreement that expired in September 2013. Second, Japan did not acquire RMB Qualified Foreign Institutional Investor (RQFII) status, which would have allowed Japanese institutional investors to invest in RMB-based assets in China. As of January 2017 institutional investors from sixteen countries besides Hong Kong and Taiwan were registered, totaling RMB 529.6 billion (US$77.2 billion) worth of quota.[129] Third, Japan has neither participated in the RMB payment settlement system nor become an RMB offshore financial center. The latter have expanded beyond Hong Kong, Taiwan, and Singapore since 2014 as the People's Bank of China issued a memorandum of understanding to allow direct access to China National Advanced Payment Systems with banks in countries including the United Kingdom, Germany, Australia, Thailand, Malaysia, and Canada. Furthermore, no Japanese banks signed on to the Cross-Border Inter-Bank Payment System (China International Payment System; CIPS), launched in October 2015, whereby foreign banks can access RMB settlement directly. All these factors effectively restrict Tokyo's role in the RMB business.

Although the political tension between the two countries has made negotiations difficult, Japan's lukewarm position on RMB internationalization between 2012 and 2018 could also be attributed to a lack of business interest due to cumbersome access to RMB.[130] Japanese financial institutions, especially globalized megabanks, have expanded their RMB business overseas, such as in Hong Kong and Singapore. In fact, the Bank of Tokyo-Mitsubishi (later Mitsubishi UFJ) and Mizuho Bank were ranked, respectively, as the third and tenth best RMB service providers by offshore

RMB in 2017, according to a poll conducted by a financial magazine, *Asia-money*.[131] At the same time, they remain reluctant to push for direct trading between the RMB and yen, which might also contribute to the internationalization of the yen.[132] The Japanese financial sector continues to see high risk in the RMB business, stemming from Japan's experience with China's highly politicized financial dealings.

The revival of Japan–China cooperation on the increased use of RMB had to wait until 2018. In response to geoeconomic uncertainty introduced by President Donald Trump's economic attack on China from 2017, Japan-China cooperation on monetary matters began to progress. On August 31, 2018, a meeting between China's finance minister, Liu Kun, and his Japanese counterpart, Tarō Asō, produced a China-Japan Finance Dialogue communiqué that promises to move all four elements of financial and monetary cooperation forward.

The Japanese government's new regional financial and monetary strategy took shape in the aftermath of the Asian financial crisis in explicit pursuit of financial stability in the region. To achieve this goal, the government has resorted to regional cooperation through ASEAN+3 and collaboration with the respective Chinese and Korean monetary authorities. The top-down initiatives of the CMI have achieved high levels of success in establishing a set institution with explicit rules. The Asian Bond Initiatives have also seen some level of success in nurturing an alternative financial channel for the region's funding needs. These initiatives have managed to reduce risks and entice the private sector to buy into the bonds around the region. The Japanese government has implemented a few initiatives in the area of currency, from internationalization of the yen to regional currency coordination, but none has seemed to gain much traction thus far.

Despite a relatively coherent domestic policy structure that has supported Japan's financial and monetary policies by the MOF and BOJ, the difficulty of inducing private-sector cooperation—especially in the area of currency—reveals an overwhelming sense of challenge as the government struggles to propagate further regional economic initiatives. Given the increasing uncertainty in the region's financial and currency environment with continuing dependence on the U.S. dollar and the rise of the RMB, the Japanese government's state-led liberal strategy has required the cooperation of the Chinese government and the solicitation of active engagement of Japan's own private sector to achieve results.

CHAPTER VII

Development and Foreign Aid

A Hybrid Path

oreign aid has been an important foreign policy instrument for Japan, which has connected the country with economies in Asia and beyond for the past sixty years.[1] Throughout Japan's rapid ascent from a small foreign aid donor in the 1950s to an aid superpower in the 1990s, the country's aid philosophy centered on the notion of "economic cooperation" (*keizai kyōryoku*), whereby the government and private sector collaborated with the recipient governments in the provision of foreign aid. As discussed in chapter 2, foreign aid played a central role in Japan's trinity economic development approach under embedded mercantilism. With solid emphasis on building physical infrastructure such as dams, roads, and ports as the basis of economic development supported by the modality of tied aid, the government focused the majority of its foreign aid bilaterally on developing countries in Asia.

In the first two decades of the twenty-first century, however, the power, modality, and focus of Japan's foreign aid have undergone dramatic changes. In addition to reducing the volume of foreign aid in the face of budgetary constraints, the government has responded to a new global consensus on "development cooperation," which emerged from the demands of new aid donors but also incorporates Japan's own development experiences. Japan has continued to emphasize infrastructure development, and it has been facing competition in this area from China in the twenty-first century. The Japanese government has begun to emphasize private business involvement through public-private partnership (PPP) arrangements and an "all-Japan" approach under Prime Minister Abe. Meanwhile, Japan has taken a new approach in establishing the global development norm of high-quality infrastructure and sound economic governance.

The government has also engaged in regional development cooperation relying on the Asian Development Bank, founded under a Japanese initiative in 1966. The use of the ADB as a focal point of regional development strategy intensified, particularly in the aftermath of the Asian financial crisis. Furthermore, with the goal of making more visible intellectual contributions to regional development and economic cooperation efforts, the government has founded and funded two regional think tanks over the past twenty years: the Asian Development Bank Institute (ADBI) and the Economic Research Institute for ASEAN and East Asia (ERIA). Unlike in the cases of trade/investment and finance/monetary relations, however, the general shift in the global norms regarding development caused Japan to rebalance between two paradigms. Its accommodation of the foreign aid modalities of the Development Assistance Committee (DAC) in the OECD, such as untied aid, social needs, and capacity building, on the one hand, and the newly emerged "development cooperation" modality emphasizing broader development and growth goals beyond poverty reduction, on the other.

After an overview of recent developments in global governance of foreign aid and development cooperation priorities, the second section of this chapter examines the institutions and politics of Japan's old-style foreign aid strategy in Asia. The third section discusses the bumpy road that Japan's foreign aid and development strategy (hereafter "regional development strategy") took during the height of its aid power and in its aftermath. Here the Japanese government not only followed but also defied the traditional foreign aid norms. After reviewing the role of Japan's businesses in the country's regional development strategy, the penultimate section examines Japan's responses to China's Belt-and-Road Initiative and to establishment of the Asian Infrastructure Investment Bank. Overall, Japan's new state-led liberal development strategy of the twenty-first century is a hybrid, where some elements of the old-style foreign aid have been clearly alive. Meanwhile, the formalization and standard-setting aspect of the new strategy also characterizes Japan's "development cooperation" in the new century.

Shifting Ground for Foreign Aid and Development Governance

In the 2000s it seemed as though there was a solid consensus governing foreign aid and development policies around the world, which primarily focused on poverty reduction and the promotion of good governance with an emphasis on social sectors as outlined by the United Nations Millennium Development Goals (MDGs).[2] Throughout the same decade, owing to the wars in Iraq and Afghanistan, there was also an increased connection between development and security, where foreign aid was channeled toward postcrisis reconstruction and peace building.[3] Meanwhile, foreign aid targeted to physical infrastructure gradually declined from 1980s through 1990s.[4] It was during this period that the World Bank began to promote the PPP modality of infrastructure development.[5]

Soon thereafter, and particularly in the aftermath of the global financial crisis, China emerged with its vast financial resources of investment to impose new challenges (or opportunities) to the global development regime. As the Chinese government, with support from the emerging powers such as Russia, began to invest heavily in physical and economic infrastructure around the developing world, concerns over China's "nondemocratic" and "nontransparent" development assistance resulted in the labeling of China as a "rogue donor."[6] China's challenge to traditional donors as well as multilateral development banks (MDBs) continued as President Xi Jinping announced in 2013 both the BRI of vast infrastructure investment around the belt (Central Asia) and road (Southeast Asia) surrounding China and the establishment of the AIIB.[7] The U.S. reaction to China's initiatives continues to be mixed. The Obama administration showed significant apprehension about the AIIB, and the U.S. government has so far stayed out of it. Meanwhile, investment in infrastructure in these economies has been welcomed. The Trump administration has started to counter the BRI through Free and Open Indo-Pacific (FOIP) initiatives with ramped up investment fund for infrastructure, especially in collaboration with Japan.

The history of foreign aid and economic development activities among traditional donors dates back to before World War II. But the bulk of the financial commitments, modalities, and institutions of foreign aid that we see today have developed since the end of that war in the context of recovery from war devastation, decolonization, political independence of countries around the world, and the emerging Cold War.[8] As aid fatigue kicked in toward the end of the Cold War, there was a visible drop in overall official development assistance in the latter half of the 1990s before it picked up in the 2000s (figure 7.1). During this time, global development efforts continued to focus on poverty alleviation and the social sector, following trends established in the 1980s, as the world moved away from infrastructure development.[9] The infrastructure investment by MDBs, particularly the World Bank and the Inter-American Development Bank, dropped from above 50 percent of loans in the 1980s to below 30 percent in the 2000s.[10] Although the Washington Consensus neoliberalism dominated this perspective, the commercial use of aid was condemned during this period.[11]

The downward trend of foreign aid reversed in the aftermath of the September 11, 2001, terrorist attacks on the United States, however, and aid efforts were also influenced by the United Nations MDGs adopted at the UN Millennium Summit in 2000.[12] In the following year the UN International Conference on Financing for Development, held in Monterrey,

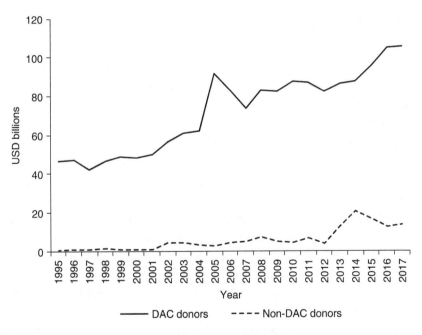

Figure 7.1 Total ODA by All Donors to All Recipients, 1995–2017.
Source: OECD, "Distribution of Net ODA," https://data.oecd.org/oda/distribution -of-net-oda.htm#indicator-chart.

Mexico, led the participating members to mobilize financial resources in support of the MDGs and toward solving the external debt issues of highly indebted economies. President George W. Bush attended the conference and made remarks directly connecting the battle against poverty with the war on terror while also committing the United States to a goal of increasing foreign aid by 50 percent between 2004 and 2006.[13] This so-called Monterrey Consensus, where the donors aimed to enhance foreign aid both in quantity (goal: 0.7 percent of the donor's respective GNP) and in quality (goal: address concerns over aid effectiveness), began a new phase of aid campaigning with an emphasis on the poorest countries—particularly in Sub-Saharan Africa—and on aid effectiveness.

Meanwhile, some East Asian countries transitioned from foreign aid recipients to foreign aid donors. Notably China, which was not only the largest aid recipient of the World Bank's soft loan window, the International Development Association, until it graduated in 1999 but also one of the two largest bilateral recipients (along with Indonesia) of Japanese ODA until 2008, began increasing its own foreign aid. China had a tradition of extending "aid" and concessional loans to neighboring countries since the beginning of its Communist rule, but it did not become a net donor of foreign aid until 2005, when it began to provide more aid than it received.[14] In 2013 China's aid was estimated to be about $7 billion, ranking sixth in comparison to the OECD DAC members.[15] Furthermore, China's Export Import Bank and China Development Bank have been actively financing infrastructure and energy projects in developing countries since the early 2000s, the amounts of which are not counted as foreign aid, but their loan portfolio by the end of 2010 had already exceeded that of the World Bank.[16] This rapidly increasing influence of Chinese money in development has raised concerns about the Chinese government's self-serving motives, which may not follow international norms.[17]

Other new Asian donors include South Korea, Taiwan, Thailand, and India.[18] With the global financial crisis hitting the Western economies hard while the emerging economies rose to join the ranks of foreign aid donors around 2010, the foreign aid paradigm shifted to accommodate not only the voices of the recipient countries in the developing world but also those of the emerging donors. Here, by "offering alternatives to aid-receiving countries, emerging donors are introducing competitive pressures into the existing system."[19] In line with such a shifting paradigm, the "Seoul Development Consensus for Shared Growth," the agenda for the G20 Summit held in Seoul in November 2010, highlighted the priority among emerging donors placed on growth and productive sectors as well as their fair share of a voice in development institutions such as the IMF and World Bank.[20] At the Busan High-Level Forum on Aid Effectiveness in the following year, a new emphasis on "development cooperation" emerged in which the foreign aid norm was recast away from single-minded poverty reduction and toward economic growth, industrial productivity, and wealth creation.[21]

"Sustainable development" became the primary goal of the new UN General Assembly resolution in September 2015, when 17 goals and 169 targets were adopted as the "2030 Agenda."[22] Reflecting the paradigmatic shift in development thinking that started at the G20 Summit in 2010, these newly adopted sustainable development goals (SDGs) are comprehensive and universal. They place less emphasis on poverty reduction and the role of ODA as a strictly bilateral relationship between donors and aid recipients in terms of "developed" and "developing" countries. In particular, the SDGs depart from MDGs in their support of an "approach to infrastructure, personal safety, resilience, private sector development, institutions and rules of law, a system-wide approach to human development."[23]

Around the same time that sustainable development was becoming the new focus of the UN General Assembly, the larger role of emerging donors materialized in 2014–2015 beyond an abstract notion of "consensus" in the form of two MDBs led by the governments of emerging powers.[24] Both aim to channel global savings mostly in emerging economies for infrastructure investment in the developing world and to expand the voices of these emerging powers in global development financial governance. One is the MDB constructed among the five BRICS (Brazil, Russia, India, China and South Africa) governments named the New Development Bank (but often called the BRICS Development Bank). It was launched in 2015 with $50 billion (to be expanded to $100 billion later), with the bank's headquarters in Shanghai and its first president, K. V. Kamath, from India. The other bank is the AIIB, proposed by the Chinese leadership in 2013. With a $100 billion starting fund, the AIIB began operating in January 2016 with its headquarters in Beijing and a Chinese economist, Jin Liqun, as its first president. Although the existing multilateral development funding institutions such as the World Bank and the ADB have announced their intentions to cofinance and cooperate with the AIIB, it is clear that the newcomers are challenging existing politics in the governance of development finance.

Facing such shifting grounds of global development governance, Japan's regional development strategy since the 1990s has generally followed the norm of the traditional donors emphasizing good governance and quality of development projects. Nonetheless, Japan also began to push its specific developmental approach during the 1990s when it was the largest aid donor in the world engaging in debates with the World Bank and other parts of the aid establishment. As the emerging donors, especially China, began to emphasize infrastructure development in the 2010s, the Japanese government has taken a hybrid path as it revisited its old-style priority with a global standard emphasizing high-quality infrastructure.

Old-Style Strategy: Japan's Ascent to Foreign Aid Superpower

Early Stage of Japan's Foreign Aid

Japan was once a recipient of American aid and World Bank financing that established a strong steel sector in the 1950s and 1960s, which helped to build hydroelectric dams as well as Japan's own *shinkansen* bullet train line extending from Tokyo to Osaka.[25] Since that time it has taken Japan about forty years to become the foreign aid superpower. Beginning with the early phase in the 1950s through the 1980s, Japan's foreign aid relationships with Asia exhibited the characteristics of the country's old-style regional geo-economic strategy of bilateralism, informal mode of operation, and an embedded mercantilist nature.

Japanese foreign aid constituted an important bilateral channel that connected the Japanese economy with the developing countries in the region. In the 1950s Japan first reestablished its diplomatic relations with Southeast Asia through war reparations. Foreign aid was also a way to link up with developing regions far away from Japan, such as the Middle East, Latin America, and Africa, particularly in the aftermath of the oil shock of the mid-1970s, in search of diversified access to natural resources. Starting from a position of very minor aid donor as it joined the OECD DAC in 1961, Japan rapidly increased its foreign aid commitments throughout the 1970s and 1980s.

Japan's foreign aid was traditionally concentrated in Asia due to historical reasons, economic ties, and geographical proximity, and despite the dramatic economic growth among many Asian economies over the past several decades, about 60 percent of Japan's bilateral foreign aid is still allocated to Asia.[26] After carrying out its war reparations, the Japanese government began to actively use foreign aid as its major foreign policy instrument in the 1970s.[27] The announcement of the Fukuda Doctrine in 1977 prompted more economic engagement with ASEAN through a rapid increase in foreign aid to the region.[28] Along with bilateral ODA, the establishment of the ADB in 1966 was an important initiative undertaken by the Japanese government in regional development during this period. Despite some pushback from Asian countries, the government succeeded in convincing the United States to come onboard as one of the two major shareholders of this new MDB, with its headquarters in Manila and its presidents from Japan.[29] During the evolution of the ADB, the Japanese government began to take a low-profile but public good–minded stance toward leadership in the area of economic development.[30]

Throughout this period, the notion of "economic cooperation" (*keizai kyōryoku*) represented the informal and mercantilist nature of Japanese foreign aid, whereby the government and the private sector closely collaborated. David Arase clearly explains this notion:

> Since its inception, *keizai kyōryoku* (economic cooperation) has been used to develop strategic resource supplies for Japanese industry, open developing country markets, help Japanese industries achieve or maintain international competitiveness, sustain domestic industries in cyclical downturns, and ease the adjustment costs of Japanese industries facing declining competitiveness. Japan's ODA has been able to promote these ends because it is incorporated into the *keizai kyōryoku* policy making system, which is designed to reconcile both state and private sector objectives.[31]

Particularly during its first decades (1960s and 1970s), Japanese foreign aid reflected this notion of *keizai kyōryoku* and prioritized national economic objectives such as access to export markets and natural resources, as well as an increased number of regional construction and purchase contracts for Japanese companies. In those early years, Japan's aid projects usually came in the form of tied aid and were concentrated in economic infrastructure building. For example, in 1972, a typical year, 65.7 percent of Japan's ODA was tied to purchases and contracts from Japan, a number that was almost twice as high as the DAC average of 34.8 percent. Yen loans (whose high concessionality qualified them as ODA) were mainly used to build physical infrastructure in support of industrialization in the region. Japanese business special interests clearly dominated Japanese foreign aid in the beginning stages of Japan's aid program. One of the standard modalities of Japanese foreign aid during this period, which also enhanced its informality, was its "request-based" policy where Japanese businesses were involved behind the scenes of recipient governments, guiding them through the foreign aid request process.[32] These governments considered that bilateral and informal consultations with the Japanese government were mutually beneficial for both parties as they were able to more freely adjust particular aid provisions, compared to the highly conditional aid provisions offered by the MDBs and "Western" OECD donors.

Aid Superpower: Conforming to Aid Norms and Defying Them?

By the mid-1980s Japanese ODA reached a point where the OECD praised Japan as one of the few aid donors that had rapidly expanded its aid commitments to developing countries.[33] Helped further by the rapid appreciation of the yen since the mid-1980s and the government's increased budget allocation, Japan's ODA had become the largest in the world by 1989, a position it maintained until 2000 (table 7.1).[34]

Japan became a more prominent economic power and a large foreign aid donor in the 1990s. After experiencing the Asian financial crisis, the government gradually began to shift its foreign aid strategy to adopt predominant development norms particularly promoted by the foreign aid and policy circles of the Western donors through the OECD DAC as well as various MDBs, including the World Bank. At the same time, however, the Japanese policy makers engaged in several debates with these establishments regarding the appropriate economic development model based on the country's own successful economic development experience.

On the one hand, the country's rapid economic growth and successful industrialization provided Japanese businesses and policy makers with tremendous confidence and pride in Japan's own economic development strategy, as well as in the success of its model across Asia, as applied through ODA and foreign direct investment. With enough empirical evidence on

TABLE 7.1
Top Ten ODA Donors, 1985–2002 (millions of current U.S. dollars)

	1985		1989		1995		2002	
1	United States	9,403	Japan	8,965	Japan	14,489	United States	12,900
2	Japan	3,797	United States	7,677	France	8,443	Japan	9,220
3	France	3,134	France	5,802	Germany	7,524	Germany	5,359
4	Germany	2,942	Germany	4,948	United States	7,367	France	5,182
5	Canada	1,631	Italy	3,613	Netherlands	3,226	United Kingdom	4,749
6	United Kingdom	1,530	United Kingdom	2,587	United Kingdom	3,202	Netherlands	3,377
7	Netherlands	1,136	Canada	2,320	Canada	2,067	Italy	2,313
8	Italy	1,098	Netherlands	2,094	Sweden	1,704	Canada	2,013
9	Sweden	840	Sweden	1,799	Denmark	1,623	Sweden	1,754
10	Australia	749	Australia	1,020	Italy	1,623	Norway	1,746
	Total DAC	30,743	Total DAC	45,735	Total DAC	58,926	Total DAC	56,911

Source: OECD, "Development Co-operation Report," http://www.oecd.org/dac/development–cooperation–report/.

the effectiveness of foreign aid loans in Asia and the important roles of infrastructure investment and human resource development for developing economies, the Overseas Economic Cooperation Fund in 1991 published its first research note criticizing the World Bank's structural adjustment approach and arguing that purely market-oriented liberalization and privatization would do more harm to recipient economies than good.[35]

In the early 1990s the Japanese government financed the World Bank's publication of a book titled *The East Asian Miracle*, which emphasized the role of the state and the importance of public policy rather than simply market forces.[36] Furthermore, the government and aid scholars began to promote the benefits of concessional loan-based foreign aid (instead of grants), as it encourages responsibility and the effective use of resources often emphasized as "self-help."[37] The very notion of "economic cooperation" had clearly exported Japan's "developmental state" structure to Asia, with a clear "visible handshake" between the Japanese government and recipient countries to facilitate Japanese investment and trade.[38] Hence the campaign of the Japanese developmentalist model and the resulting success observed in the East Asian economies through foreign aid have become pillars of Japan's foreign aid principles.[39]

On the other hand, Japanese foreign aid practices began to follow the global norms and standards of aid giving set by the OECD. The first significant change, despite the emphasis on physical infrastructure, was the decrease of tied aid. International pressure to phase out tied aid came in the form of various agreements at the OECD level, and finally, in 1991, the Helsinki Disciplines imposed restrictions on using tied aid.[40] The data show that the amount of Japan's tied aid indeed declined notably from the late 1970s into the late 1990s, and that the level stayed lower than 10 percent throughout the first decade of the twenty-first century (figure 7.2). By the early 2000s average tied aid for Japan remained at around 6 percent of Japan's entire ODA, which is quite comparable to the low levels of tied aid provided by many European donors between 2003 and 2012, such as France (7 percent), Germany (5 percent), and the United Kingdom (0 percent).[41] Meanwhile, the United States kept 31 percent of its aid tied over this period.[42] This was a visible way in which the traditional neomercantilism aspect of old-style Japan's foreign aid, where Japanese aid was used as a way to obtain and expand Japanese businesses in recipient countries, has waned.[43]

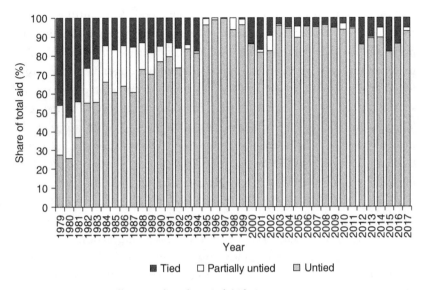

Figure 7.2 Tied, Partially Untied, and Untied Aid, 1979–2017.
Source: OECD, "Aid (ODA) Tying Status," https://stats.oecd.org/viewhtml.aspx?dataset code=TABLE7B&lang=en#.

In fact, during this period the share of ODA-related contracts and procurements awarded to Japanese businesses declined from nearly 70 percent in the 1980s to just 19 percent in 1999, as many high-income developing countries, such as South Korea, and later China and India, began to compete successfully against Japanese companies in bidding.[44] Some argue that this low level of contracts not only created frustration on the part of the Japanese business community but also led to the weakening of support for ODA.[45] Others reverse the causality and contend that the very increase in competitiveness of Japanese firms made it unnecessary for them to rely on foreign aid bidding for their business.[46] Regardless, the reduction of tied aid and a tight budgetary environment in Japan led the government to devise alternative ways to involve the private sector through partnership arrangements for Japan's ODA and development projects.

The other aspect of the change in Japanese foreign aid and development strategy in line with global norms came in the form of its engagement with civil society. Since the early 1990s the Ministry of Foreign Affairs has cultivated its relationship with nongovernmental organizations. The government began to fund foreign aid projects carried out by Japanese NGOs in

1989, and this funding expanded rapidly from merely $16.2 million in 1991 to $112.6 million in 2001.[47] In addition to securing increased funding and project-based collaboration, these NGOs have been actively involved in policy dialogue with various Japanese government agencies. Since 1996 MOFA's aid-related divisions and NGO member representatives have had several meetings per year to engage in government-NGO policy dialogues.[48] And in 1998 a number of legal changes eased restrictions on the incorporation of NGOs, enabling them to engage with foreign aid activities even further.[49] MOFA began providing financial support to NGOs to implement some of Japan's foreign aid projects through the ministry's newly established NGO Assistance Division, whose funding grew tenfold from its founding in 1989 to 1997. The number of foreign aid volunteers managed by MOFA through the Japan Overseas Cooperation Volunteers (JOCV) also increased significantly, to a total of forty thousand volunteers around the world by 2015.[50] All these efforts were further assisted by an "NGO and NPO boom" in Japan in the 1990s, when their image of idealistic, clean, and grass-roots activities gained wide public appeal and allowed MOFA to also gain greater public support.[51]

Domestic Foreign Aid Institutions

A visible bifurcation in Japan's foreign aid posture has occurred particularly since the 1990s as its emphasis on infrastructure building and humanitarian objectives emerged from Japan's fragmented budgetary, bureaucratic, and public support structure that remained intact into the twenty-first century.[52] First, there have been two clear sets of ODA funding mechanisms in Japan. Unlike many other aid donors that provide foreign aid predominantly in the form of grants, Japan's ODA has been dominated by concessional yen loans, whose source of funding is the Fiscal Investment Loan Program (FILP or *Zaisei Tōyushi*).[53] Although these yen loans carry extremely low or almost no interest and qualify as ODA according to the DAC definition, the predominance of concessional loans (as opposed to grants) caused Japan to become the aid donor with the lowest grant ratio of all DAC member countries by the mid-1990s. Although the government continually justified the use of these loans instead of grants as a way to make the recipient governments more responsible while reducing waste and corruption, such a funding modality made it inevitable that Japan would focus its aid on relatively high-income Asian nations and on infrastructure that had greater potential for economic returns. Meanwhile, the government began to allocate its grant aid to low-income countries in South Asia and Africa.

Second, Japan's foreign aid bureaucracy has encompassed various ministries and has been quite fragmented.[54] Traditionally it comprised a four-ministry structure (*yonshō-taisei*) that included the MOFA, MOF, MITI (named METI since 2001), and the Economic Planning Agency (which was absorbed into the Cabinet Office in 2001). As foreign aid became one of the few growing budgetary items in the 1990s besides social welfare provisions, however, another nine ministries engaged in ODA activities, further complicating the coordination of ODA planning. In general, MOF and METI dealt with the yen loans, while MOFA was in charge of the aid grants and technical cooperation. There were two major implementation agencies, the OECF and the Japan International Cooperation Agency (JICA), which managed the yen loans and technical cooperation, respectively.

Third, distinct domestic constituencies of the ministries have created further fragmentation in Japanese foreign aid policy, as these distinct social groups pressure the ministries to satisfy their respective interests through ODA. On the one hand, METI- and MOF-led foreign aid has long supported the economic development and industrial upgrading of many Southeast Asian countries, and Japan's old-style foreign aid strategy has constituted the most important link tying Japanese businesses with the government in constructing a strong and stable regional economy and regional production network.[55] The METI Committee also recommended that Japan's financial assistance to developing countries should be used primarily to lower the risks that accompany infrastructure investment undertaken by private investors, and that ODA should be used to underwrite the elements of each project having a public aspect.[56] Obviously, these recommendations made Japanese businesses strong supporters of traditional aid mercantilism. On the other hand, while MOFA did not have a specific domestic clientele, it had always succeeded in invoking an altruistic and positive image of foreign aid to garner public support.[57] Because the Japanese public is often quite sensitive about Japan's international image, its status as a "foreign aid superpower" that has contributed to helping the poor and supporting the United Nations provided MOFA with solid support in the arena of public opinion.

Regional Institution-Building Efforts

Until the late 1990s Japanese foreign aid went to East Asia through mostly bilateral channels. Although the Japanese government led in establishing the ADB in the 1960s as a way to increase its regional presence in development finance, the government was not aggressive in utilizing the ADB to promote its own development strategy.[58] Such a passive position changed to a more active one in the 1990s along with Japan's debate with the World Bank and in the aftermath of the Asian financial crisis, as the government began to shift its attention regionally. Facing the crisis, the government scrambled to establish a regional financial mechanism for emergency funding, and ASEAN members requested the setting up of the Regional Economic Monitoring Unit (REMU) to further monitor the crisis. In March 1999 the ADB authorized Japan's Special Fund, the "Asian Currency Crisis Support Facility," with ¥7.5 billion ($68 million at the 1999 exchange rate) in cash for interest payments and technical assistant grants, as well as ¥360 billion ($3.3 billion) in guarantees.[59] In the same year, the Asian Recovery Information Center was set up to support the economic recovery of the region with a $1 billion contribution from the MOF. Many regional financial cooperation activities after the Asian financial crisis took place within the newly established ASEAN+3 meetings (see chapter 6), and the ADB has continued to support regional financial and development efforts, particularly under Haruhiko Kuroda, who became the ADB president in February 2005.[60]

Under President Kuroda, the ADB upgraded the REMU to the Office of Regional Economic Integration (OREI) in April 2005, an act that "substantially raised the ADB's capacity to address regional cooperation and integration issues" with a much larger staff devoted to the cause.[61] It was in this context that the OREI, headed by the prominent Japanese economist Masahiro Kawai, took on the issue of a regional currency unit at the ADB (see chapter 6). The ADB has become a conduit for regional integration efforts in other areas of Japan's regional economic strategy, such as promoting the ASEAN+6 arrangement or Comprehensive

Economic Partnership Agreement for a regional free trade area (see chapter 5) to overcome the region's noodle bowl phenomenon of bilateral FTAs.[62] To formalize these efforts, the ADB adopted in 2006 the Regional Cooperation and Integration (RCI) strategy with four pillars: cross-border infrastructure development, trade and investment, monetary and financial cooperation, and regional public goods. Above all, regional connectivity efforts helped ASEAN to develop its Master Plan on Connectivity, including physical, institutional, and people-to-people connectivity for economic community building.[63] Japan's initiatives at the ADB in the form of "developmental regionalism" are advocated where "development, regionalism, and capacity-building" are linked together. The Japanese government's aims seem to be fully in line with what Christopher M. Dent describes: "The creation of more coherent regional economic spaces is conducive to the operation of more efficient internationalised and transnational business activities, and regional cooperation and integration (RCI) activities that the ADB has promoted . . . have generally been devised with at least some acknowledgement of this principle."[64]

Hence the Japanese government began to resort to the ADB as an institutional framework for its regional development strategy following the Asian financial crisis. By channeling some special funds coupled with a strong Japanese official representation in the bank, Japan was able to enhance its regional development framework.

In addition, and in the context of emerging (and competing) regional economic frameworks in the mid-2000s, METI proposed an "OECD-like" think tank in Asia called the Economic Research Institute for ASEAN and East Asia (ERIA), which could formulate policy proposals and coordinate networks of research associated with regional economic integration.[65] Under METI's "Global Economic Strategy" of April 2006, presided over by Trade Minister Toshihiro Nikai (often called the "Nikai Initiative"), the Japanese government formulated its strategies toward the establishment of an appropriate regional order and steps toward integration, as well as an approach to maintain Japan's presence in the region.[66] With the opening of the institute in Jakarta in 2008 with an $80 to $100 million contribution from the Japanese government, ERIA began contributing to Japan's efforts toward deeper regional economic integration by promoting the ASEAN+6 CEPEA and supporting the East Asian Summit.[67]

Norm Building and Pursuit of National Economic Interest Through Foreign Aid

Constraining Funding Resources and Sharpening Objectives

From the late 1990s, Japan's ODA began to decline because of the deteriorating fiscal balance as the country faced sluggish economy after the burst of the economic bubble in the early 1990s. Japan's foreign aid funding had begun to contract in 1997, as Prime Minister Ryūtaro Hashimoto announced the first ODA budget cut. This ODA reduction did not materialize, however, for the next few years owing to the sudden economic hardship that hit East Asian countries in the aftermath of the Asian financial crisis. The crisis motivated the Japanese government to commit $30 billion through the New Miyazawa Initiative, announced in October 1998 (see chapter 6 and next section).[68] The actual reduction in Japanese foreign aid finally started in 2001 when the ODA budget was cut by 10 percent. Additionally, the FILP reforms of the late 1990s also put pressure on the source of yen loans.

Since then, Japanese aid volume has declined in both absolute terms and relative to other donors. In 2011 Japan's ODA net flow stood at $8.1 billion, which approximates the level of its foreign aid in the mid-1980s, while the United States more than tripled its aid net flows from mid-1990s levels to $34.1 billion. Such shifts in foreign aid provision caused Japan to fall to fifth in rank among OECD donors in 2011, following the United States, Germany ($12.6 billion), the United Kingdom ($12.2 billion), and France ($11 billion).[69] Accordingly, the share of Japan's foreign aid as a percentage of the total foreign aid from DAC members declined from above 18 percent in the late 1990s to about 6 percent in 2011. Japan is, however, still a large Asian aid donor compared to emerging Asian donors such as South Korea ($1.4 billion) or Taiwan (about $0.5 billion).

During this period, popular support of Japan's foreign aid also saw a significant decline. According the Cabinet Office's annual opinion poll on diplomacy (*gaikō ni kansuru yoron chōsa*), the support for more foreign aid dipped to around 19 percent from 2002 to 2006, a significant decline from its high in the upper 30–40 percent range during the mid-1990s (figure 7.3).[70]

A shrinking budget, along with the shifting priorities and sagging popularity of foreign aid, has had a constructive impact on Japan's new

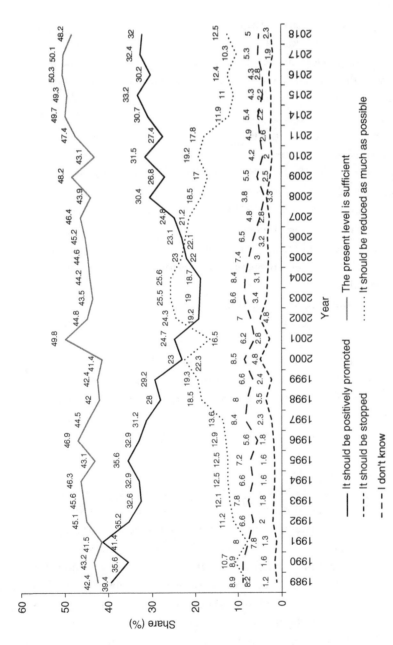

Figure 7.3 Public Opinion Polls on Foreign Aid, 1989–2018. The Ministry of Foreign Affairs did not include a question on development assistance in its 2012 and 2013 polls, so these years are excluded.

Source: Cabinet Office, "Public Opinion Polls on Development Assistance," https://survey.gov-online.go.jp/h30/h30-gaiko/2-2.html.

state-led foreign aid strategy as the government began to formalize its objectives through increasingly explicit foreign aid charters. Japan's first ODA Charter (ODA Taikō) was adopted at the height of Japan's rising ODA in 1992 with four priorities: environmental conservation, nonmilitary use, no support to countries with large military expenditures, and attention to other values such as democracy, market-oriented economies, and human rights and freedom.[71] But this short charter did very little to elaborate on the agreed-on objectives of foreign aid by its stakeholders.

In 2002 continued active discussion on ODA policy among many of its stakeholders—ranging from the Prime Minister's Task Force to the Board of Comprehensive ODA Strategy, advisory boards and ministerial public comment panels, as well as involvement of the Liberal Democratic Party ODA Reform Working Group together with recommendations from Keidanren—produced the "New ODA Charter." This much longer document was the codification of where the policy makers saw Japan's foreign aid going from there. There are two notable elements in the new charter: First, it is a broad synthesis of views from various groups in relation to ODA.[72] Second, it clearly acknowledges and highlights the two-tier system of (a) pursuing Japan's national interest in the areas of both security and prosperity and (b) providing public goods in the areas of human security and governance.[73] Furthermore, the utilization of Japan's own experience in economic and social development was highlighted.[74]

Declining financial resources also motivated the Japanese government to emphasize humanitarian values. An emphasis on humanitarian goals, including basic human needs, poverty alleviation, women in development, and sustainable development in foreign aid goals, emerged under the MOFA initiative.[75] Extending this avenue and adding the country's unique foreign policy profile of a "peaceful nation," the Japanese government began to articulate the concept of human security at the United Nations Development Program in the mid-1990s, where advocates drew attention to the security of each human being and communities of people and not only that of states.[76] Championed by Amartya Sen, winner of the 1998 Nobel Prize in Economics, and Sadako Ogata, former UN high commissioner for refugees (1991–2001), this human security concept was adopted by scholars and practitioners of development throughout the UNDP, from donor governments to NGOs.[77] In Japan, Prime Minister Keizō Obuchi (1998–2000) became the first leader to emphasize the human security–centered approach with his speech (then as foreign minister) in Singapore in May 1998, in which he linked Japan's ODA to the needs of the people affected by the economic crisis.

In the ODA policy review of 2005, the Japanese government emphasized four aspects of its foreign aid policy—poverty reduction, sustainable development, global issues, and peace building—all of which touch on human security. It has also made a conscious effort to support the "Human Security Network" (established under an initiative by Canada and Norway in 1999) and promote civil society groups in support of human security by establishing the group "Friends of Human Security" in 2006.[78] In practice, the concept of human security has been promoted across the board since the early 2000s not only in relation to Japan's development aid and postdisaster humanitarian assistance, such as the 2004 Indian Ocean earthquake and tsunami relief, but also in the context of Japan's peace-making and peace-building diplomacy from East Timor and Cambodia to Afghanistan and Iraq.[79]

The Japanese government issued two more foreign aid and "development cooperation" charters (as of 2019); the ODA review of 2010 and the Development Cooperation Charter of 2015. The former, published under the Democratic Party of Japan government, emphasizes "enlightened national interest" where Japan can share its knowledge, technology, and institutions that helped the country successfully develop. It also highlighted the importance of installing measures to support sustainable development by focusing on environment, infrastructure, and legal systems.[80] The 2015 charter has gone further on the same path but emphasizes comprehensive development through self-help and "quality growth."[81]

In addition to articulating the objectives and values of foreign aid surrounding human security, the Japanese government worked to reorganize the ODA chain of command to streamline the strategic planning and implementation of Japan's foreign aid. These efforts took place throughout the late 1990s and early 2000s.[82] The first step was the establishment of the Overseas Economic Cooperation Council in 2006 directly under the prime minister, where foreign aid policy is discussed and coordinated with the cabinet secretary, foreign minister, finance minister, and economic minister. After being dormant during the DPJ's rule from September 2009 to the end of 2012, this council was revived as the Joint Committee on Economic Cooperation and Infrastructure under Prime Minister Abe in March 2013.[83] At the ministry level, the MOF became the single coordinator of foreign aid in August 2006 and established the International Cooperation Bureau directly under the International Planning Headquarters housed in MOFA. Most of the ODA channels were finally consolidated in the New JICA in October 2008, which has since become the largest foreign aid implementing agency in the world.[84] Since then the strengthened New JICA has implemented ODA projects utilizing all three ODA resources: concessional yen loans, grant aid, and technical cooperation. On the other hand, the Japan Bank for International Cooperation (JBIC), which used to house the former OECF's foreign aid loan function from 1999 to 2007, became the policy-based financing agency providing non-ODA (Other Official Flows) lending.

Changing Government-Business Relationship

Efforts to Relink the Government and Business Through PPP

As discussed previously, Japanese developmental strategy has long been bifurcated between the humanitarian track and one that emphasizes infrastructure building and economic growth. In the twenty-first century the government appeared as though it was putting a lot more emphasis on the latter, revisiting aspects of its old-style foreign aid. Japanese ODA drastically decreased traditional tied aid in the 1990s, following the OECD standard. But the exceptional reversal was made in the aftermath of the Asian financial crisis as Japan's tied aid came back into prominence in the form of the New Miyazawa Initiative announced in October 1998. This was a plan to assist Japan's neighboring countries hit by the financial crisis, which included approximately ¥600 billion ($5 billion) in yen loans for infrastructural development to promote growth, employment, and economic restructuring in those countries. These yen loans were disbursed in the form of tied aid, with a large portion extended for three years (until 2002) and procured from Japanese companies only when the Japanese economy itself was struggling to recover from the series of financial crises. Lee Poh Ping notes that "Japanese officials readily admit that much of the aid is tied to projects to stimulate demand for Japanese goods and service and to boost the role of the yen."[85] Since then, the ODA budget has declined significantly, and Japan's tied aid has remained low for about another decade.

Furthermore, the debate over the causes of the Asian financial crisis strengthened the government's conviction that the battle of ideas is critical in establishing the country as one of the respected leaders in the field of development financing and foreign aid.[86] In this context, the government began to implement a kind of foreign aid strategy that establishes Japan as a "soft power" based on its economic success. The Koizumi administration promoted the Initiative for Development in East Asia (IDEA) to set up a basis for an exchange of views regarding development and regional cooperation "based on the countries' development experience and knowledge."[87]

Sector allocation of Japan's foreign aid, which had somewhat shifted from the economic infrastructure and production sectors to the social sector following global trends and responding to international pressure, still housed a substantial level of economic infrastructure development. By 2010 more than 20 percent of Japan's ODA was targeted at the social sector, a clear improvement from the 3.7 percent of the early 1970s and slightly above the 10 percent of the early 1990s.[88] Particularly since the global financial crisis (2008–2009), nonetheless, the allocation of Japan's ODA to economic infrastructure began to bounce back as Japan struggled to recover from the crisis. By 2014 the allocation to the economic infrastructure sector had gone up as high as 50 percent of bilateral aid.[89] This sector includes transportation, communication, energy, and other businesses such as finance, and where infrastructure was crucial in attracting private direct investment from Japan and elsewhere for industrialization and increasing exports. Two additional factors associated with this sector are the regional concentration of Japanese foreign aid in relatively high-income Asian countries and its financial makeup dominated by yen loans.

Under the increasing fiscal constraints, however, the Japanese government began to direct its interest in the public-private partnership arrangements during this time to utilize funds and expertise from the private sector to sustain infrastructure-oriented projects.[90] This led to the devising of the Special Terms of Economic Partnership (STEP) by JICA, where Japan's ODA became explicitly tied to procurement from Japan, and funding was given to the leading partners from Japan. This should also be used to promote the country's superior technology.[91] The PPP modality had been popular among advanced economies for their domestic infrastructure investment since the 1980s, when privatization and fiscal constraints led the state to collaborate closely with the private sector and run what used to be public-sector responsibilities such as public transportation or infrastructure. This was expanded into the development world and MDB foreign assistance from the mid-1990s.

By 2005 Japan's Ministry of Economy, Trade, and Industry became keen on applying the PPP modality to Asia's infrastructure development. METI's definition of PPP is revealing in that it focuses on "the division of labor between the public and private in infrastructure building and administrative services, as the two entities share adequate cost and risk."[92] In relation to this, the Japanese government began to promote a "Japan package" ODA modality in which the Japanese government would engage in planning with aid recipient governments to provide a package-type aid, which included everything from identifying possible infrastructure projects, public and private financing, and construction to maintenance.[93] Along with these major initiatives, the Japanese government began increasing Japan's explicitly tied aid, not only to secure the procurement and contracts of Japanese businesses but also to prevail over foreign aid competition from China. For example, the new phase of Japanese foreign aid loans of approximately ¥198.9 billion to the newly democratized Myanmar announced in January 2013 became all tied, and no international bidding was opened.[94] Furthermore, a large (¥240 billion in yen loans) foreign aid project in the Philippines, a railroad construction project that connects Manila and Malolos, agreed on and signed in November 2015, is tied to procurement from Japan.[95]

Although there are similarities between the PPP scheme and Japan's old "request base" aid modality, there are some critical differences, both on the supply side (Japan) and on the demand side (recipient countries). These differences have actually led Japanese aid agencies and ministries to struggle with moving this scheme forward in an effort to enhance Japan's economic presence in Asia's development.

On the supply side, the challenge comes from the risks and costs associated with privately funded infrastructure projects. Unlike earlier foreign aid, where the bulk of funding came from the government and comprised only a single project that a private company had to manage (i.e., the so-called engineering, procurement, and construction [EPC] projects), PPP arrangements counted on private firms to fund several phases of aid projects, with the government providing the official loans as well as trade and investment insurance.[96] This new modality is not what Japanese companies are used to nor comfortable with, and the cost of Japan's services is often very high.[97] Japanese businesses' high sensitivity to financial risks associated with infrastructure projects has prevented the expansion of Japan's infrastructure investments. As noted previously, Japanese firms have robust expertise in EPC schemes where they have well-identified and limited operational and financial responsibilities, which reduce uncertainty and risk. Meanwhile, many infrastructure projects in emerging Asian economies in the twenty-first century come mainly in the form of "concessions," in which private firms take responsibility not only for the operation and maintenance of the invested assets but also for the financing and managing of all required investment and hence take risks with respect to both condition of the assets and the investments themselves.[98] Japanese businesses are not used to such schemes, and they consider the associated risks to be too high.[99] There is also some mismatch between the loan and evaluation cycles of the Japanese loan agencies, such as JICA and JBIC, and Japan's private sector. As a result, the amount of PPP projects supported by the STEP loans did not expand as much as the government had hoped.[100]

On the demand side, the recipient governments have increasingly taken ownership of development cooperation as they communicate with the respective Japanese aid agency in both the planning of the projects and their responsibility in implementing them. Particularly in the aftermath of the Asian financial crisis, the ASEAN governments moved toward decentralization and the direct funding of public projects through bonds, which made it less likely for Japanese ODA to be the critical factor in their infrastructure financing.[101] These governments, including less experienced ones like Vietnam, insist on managing their aid-funded projects despite the country's still weak legal and governance institutions. This has led the Japanese private sector to become hesitant to get involved and has also led Japanese aid agencies to turn to either fiscal support or legal and governance capacity-building for these countries.[102] In sum, the Japanese government has struggled to put in place an effective PPP arrangement where it could count on the private sector's direct involvement. Notwithstanding, Japan has continued to promote infrastructure investment and exports as a way to nurture an accommodative economic environment for Japanese businesses, particularly in Asia.

Aid and Its "Vanguard" Effects

As a part of Japan's regional development strategy in the twenty-first century, the government has sought to involve Japanese businesses by improving the business environment in developing regions. In a JBIC survey in 2015, 607 manufacturing companies were asked how the level of infrastructure development influenced their business decisions on whether to operate in a certain developing country. More than 72.2 percent of auto-manufacturing firms and 81.9 percent of electronics firms responded that they would be hesitant to invest in countries with poor infrastructure. Only 2.2 percent of auto manufacturers responded that infrastructure deficiency does not affect their decision, while none (0 percent) said so among firms in the electronics sector.[103]

Such a business attitude underlies what Hidemi Kimura and Yasuyuki Todo call a "vanguard effect" of Japanese aid, where aid can prepare the business environment in local developing economies to invite foreign direct investment from Japan.[104] It is not infrastructure building per se that would lead to an increase in *total* FDI regardless of the investment origin, but rather the role of Japanese ODA that leads private investments from Japan. Todo explains that there are two fundamental reasons for this effect: One is foreign aid's utility as a penetrating method to gather information on the political, economic, legal, and institutional conditions of the recipient countries. The other is to spread those elements of business environments favored by Japanese companies through foreign aid projects, including Japanese-style business practices and customs.[105]

In this vein, the Japanese government has also implemented projects to directly strengthen the legal systems in many of the less advanced Asian countries since the late 1990s, so that the Japanese private sector can more actively engage with development projects. The Japanese government hence began considering support for legal system improvements as an important component of good governance and in support of developing countries' economic development and democracy.[106] This effort has taken place in the context of soft aid and intellectual support. For example, in the Ishikawa Project (1995–2001), which conducted extensive research on the institutional needs of Vietnam in the country's transition to a market economy, the first phase of law training (Legal System Development Support Phase 1) started with Vietnam and Cambodia in 1996.[107] That year, the International

Civil and Commercial Law Center (ICCLC), a public foundation, was set up to help these developing countries develop their legal systems, as the founders (i.e., Ministry of Justice) believed that "it is desirable that we mutually cultivate an understanding of each country's legal system and its application, and encourage mutual research on a better legal structure for international economic activity in order to promote and facilitate further economic interaction and mutual prosperity."[108] The Ministry of Justice established the International Cooperation Department in 2001 to expand legal training and legal assistance in several Asian countries, including Vietnam, Cambodia, Laos, Indonesia, Mongolia, Bangladesh, and Uzbekistan.[109]

The Japanese government has placed strong emphasis on governance issues since 2009, when the Basic Policy for Legal System Development Support was announced through the Cabinet Office after in-depth consultation with several relevant ministries.[110] In 2013 the revised basic policy included the five main objectives of this development assistance: (a) promote the rule of law in developing countries; (b) enhance legal environments that will allow the countries to abide by global rules and maintain sustainable growth; (c) share Japan's experience and institutions while enhancing economic partnerships that will constitute the foundation of regional partnerships and integration; (d) support a useful environment for trade and investment for Japanese business operations; and (e) enhance capacities for governance.[111]

In sum, foreign aid has served as a catalyst for the Japanese government to foster economic development in East Asia. Japan's recent regional development strategy has focused, nonetheless, not on the direct mercantilistic connection between the government and the big businesses but on the government's role in cultivating an amicable business environment in the region.

Japan Faces China's Belt-and-Road Initiative and the AIIB

China's Challenge to Development Cooperation Paradigm

Japan's long-held belief in the importance of infrastructure investment began to come under the spotlight by the 2010s not so much due to Japan's own efforts but mostly because of the increasing prominence of China as a large provider of development funding with an emphasis on physical infrastructure. It is indeed ironic that China's infrastructure development initiatives have parts of their roots in the country's own experience as a major recipient of economic aid from Japan in the 1980s and the 1990s.[112] In addition, with the rise of the "sustainable development goals" paradigm after the 2011 Busan forum, the Japanese government was vindicated as the world started to acknowledge the value of "development cooperation" with an emphasis on economic growth (rather than poverty reduction) and infrastructure investment, all of which Japan had advocated and practiced in the past. According to Tatsufumi Yamagata, "the [new] Sustainable Development Goals enabled Japan to formulate a more self-oriented international cooperation policy."[113] Moreover, these shifting priorities have enabled Japan to engage in private-sector-based support to developing countries in addition to capacity development, governance, and empowerment.[114]

During this period China has also emerged as a chief foreign aid rival to Japan, especially in Asia.[115] In fall 2013 China's president Xi Jinping launched the Belt-and-Road Initiative, a vast economic connectivity scheme. These initiatives emerged as a way to sustain China's economic growth by expanding its regional and global influence as well as engaging in international development dialogues based on the country's own development experience.[116] China's infrastructure investment can help meet the infrastructure investment shortage around the world. Asia alone, according to ADB's 2009 estimates, requires roughly $8 trillion in the ten years between 2010 and 2020 to fill the existing infrastructure investment gap.[117] Although the BRI houses a much larger connectivity scheme apart from just infrastructure development and investment, and the coverage goes beyond the immediate region, the proposed $1 trillion fund to help with the vast infrastructure investment needs in Asia has made this issue the central focus of China's new enterprise.

In support of infrastructure investment, the BRI was accompanied by a proposal to establish a brand new multilateral development bank, the Asian Infrastructure Investment Bank, with an initial capital funding of $50 billion, along with China's bilateral funding institutions such as the China Development Bank and the Export-Import Bank of China.[118] In October 2014 twenty-one countries sent delegates to the AIIB launch ceremony to start the process.[119] The AIIB's capital subscription was expanded to $100 billion in June 2014; hence its capital base has reached 61 percent of that of the Asian Development Bank ($163 billion) and slightly over 35 percent of the World Bank's scale ($283 billion). By the time the AIIB's official deadline for joining it as a prospective founding member (PFM) came at the end of March 2015, fifty-seven countries, including many in Europe as well as most of the Asia-Pacific except Japan and the United States, had signed up. The AIIB was officially launched at its inaugural ceremony in Beijing on January 16, 2016. By late 2019 the membership had expanded to one hundred countries, and the AIIB has since approved sixty-three projects, almost all in physical infrastructure development in the widely defined region of Asia.

Japan's Hybrid Strategy to Respond to the BRI

In the early 2010s the Japanese government moved back in time to resort to the old regional development strategy of infrastructure investment through tied aid in the face of China's challenges. The Abe government (December 2012–present) had already launched "all-Japan" public-private sales efforts of Japanese products and services to foreign nations led by the prime minister and other economic ministers. These efforts constitute part of Japan's economic revitalization strategy of Abenomics. In addition, "close partnership between the government and business groups also underpin effective policy formulation and implementation by facilitating the reflection of practical needs of private actors on government policies."[120] The government also increased funding for infrastructure investment and changed the laws and rules on funding to allow more risk tolerance for Japan's infrastructure financing in response to the rise of the BRI. The top-down initiatives by the prime minister allowed policy harmonization among government agencies and enabled the government to lead its geo-economic strategy of infrastructure investment and exports. At the same time, an element of the state-led liberal strategy is apparent as the Japanese government also pursued standard setting and rulemaking while it promoted quality infrastructure development in the context of both regional and global forums, such as the Free and Open Indo-Pacific (FOIP), the G7 Ise-shima Summit (2016), and the G20 Osaka Summit (2019).

To meet the challenge of China's BRI and its infrastructure investments, Prime Minister Abe and Finance Minister Tarō Asō unveiled in 2015 Japan's plan to respond to the vast infrastructure needs in Asia by providing "quality infrastructure" investment. This "Partnership for Quality Infrastructure" (PQI), announced by Prime Minister Abe at the 21st International Conference on the Future of Asia on May 21, 2015, consists of four pillars, two of which focus on Japanese economic cooperation.[121] One of these is the introduction of economic cooperation tools for Japan such as the PPP to increase funds for infrastructure investment. Through these instruments, the government promises to increase its commitment to infrastructure support in Asia by 25 percent. Furthermore, in November 2015 the Japanese government issued several follow-up measures within the context of the PQI with Asia, including (a) acceleration of yen-loan approval procedures; (b) establishment of dollar-denominated ODA loans; (c) possible exemption of recipient government funding guarantees on a case-by-case basis; and (d) promotion of "developing relevant" international standards for quality infrastructure investment.[122] Another pillar is an increase in the JBIC's capacity to provide loans to relatively high-risk projects with a longer cost-accounting timeframe by revising the JBIC Law and adding a financial cushion to sustain higher risk.[123] The law that passed in May 2016 has made the JBIC more risk-tolerant, so that the bank can overcome existing difficulties in identifying appropriate infrastructure projects in Asia due to risk concerns.[124]

As a part of its dialogue with Southeast Asian governments, the Japanese government also began to lobby for changes in the contract bidding procedures to take into consideration not only low prices but also the quality of infrastructure.[125] Based on this principle, the Abe administration has sought to spread the gospel of quality infrastructure among like-minded countries around the Asia Pacific and beyond through its FOIP strategy, poised to counter China's BRI.[126]

Utilizing the spotlight opportunities of the G7 Ise-Shima Summit in 2016 as its host, the Japanese government and the leaders of member governments agreed on the "G7 Ise-Shima Principles for Promoting Quality Infrastructure Investment," which include five principles around effective governance and implementation of infrastructure investment.[127] At the G20 Osaka Summit in June 2019, the "G20 Principles for Quality Infrastructure Investment" were adopted by the participating leaders (including China), with six principles emphasizing consideration of life-cycle cost of infrastructure investment and debt-sustainability. Finance Minister Asō was quoted as noting that he was very proud to be able to "explicitly codify and publicize" these principles among the G20 leaders in order to establish a global standard for infrastructure investment.[128]

Regional Infrastructure Initiative

Meanwhile, the establishment of the AIIB posed some challenges to Japan's regional institution-building in Asia. Initially Japan's reaction to China's AIIB proposal throughout 2014 was one of low enthusiasm and suspicion. On a geoeconomic level, the Japanese leadership perceived China's AIIB proposal as a challenge to Japanese and American dominance at the ADB and viewed China's moves as aiming to diminish Japan's important economic leadership role in the region.[129] The fact that the U.S. government was dubious of China's intentions boosted Japan's reluctance to endorse the AIIB. Both governments and many practitioners were also concerned about the AIIB's apparent lack of transparency, good governance structure, and credibility.[130] Various circles in Japan began to engage in brainstorming about whether Japan should join the AIIB in the near future. Of course, the major opposition party, the DPJ, was very critical of the government's misstep, calling it a "massive foreign policy blunder."[131]

In response, Prime Minister Abe was reported to have ordered the LDP to engage in serious discussion about the course of Japan's future decision regarding AIIB membership. From April 1, 2015, three LDP committees (Foreign Affairs, Treasury and Finance, and Regional Diplomatic and Economic Partnership) belatedly began to meet and discuss whether Japan should join this new institution. After six meetings, the opinions of economists and experts from the private sector, mass media, and academia were split, and hesitant LDP members wary of China's successful initiative settled on a "wait-and-see" position by June, as the United States also sat on the sidelines.[132]

Meanwhile, Japan (and the United States) kicked in important changes in the ADB.[133] This ADB reform proposal, in place since 2013, to expand ADB loans by 50 percent passed a board meeting in 2015. As a result, the ADB's new loan capacity includes a component for quality infrastructure (cofinanced with Japan) of $110 billion for the next five years. At the same time, the ADB moved to accelerate the loan approval process, hence shortening the approval time from twenty-one months to fifteen months. In addition to these institutional and procedural changes, the ADB president,

Takehiko Nakao, met with AIIB president-designate Jin Liqun several times over the course of AIIB setup to share the experience of the ADB and to discuss cofinancing of projects. World Bank then-president Jim Yong Kim has also expressed his willingness to support the AIIB.[134]

In Japan's domestic political response to the AIIB, differences among the ministries were evident. Among the main ministries in Japan, the Ministry of Finance saw the Chinese infrastructure initiatives, particularly the AIIB, as a threat to Japan's (at least #2) position in development finance. The AIIB would challenge the authority of the ADB (whose presidents are usually the MOF *amakudari* officials) and Japan's influence in the World Bank and other international financial institutions. The MOF was also very wary of the financial contribution that the government would have to make in support of the AIIB if Japan were to participate under a China-dominant governance structure.[135] There were additional concerns of Japan being "used," especially in the early stages, to help the AIIB bonds obtain a higher credit rating—particularly, prior to advanced countries signing on to the AIIB.[136] The Ministry of Foreign Affairs was also reluctant owing to the U.S. position of suspicion regarding the AIIB.[137] The MOFA also insisted that it would be difficult to support the AIIB until its governance structure became clearer and more transparent.[138]

In line with the economic growth strategy laid out particularly under Abenomics, the METI was more amenable to the AIIB idea because it would mean greater business opportunities for Japan and a way to provide much-needed infrastructure in the region. For Japanese businesses with high stakes in China (and hence for METI), it has become increasingly important to please the Chinese authorities and to be viewed favorably. But these are diffuse interests. METI had a hard time pushing other reluctant ministries to favor the AIIB without solid backing from the industries that stood to directly benefit from the agreement.[139] In support of the anti-AIIB position against METI, MOF officials pitched seemingly limited benefits that the AIIB would accrue in the way of direct business opportunities for Japanese companies and banks. The MOF frequently quoted statistics from the ADB showing that, even in the multilateral development banks where Japanese power dominates, only 0.5 percent of ADB infrastructure contracts had been awarded to Japanese companies in recent years.[140] Reportedly, the MOF has on every occasion mentioned this low rate of business success in order to convince those who worry about a potential loss of business opportunities from failing to participate in the AIIB.[141]

Reactions by Japan's big businesses to the BRI and AIIB have also been mixed. Peak business associations such as the Keidanren refrained from voicing strong views on the AIIB, claiming insufficient information.[142] Japanese financial industries were also reluctant to commit to Asia's infrastructure funding, whose governance structure and project assessment criteria are not yet clear.[143] Even as the Abe administration began to show a positive stance toward the BRI during its BRI summit in 2017, Japanese businesses remained concerned about the high risks of the various infrastructure projects undertaken by the BRI. Meanwhile, Japanese businesses continue to rely for their funding on the JBIC, which actually has a larger funding base than the AIIB.

Consolidation of Domestic Institution Behind Quality Infrastructure Investment

During the course of this final round of competition with China, the Japanese government experienced a major blow as it lost the bid to build the Jakarta-Bandung High-Speed Rail. As a part of its own infrastructure export push, the JICA was involved in the feasibility study and planning of this high-speed rail line since 2008, under Indonesia's former president Yudhoyono (2004–2014). With the electoral victory of Joko Widodo (who goes by President Jokowi) in July 2014, however, the government shifted its focus toward redistribution in the face of the country's difficult fiscal and balance-of-payments positions. This was the time when the Chinese leadership began keenly courting Indonesia to engage in infrastructure development with China, emphasizing that the Chinese-supported project would meet President Jokowi's three conditions of (a) not using Indonesia's fiscal resources, (b) not requiring any government guarantees for loans, and (c) implementing the projects on business-to-business basis. By October 2015 China had won the project, which broke ground in January 2016.[144]

To counter the rise of the BRI and AIIB in the midst of Japan's loss against China over the high-speed rail contract in Indonesia, Prime Minister Abe and the Cabinet Office spearheaded efforts to consolidate a team to support Japan's infrastructure exports.[145] Such efforts included promoting the PPP projects with a newly revised ODA system of tied aid and information sharing, as well as launching "top-level sales" activities around

Asia to sell Japan's technology and quality in infrastructure development. This "all-Japan" partnership, reminiscent of the 1970s and 1980s, aims to deploy effective support for Japan's infrastructure exports by harmonizing the interests and policies of the usually fragmented ministries in Japan, and it simultaneously nurtures the close partnership between Japan's government and businesses.[146] This economic strategy reversal arose primarily as a way for Japan to meet the Chinese challenge, while making infrastructure competition that of quality and standard.

The Japanese government's motivations lie in the fact that infrastructure exports continue to be an important business and a part of their economic growth strategy. As discussed, Japan's foreign aid policy gradually converged with OECD norms (decreased tied aid and high governance standards, for example) over the course of the 1990s and into the 2000s. Japanese businesses, facing increased competition with new entrants along with high costs and risk averseness, have suffered significant losses in opportunities for infrastructure business in Asia. Nonetheless, and particularly owing to Japan's slow or negative growth in the aftermath of the global financial crisis, the government saw infrastructure exports to rapidly recovering Asian countries as one of the few avenues to bolster Japan's own economic recovery and growth. Given Japan's constraints due to a shortage of fiscal resources, difficulty in motivating or controlling business behavior, and fragmented bureaucratic interests, it took the threat of China's geoeconomic challenge for Japan to finally energize its own infrastructure export push. Notwithstanding, discord remains among major players in infrastructure development.

The longer-term evolution of Japan's new regional development and aid strategy has taken a winding and hybrid path, especially under the fluctuating global development and foreign aid paradigm of the twenty-first century and in the face of China's rise as a large foreign aid power. Nonetheless, the embedded mercantilist nature of Japan's foreign aid that characterized it in the 1970s has faded away, while the Japanese government's efforts to involve its business sector and enhance the space for Japan's development cooperation continue. Meanwhile, the government has become much more transparent in its aid priorities, with an emphasis on human security and efforts toward rulemaking and institution building for better business environments.

Conclusion

This study has focused on the Japanese government and the geo-economic strategy it pursues in the region to promote its national interests. The government's old-style regional geoeconomic strategy exhibited its most notable and defining characteristics prior to the mid-1990s, when the Japanese economy was robust and much larger relative to the other Asian economies. This strategy was characterized by bilateralism, informal rules, and embedded mercantilism (chapter 1). Since then, Japan has adopted a much more regional and formalistic approach in its regional geoeconomic strategy with a strong emphasis on rule setting and institution building, all of which shows liberal tendencies and largely follows global standards.

Such transformations came from various sources clustered in two dimensions: The first is the geoeconomics of the Asia-Pacific, which shapes the broad contours of Japan's regional geoeconomic strategy. The second is the domestic dimension, which reflects the transformation of Japanese domestic politico-economic institutions with an arm's-length relationship between the government and big businesses, as Japanese firms have become larger and expanded their operations around the world. The government itself has experienced institutional changes through economic, political, and administrative reforms. Hence Japan's strategies have developed in the context of a rapidly expanding regional economy and changing power balance in East Asia and the Asia-Pacific. Although such dynamics have widened the range of Japan's options for potential strategies, they also constrained its policy effectiveness.

Japan's Regional Geoeconomic Strategy

Geoeconomics and Domestic Institutions

The regional dimension that has motivated Japan's new regional geoeconomic strategy rests heavily on the geostrategic and geoeconomic dynamics of the Asia-Pacific region. As discussed in chapter 3, the rise of China with its dramatic economic growth has compelled a shift in the regional economic balance. At the same time, other Asian economies have undergone rapid transformation through their own economic growth and globalization. Although Japan continues to be a significant trading partner and investor for many of these Asian economies, including China, the balance between increasing Asia's importance to Japan (especially relative to the United States) and decreasing Japan's importance to Asia (especially relative to China) has made Japan's new regional geoeconomic strategy its high priority. Throughout this period, economic integration and the expansion of supply chains throughout Asia have continued to connect the regional economy, and Japan has relied more and more on the other Asian economies as sources to fuel its own economic growth. Hence the government is motivated to protect the region from financial or currency crises and continually strives to construct the region's market into one that is more accommodating to Japan's economic presence, especially through investment. In this context, the U.S.-promoted Trans-Pacific Partnership became an attractive opportunity for the Japanese government to prod the developing Asian members to further reform, with the hope that someday China will also sign on to this liberal economic coalition.

In particular, the domestic dimension reflects Japan's maturing economy and changing political underpinning. As discussed in chapter 4, the distance between the Japanese government and big businesses has widened significantly since the mid-1990s. From the business side, there has been a fairly consistent outflow of production capacity from Japan to Asia (including China) in the past twenty years, following several *yen-daka* episodes. The exit was also based on business calculations that range from high production costs and shrinking markets to cumbersome regulations in Japan and expanding markets and business opportunities in Asia. Survey analysis by Michio Muramatsu and Ikuo Kume has also revealed a weakening of government control over businesses and an increasing distance between the bureaucracy and businesses.[1] Furthermore, continuing economic stagnation and a host of corruption scandals involving bureaucrats and politicians throughout the 1990s blocked the information flow between the government and big business and triggered various reforms. Most prominently, the administrative reforms of the late 1990s challenged many of the consultative (or collusive) arrangements and institutions of the government, from the advisory council (*shingi-kai*) system, *amakudari* and off-business gatherings or gifting, to public financing channels. The electoral reform of 1994 as well as changes in the majority party in both the Upper House and the Lower House during this period contributed to the weakening of special interests in politics. Now the old convoy system between businesses and the government, which constituted the foundation of embedded autonomy and embedded mercantilism, is being undone, leading it to become "disembedded" from the government's economic strategy as the government loses control over the country's large businesses.

In short, the region's geoeconomic environment shaped the Japanese government's regional geoeconomic strategy into one that now pursues regionalism, formal rules, and a global standard. Nonetheless, as detailed in chapters 5 through 7, the implementation of concrete policies by the Japanese government in each economic issue area has exhibited a certain level of idiosyncrasies.

Diverse Paths of Implementation

The three issue areas investigated in this study took different paths to realize the Japanese government's goals through the state-led liberal strategy. In regional trade and investment strategy (chapter 5), formal agreements in the form of economic partnership agreements took off in the early 2000s and finally led to Japan's participation in TPP negotiations in 2013, which enhanced the government's bargaining power in the China-Japan-Korea Free Trade Agreement and the Regional Comprehensive Economic Partnership. Overall, this has been a gradual path where implementation of the liberal strategy started slowly but later became more assertive with the TPP. Any remaining hints of bilateralism that lingered in the early parts of Japan's regional trade strategy gradually gave way to trade regionalism, yet the multilayered structure of regional institution-building persists. As for the extent to which Japan is adopting global standards, the early bilateral EPAs still housed some embedded mercantilist elements of agricultural protection, exemptions, and carve-outs, while the TPP embodied very little of such ideology. It is noteworthy, nonetheless, that the Japanese government did not give up on promoting a high standard of liberal trade and investment order in the Asia-Pacific even after the U.S. government withdrew from the TPP in 2017 under newly inaugurated president Donald Trump. Since the eleven-member Comprehensive and Progressive Agreement for the Trans-Pacific Partnership officially came into effect on December 30, 2018, the Japanese government has been hailed as the new champion of the liberal economic order in the Trump era.

In the area of monetary and financial affairs (chapter 6), the most prominent feature of the transition in Japan's strategy in East Asia is its move toward regionalism, a conscious effort to create an explicit grouping among ASEAN+3 members for emergency funding, macroeconomic governance, and financial monitoring. In this case, the Asian financial crisis was the critical juncture influencing the institutional evolution of the region, and this path has continued.[2] With the external shock, this strategic move was swift, but since the initial efforts of the late 1990s into the early 2000s, the coherent outlook of this regional financial strategy has become uneven. On the rules front, the Japanese government has managed to promote formal rules and standards that will allow market discipline to guide Asia's financial and monetary affairs. To avoid another regional financial crisis, Japanese efforts came with prudent financial surveillance and supervision via regional institutions such as the ASEAN+3 Macroeconomic Research Office, along with concrete agreements of currency-swap activation for the Chiang Mai Initiative Multilateralization emergency funding. The Asian Bond Market progressed under the powers of market forces, but the currency arrangements, which rely heavily on business involvement, did not make much progress.

Finally, the Japanese government's regional strategy in the area of development and foreign aid (chapter 7) has undergone limited changes in terms of its modality of bilateralism. With the important exception of the government's intense commitment to the Asian Development Bank, other foreign aid efforts have largely taken place on a government-to-government basis with some involvement of local governments and civil societies on both the donor and recipient sides. In terms of norms, nonetheless, a much more value-based policy dialogue has taken place between Japan and its aid recipients. Particularly interesting are the cases of Vietnam and some less advanced Southeast Asian economies, where the Japanese government is actively engaged in technical assistance for the development of these countries' legal systems (chapter 7). The implementation of the liberal strategy in this issue area is still mixed. Nevertheless, the intimate connection between Japanese businesses and foreign aid, which was the hallmark of Japan's mercantilist behavior in Asia, has weakened. In the context of Japan's new development strategy, the government, facing tight funding conditions, has sought to engage Japanese big businesses in this process. But as demonstrated by the reluctance of businesses to engage in government-led public-private partnership initiatives or even to support the government's participation in the Asian Infrastructure Investment Bank, these arrangements target high-quality standards.

Factors Leading to Distinct Paths

In chapter 1, table 1.1 organizes the difference in levels of transformation in the Japanese government's regional economic strategy in the three issue areas. Here we question why some institutional changes are gradual and slow and others uneven. Phillip Lipscy's insight in applying industrial organization theory is that interstate bargaining among members shapes the trajectory of institutional change.[3] The present study points to the claim that while there is a macro- and geoeconomic foundation for the general contour of member states' strategy, the concrete policy changes are guided by institutional path-dependence, occasionally interrupted by shocks and crises. Although more research is required to provide a conclusive analysis of the variation in each area, this study uncovers several insights.

First, it is essential to consider the goal of geoeconomic strategy in terms of what to balance or against what the strategy is devised. In this study, in particular, the question is who Japan is trying to counter. In the changing geoeconomic environment of the Asia-Pacific, the challenges and pressures that the Japanese government had to operate under varied depending on the relevant time frames and issue areas. For example, in the aftermath of the Asian financial crisis, U.S. pressure and neoliberal economic policies imposed by the IMF motivated the Japanese government to lead financial regionalism. Concomitantly, cohesion in the East Asian region is much more potent when the Japanese and Asian strategy have an extra-regional "other" against which to band together, such as the IMF's neoliberal policy imposition or the American double standard. Meanwhile, a large part of Japan's adaptation of liberal and global rules, included in the TPP, legal system development, and value-oriented diplomacy, is an attempt to capitalize on such global values to pit Japan's regional leadership against China's rapid rise and its statist strategy. Of course, in such cases, regional grouping can quickly become complicated, with two major powers in the region competing for leadership against each other while simultaneously trying to make favorable groupings, sometimes with overlapping states.

Second, on the policy implementation front, institutional path-dependence and embedded institutional interests have slowed down the implementation of this new strategy. For example, in a scenario where there already existed a relatively established channel to conduct regional economic strategy in Asia, such as in the case of foreign aid with a set ministry (or implementation agency) in charge of policy making and the task, the shift that could remove the responsibilities of these ministries has been difficult. Even in the case of free trade agreements, the dominance of the Ministry of Foreign Affairs' preferred bilateral modality prevailed, at least in the early rounds of negotiations. Meanwhile, with limited institutional precedent, Japan's regional financial initiatives proceeded quite smoothly in a region-wide framework, as seen in the emergence of the Ministry of Finance's role in proposing Asia's financial cooperation. As demonstrated in the case of Japan's energetic engagement with the TPP since 2013 (chapter 5), the implementation of a liberal regional trade strategy was facilitated by the modification of administrative modality as well as the control of domestic opposition.

Finally, the state-business relationship is crucial in understanding the formation of concrete foreign economic policies. For this study, the vital component to uncover the effectiveness of Japan's state-led liberal strategy in different issue areas or even across areas comes from the way in which the government can engage with the country's big businesses. As discussed in chapter 4, Japanese big businesses have expanded their operations globally over the past several decades. In particular, Japan's production network has expanded across Asia since the 1990s. Furthermore, the disembedding of these businesses from the government's interventionist control has fragmented the traditional trinity approach of Japan's engagement with developing Asian countries. Hence, even as Japanese businesses operate actively in the region, bottom-up pressure from such businesses on the government has been spotty, sporadic, or firm-specific. Such variation in business involvement in the government's regional geoeconomic strategy leads to uneven outcomes, even within the same issue area.

For example, in the area of finance, the Chiang Mai Initiative was much easier to achieve since it did not necessitate the involvement of Japanese business. Meanwhile, the government's efforts to internationalize the yen in the region or to create a regional monetary unit did not bear fruit, as neither Japanese financial industries nor the market responded to such efforts (chapter 6). In the area of free trade agreements, the strong push to conclude the FTA with Mexico, an extraregional and very small trading partner of Japan, came from the coherent and strong business involvement in the negotiation process, while other similar FTAs being negotiated with East Asia suffered from either diffuse or conflicting Japanese business interests and thus lacked bottom-up involvement. A shortage in active business participation introduces challenges to Japan's infrastructure development ventures, as the government seeks private financial commitment to these projects. In the past, the business "glue" facilitated a strong coherence in the Japanese embedded mercantilist strategy under the trinity approach. More recently, however, it is evident that the government's current strategy lacks such glue or uniform support from the business sector. The fragmented state structure in conducting regional geoeconomic strategy without consistent business involvement reinforces eclectic approaches and hence limits the effectiveness of policies associated with Japan's evolving regional geoeconomic strategy.

The State's Role in Markets

What, then, is the role of a state in managing the market? What kind of instruments are available for the state, and which ones are effective in shaping the market? These have been vital questions in comparative and international political economy. Karl Polanyi's original thesis of "double movement," where market society emerged under social dislocation and protection, emphasizes the essential role of state in shaping market.[4] More recently, Steven K. Vogel argues that not only the regulated markets but liberal markets are also crafted by states.[5] On a policy ground, the famous "East Asian miracle" debates over the role of the state and public policy in economic development lingered from the publication by the World Bank of the book on the subject in 1993.[6] Despite some skepticism over exactly what constituted the core of the "developmental state," the fact that states have played a major role in the economic catchup process of East Asia is strongly supported. The case of Japan in this study constitutes an interesting extension: Does the state's interventionist role and its ideology live beyond its usefulness?

Japan by the late 1990s was undoubtedly the first, and arguably the only, large economy advanced enough to shed its developmentalist shell, at least in the context of Asia (chapter 2).[7] The public mobilization of resources for investment and the government's heavy intervention in the market were phased out. The convoy system was slowly dismantled as Japan's competitive industries distanced themselves from the government, while the weak and uncompetitive sectors (including agriculture) continue to expect the government's protection, which also was gradually scaled back (chapter 4). The globalization of the Japanese economy is taking place through large amounts of foreign investment flowing into Japan from many regions, particularly Asia, and the presence of foreign ownership and the increasing weight of outside voices over time (chapters 3 and 4).

Through such a process, the interventionist role of the state implemented by Japan's economic bureaucracy slowly declined. With various political powers trying to chip away at the authority and control of the bureaucracy over the economy, elected politicians, especially the prime minister and the Cabinet Office, have increased their influence. The state also lost much of its control over big businesses as they grew and globalized and the state began to experience a squeeze on financial and institutional resources needed to exercise this authority (chapter 4). The weakening of state control is attributed, on the one hand, to the success of developmentalism in the form of the expansion and globalization of Japan's big businesses. On the other hand, it comes from the economy's failures, including continued domestic economic stagnation, overstretched fiscal commitment, and the loss of public trust as well as a perceived lack of usefulness in the eyes of successful businesses.

Under these conditions, the government's new state-led regional geo-economic strategy represents a possible avenue for the state to reinvent its usefulness in the regional setting. A stable monetary and financial environment with a solid legal framework as well as developed human capital and infrastructure in East Asia is desirable for business activities, and adapting a liberal and global standard provides friendly business environments. While this is a seemingly natural progression for Japan as it graduates from developmentalism and interventionism to postdevelopmentalism, the transformation embodies two ironies that have imposed difficulties that Japan's recent efforts have encountered.

First, there is an inherent clash between Japan's customary developmentalist belief and identity, including interventionist ideology, and its liberal economic strategy. Japan was and continues to be the most successful example of the "East Asian miracle," and many of the country's leaders still believe in the effectiveness of state guidance. This is evidenced by efforts on the part of the government to disseminate such an approach via technical assistance and foreign aid to other parts of the world. Conversely, however, many of the developmentalist measures, ranging from heavy intervention and financial repression to government subsidies, commonly employed by Asian governments, particularly China, are problematic obstacles for investors and foreign business partners. Being one of the largest traders, investors, and creditors in the region, Japan sees its economic interests exposed in the region. Liberal rulemaking as well as open and global standards are the Japanese economy's choice for regional engagement, although the same marketcraft ideology does not necessarily apply domestically.[8]

The second irony comes in the form of Japan's government-business relations. The government has ventured into uncharted territory by signing on to the TPP and insisting on the high standards to construct a favorable business environment in the region. Such incentives promised by the government to secure the private sector's support hardly entice businesses to work toward national goals. As discussed previously, the government's last-ditch effort to internationalize the yen in the late 1990s to the early 2000s failed largely because Japanese businesses were not interested in forgoing the existing benefits of the foreign-exchange business and making the initial investment of switching and moving away from the dollar. Efforts to capture large infrastructure projects with significant private financing through the public-private partnership scheme have hardly paid off for Japan, either. Furthermore, Japan's efforts to construct its own rules based on its developmental experience and to create an advantage for the country in general have only recently begun.[9] Hence the government's regional geoeconomic strategy has yet to significantly affect regional economic governance.

Japan's Regional Geoeconomic Strategy in the Late 2010s: Policy Reversal or the Leader of the Free (Market) World?

The second Abe administration seems painfully aware of the weakness in the government's regional geoeconomic strategy, which seems to arise from geoeconomic competition with China, as Japan's policy implementation has lagged owing to disembedding and fragmentation. At the same time, Japan's strategic advantage in the regional geoeconomic context seems to have expanded in the late 2010s.

In the late 2010s the geoeconomics of the Asia-Pacific have taken a more precarious turn under the Trump administration's "America First" policy and the increasingly forceful regional expansion under Chinese president Xi's policies. The contrast of the Japanese government's proactive strategies vis-à-vis the TPP (chapter 5) and its ambivalence to the Belt-and-Road and AIIB Initiatives (chapter 7) reveals where Japan stands. There is no doubt that the recent economic conflict and the trade war between China and the United States have provided a strategic opportunity for Japan to influence this power balance and shape the dynamics of the regional economic order at a time when Japan needs it most. This timing was also opportune, as the Japanese political leadership since the end of 2012 has been quite stable under the Liberal Democratic Party majority and Prime Minister Abe, who has had no obvious competing candidates around to unseat him. Nonetheless, Japan's contemporary political economy inherently houses stark dilemmas. Japan's key predicaments are as follows.

First, as the regional mechanism develops, the membership challenge, which has long plagued Asia's (East Asia/Asia-Pacific) regionalism, becomes starker. Starting out quite ambivalently and eclectically as the Japanese regional geoeconomic strategy began to take shape after the Asian financial crisis in the early 2000s (chapters 5, 6, and 7), the Japanese government was increasingly pushed by China's enhanced influence in the region to cling to U.S. inclusion in the integration of the Asia-Pacific. Furthermore, Japan has welcomed the inclusion of Australia, New Zealand, and India into the "region" so as to create a coalition of democracies with which to counter China. ASEAN has been at the core of most regional integration efforts in recent years. But the TPP draws a line through this Southeast Asian entity, whose economic community building is progressing, between TPP members (Singapore, Brunei, Malaysia, and Vietnam) and nonmembers (Cambodia, Indonesia, Laos, Myanmar, Philippines, and Thailand).

Second, Japan's relationship with China is probably the most unambiguous dilemma for Japan. This relationship involves significant rivalry, tensions, and a complex history, on the one hand, but is also built on strong economic interdependence, with China emulating at least part of Japan's developmentalist economic model, on the other.[10] Hence some of the Chinese regional development initiatives are very similar to what Japan conducted in the past, and these strategies would still feel comfortable unless they impose challenges to Japan. Some Japanese political leaders and businesses welcome the type of interventionist initiatives taken up by Chinese leadership even today, as they embody remnants of Japan's developmentalist institutions and ideals. It is ironic that the embedded mercantilist elements in China's current strategy are propelling the Japanese government to switch from its own old model in favor of a more neoliberal approach to regional economic integration supporting the United States.

There are also signs of the Japanese government's ambivalence between its current liberal strategy and its old-style strategy in responding to China's regional expansion. As of the mid-2010s Prime Minister Abe began to emphasize the "all Japan" modality in infrastructure exports, aiming to revisit the power the government possessed in the good old days, and to try to compete with China by invoking the old regional geoeconomic strategy.[11] It is premature to conclude how such competition with China will lead to Japan's return to its old-style strategy in the future. These two countries' political regimes, one democratic and the other autocratic, also heavily influence how much the respective government can control the country's business behavior. Suffice it to say, however, that in some issue areas, such as development, the Japanese government is tempted to use its state interventionist power more than in other areas. The apparent disengagement of the United States from the role as the guardian of liberal international order particularly under President Trump adds a complication to the ambivalence of the Japanese government's strategy.

Third, Japan's government-business relationship also affects Japan's recent actions. These days, it is clear that the government needs the help of big businesses, not the other way around (like the old days), despite the supportive posture of the Keidanren regarding the government's active engagement in Asia's economic development. As public resources would not be adequate in guiding its regional development strategy and supporting Japanese business needs, the government must devise all sorts of schemes to lower risks, entice businesses to engage in development projects, and somehow convince middle-income recipient governments of the superiority of Japan's reliable technology (despite its high costs). Meanwhile, rule-setting competition, which was evident in the TPP, is arguably a more efficient way for the Japanese regional geoeconomic strategy to create broad (though diffuse) impacts on the region's economic order.

Finally, the underpinning of the open and liberal regional economic order is facing a massive challenge as President Trump withdrew from the TPP, engaged in a blatant trade war with China, and forced (re)negotiations of several bilateral trade deals with U.S. allies to extract more gains for the United States. Now the Japanese government confronts yet another changing geoeconomic landscape in the region. On the one hand, it acquired the title of champion of the liberal economic order, as it took a very visible and uncharacteristic lead to conclude the CPTPP among the remaining TPP-11 members in 2018.[12] On the other hand, the Japanese government (as well as Chinese leadership) has quickly moved to hedge against the U.S. actions by mending Sino-Japanese relations through a series of high-level talks and expanded economic engagement. These two movements could well be compatible where the Japanese government's strategy to spread liberal rules will reach China through Japan's active engagement. Or instead, these could be a sign of the Japanese government having to juggle two conflicting pressures yet again. One set of pressures is to carry the torch of the liberal economic order in the region by itself without the help of the United States in facing China's challenge. The other set of challenges is to resist being drawn back to its old ways of mercantilist business heavily influenced by Chinese practices either through collaboration or via competition.

The Future of Regionalism and Regional Governance in Asia

This study also contemplates the future of regionalism and regional governance. In the twenty-first century a sizable scholarly community has developed with an interest in analyzing the evolution of regionalism in East Asia.[13] Some see regionalism as part of power dynamics capitalizing on state interactions in pursuit of national goals.[14] Others are more interested in the design and the substance of regionalism, from emerging regional identities and institutional setups to the roles of business networks and the epistemic community.[15] There are efforts to analyze the dynamics in specific issue areas,[16] and efforts to apply theories of regionalism from other regions of the world (particularly Western Europe) to East Asia.[17] In most cases, these studies illuminate each aspect of regionalism they cover specifically, while cross-issue tensions and connections as well as the domestic-regional political nexus often get left out of the analysis.[18] In contrast, this study centers on an agent behind regionalism dynamics. By focusing on an influential member of the region, Japan, it covers several economic issue areas and examines the domestic-regional nexus through an analysis of Japan's regional economic strategy.

How does Japan's new regional geoeconomic strategy, then, influence the course of regional economic governance and regionalism? Granted that Japan is only one of many pieces that serve to construct economic integration and regionalism in East Asia or the Asia-Pacific, it is nonetheless an important piece. This study has led to three preliminary observations. First, in recent years Japan has been and will continue to be an important agent of policy diffusion that channels the pressure of convergence on Asia to embrace the liberal world order and rule-based open economic system. The days when the Japanese government wanted and could manage a Japan-centered block in East Asia are long gone, and now, with the large Chinese presence in the region, Japan has to enhance its influence by becoming the pivotal state of policy diffusion. Japan's adaptation of the "platinum standard" of the TPP and other liberal norms guiding its foreign aid policy, among others, are part of the government's regional geoeconomic strategy to enhance the country's interests throughout the region, particularly with the aim of countering China's influence.

Second, although domestic interests and domestic policy-making forces among the major powers continue to influence the regional economic order (inside out), these forces are also influenced by geoeconomic dynamics (outside in). As the agents leading the geoeconomic strategy, governments will work to shape institutions and incentive structures to achieve their goals via establishing a broad contour of the country's regional geoeconomic strategy. The important question here is whether governments have enough instruments at their disposal to motivate businesses to follow their lead. On this point, China's centralized (and authoritarian) regime, which provides a government with strong control over businesses, has the upper hand over Japan, which has disembedded government-business relations.

Finally, the ironic clash between Japan's developmental identity and its instrumental adaptation of a rule-based liberal approach to regional geo-economic strategy will be the future of many advanced Asian economies, arguably including China. Broadly speaking, the government of a creditor and a major investor around the region and the world uses its geoeconomic policy to protect the country's overseas economic interests. As such, it is remarkable, as discussed by William W. Grimes, that the governments of Japan and China, two large creditor nations, can be on the same page in providing financial stability with macroeconomic discipline in the region through the Chiang Mai Initiative Multilateralization and the monitoring process conducted by the ASEAN+3 Macroeconomic Research Office.[19] One hopes, as regional development continues, that these strategies on the part of advanced Asian states will not translate into another round of these economies "kicking away the ladder" for the late-comers.[20]

Japan's regional geoeconomic strategy is facing a new regional reality under a dramatically shifting geoeconomic environment, on the one hand, and through slowly changing the domestic politics of institutions that influence foreign policy, on the other. The dynamics could present the Japanese government with its greatest opportunity to shape the regional economic order in the Asia-Pacific for decades to come. This could also be the most difficult challenge for the government as it reinvents its role in the face of globalizing businesses and changing society.

Notes

Introduction

1. The definition of geoeconomics is not standardized. A recent study by Robert D. Blackwill and Jennifer M. Harris defines it as "the systemic use of economic instruments to accomplish geopolitical objectives." See Blackwill and Harris, *War by Other Means: Geoeconomics and Statecraft* (Cambridge, Mass.: Harvard University Press, 2016), 1. For a good overview of recent scholarly work on geoeconomics, see Mikael Mattlin and Mikael Wigell, "Geoeconomics in the Context of Restive Regional Powers," *Asia Europe Journal* 14, no. 2 (2015): 125–34.

2. T. J. Pempel, "How Bush Bungled Asia: Militarism, Economic Indifference and Unilateralism Have Weakened the United States Across Asia," *Pacific Review* 21, no. 5 (2008): 547–81.

3. David Shambaugh, *China Goes Global: The Partial Power* (New York: Oxford University Press, 2013).

4. On China's influence in Latin America, see, for example, Kevin Gallagher and Roberto Porzecanski, *The Dragon in the Room: China and the Future of Latin American Industrialization* (Stanford, Calif.: Stanford University Press, 2010). On its push in Africa, see Deborah Bräutigam, *The Dragon's Gift: The Real Story of China in Africa* (New York: Oxford University Press, 2009).

1. Japan's Regional Geoeconomic Strategy

1. Robert O. Keohane and Joseph S. Nye, *Power and Interdependence: World Politics in Transition* (Boston: Little, Brown, 1977).

2. Albert Hirschman, *National Power and the Structure of International Trade* (Berkeley: University of California Press, 1945); David A. Baldwin, *Economic Statecraft* (Princeton, N.J.: Princeton University Press, 1985); Daniel W. Drezner, *The Sanctions Paradox: Economic Statecraft and International Relations* (New York: Cambridge University Press, 1999); Jonathan Kirshner, *Currency and Coercion: The Political Economy of International Monetary Power* (Princeton, N.J.: Princeton University Press, 1997); Leslie Elliott Armijo and Saori N. Katada, "Theorizing the Financial Statecraft of Emerging Powers," *New Political Economy* 20, no. 1 (2015): 42–62.

3. For an analysis of regional security order with the role of great power struggles and security as public goods, see Evelyn Goh, *The Struggle for Order: Hegemony, Hierarchy, and Transition in Post–Cold War East Asia* (Oxford: Oxford University Press, 2013).

4. As I will discuss, the results of the regional institution building also depend on other players in the region. But the point here is that large countries can have more influence in initiating these efforts.

5. On capturing relative gains, see Joseph M. Grieco, "Systemic Sources of Variation in Regional Institutionalization in Western Europe, East Asia, and the Americas," in *The Political Economy of Regionalism*, ed. Edward D. Mansfield and Helen V. Milner (New York: Columbia University Press, 1997). On rule-setting competition, see Junji Nakagawa, "Competitive Regionalism Through Bilateral and Regional Rule-Making: Standard Setting and Locking-In," in *Competitive Regionalism: FTA Diffusion in the Pacific Rim*, ed. Mireya Solís, Barbara Stallings, and Saori N. Katada, International Political Economy Series (Basingstoke, UK: Palgrave Macmillan, 2009); and Melissa K. Griffith, Richard H. Steinberg, and John Zysman, "From Great Power Politics to a Strategic Vacuum: Origins and Consequences of the TPP and TTIP," *Business and Politics* 19, no. 4 (2017): 573–92.

6. G. John Ikenberry, *After Victory: Institutions, Strategic Restraint, and the Rebuilding of Order After Major Wars*, Princeton Studies in International History and Politics (Princeton, N.J.: Princeton University Press, 2001); Robert D. Blackwill and Jennifer M. Harris, *War by Other Means: Geoeconomics and Statecraft* (Cambridge, Mass.: Harvard University Press, 2016); Mikael Mattlin and Mikael Wigell, "Geoeconomics in the Context of Restive Regional Powers," *Asia Europe Journal* 14, no. 2 (2015): 125–34. An interesting contrast can be seen in the Cold War tension between the U.S.-led bloc and the Soviet-led bloc, which had a very small economic component in the context of the blocs' limited economic relationship, compared with the post–Cold War competition and rivalries that have taken place under vast economic interdependence among the major powers.

7. John Ravenhill, "The 'New East Asian Regionalism': A Political Domino Effect," *Review of International Political Economy* 17, no. 2 (2010): 178–208; William Wallace, "Political Cooperation: Integration Through Intergovernmentalism," in *Policy-Making in the European Community*, ed. Helen S. Wallace, William Wallace, and Carole Webb (New York: Wiley, 1983).

8. Andrew Moravcsik, "Taking Preferences Seriously: A Liberal Theory of International Politics," *International Organization* 51, no. 4 (1997): 513–53.

9. Kanishka Jayasuriya, "Embedded Mercantilism and Open Regionalism: The Crisis of a Regional Political Project," *Third World Quarterly* 24, no. 2 (2003): 339–55; John Gerard Ruggie, "International Regimes, Transactions, and Change: Embedded Liberalism in the Postwar Economic Order," *International Organization* 36, no. 2 (1982): 379–415; T. J. Pempel, *Regime Shift: Comparative Dynamics of the Japanese Political Economy* (Ithaca, N.Y.: Cornell University Press, 1998).

10. Saori N. Katada and Mireya Solís, "Domestic Sources of Japanese Foreign Policy Activism: Loss Avoidance and Demand Coherence," *International Relations of the Asia-Pacific* 10, no. 1 (2010): 129–57.

11. Ezra F. Vogel, *Japan as Number One: Lessons for America* (Cambridge, Mass.: Harvard University Press, 1979); Douglas McGray, "Japan's Gross National Cool," *Foreign Policy* 130, no. 1 (2002): 44–54.

12. Thomas U. Berger, "From Sword to Chrysanthemum: Japan's Culture of Anti-militarism," *International Security* 17, no. 4 (1993): 119–50; Courtney Purrington, "Tokyo's Policy Responses During the Gulf War and the Impact of the 'Iraqi Shock' on Japan," *Pacific Affairs* 65, no. 2 (1992): 161–81.

13. Kenneth B. Pyle, *The Japanese Question: Power and Purpose in a New Era* (Washington, D.C.: American Enterprise Institute, 1996).

14. Kent E. Calder, "Japanese Foreign Economic Policy Formation: Explaining the Reactive State," *World Politics* 40, no. 4 (1988): 517–41. A cottage scholarly industry emerged from the "reactive state" thesis after its publication. See, for example, Akitoshi Miyashita, "Gaiatsu and Japan's Foreign Aid: Rethinking the Reactive-Proactive Debate," *International Studies Quarterly* 43, no. 4 (1999): 695–731; Leonard J. Schoppa, "Two-Level Games and Bargaining Outcomes: Why Gaiatsu Succeeds in Japan in Some Cases but Not Others," *International Organization* 47, no. 3 (1993): 353–86; and Saori N. Katada, "Two Aid Hegemons: Japanese-US Interaction and Aid Allocation to Latin America and the Caribbean," *World Development* 25, no. 6 (1997): 931–45.

15. Henrik Schmiegelow and Michele Schmiegelow, "How Japan Affects the International System," *International Organization* 44, no. 4 (1990): 553–88.

16. Eric Heginbotham and Richard J. Samuels, "Mercantile Realism and Japanese Foreign Policy," *International Security* 22, no. 4 (1998): 171–203; Pempel, *Regime Shift.*

17. David Arase, "Japan, the Active State? Security Policy After 9/11," *Asian Survey* 47, no. 4 (2007): 560–83; Thomas U. Berger, "The Pragmatic Liberalism of an Adaptive State," in *Japan in International Politics: The Foreign Policies of an Adaptive State*, ed. Thomas U. Berger, Mike Mochizuki, and Jitsuo Tsuchiyama (Boulder, Colo.: Lynne Rienner, 2007).

18. For a comprehensive, concise, and excellent summary of Japan's debates over its "grand strategies," see Richard J. Samuels, *Securing Japan: Tokyo's Grand Strategy and the Future of East Asia* (Ithaca, N.Y.: Cornell University Press, 2007), esp. chap. 1 and fig. 1.

19. Ichiro Ozawa, *Nihon kaizo keikaku* (A plan to transform Japan) (Tokyo: Kodansha, 1993); Hanns W. Maull, "Germany and Japan: The New Civilian Powers," *Foreign Affairs* 69 (1989): 91–106; Yoichi Funabashi, *Nihon no taigai kōsō: Reisen go no bijon wo kaku* (Japan's foreign strategy: Drafting the post–Cold War vision) (Tokyo: Iwanami Shoten, 1993).

20. Yoshihide Soeya, *Japan's "Middle Power" Diplomacy: Post-War Japan's Choice and Strategy* (Tokyo: Chikuma Shobo, 2005).

21. For example, Maull, "Germany and Japan"; Thomas U. Berger, *Cultures of Antimilitarism: National Security in Germany and Japan* (Baltimore: Johns Hopkins University Press, 1998); Wolfgang Streeck and Kozo Yamamura, eds., *The Origins of Nonliberal Capitalism: Germany and Japan in Comparison* (Ithaca, N.Y.: Cornell University Press, 2005); Jennifer Lind, *Sorry States: Apologies in International Politics* (Ithaca, N.Y.: Cornell University Press, 2008).

22. Peter J. Katzenstein, *A World of Regions: Asia and Europe in the American Imperium* (Ithaca, N.Y.: Cornell University Press, 2005).

23. Christopher Hemmer and Peter J. Katzenstein, "Why Is There No NATO in Asia? Collective Identity, Regionalism, and the Origins of Multilateralism," *International Organization* 56, no. 3 (2002): 575–607; Katzenstein, *A World of Regions.*

24. William S. Borden, *The Pacific Alliance: United States Foreign Economic Policy and Japanese Trade Recovery, 1947–1955* (Madison: University of Wisconsin Press, 1984).

25. Robert S. Chase, Emily B. Hill, and Paul Kennedy, "Pivotal States and U.S. Strategy," *Foreign Affairs* 75 (1996): 33–51. Examples of pivotal states are traditionally Turkey, Brazil, and Egypt. Tim Sweijs and colleagues also identify about thirty pivot states around the world and categorize them into four types. See Tim Sweijs et al., "Why Are Pivot States So Pivotal? The Role of Pivot States in Regional and Global Security," in *Strategic Monitor 2014: Four Strategic Challenges* (Netherlands: Hague Centre for Strategic Studies, 2014).

26. Mireya Solís and Saori N. Katada, "Unlikely Pivotal States in Competitive Free Trade Agreement Diffusion: The Effect of Japan's Trans-Pacific Partnership Participation on Asia-Pacific Regional Integration," *New Political Economy* 20, no. 2 (2015): 155–77.

27. Ian Bremmer, *Every Nation for Itself: Winners and Losers in a G-Zero World* (New York: Penguin, 2012); Sweijs et al., "Why Are Pivot States So Pivotal?"

28. These is a massive literature on this topic, starting with Peter J. Katzenstein, *Between Power and Plenty: Foreign Economic Policies of Advanced Industrial States* (Madison: University of Wisconsin Press, 1978); and Keohane and Nye, *Power and Interdependence.*

29. Mikko Kuisma, "Social Democratic Internationalism and the Welfare State After the 'Golden Age,'" *Cooperation and Conflict* 42, no. 1 (2007): 9–26.

30. Alexander Gerschenkron, *Economic Backwardness in Historical Perspective: A Book of Essays* (Cambridge, Mass.: Harvard University Press, 1962).

31. Mitchell Bernard and John Ravenhill, "Beyond Product Cycles and Flying Geese: Regionalization, Hierarchy, and the Industrialization of East Asia," *World Politics* 47, no. 2 (1995): 171–209.

32. Alice H. Amsden, "Diffusion of Development: The Late-Industrializing Model and Greater East Asia," *American Economic Review* 81, no. 2 (1991): 282–86.

33. Shōjirō Tokunaga, *Japan's Foreign Investment and Asian Economic Interdependence: Production, Trade, and Financial Systems* (Tokyo: University of Tokyo Press, 1992); Walter Hatch and Kozo Yamamura, *Asia in Japan's Embrace: Building a Regional Production Alliance* (Cambridge: Cambridge University Press, 1996).

34. Hatch and Yamamura, *Asia in Japan's Embrace*; Edward J. Lincoln, *Japan's New Global Role* (Piscataway, N.J.: Transaction, 1993); Takashi Shiraishi, "Japan and Southeast Asia," in *Network Power: Japan and Asia*, ed. Peter J. Katzenstein and Takashi Shiraishi (Ithaca, N.Y.: Cornell University Press, 1997).

35. Peter Cowhey, "Pacific Trade Relations After the Cold War: GATT, NAFTA, ASEAN and APEC," in *United States–Japan Relations and International Institutions After the Cold War*, ed. Peter A. Gourevitch, Takashi Inoguchi, and Courtney Purrington (La Jolla: Graduate School of International Relations and Pacific Studies, University of California, San Diego, 1995), 193–94.

36. Nobuo Okawara and Peter J. Katzenstein, "Japan and Asian-Pacific Security: Regionalization, Entrenched Bilateralism and Incipient Multilateralism," *Pacific Review* 14, no. 2 (2001): 165–94.

37. T. J. Pempel, "Challenges to Bilateralism: Changing Foes, Capital Flows, and Complex Forums," in *Beyond Bilateralism: US–Japan Relations in the New Asia Pacific*, ed. Ellis S. Krauss and T. J. Pempel (Stanford, Calif.: Stanford University Press, 2004), 5.

38. Shintaro Hamanaka, *Asian Regionalism and Japan: The Politics of Membership in Regional Diplomatic, Financial and Trade Groups* (London: Routledge, 2009), 38–46; Mie Oba, *Ajia taiheiyō chiiki keisei he no doutei: Kyōkai kokka Nichigō no aidentiti mosaku to chiiki-shugi* (Road to the creation of the Asia-Pacific region: Japan's and Australia's search for their identity as a boundary nation and the regionalism) (Kyoto: Minerva Shobo, 2004), 98–102.

39. Hemmer and Katzenstein, "Why Is There No NATO in Asia?"; Donald K. Crone, "Does Hegemony Matter? The Reorganization of the Pacific Political Economy," *World Politics* 45, no. 4 (1993): 501–25.

40. Kevin G. Cai, *The Political Economy of East Asia: Regional and National Dimensions*, International Political Economy Series (Hampshire, UK: Palgrave Macmillan, 2008), chap. 4.

41. Irving M. Destler, Haruhiro Fukui, and Hideo Satō, *The Textile Wrangle: Conflict in Japanese-American Relations, 1969–1971* (Ithaca, N.Y.: Cornell University Press, 1979); C. Fred Bergsten and Marcus Noland, *Reconcilable Differences? United States-Japan Economic Conflict* (Washington, D.C.: Institute for International Economics, 1993); Leonard J. Schoppa, *Bargaining with Japan: What American Pressure Can and Cannot Do* (New York: Columbia University Press, 1997).

42. Jeffrey A. Frankel, *The Yen-Dollar Agreement: Liberalizing Japanese Capital Markets* (Cambridge, Mass.: MIT Press, 1984); Frances McCall Rosenbluth, *Financial Politics in Contemporary Japan* (Ithaca, N.Y.: Cornell University Press, 1989).

43. Terutomo Ozawa, "Foreign Direct Investment and Economic Development," *Transnational Corporations* 1, no. 1 (1992): 27–54. Unilateralism is an additional regional economic strategy tool for building bilateral relations, where some moves such as trade liberalization and economic reforms based on "open regionalism" were carried out by Asian governments on a voluntary basis. See John Ravenhill, *APEC and the Construction of Pacific Rim Regionalism* (Cambridge: Cambridge University Press, 2001).

44. Miles Kahler, "Legalization as Strategy: The Asia-Pacific Case," *International Organization* 54, no. 3 (2000): 549–71; David P. Rapkin, "The United States, Japan, and the

Power to Block: The APEC and AMF Cases," *Pacific Review* 14, no. 3 (2001): 373–410.

45. Karen J. Alter, *The New Terrain of International Law: Courts, Politics, Rights* (Princeton, N.J.: Princeton University Press, 2014); Kahler, "Legalization as Strategy," 560.

46. Amitav Acharya, *Whose Ideas Matter? Agency and Power in Asian Regionalism* (Ithaca, N.Y.: Cornell University Press, 2009).

47. The Japanese government's aversion to legal measures is often attributed to cultural sources. For a discussion on law and society in Japan, see Frank K. Upham, *Law and Social Change in Postwar Japan* (Cambridge, Mass.: Harvard University Press, 2009).

48. The Association of Southeast Asian Nations (ASEAN), established in 1967, is the oldest post–World War II regional institution in East Asia. Japan has actively engaged in and supported ASEAN, particularly since the announcement of the Fukuda Doctrine in 1977. See Sueo Sudo, *The Fukuda Doctrine and ASEAN: New Dimensions in Japanese Foreign Policy* (Singapore: Institute of Southeast Asian Studies, 1992).

49. Andrew Hurrell, *Regionalism in World Politics: Regional Organization and International Order* (New York: Oxford University Press, 1995); Edward D. Mansfield and Helen V. Milner, "The New Wave of Regionalism," *International Organization* 53, no. 3 (1999): 589–627. This phenomenon kicked off active research on the reasons that East Asia did not develop formal regional institutions. Grieco presents a realist thesis that places the source of reluctance toward institutionalization on the rapidly shifting capabilities among the major powers in the Asia-Pacific; Peter J. Katzenstein and Takashi Shiraishi emphasize the network of relations that had made the formalization of relations less important; and Gilbert Rozman focuses on the tension among the major economies in the region that had "stunted" East Asian regionalism. See Grieco, "Systemic Sources of Variation"; Katzenstein and Shiraishi, *Network Power: Japan and Asia* (Ithaca, N.Y.: Cornell University Press, 1997) and *Beyond Japan: The Dynamics of East Asian Regionalism* (Ithaca, N.Y.: Cornell University Press, 2006); and Rozman, *Northeast Asia's Stunted Regionalism: Bilateral Distrust in the Shadow of Globalization* (Cambridge: Cambridge University Press, 2004).

50. Kuniko Ashizawa, "Japan's Approach Toward Asian Regional Security: From 'Hub-and-Spoke' Bilateralism to 'Multi-tiered,'" *Pacific Review* 16, no. 3 (2003): 361–82; Paul Bowles, "Asia's Post-Crisis Regionalism: Bringing the State Back In, Keeping the (United) States Out," *Review of International Political Economy* 9, no. 2 (2002): 244–70; Douglas Webber, "Two Funerals and a Wedding? The Ups and Downs of Regionalism in East Asia and Asia-Pacific After the Asian Crisis," *Pacific Review* 14, no. 3 (2001): 339–72; Michael Wesley, "The Asian Crisis and the Adequacy of Regional Institutions," *Contemporary Southeast Asia* 21, no. 1 (1999): 54–73.

51. T. J. Pempel, "Regime Shift: Japanese Politics in a Changing World Economy," *Journal of Japanese Studies* 23, no. 2 (1997): 333–61; Pempel, *Regime Shift*; Ruggie, "International Regimes."

52. Jayasuriya, "Embedded Mercantilism."

53. Mireya Solís, *Banking on Multinationals: Public Credit and the Export of Japanese Sunset Industries* (Stanford, Calif.: Stanford University Press, 2004); Lincoln, *Japan's New Global Role*, 145.

54. Gerschenkron, *Economic Backwardness*; Ha-Joon Chang, *Kicking Away the Ladder: Development Strategy in Historical Perspective* (London: Anthem Press, 2002).

55. Hatch and Yamamura, *Asia in Japan's Embrace.*

56. Mitsuya Araki, "Japan's Official Development Assistance: The Japan ODA Model That Began Life in Southeast Asia," *Asia-Pacific Review* 14, no. 2 (2007): 17–29.

57. David Arase, *Buying Power: The Political Economy of Japan's Foreign Aid* (Boulder, Colo.: Lynne Rienner, 1995). We can also find this type of close government-business collaboration beyond Asia in the 1970s, such as in the "national projects" in Brazil. See Fumiko Kurihara, *Nihon no taibei taika chokusetsu toshi no shin tenkai* (New developments in Japan's foreign direct investments in the United States and Latin America), vol. 31 (Tokyo: Ochanomizu Chiri, 1990).

58. Steven K. Vogel, *Marketcraft: How Governments Make Markets Work* (New York: Oxford University Press, 2018).

59. Peter J. Katzenstein, "East Asia—Beyond Japan," in *Beyond Japan: The Dynamics of East Asian Regionalism*, ed. Peter J. Katzenstein and Takashi Shiraishi (Ithaca, N.Y.: Cornell University Press, 2006).

60. Katzenstein and Shiraishi, *Network Power*; Paul Evans, "Between Regionalism and Regionalization: Policy Networks and the Nascent East Asian Institutional Identity," in *Remapping East Asia: The Construction of a Region*, ed. T. J. Pempel (Ithaca, N.Y.: Cornell University Press, 2005). In comparison to other regions, Asia overall still has relatively underdeveloped regionalism in relation to its quite developed economic integration through regionalization. See Anja Jetschke and Saori N. Katada, "Asia," in *The Oxford Handbook of Comparative Regionalism*, ed. Tanja Borzel and Thomas Risse (Oxford: Oxford University Press, 2016).

61. Keiichi Tsunekawa, "Why So Many Maps There? Japan and Regional Cooperation," in *Remapping East Asia: The Construction of a Region*, ed. T. J. Pempel (Ithaca, N.Y.: Cornell University Press, 2004); Saadia Pekkanen, ed. *Asian Designs: Governance in the Contemporary World Order* (Ithaca, N.Y.: Cornell University Press, 2016).

62. Ernst B. Haas and Philippe C. Schmitter, "Economics and Differential Patterns of Political Integration: Projections About Unity in Latin America," *International Organization* 18, no. 4 (1964): 705–37; Naoko Munakata, "Has Politics Caught Up with Markets? In Search of East Asian Economic Regionalism," in *Beyond Japan: The Dynamics of East Asian Regionalism*, ed. Peter J. Katzenstein and Takashi Shiraishi (Ithaca, N.Y.: Cornell University Press, 2006).

63. Ravenhill, "The 'New East Asian Regionalism.'"

64. Richard Higgott, "The Asian Economic Crisis: A Study in the Politics of Resentment," *New Political Economy* 3, no. 3 (1998): 333–56; Takashi Terada, "Constructing an 'East Asian' Concept and Growing Regional Identity: From EAEC to ASEAN+3," *Pacific Review* 16, no. 2 (2003): 251–77.

65. T. J. Pempel, *Remapping East Asia: The Construction of a Region* (Ithaca, N.Y.: Cornell University Press, 2005), 4.

66. Hamanaka, *Asian Regionalism and Japan.*

67. Robert O. Keohane, *After Hegemony: Cooperation and Discord in the World Political Economy* (Princeton, N.J.: Princeton University Press, 1984); B. Peter Rosendorff and

Helen V. Milner, "The Optimal Design of International Trade Institutions: Uncertainty and Escape," *International Organization* 55, no. 4 (2001): 829–57.

68. Kenneth W. Abbott and Duncan Snidal, "Hard Law and Soft Law in International Governance," *International Organization* 54, no. 3 (2000): 420–33.

69. Grieco, "Systemic Sources of Variation."

70. David A. Lake, "Delegating Divisible Sovereignty: Sweeping a Conceptual Minefield," *Review of International Organizations* 2, no. 3 (2007): 219–37; Stephan Haggard, "The Liberal View of the International Relations of Asia," in *The Oxford Handbook of the International Relations of Asia*, ed. Saadia M. Pekkanen, John Ravenhill, and Rosemary Foot (New York: Oxford University Press, 2014).

71. As discussed by Randall W. Stone, all institutions maintain some degree of informal rules. Hence Japan's "formal turn" does not mean that all the informal means of influence have been totally left behind. See Stone, *Controlling Institutions: International Organizations and the Global Economy* (Cambridge: Cambridge University Press, 2011).

72. Yong Wook Lee, "Japan and the Asian Monetary Fund: An Identity–Intention Approach," *International Studies Quarterly* 50, no. 2 (2006): 339–66. Although John Ikenberry argues that liberal institutionalism is not the same as neoliberalism or market-fundamentalism, these approaches to economy constitute a subgroup within the rule-based liberal economic order promoted largely by the United States through these institutions, particularly since the 1980s. See G. John Ikenberry, "The Future of the Liberal World Order," *Foreign Affairs* 90, no. 3 (2011): 56–68.

73. The Singapore issues includes transparency in government procurement, custom issues (trade facilitation), investment and trade, as well as competition issues. These issues pursued by Japan, South Korea, and Europe were shelved at the WTO ministerial conference in Cancun in 2003, except for trade facilitation. See WTO, https://www.wto.org/english/thewto_e/whatis_e/tif_e/bey3_e.htm.

74. The 1840s through the 1850s were the height of British "gunboat diplomacy," wherein military force was deployed to protect overseas nationals and their investments. These measures became less acceptable over time and gave way to investment laws and arbitration. O. Thomas Johnson and Jonathan Gimblett, "From Gunboats to BITs: The Evolution of Modern International Investment Law," in *Yearbook on International Investment Law & Policy 2010–2011*, ed. Karl P. Sauvant (New York: Oxford University Press, 2010).

75. In relation to Japan's reluctance to sanction China for the Tiananmen Incident of 1989 on the basis of human rights abuses, see, for example, Saori N. Katada, "Why Did Japan Suspend Foreign Aid to China? Japan's Foreign Aid Decision-making and Sources of Aid Sanction," *Social Science Japan Journal* 4, no. 1 (2001): 39–58. On Japan's values-oriented diplomacy, see Yul Sohn, "Japan's New Regionalism: China Shock, Values, and the East Asian Community," *Asian Survey* 50, no. 3 (2010): 497–519.

76. Robert Wade, "The Asian Debt-and-Development Crisis of 1997–?: Causes and Consequences," *World Development* 26, no. 8 (1998): 1535–53; William W. Grimes, *Currency and Contest in East Asia: The Great Power Politics of Financial Regionalism*, Cornell Studies in Money (Ithaca, N.Y.: Cornell University Press, 2009).

77. Joshua Cooper Ramo, *The Beijing Consensus: Notes on the New Physics of Chinese Power* (London: Foreign Policy Centre, 2004); Ian Bremmer, "State Capitalism Comes of Age," *Foreign Affairs* 88, no. 3 (2009): 40–55.

78. Katzenstein and Shiraishi, *Network Power*; Hatch and Yamamura, *Asia in Japan's Embrace.*

79. Grieco, "Systemic Sources of Variation."

80. Schoppa, *Bargaining with Japan.*

81. Bela Balassa, *The Theory of Economic Integration* (Homewood, Ill.: Routledge, 1961).

82. Phillip Y. Lipscy, *Renegotiating the World Order: Institutional Change in International Relations* (New York: Cambridge University Press, 2017).

83. Blackwill and Harris, *War by Other Means*, 8.

84. Walter Hatch, *Asia's Flying Geese: How Regionalization Shapes Japan* (Ithaca, N.Y.: Cornell University Press, 2010).

2. Foreign Economic Policy, Domestic Institutions, and Regional Governance

1. Peter J. Katzenstein, *Between Power and Plenty: Foreign Economic Policies of Advanced Industrial States* (Madison: University of Wisconsin Press, 1978).

2. G. John Ikenberry, David A. Lake, and Michael Mastanduno, "Introduction: Approaches to Explaining American Foreign Economic Policy," *International Organization* 42, no. 1 (1988): 1–14. In the concluding article of this issue, Ikenberry succinctly summarizes the three approaches of foreign economic policy making. "System-centered approaches trace policy to demands or opportunities generated within the international political economy. Prevailing distributions of power, the norms and principles embedded in international regimes, or the imperatives of international economic structures have all been invoked as systemic explanations of American foreign economic policy. Society-centered approaches trace policy to the demands placed on government by private groups, sectors, or classes within the national political system. State-centered approaches trace policy to either the active role of government officials pursuing autonomous goals or to the shaping and constraining role of the state's organizational structure." See G. John Ikenberry, "Conclusion: An Institutional Approach to American Foreign Economic Policy," *International Organization* 42, no. 1 (1988): 219–43.

3. Robert D. Putnam, "Diplomacy and Domestic Politics: The Logic of Two-level Games," *International Organization* 42, no. 3 (1988): 427–60.

4. For the most concise and authoritative discussion of OEP, see David A. Lake, "Open Economy Politics: A Critical Review," *Review of International Organizations* 4, no. 3 (2009): 219–44. For a well-cited critique of the OEP approach, see Thomas Oatley, "The Reductionist Gamble: Open Economy Politics in the Global Economy," *International Organization* 65, no. 2 (2011): 311–41.

5. Nicola Phillips, "Bridging the Comparative/International Divide in the Study of States," *New Political Economy* 10, no. 3 (2005): 335–43.

6. In the Ikenberry, Lake, and Mastanduno volume mentioned in note 2, Lake examines the U.S. tariff-making process of 1887 to 1894 to highlight the importance of political leadership in making strategic choices in a country's foreign policy.

7. Stephen Chaudoin, Helen V. Milner, and Xun Pang, "International Systems and Domestic Politics: Linking Complex Interactions with Empirical Models in International Relations," *International Organization* 69, no. 2 (2015): 275–309.

8. Peter Gourevitch, "The Second Image Reversed: The International Sources of Domestic Politics," *International Organization* 32, no. 4 (1978): 881–912.

9. Oatley, "The Reductionist Gamble."

10. Kent E. Calder, "Japanese Foreign Economic Policy Formation: Explaining the Reactive State," *World Politics* 40, no. 4 (1988): 517–41.

11. T. J. Pempel, "Structural Gaiatsu: International Finance and Political Change in Japan," *Comparative Political Studies* 32, no. 8 (1999): 907–32; Leonard J. Schoppa, *Bargaining with Japan: What American Pressure Can and Cannot Do* (New York: Columbia University Press, 1997).

12. Lake explains that OEP "begins with individuals, sectors, or factors of production as the units of analysis and derives their interests over economic policy from each unit's position within the international economy. It conceives of domestic political institutions as mechanisms that aggregate interests (with more or less bias) and structure the bargaining of competing societal groups. Finally, it introduces, when necessary, bargaining between states with different interests." See Lake, "Open Economy Politics," 225.

13. Frances McCall Rosenbluth and Michael F. Thies, *Japan Transformed: Political Change and Economic Restructuring* (Princeton, N.J.: Princeton University Press, 2010).

14. Megumi Naoi, *Building Legislative Coalitions for Free Trade in Asia: Globalization as Legislation* (New York: Cambridge University Press, 2015); Amy Catalinac, *Electoral Reform and National Security in Japan: From Pork to Foreign Policy* (New York: Cambridge University Press, 2016).

15. The crises instigated by shifting political coalitions often trigger opportunities for change from within where "old relationships crumble and new ones have to be constructed." See Peter Gourevitch, *Politics in Hard Times: Comparative Responses to International Economic Crises* (Ithaca, N.Y.: Cornell University Press, 1986), 9.

16. Yong Wook Lee, "Japan and the Asian Monetary Fund: An Identity–Intention Approach," *International Studies Quarterly* 50, no. 2 (2006): 339–66.

17. Chaudoin, Milner, and Pang, "International Systems and Domestic Politics," 304.

18. Steven K. Vogel, *Freer Markets, More Rules: Regulatory Reform in Advanced Industrial Countries* (Ithaca, N.Y.: Cornell University Press, 1996).

19. Richard E. Baldwin, "The Causes of Regionalism," *World Economy* 20, no. 7 (1997): 865–88; John Ravenhill, "The 'New East Asian Regionalism': A Political Domino Effect," *Review of International Political Economy* 17, no. 2 (2010): 178–208.

20. William W. Grimes, "Internationalization of the Yen and the New Politics of Monetary Insulation," in *Monetary Orders: Ambiguous Economics, Ubiquitous Politics*, ed.

Jonathan Kirshner (Ithaca, N.Y.: Cornell University Press, 2003); Carlo Perroni and John Whalley, "The New Regionalism: Trade Liberalization or Insurance?," *Canadian Journal of Economics* 33, no. 1 (2000): 1–24.

21. Zachary Elkins, Andrew T. Guzman, and Beth A. Simmons, "Competing for Capital: The Diffusion of Bilateral Investment Treaties, 1960–2000," *International Organization* 60, no. 4 (2006): 811–46.

22. Mireya Solís and Saori N. Katada, "Explaining FTA Proliferation: A Policy Diffusion Framework," in *Competitive Regionalism: FTA Diffusion in the Pacific Rim*, ed. Mireya Solís, Barbara Stallings, and Saori N. Katada (Basingstoke, UK: Palgrave Macmillan, 2009).

23. Ha-Joon Chang, *Kicking Away the Ladder: Development Strategy in Historical Perspective* (London: Anthem Press, 2002).

24. Stephan Haggard, *Developmental States*, Cambridge Elements: Politics of Development (New York: Cambridge University Press, 2018); Robert Wade, "The Developmental State: Dead or Alive?," *Development and Change* 49, no. 2 (2018): 518–46.

25. For the overview of the developmental state discussion, see Meredith Woo-Cumings, *The Developmental State* (Ithaca, N.Y.: Cornell University Press, 1999). After the publication of Chalmers Johnson's *MITI and the Japanese Miracle: The Growth of Industrial Policy: 1925–1975* (Stanford, Calif.: Stanford University Press, 1982), a major debate erupted regarding the source of Japan's economic "miracle." Some followed Johnson's thesis and expanded "developmental state" discussion that later led to works of the gang-of-four Japan revisionists—Johnson, Karel Van Wolferen, James Fallows, and Clyde Prestowitz—while others, such as David Bennett Friedman and Scott Callon, criticized the almighty importance of the Ministry of International Trade and Industry (MITI) behind Japan's dynamic economic growth. See Karel Van Wolferen, *The Enigma of Japanese Power: People and Politics in a Stateless Nation* (New York: Vintage, 1989); James Fallows, *Looking at the Sun: The Rise of the New East Asian Economic and Political System* (New York: Vintage, 1994); Clyde Prestowitz, *Trading Places: How We Are Giving Our Future to Japan & How to Reclaim It* (New York: Basic Books, 1990); David Bennett Friedman, *The Misunderstood Miracle: Industrial Development and Political Change in Japan* (Ithaca, N.Y.: Cornell University Press, 1988); Scott Callon, *Divided Sun: MITI and the Breakdown of Japanese High-tech Industrial Policy, 1975–1993* (Stanford, Calif.: Stanford University Press, 1997).

26. See Chang, *Kicking Away the Ladder*; Alexander Gerschenkron, *Economic Backwardness in Historical Perspective: A Book of Essays* (Cambridge, Mass.: Harvard University Press 1962). These economies at the early stage of industrial catch-up are, in theory, scarce in capital and technology, while they are abundant in (usually unskilled) labor that can be mobilized to produce simple goods (such as toys or shoes) cheaply.

27. On Japan, see Johnson, *MITI and the Japanese Miracle*. On South Korea, see Alice H. Amsden, *Asia's Next Giant: South Korea and Late Industrialization* (New York: Oxford University Press, 1992). On Taiwan, see Robert Wade, *Governing the Market: Economic Theory and the Role of Government in East Asian Industrialization* (Princeton, N.J.: Princeton University Press, 1990).

28. Peter B. Evans, *Embedded Autonomy: States and Industrial Transformation* (Princeton, N.J.: Princeton University Press, 1995).

29. Chapter 3 addresses the question of how China could continue following the developmental state model especially in the aftermath of the global financial crisis of 2008. Suffice it to note here that by the late 1990s the Chinese model had not yet become a major part of the scholarly debate.

30. For a critique of the "obsolescence of the developmental state" thesis in the post–Cold War period and under globalization, see Shigeko Hayashi, "The Developmental State in the Era of Globalization: Beyond the Northeast Asian Model of Political Economy," *Pacific Review* 23, no. 1 (2010): 45–69.

31. A vibrant debate and much research exists regarding this question, including Susan Strange, *The Retreat of the State: The Diffusion of Power in the World Economy* (New York: Cambridge University Press, 1996); Philip G. Cerny, *The Changing Architecture of Politics: Structure, Agency and the Future of the State* (London: Sage, 1990); Eric Helleiner, *States and the Reemergence of Global Finance: from Bretton Woods to the 1990s* (Ithaca, N.Y.: Cornell University Press, 1996); David M. Andrews, "Capital Mobility and State Autonomy: Toward a Structural Theory of International Monetary Relations," *International Studies Quarterly* 38, no. 2 (1994): 193–218; Layna Mosley, "Room to Move: International Financial Markets and National Welfare States," *International Organization* 54, no. 4 (2000): 737–73.

32. Richard Higgott, "The Asian Economic Crisis: A Study in the Politics of Resentment," *New Political Economy* 3, no. 3 (1998): 333–56; Rodney Bruce Hall, "The Discursive Demolition of the Asian Development Model," *International Studies Quarterly* 47, no. 1 (2003): 71–99.

33. Thomas Kalinowski, "Korea's Recovery Since the 1997/98 Financial Crisis: The Last Stage of the Developmental State," *New Political Economy* 13, no. 4 (2008): 447–62.

34. Andrew J. MacIntyre, T. J. Pempel, and John Ravenhill, *Crisis as Catalyst: Asia's Dynamic Political Economy* (Ithaca, N.Y.: Cornell University Press, 2008).

35. Mark Beeson, "Politics and Markets in East Asia: Is the Developmental State Compatible with Globalisation?," in *Political Economy and the Changing Global Order*, ed. Richard Stubbs and Geoffrey R.D. Underhill (Oxford: Oxford University Press, 2005).

36. Wade, "The Developmental State," 534.

37. Iain Pirie, "Korea and Taiwan: The Crisis of Investment-Led Growth and the End of the Developmental State," *Journal of Contemporary Asia* 48, no. 1 (2018): 133–58.

38. Of course, a smooth transition from a middle-income country to a high-income one is rare. In reality, government officials in emerging economies and economic developmental practitioners have worried about "middle-income traps," in which a country that has achieved middle-income levels of economic development gets trapped in that status, unable to advance to the level of an advanced economy. See Indermit Gill and Homi Kharas, *An East Asian Renaissance: Ideas for Economic Growth* (Washington, D.C.: World Bank, 2007); "The Middle-Income Trap Turns Ten," *Policy Research Working Paper* 7403 (2015), https://elibrary.worldbank.org/doi/abs/10.1596/1813-9450 -7403.

39. Nancy Birdsall and Francis Fukuyama, "The Post-Washington Consensus: Development After the Crisis," *Foreign Affairs* 90, no. 2 (2011): 45–53; Haggard, *Developmental States.*

40. Mark Beeson, "What Does China's Rise Mean for the Developmental State Paradigm?," in *Asia After the Developmental State: Disembedding Autonomy*, ed. Toby Carroll and Darryl S. L. Jarvis (Cambridge: Cambridge University Press, 2017), 177.

41. Robert Devlin and Graciela Moguillansky, *Breeding Latin American Tigers: Operational Principles for Rehabilitating Industrial Policies* (Washington, D.C.: United Nations Economic Commission for Latin America and the Caribbean and the World Bank, 2011); Laura Routley, "Developmental States in Africa? A Review of Ongoing Debates and Buzzwords," *Development Policy Review* 32, no. 2 (2014): 159–77.

42. Wade, "The Developmental State," 535; Elizabeth Thurbon, *Developmental Mindset: The Revival of Financial Activism in South Korea* (Ithaca, N.Y.: Cornell University Press, 2016).

43. Richard Stubbs, "What Ever Happened to the East Asian Developmental State? The Unfolding Debate," *Pacific Review* 22, no. 1 (2009): 1–22.

44. Thurbon, *Developmental Mindset.*

45. Robyn Klingler-Vidra and Ramon Pacheco Pardo, "Legitimate Social Purpose and South Korea's Support for Entrepreneurial Finance Since the Asian Financial Crisis," *New Political Economy*, January 8, 2019: 1–17; Christopher M. Dent, "East Asia's New Developmentalism: State Capacity, Climate Change and Low-Carbon Development," *Third World Quarterly* 39, no. 6 (2018): 1191–210.

46. Roselyn Hsueh, *China's Regulatory State: A New Strategy for Globalization* (Ithaca, N.Y.: Cornell University Press, 2011).

47. Wade, "The Developmental State," 536.

48. David W. Soskice and Peter A. Hall, *Varieties of Capitalism: The Institutional Foundations of Comparative Advantage* (New York: Oxford University Press, 2001), quoted on 9.

49. John Zysman, *Governments, Markets, and Growth: Financial Systems and the Politics of Industrial Change* (Ithaca, N.Y.: Cornell University Press, 1984); Johnson, *MITI and the Japanese Miracle.*

50. Wolfgang Streeck, "Introduction: Explorations into the Origins of Nonliberal Capitalism in Germany and Japan," in *The Origins of Nonliberal Capitalism: Germany and Japan in Comparison*, ed. Wolfgang Streeck and Kozo Yamamura (Ithaca, N.Y.: Cornell University Press, 2005), 6. There is limited discussion on the dynamic changes of these economies and models over time. See Richard Deeg and Gregory Jackson, "Towards a More Dynamic Theory of Capitalist Variety," *Socio-Economic Review* 5, no. 1 (2007): 149–79.

51. Steven K. Vogel, *Marketcraft: How Governments Make Markets Work* (New York: Oxford University Press, 2018). Vogel quotes Polanyi's famous phrase that "laissez-faire was planned" (4).

52. Walter Hatch and Kozo Yamamura, *Asia in Japan's Embrace: Building a Regional Production Alliance* (Cambridge: Cambridge University Press, 1996); Kenichi Ohno, *Tojōkoku Nippon no Ayumi: Edo kara Heisei madeno Keizai Hatten* (The path traveled by

Japan as a developing country: Economic growth from Edo to Heisei) (Tokyo: Yūhikaku, 2005).

53. Yasuyuki Sawada and Yasuyuki Todo, "Tojōkoku no hinkon sakugen ni okeru seifu kaihatsu enjo no yakuwari" (The role of official development assistance in reducing poverty among developing countries), *RIETI Policy Discussion Paper Series* 10-P-021 (2010), http://www.dl.ndl.go.jp/view/download/digidepo_8703930_po_10p021.pdf ?contentNo=1&alternativeNo=.

54. Kazuhito Ikeo, *Kaihatsu shugi no bosō to hoshin: Kinyū sisutemu to heisei keizai* (Runaway state and self-preservation of developmentalism) (Tokyo: NTT, 2006).

55. Wade, "The Developmental State."

56. On the doubts, see Susan Carpenter, *Why Japan Can't Reform* (London: Palgrave Macmillan, 2008). On the changes in strategy and governance, see Ulrike Schaede, *Choose and Focus: Japanese Business Strategies for the 21st Century* (Ithaca, N.Y.: Cornell University Press, 2008); and Steven K. Vogel, *Japan Remodeled: How Government and Industry Are Reforming Japanese Capitalism* (Ithaca, N.Y.: Cornell University Press, 2006).

57. Leonard J. Schoppa, *Race for the Exits: The Unraveling of Japan's System of Social Protection* (Ithaca, N.Y.: Cornell University Press, 2008).

58. Linda Weiss argues, however, that a strong private sector does not immediately lead to a weaker state. See Weiss, "Governed Interdependence: Rethinking the Government-Business Relationship in East Asia," *Pacific Review* 8, no. 4 (1995): 589–616.

59. Taiwan and South Korea followed the trend in the late 1990s, and China arguably did so since its "going global" strategy of 1999, or at least in the 2010s.

60. Dennis Tachiki, "Between Foreign Direct Investment and Regionalism: The Role of Japanese Production Networks," in *Remapping East Asia: The Construction of a Region*, ed. T. J. Pempel (Ithaca, N.Y.: Cornell University Press, 2005), 149.

61. Henry Wai-chung Yeung defines "strategic coupling" as a firm-specific strategy in the evolution of state-firm relations, in which firms decouple from their domestic structures and recouple with lead firms in global production networks. See Yeung, "Governing the Market in a Globalizing Era: Eevelopmental States, Global Production Networks and Inter-firm Dynamics in East Asia," *Review of International Political Economy* 21, no. 1 (2014): 70–101; and *Strategic Coupling: East Asian Industrial Transformation in the New Global Economy* (Ithaca, N.Y.: Cornell University Press, 2016).

62. Yeung, "Governing the Market in a Globalizing Era," 81.

63. Joseph Wong, *Betting on Biotech: Innovation and the Limits of Asia's Developmental State* (Ithaca, N.Y.: Cornell University Press, 2011).

64. Toby Carroll and Darryl S. L. Jarvis, *Asia After the Developmental State: Disembedding Autonomy* (Cambridge: Cambridge University Press, 2017).

65. Richard Katz, *Japan: The System That Soured: The Rise and Fall of the Japanese Economic Miracle* (Armonk, N.Y.: M. E. Sharpe, 1998); Jennifer A. Amyx, *Japan's Financial Crisis: Institutional Rigidity and Reluctant Change* (Princeton, N.J.: Princeton University Press, 2004); Edward J. Lincoln, *Arthritic Japan: The Slow Pace of Economic Reform* (Washington, D.C.: Brookings Institution Press, 2004); Mark Beeson, "Japan's Reluctant Reformers and the Legacy of the Developmental State," in *Governance and Public*

Sector Reform in Asia: Paradigm Shifts or Business as Usual?, ed. Anthony B. L. Cheung and Ian Scott (New York, N.Y.: RoutledgeCurzon, 2003); William W. Grimes, *Unmaking the Japanese Miracle: Macroeconomic Politics, 1985–2000* (Ithaca, N.Y.: Cornell University Press, 2002).

66. Kent E. Calder, *Circles of Compensation: Economic Growth and the Globalization of Japan* (Stanford, Calif.: Stanford University Press, 2017); Walter Hatch, *Asia's Flying Geese: How Regionalization Shapes Japan* (Ithaca, N.Y.: Cornell University Press, 2010).

67. Vogel, *Marketcraft*.

68. Steven R. Reed, "Is Japanese Government Really Centralized?," *Journal of Japanese Studies* 8, no. 1 (1982): 133–64; Hidetaka Yoshimatsu, "Japan's Quest for Free Trade Agreements: Constraints from Bureaucratic and Interest Group Politics," in *Japan's Future in East Asia and the Pacific* ed. Mari Pangestu and Ligang Song (Canberra: ANU Press, 2007).

69. Aurelia George Mulgan, "Japan's 'Un-Westminster' System: Impediments to Reform in a Crisis Economy," *Government and Opposition* 38, no. 1 (2003): 73–91.

70. Ironically, this is reminiscent of the claim that the U.S. government was using against Japan over its bilateral trade imbalance in the 1980s and the first half of the 1990s.

3. Geoeconomics of the Asia-Pacific

1. William S. Borden, *The Pacific Alliance: United States Foreign Economic Policy and Japanese Trade Recovery, 1947–1955* (Madison: University of Wisconsin Press, 1984).

2. New trade tension is emerging between Japan and the United States under President Trump as he has complained about Japan's trade surplus with the United States. The two countries concluded a bilateral trade deal in late 2019.

3. Gerald L. Curtis, "U.S. Relations with Japan," in *The Golden Age of the U.S.-China-Japan Triangle, 1972–1989*, ed. Ezra F. Vogel, Ming Yuan, and Akihiko Tanaka (Cambridge, Mass.: Harvard University Press, 2002).

4. Saori N. Katada, "Why Did Japan Suspend Foreign Aid to China? Japan's Foreign Aid Decision-Making and Sources of Aid Sanction," *Social Science Japan Journal* 4, no. 1 (2001): 39–58; Quansheng Zhao, "Japan's Aid Diplomacy with China," in *Japan's Foreign Aid: Power and Policy in a New Era*, ed. Bruce Koppel and Robert Orr (Boulder, Colo.: Westview Press, 1993).

5. T. J. Pempel, "How Bush Bungled Asia: Militarism, Economic Indifference and Unilateralism Have Weakened the United States Across Asia," *Pacific Review* 21, no. 5 (2008): 547–81.

6. David Shambaugh, *China Goes Global: The Partial Power* (New York: Oxford University Press, 2013).

7. Richard E. Baldwin, "Multilateralising Regionalism: Spaghetti Bowls as Building Blocs on the Path to Global Free Trade," *World Economy* 29, no. 11 (2006): 1451–518.

8. Arvind Subramanian, *Eclipse: Living in the Shadow of China's Economic Dominance* (Washington, D.C.: Peterson Institute for International Economics, 2011).

9. The Chinese economy is the largest in the world since 2014 based on the purchasing power parity calculation done by the IMF. China's GDP growth rate, however, has slowed since 2015.

10. Saadia Pekkanen and Kellee Tsai, *Japan and China in the World Political Economy* (New York: Routledge, 2006); Elizabeth Thurbon and Linda Weiss, "The Developmental State in the Late Twentieth Century," in *Handbook of Alternative Theories of Economic Development*, ed. Erik S. Reinert, Jayati Ghosh, and Rainer Kattel (Cheltenham, UK: Edward Elgar, 2016).

11. Ian Bremmer, "State Capitalism Comes of Age," *Foreign Affairs* 88, no. 3 (2009): 40–55.

12. On the Washington Consensus, see John Williamson, "What Washington Means by Policy Reform," in *Latin American Adjustment: How Much Has Happened*, ed. John Williamson (Washington, D.C.: Institute for International Economics, 1990). On the Beijing Consensus, see Joshua Cooper Ramo, *The Beijing Consensus* (London: Foreign Policy Centre 2004); and Arif Dirlik, "Beijing Consensus: Beijing 'Gongshi.' Who Recognizes Whom and to What End?," *Globalization and Autonomy Online Compendium* (2006). For its critique, see Scott Kennedy, "The Myth of the Beijing Consensus," *Journal of Contemporary China* 19, no. 65 (2010): 461–77.

13. Eswar S. Prasad, *Gaining Currency: The Rise of the Renminbi* (New York: Oxford University Press, 2017).

14. G. John Ikenberry, "The Future of the Liberal World Order," *Foreign Affairs* 90, no. 3 (2011): 56–68.

15. There are many books written on the subject. For example, Martin Wolf, *Fixing Global Finance* (Baltimore: JHU Press, 2010); *The Shifts and the Shocks: What We've Learned— and Have Still to Learn—from the Financial Crisis* (London: Penguin, 2014); Raghuram Rajan, *Fault Lines* (New York: HarperCollins, 2012); Alan S. Blinder, *After the Music Stopped: The Financial Crisis, the Response, and the Work Ahead* (New York: Penguin, 2013); Andrew Sheng, *From Asian to Global Financial Crisis: An Asian Regulator's View of Unfettered Finance in the 1990s and 2000s* (New York: Cambridge University Press, 2009); Eric Helleiner, *The Status Quo Crisis: Global Financial Governance After the 2008 Meltdown* (New York: Oxford University Press, 2014); Nouriel Roubini and Stephen Mihm, *Crisis Economics: A Crash Course in the Future of Finance* (London: Penguin Group, 2010).

16. For an interesting comparison of various estimates of the costs associated with the crisis, see David Luttrell, Tyler Atkinson, and Harvey Rosenblum, "Assessing the Costs and Consequences of the 2007–09 Financial Crisis and Its Aftermath," *Economic Letter* 8, no. 7 (2013): 1–4.

17. Nancy Birdsall and Francis Fukuyama, "The Post-Washington Consensus: Development after the Crisis," *Foreign Affairs* 90, no. 2 (2011): 45–53; Robert Wade, "The First-World Debt Crisis of 2007–2010 in Global Perspective," *Challenge* 51, no. 4 (2008): 23–54.

18. As will be discussed in chapter 6, the G20 was actually put in place in 1999 in the aftermath of the Asian financial crisis as a meeting of finance ministers. But following

the global financial crisis, the G20 meeting was promoted to a head-of-state summit, the first of which was held in Washington, D.C., in November 2008.

19. Arturo C. Porzecanski, *Latin America: The Missing Financial Crisis*, vol. 6 (New York: United Nations, 2010); Carol Wise, Leslie Elliott Armijo, and Saori N. Katada, *Unexpected Outcomes: How Emerging Economies Survived the Global Financial Crisis* (Washington, D.C.: Brookings Institution Press, 2015).

20. Shaun Breslin, "Chinese Financial Statecraft and the Response to the Global Financial Crisis," in *Unexpected Outcomes: How Emerging Economies Survived the Global Financial Crisis*, ed. Carol Wise, Leslie E. Armijo, and Saori N. Katada (Washington, D.C.: Brookings Institution Press, 2015).

21. The connection between the stagnation of the WTO and the proliferation of the PTAs is discussed as an insurance policy. See Carlo Perroni and John Whalley, "The New Regionalism: Trade Liberalization or Insurance?," *Canadian Journal of Economics* 33, no. 1 (2000): 1–24.

22. The call for expansion of the IMF subscription began right after the onset of the global financial crisis. In April 2009 the G20 governments agreed to expand IMF funding resources from $250 billion to $750 billion in order to respond to the crisis. Meanwhile, the four original BRIC governments created a caucus-like group in the G20 from 2009. South Africa entered in 2010, and the "s" in the BRICs became capitalized to show its incorporation.

23. Cynthia A. Roberts, Leslie Elliott Armijo, and Saori N. Katada, *The BRICS and Collective Financial Statecraft* (New York: Oxford University Press, 2017).

24. Robert Wade, "The Asian Debt-and-Development Crisis of 1997–?: Causes and Consequences," *World Development* 26, no. 8 (1998): 1535–53; Richard Higgott, "The Asian Economic Crisis: A Study in the Politics of Resentment," *New Political Economy* 3, no. 3 (1998): 333–56. See also Joseph Stiglitz's criticism when he was the chief economist of the World Bank: "The Role of International Financial Institutions in the Current Global Economy," address to the Chicago Council on Foreign Relations, February 27, 1998, http://web.worldbank.org/WBSITE/EXTERNAL/NEWS/0,,contentMDK: 20024294~menuPK:34474~pagePK:34370~piPK:34424~theSitePK:4607,00.html.

25. For example, Jonathan D. Ostry et al., "Tools for Managing Financial-Stability Risks from Capital Inflows," *Journal of International Economics* 88, no. 2 (2012): 407–21. For a detailed analysis of the transformation in the policies and politics of capital control, see Kevin Gallagher, *Ruling Capital: Emerging Markets and the Reregulation of Cross-Border Finance*, Cornell Studies in Money (Ithaca, N.Y.: Cornell University Press, 2015).

26. Besides the quota reform, criticism was directed at the practice of selecting the managing director of the IMF from Europe and that of the World Bank from the United States. See Roberts, Armijo, and Katada, *The BRICS*.

27. A prominent proponent of the "Asian Century" is Kishore Mahbubani. See Mahbubani, *The New Asian Hemisphere: The Irresistible Shift of Global Power to the East* (New York: PublicAffairs, 2008). U.S. leaders seem to acknowledge the power shift, as then-secretary of state Hillary Clinton gave a famous speech in Hawaii in 2011 titled

"America's Pacific Century" (http://foreignpolicy.com/2011/10/11/americas-pacific
-century/).

28. The OECD Economic Outlook for Southeast Asia, China, and India 2016 reports
that Malaysia's best scenario predicts the country to be in the high-income group by
2021, China by 2026, and Indonesia by 2042.

29. Mitchell Bernard and John Ravenhill, "Beyond Product Cycles and Flying Geese:
Regionalization, Hierarchy, and the Industrialization of East Asia," *World Politics* 47,
no. 2 (1995): 171–209; Walter Hatch and Kozo Yamamura, *Asia in Japan's Embrace:
Building a Regional Production Alliance* (Cambridge: Cambridge University Press, 1996).

30. Richard Baldwin calls this phenomenon "Factory Asia." See Baldwin, "Multilateralising Regionalism."

31. Hatch and Yamamura, *Asia in Japan's Embrace*.

32. Prior to the Asian financial crisis, many Southeast Asian economies faced a lack of
domestic regulatory capacity, which was considered a major factor in inhibiting
regional economic cooperation. See Natasha Hamilton-Hart, "Asia's New Regionalism: Government Capacity and Cooperation in the Western Pacific," *Review of International Political Economy* 10, no. 2 (2003): 222–45.

33. Amitav Acharya, "Realism, Institutionalism, and the Asian Economic Crisis," *Con-
temporary Southeast Asia* 21, no. 1 (1999): 1–29; Takashi Shiraishi, "The Third Wave:
Southeast Asia and Middle-Class Formation in the Making of a Region," in *Beyond
Japan: The Dynamics of East Asian Regionalism*, ed. Peter J. Katzenstein and Takashi
Shiraishi (Ithaca, N.Y.: Cornell University Press, 2006).

34. T. J. Pempel, *The Politics of the Asian Economic Crisis*, Cornell Studies in Political Economy (Ithaca, N.Y.: Cornell University Press, 1999); Andrew J. MacIntyre, T. J. Pempel, and John Ravenhill, *Crisis as Catalyst: Asia's Dynamic Political Economy* (Ithaca,
N.Y.: Cornell University Press, 2008).

35. Yuchao Zhu, " 'Performance Legitimacy' and China's Political Adaptation Strategy,"
Journal of Chinese Political Science 16, no. 2 (2011): 123–40.

36. Natasha Hamilton-Hart, "Monetary Politics in Southeast Asia: External Imbalances
in Regional Context," *New Political Economy* 19, no. 6 (2014): 872–94; Andrew Walter, *Governing Finance: East Asia's Adoption of International Standards* (Ithaca, N.Y.: Cornell University Press, 2008).

37. Saori N. Katada and C. Randall Henning, "Currency and Exchange Rate Regime
in Asia," in *The Oxford Handbook of the International Relations of Asia*, ed. Saadia M.
Pekkanen, John Ravenhill, and Rosemary Foot (New York: Oxford University Press,
2014).

38. Hamilton-Hart, "Monetary Politics in Southeast Asia"; Joshua Aizenman and Jaewoo Lee, "Financial Versus Monetary Mercantilism: Long-Run View of Large International Reserves Hoarding," *World Economy* 31, no. 5 (2008): 593–611.

39. Saori N. Katada, "Mission Accomplished, or a Sisyphean Task? Japan's Regulatory
Response to the Global Financial Crisis," in *Global Finance in Crisis: The Politics of
International Regulatory Change*, ed. Eric Helleiner, Stefano Pagliari, and Hubert Zimmermann (New York: Routledge, 2009); Barbara Stallings, "Korea's Victory Over
the Global Financial Crisis of 2008–09," in *Unexpected Outcomes: How Emerging*

Economies Survived the Global Financial Crisis, ed. Carol Wise, Leslie E. Armijo, and Saori N. Katada, How Emerging Economies Survived the Global Financial Crisis (Washington, D.C.: Brookings Institution Press, 2015).

40. Wise, Armijo, and Katada, *Unexpected Outcomes*; Harinder S. Kohli and Ashok Sharma, *A Resilient Asia Amidst Global Financial Crisis: From Crisis Management to Global Leadership* (New Delhi: SAGE Publications and Asian Development Bank, 2010).

41. Wade, "The First-World Debt Crisis"; Helleiner, *The Status Quo Crisis*.

42. The only two FTAs in place as of 2008 in the Asia-Pacific region were the U.S. bilateral agreements with Singapore (in effect from 2004) and Australia (in effect from 2005). The FTA negotiations with Thailand and Malaysia had failed, and the Korea--U.S. FTA (KORUS), signed in spring 2007, was facing difficult ratification politics in Washington. After having lost the Trade Promotion Authority in summer 2007, U.S. executive branch found it increasingly difficult to pursue an active FTA policy.

43. The entire manuscript of Secretary Clinton's speech was published in "America's Pacific Century," *Foreign Policy*, no. 189 (2011): 56–63.

44. For an excellent analysis of the U.S. pivot strategy by one of its architects, see Kurt Campbell, *The Pivot: The Future of American Statecraft in Asia* (London: Hachette, 2016).

45. Bonnie S. Glaser, "Pivot to Asia: Prepare for Unintended Consequences," *Center for Strategic and International Studies: 2012 Global Forecast* (2012), https://www.csis.org/analysis/pivot-asia-prepare-unintended-consequences.

46. Ann Capling and John Ravenhill, "Multilateralising Regionalism: What Role for the Trans-Pacific Partnership Agreement?," *Pacific Review* 24, no. 5 (2011): 553–75.

47. Hence, throughout the TPP negotiations, the negotiators were taking China's future accession into consideration. That is why certain TPP chapters such as the one on state-owned enterprises became important. Solís calls China a "shadow negotiator" of the TPP. See Mireya Solís, "The Trans-Pacific Partnership: Can the United States Lead the Way in Asia-Pacific Integration?," *Pacific Focus* 27, no. 3 (2012): 319–41.

48. The two largest countries in the TPP negotiations, the United States and Japan, constituted about 78 percent of the total GDP of the twelve negotiating members as of 2014.

49. For example, in Sri Lanka, China's investment in Hambantota International Port and the Sri Lankan government's inability to repay its loans led a Chinese company to acquire the port's ninety-nine-year leasing rights in 2017.

50. Roberts, Armijo, and Katada, *The BRICS*.

4. Transformation in the Japanese Political Economy

1. Brian Woodall, *Japan Under Construction: Corruption, Politics, and Public Works* (Berkeley: University of California Press, 1996); James C. Abegglen, *The Strategy of Japanese Business* (Cambridge, Mass.: Ballinger, 1984); Michael L. Gerlach, *Alliance Capitalism: The Social Organization of Japanese Business* (Berkeley: University of California Press, 1992).

2. Edward J. Lincoln, *Japan's New Global Role* (Piscataway, N.J.: Transaction, 1993); Walter Hatch and Kozo Yamamura, *Asia in Japan's Embrace: Building a Regional Production Alliance* (Cambridge: Cambridge University Press, 1996); David Arase, *Buying Power: The Political Economy of Japan's Foreign Aid* (Boulder, Colo.: Lynne Rienner, 1995).

3. Chalmers A. Johnson, *Japan: Who Governs? The Rise of the Developmental State* (New York: Norton, 1995).

4. T. J. Pempel, *Regime Shift: Comparative Dynamics of the Japanese Political Economy* (Ithaca, N.Y.: Cornell University Press, 1998); Gerald L. Curtis, *The Logic of Japanese Politics: Leaders, Institutions, and the Limits of Change* (New York: Columbia University Press, 2000).

5. Michio Muramatsu and Ikuo Kume, *Nihon seiji hendō no 30 nen: Seijika/kanryō/dantaichōsa nimiru kōzō henyō* (Thirty years of political changes in Japan: Structural transformation of politicians, bureaucrats, and organizational surveys) (Tokyo: Tōyō Keizai Shinposha, 2006). Details of the surveys can be found in Michio Muramatsu, *Seikan sukuramu gata rīdāshippu no houkai* (Collapse of leadership created by a unified front of politicians and bureaucrats) (Tokyo: Tōyō Keizai Shinpōsha, 2010), 283–99. The surveys of politicians and bureaucrats were taken in 1976–1977, 1986–1987, and 2003. The surveys of industry organizations were taken in 1980, 1994, and 2003–2004.

6. On the frequency of contact, see Muramatsu, *Seikan sukuramu gata rīdāshippu no houkai*, 49–53, 257; Ikuo Kume, "Rieki dantai seiji no henyō" (Changes in the politics of interest groups)," in *Nihon seiji hendō no 30 nen: Seijika/kanryō/dantaichōsa nimiru kōzō henyō*, ed. Michio Muramatsu and Ikuo Kume (Tokyo: Tōyō Keizai Shinpōsha, 2006), 260–64. On the view on the contact, see Masaru Mabuchi, "Kanryosei no henyo; ishuku suru kanryo" (Changes of the bureaucratic system; cowering bureaucrats), in *Nihon seiji hendō no 30 nen: Seijika/kanryō/dantaichōsa nimiru kōzō henyō*, ed. Michio Muramatsu and Ikuo Kume (Tokyo: Tōyō Keizai Shinpōsha, 2006), 508. On trust and ethics, see Muramatsu, *Seikan sukuramu gata rīdāshippu no houkai*, 79, 258–59.

7. Sources of the data for this section are Mitsutoshi Ito, "Kokkai 'shūgō zai' moderu" (Collective goods model of parliament)," in *Nihon seiji hendō no 30 nen: Seijika/kanryō/dantaichōsa nimiru kōzō henyō*, ed. Michio Muramatsu and Ikuo Kume (Tokyo: Tōyō Keizai Shinpōsha, 2006), 40; Masahiko Tatebayashi, "Seitō naibu soshiki to seitō kan kōshō katei no henyō" (Transformation of inside organizations of political parties and the process of intraparty negotiation), in *Nihon seiji hendō no 30 nen: Seijika/kanryo/dantaichōsa nimiru kōzō henyō*, ed. Michio Muramatsu and Ikuo Kume (Tokyo: Tōyō Keizai Shinpōsha, 2006), 76–77; Muramatsu, *Seikan sukuramu gata rīdāshippu no houkai*, 83; 228–29; and Muramatsu and Kume, *Nihon seiji hendō no 30 nen*.

8. Muramatsu, *Seikan sukuramu gata rīdāshippu no houkai*, 235–39. The first two are a "zero sum" game of Japan's leadership, which has constituted a core of the scholarly debate on Japanese politics of the 1980s to 1990s. Muramatsu argues that there are possibilities of positive sum (which he calls the politician-bureaucratic scrummage leadership) and a game of negative sum where the state collectively loses over the private sector.

9. Muramatsu, *Seikan sukuramu gata rīdāshippu no houkai*.

10. The disasters include the continuing economic crisis in Europe; the Dubai crisis; the triple disaster of earthquake, tsunami, and nuclear plant meltdown; and heightened conflict with the United States and China. On the election, see Steven R. Reed et al., "The 2012 Election Results: The LDP Wins Big by Default," in *Japan Decides 2012: The Japanese General Election*, ed. Robert J. Pekkanen, Steven R. Reed, and Ethan Scheiner (New York: Springer, 2013).

11. The DPJ electoral campaign manifesto outlined five large thematic goals: ending wasteful spending, child-rearing and education, pension and medical care, regional sovereignty, and employment and the economy. Kenji Kushida and Phillip Lipscy cite the newspaper *Yomiuri* in stating that "only 30 of the DPJ's 170 original proposals had been implemented." See Kushida and Lipscy, *Japan Under the DPJ: The Politics of Transition and Governance* (Stanford, Calif.: Walter H. Shorenstein Asia-Pacific Research Center, 2013), 24.

12. Tomohito Shinoda, "Japan's Failed Experiment: The DPJ and Institutional Change for Political Leadership," *Asian Survey* 52, no. 5 (2012): 799–821.

13. The Upper House (House of Councillors) carried out a major electoral reform in 1982 with the combination of proportional representation and multimember districts. The system did not change in 1994, except for adjustments in the number of delegates in some districts.

14. Frances McCall Rosenbluth and Michael F. Thies, *Japan Transformed: Political Change and Economic Restructuring* (Princeton, N.J.: Princeton University Press, 2010); J. Mark Ramseyer and Frances McCall Rosenbluth, *Japan's Political Marketplace* (Cambridge, Mass.: Harvard University Press, 1993).

15. Tomohito Shinoda, *Contemporary Japanese Politics: Institutional Changes and Power Shifts* (New York: Columbia University Press, 2013).

16. Rosenbluth and Thies, *Japan Transformed*.

17. For an excellent discussion of the administrative reform, see Aurelia George Mulgan, "Japan's Political Leadership Deficit," *Australian Journal of Political Science* 35, no. 2 (2000): 183–202.

18. Ko Mishima, "The Changing Relationship Between Japan's LDP and the Bureaucracy: Hashimoto's Administrative Reform Effort and Its Politics," *Asian Survey* 38, no. 10 (1998): 968–85.

19. Jennifer A. Amyx, *Japan's Financial Crisis: Institutional Rigidity and Reluctant Change* (Princeton, N.J.: Princeton University Press, 2004), especially app. 2.

20. Based on *Jiji yoron chosa*, various issues.

21. Harukata Takenaka, *Shushō shihai: Nihon seiji no henbō* (Dominance of the prime minister: Transfiguration of Japanese politics) (Tokyo: Chuo koron Shinsha, 2006).

22. Ko Mishima, "Grading Japanese Prime Minister Koizumi's Revolution: How Far has the LDP's Policymaking Changed?," *Asian Survey* 47, no. 5 (2007): 727–48.

23. Mulgan claims that owing to structural difficulties in Japan, the Koizumi revolution was destined to fail. See Aurelia George Mulgan, *Japan's Failed Revolution: Koizumi and the Politics of Economic Reform* (Canberra: Asia Pacific Press, 2002). Ikuo Kabashima and Gill Steel recognize that Koizumi's popularity and electoral success allowed him to stay in office for a long time to carry out many of his revolutionary reform

policies. See Kabashima and Steel, "The Koizumi Revolution," *PS: Political Science & Politics* 40, no. 1 (2007): 79–84.

24. Mulgan, "Japan's Political Leadership Deficit."

25. On the prime minister–led foreign policy (*kantei gaikō*) under Koizumi, see Tomohito Shinoda, *Kantei gaikō: Seiji rīdāshippu no yukue* (Diplomacy by Prime Minister's Office: Whither political leadership?) (Tokyo: Asahi Shimbun Shuppan, 2004).

26. Amyx, *Japan's Financial Crisis*, 222–23.

27. The quote is the response to a questionnaire distributed by the National Personnel Authority to two hundred experts from industries, media, academia, labor unions, and civil society organizations. Some 51.2 percent of respondents answered as noted. See http://www.jinji.go.jp/hakusho/h14/jine200302_2_087.html#fb2.1.1.

28. Also translated as deliberation council. These are usually informal meetings organized by ministries on specific policy matters where experts and social (or interest) group representatives chosen by the ministries gather to exchange views. For a detailed study of *shingi-kai*, see Frank J. Schwartz, *Advice and Consent: The Politics of Consultation in Japan* (Cambridge: Cambridge University Press, 2001). On the recent changes in the *shingi-kai* structure, see Akiko Nishikawa, "Shingikai nado shiteki shimonkikan no genjō to ronten" (Current status and issues of advisory bodies of the central government), *National Diet Library Research and Legislative Reference* 57, no. 5 (2007): 59–73.

29. Yung Ho Park, "The Governmental Advisory Commission System in Japan," *Administration & Society* 3, no. 4 (1972): 435–67.

30. Schwartz, *Advice and Consent*, 69. On the criticism of how the special-interest groups protected their interests through connection to ministries, see also Atsushi Kusano, "Tettei kenshō: Shingikai wa kakuremino dearu" (Thorough investigation: Commissions are used as a cover), *Shokun* 27, no. 7 (1995): 98–110.

31. The 1996 number was reported in *Nihon keizai shimbun*, August 9, 1996, while the 2006 number was reported in Nishikawa, "Shingikai nado shiteki shimonkikan no genjō to ronten," 69–73.

32. Nishikawa, "Shingikai nado shiteki shimonkikan no genjō to ronten," 64.

33. Gene Park, *Spending Without Taxation: FILP and the Politics of Public Finance in Japan* (Stanford: Stanford University Press, 2011); Kent E. Calder, "Japan's Changing Political Economy," in *Japan's Emerging Global Role*, ed. Daniel Unger and Paul Blackburn (Boulder, Colo.: Lynne Rienner, 1993), 59.

34. Masahiro Higo notes that in 1999, 58 percent of the funding that the governmental financial institutions extended to private corporations using the FILP source was for the big businesses. See Higo, "Zaiseitōyūshi no genjō to kadai: 2001 nendo kaikaku ga Zaitō no kinō ni ataeru eikyō" (Current state and challenges of Fiscal Investment and Loan Program: How 2001 reform affects the function of Fiscal Investment and Loan Program), *Bank of Japan Working Paper Series* WP01.1 (2001).

35. Calder, "Japan's Changing Political Economy."

36. Section 2 of article 103 of the Revised National Public Service Act reads: "Officials shall not, for a period of two years after separation from the service, accept or assume a position with a profit-making enterprise with a close connection to any agency of

the State defined by rules of the National Personnel Authority, any specified independent administrative institution or the Japan Post, with which such persons were formerly employed within five years prior to separation from the service."

37. Kimio Kobayashi, "Kokka kōmuin no amakudari konzetsu ni muketa kinnen no torikumi" (Recent efforts to eliminate golden parachute deal for national government officials), *Leviathan* 62, no. 8 (2012): 27–63.

38. Ko Mishima, "A Missing Piece in Japan's Political Reform," *Asian Survey* 53, no. 4 (2013): 703–27.

39. Ethan Scheiner et al., "When Do Interest Groups Contact Bureaucrats Rather than Politicians? Evidence on Fire Alarms and Smoke Detectors from Japan," *Japanese Journal of Political Science* 14, no. 3 (2013): 283–304.

40. Leonard J. Schoppa, *Race for the Exits: The Unraveling of Japan's System of Social Protection* (Ithaca, N.Y.: Cornell University Press, 2008).

41. Leonard J. Schoppa, *Bargaining with Japan: What American Pressure Can and Cannot Do* (New York: Columbia University Press, 1997).

42. Jeffrey A. Frankel, *The Yen-Dollar Agreement: Liberalizing Japanese Capital Markets* (Cambridge, Mass.: MIT Press, 1984); Frances McCall Rosenbluth, *Financial Politics in Contemporary Japan* (Ithaca, N.Y.: Cornell University Press, 1989).

43. Steven K. Vogel, *Marketcraft: How Governments Make Markets Work* (New York: Oxford University Press, 2018).

44. Amyx, *Japan's Financial Crisis*; William W. Grimes, *Unmaking the Japanese Miracle: Macroeconomic Politics, 1985–2000* (Ithaca, N.Y.: Cornell University Press, 2002).

45. The financial crisis continued in Japan in 1998 when the Long-Term Credit Bank of Japan and the Nippon Credit Bank were both nationalized.

46. Edward J. Lincoln, "Japan's Financial Mess," *Foreign Affairs* 77 (1998): 57–66. An earlier incident of the Japan Premium appeared in summer of 1995 as some Japanese banks began to collapse, and it worsened later that year as the Federal Reserve discovered Daiwa Bank's $1 billion derivative loss cover-up. What made this situation worse was the delay in MOF's reporting of the matter to the Federal Reserve. See Thomas F. Cargill, Michael M. Hutchison, and Takatoshi Ito, *The Political Economy of Japanese Monetary Policy* (Cambridge, Mass.: MIT Press, 2003), 123.

47. Tetsuro Toya and Jennifer A. Amyx, *The Political Economy of the Japanese Financial Big Bang: Institutional Change in Finance and Public Policymaking* (Oxford: Oxford University Press, 2006), 130. To deal with the financial crises and mounting NPLs during this time, the government also put in place a series of financial reconstruction measures from 1998 through 2002 under Prime Minister Koizumi. See Amyx, *Japan's Financial Crisis*.

48. Takatoshi Ito and Michael Melvin, "Japan's Big Bang and the Transformation of Financial Markets," *National Bureau of Economic Research Working Paper* No. 7247 (1999), https://www.nber.org/papers/w7247.

49. See Schoppa, *Race for the Exits*, 10–11. Schoppa describes the broader "convoy system" as a large number of policies and practices that during the rapid growth era (1950s) into the 1980s fit neatly with one another to generate economic growth and protection. The convoy is the government system that had successfully managed to

regulate economic and social activities of the Japanese firms and people to secure a predictable business environment.

50. Steven K. Vogel, *Japan Remodeled: How Government and Industry Are Reforming Japanese Capitalism* (Ithaca, N.Y.: Cornell University Press, 2006).

51. One of the big-bang reforms allowed the establishment of holding companies through revision of antitrust law in 1997, which became the foundation of the establishment of the megabanks.

52. Nissei Kiso Kenkyūjo (Nihon Life Institute), *Kabushiki mochiai jōkyōchōsa*, http://www.nli-research.co.jp/report/detail/id=36431. This report was discontinued in 2004 owing to rapid decline in cross-shareholding in Japan. However, Dan Hu reports that there has been an uptick of cross-shareholding since 2005. See Hu, "The Relevance of Japanese Horizontal Keiretsu Affiliated Firms from the Perspective of Disclosure Quality," *SSRN Working Paper* (2014).

53. Japan Exchange Group, *Kabushiki bunpu jōkyō chōsa*, various issues, http://www.jpx.co.jp/markets/statistics-equities/examination/01.html. In addition, there was relatively high foreign ownership of major Japanese corporations by 2005, ranging from Nissan (64.3 percent), Sony (40.1), and Toyota (21.3) to Mizuho (20.4). See Vogel, *Japan Remodeled*, 164–65.

54. Nonregular workers increased from about 20 percent of the employed workforce in 1990 to 33 percent in 2006 and 37.4 percent in 2014. See Ministry of Internal Affairs and Communication, *Rōdōryoku chōsa*, various issues; Ulrike Schaede, *Choose and Focus: Japanese Business Strategies for the 21st Century* (Ithaca, N.Y.: Cornell University Press, 2008), chap. 9.

55. Schaede, *Choose and Focus*; Michael A. Witt, *Changing Japanese Capitalism: Societal Coordination and Institutional Adjustment* (Cambridge: Cambridge University Press, 2006); Susan Carpenter, *Why Japan Can't Reform* (London: Palgrave Macmillan, 2008); Vogel, *Japan Remodeled*. For more discussion on the institutional continuity and changes through neoliberal reforms, see Yong Wook Lee and Sun Young Kwak, "Neo-liberal Korea and Still Developmentalist Japan: Myth or Reality?," *Global Economic Review* 38, no. 3 (2009): 277–95.

56. Until 1994 Keidanren allocated political donation obligation to each industry association, but then it stopped playing such a role. By 2005 Keidanren, under its president, Okuda, ended its role of even coordinating any political donation activities to the LDP. See Megumi Naoi and Ellis Krauss, "Who Lobbies Whom? Special Interest Politics Under Alternative Electoral Systems," *American Journal of Political Science* 53, no. 4 (2009): 874–92.

57. Pempel, *Regime Shift*; Hatch and Yamamura, *Asia in Japan's Embrace*.

58. Kiyoshi Kojima, "The "Flying Geese" Model of Asian Economic Development: Origin, Theoretical Extensions, and Regional Policy Implications," *Journal of Asian Economics* 11, no. 4 (2000): 375–401; Terutomo Ozawa, "Foreign Direct Investment and Economic Development," *Transnational Corporations* 1, no. 1 (1992): 27–54; Schoppa, *Race for the Exits*.

59. Walter Hatch, *Asia's Flying Geese: How Regionalization Shapes Japan* (Ithaca, N.Y.: Cornell University Press, 2010).

60. Mireya Solís, *Banking on Multinationals: Public Credit and the Export of Japanese Sunset Industries* (Stanford, Calif.: Stanford University Press, 2004).

61. Schaede, *Choose and Focus*, 142; Hideo Kobayashi, *Sangyō kūdōka no kokufuku: Sangyō tenkanki no Nihon to Ajia* (Conquering hollowing-out: Japan at the time of industrial structure transition and Asia) (Tokyo: Chuo Koron Shinshan, 2003).

62. *METI Wagakuni kikyō no kaigai jigyō katsudō kekka gaiyō*, various issues (http://www.meti.go.jp/statistics/tyo/kaigaizi/result-1.html).

63. Junko Shimizu and Kiyotaka Sato, "Abenomics, Yen Depreciation, Trade Deficit, and Export Competitiveness," *RIETI Discussion Paper Series* 15-E-020 (2015): 1–31.

64. MITI defined hollowing out as "decrease in domestic production, investment or employment due to increase in foreign direct investment" (METI White Paper, 1986).

65. Schoppa, *Race for the Exits*.

66. Schaede, *Choose and Focus*. Some, such as Solís, *Banking on Multinationals*, argue that Japan's outward FDI tends to concentrate on the "standardized products," while high value-added production remains in Japan.

67. In the annual METI questionnaire in 2012, when companies were asked whether hollowing out was taking place in Japan, close to 70 percent answered yes; when asked whether they saw their business partners engage in FDI that led to hollowing out, about 50 percent said yes. Meanwhile, when asked whether the company itself was contributing to create hollowing out, only about 20 percent said yes, while 50 percent said no. METI, White Paper, 2014, http://www.meti.go.jp/report/tsuhaku2012/2012honbun/html/i3120000.html.

68. The amount of Japan's outward FDI was more than ¥4 trillion against less than ¥1 trillion in inward FDI. See Masako Suginohara, "The Politics of Economic Nationalism in Japan: Backlash Against Inward Foreign Direct Investment?," *Asian Survey* 48, no. 5 (2008): 839–59. As for cross-country comparison, the respective inward FDI stock as a percentage of the country's GDP in 2000 was France, 19.9 percent; Germany, 25.2 percent; United Kingdom, 30.5 percent; and United States, 12.4 percent. For Japan that year it was 1.1 percent. *UNCTAD World Investment Report*, 2003, annex table B.6, 278–79.

69. Suginohara, "The Politics of Economic Nationalism in Japan"; Jennifer A. Amyx, "Regional Financial Cooperation in East Asia Since the Asian Financial Crisis," in *Crisis as Catalyst: Asia's Dynamic Political Economy*, ed. Andrew MacIntyre, T. J. Pempel, and John Ravenhill, Cornell Studies in Political Economy (Ithaca, N.Y.: Cornell University Press, 2008), 117–39.

70. Hatch and Yamamura, *Asia in Japan's Embrace*; Dennis Tachiki, "Between Foreign Direct Investment and Regionalism: The Role of Japanese Production Networks," in *Remapping East Asia: The Construction of a Region*, ed. T. J. Pempel (Ithaca, N.Y.: Cornell University Press, 2005).

71. René Belderbos and Leo Sleuwaegen, "Japanese Firms and the Decision to Invest Abroad: Business Groups and Regional Core Networks," *Review of Economics and Statistics* 78, no. 2 (1996): 214–20; René Belderbos, Giovanni Capannelli, and Kyoji Fukao, "Local Procurement by Japanese Manufacturing Affiliates Abroad," in

Multinational Firms and Impacts on Employment, Trade and Technology: New Perspectives for a New Century, ed. Robert E. Lipsey and Jean-Louis Mucchielli (London: Routledge, 2002).

72. Seishi Kimura, "Changing Context of Firm-Based Late Industrialization in the Global Business Transformation," in *The Challenges of Late Industrialization: The Global Economy and the Japanese Commercial Aircraft Industry*, ed. Seishi Kimura (Hampshire, UK: Palgrave Macmillan, 2007), 100. Schaede, *Choose and Focus*, argues that the modularization has elevated the importance of the first-tier suppliers' role as these suppliers become the critical player in producing preassembled parts and coordinating all the subcontracting suppliers. The level and the importance of supply chain for manufacturing production made some Japanese firms vulnerable for disruption of the chain, as seen at in 2011 at the time of the triple disaster (March 11, 2011) and the massive flooding in Thailand (March–April 2011).

73. Hidetaka Yoshimatsu, *Japan and East Asia in Transition: Trade Policy, Crisis and Evolution, and Regionalism* (New York: Palgrave Macmillan, 2003). Yoshimatsu gives the example of Honda Motors and Hainan Sundiro Motorcycle (106).

74. Andrew Staples, *Responses to Regionalism in East Asia: Japanese Production Networks in the Automotive Sector* (New York: Palgrave Macmillan, 2008), 233. Meanwhile, Mark S. Manger emphasizes the importance of FDI on FTA formation in Asia. Manger, *Investing in Protection: The Politics of Preferential Trade Agreements Between North and South* (Cambridge: Cambridge University Press, 2009).

5. Trade and Investment

1. FTAs are preferential trade agreements (PTAs) among the agreed members to reduce or eliminate trade barriers. FTAs bear different titles depending on the members and the principles of the agreement and arrangements. The WTO lists all FTAs under regional trade agreements (RTAs), for example. The Japanese government prefers to label its FTAs as economic partnership agreements (EPAs) or comprehensive economic partnership (CEP) agreements. According to the *Asahi shimbun*, January 15, 2002, the government is hesitant to use the term "free trade" because it appears to represent full liberalization of trade without exception.

2. The only bilateral EPA that does not include the investment chapter is the one with Vietnam. The Japanese government concluded a separate bilateral investment treaty with Vietnam in 2003.

3. Trade multilateralism is characterized by the liberal perspective as the "liberal world order" established after World War II under U.S. hegemony that is open and rule-based. See G. John Ikenberry, "The Future of the Liberal World Order," *Foreign Affairs* 90, no. 3 (2011): 56–68. The reasons behind the waning of multilateralism and the rise of bilateralism are beyond the scope of this project.

4. Edward D. Mansfield and Helen V. Milner, "The New Wave of Regionalism," *International Organization* 53, no. 3 (1999): 589–627.

5. For details of the Uruguay Round and the rules and framework established in the WTO, see Amrita Narlikar, Martin Daunton, and Robert M. Stern, eds., *The Oxford Handbook on the World Trade Organization* (Oxford: Oxford University Press, 2012).

6. The Singapore issues were introduced at the December 1996 WTO Ministerial Conference in Singapore and included four items: investment, competition policy, transparency in government procurement, and trade facilitation. They were placed in the WTO Doha Development Round, but WTO members failed to reach an agreement to pursue them at the 2003 Cancun meeting. On the dynamics of NGO and protectionist business opposition to these initiatives, see Andre Walter, "NGOs, Business, and International Investment: The Multilateral Agreement on Investment, Seattle, and Beyond," *Global Governance* 7, no. 1 (2001): 51–73.

7. For the data, see the UNCTAD IIA/BIT database, http://investmentpolicyhub .unctad.org/IIA.

8. Robert Zoellick, "The United States, Europe, and the World Trading System," remarks before the Kangaroo Group, May 15, 2001, https://ustr.gov/archive/assets /Document_Library/USTR_Speeches/2001/asset_upload_file206_4282.pdf.

9. The Closer Economic Partnership Agreement was signed with Hong Kong in June 2003 and with Macao in October 2003. The Framework Agreement of China's Comprehensive Economic Cooperation was signed in November 2002.

10. The Early Harvest Program was a way to increase confidence on the part of ASEAN countries regarding China's commitment to its FTA with ASEAN by providing early tariff reductions on certain agricultural and industrial products. See Elaine Kwei, "Chinese Trade Bilateralism: Politics Still in Command," in *Bilateral Trade Agreements in the Asia-Pacific: Origins, Evolution, and Implication*, ed. Vinod K. Aggarwal and Shujiro Urata (Abingdon-on-Thames, UK: Routledge, 2006), 134. Yoshimatsu also discusses how China's EHP, combined with other incentives such as debt write-off, "contributed to the enhancement of China's credibility in term of policy commitments," as China was willing to accept disadvantageous conditions and had decided not to take advantage of the asymmetries of power. See Hidetaka Yoshimatsu, "Regional Cooperation in Northeast Asia: Searching for the Mode of Governance," *International Relations of the Asia-Pacific* 10, no. 2 (2010): 247–74.

11. Gregory Chin and Richard Stubbs, "China, Regional Institution-Building and the China-ASEAN Free Trade Area," *Review of International Political Economy* 18, no. 3 (2011): 277–98.

12. Agata Antkiewicz and John Whalley, "China's New Regional Trade Agreements," *World Economy* 28, no. 10 (2005): 1539–57.

13. Saori N. Katada, *Banking on Stability: Japan and the Cross-Pacific Dynamics of International Financial Crisis Management* (Ann Arbor: University of Michigan Press, 2001).

14. Kuniko Ashizawa, "Japan's Approach Toward Asian Regional Security: From 'Hub-and-Spoke' Bilateralism to 'Multi-tiered,'" *Pacific Review* 16, no. 3 (2003): 361–82; Mie Oba, *Jūsōteki chiiki toshiteno Ajia: Tairitsu to kyōzon no kōzu* (Asia as a multilayered region: Framed by conflicts and coexistence) (Tokyo: Yuhikaku, 2014).

15. Currency and macroeconomic policies as well as financial liberalization were also addressed in the 1985 Plaza Accord and multiple G7 summits.

16. Christina L. Davis, *Food Fights Over Free Trade: How International Institutions Promote Agricultural Trade Liberalization* (Princeton, N.J.: Princeton University Press, 2003), chaps. 5 and 6.

17. There are many reasons why the U.S. government softened its liberalization pressure on Japan. One is the improvement in the U.S. economy and the shifting of its growth focus to Wall Street and the rapid innovation of information technology during the dot-com boom of the late 1990s. On the Japanese side, in addition to substantial trade liberalization up to that point (except for some agricultural products), Japanese companies rapidly increased production in the United States. The establishment of the WTO also helped Japan to direct some of the conflict to its dispute settlement mechanism. See Saadia M. Pekkanen, *Japan's Aggressive Legalism: Law and Foreign Trade Politics Beyond the WTO* (Stanford, Calif.: Stanford University Press, 2008). Finally, since the 2000s, the rapid growth of exports from China to the United States has made China the focus of bilateral trade conflicts with the United States.

18. Takashi Terada, "The Origins of Japan's APEC Policy: Foreign Minister Takeo Miki's Asia-Pacific Policy and Current Implications," *Pacific Review* 11, no. 3 (1998): 337–63; Peter J. Katzenstein, "Introduction: Asian Regionalism in Comparative Perspective," in *Network Power: Japan and Asia*, ed. Peter J. Katzenstein and Takashi Shiraishi (Ithaca, N.Y.: Cornell University Press, 1997); Shintaro Hamanaka, *Asian Regionalism and Japan: The Politics of Membership in Regional Diplomatic, Financial and Trade Groups* (London: Routledge, 2009), 127–41.

19. By the end of 2000 there were already 153 FTAs and 2,099 BITs in the world. The early BITs that Japan signed were with Egypt (1977), Sri Lanka (1982), China (1988), Turkey (1992), Hong Kong (1997), Pakistan (1998), Bangladesh (1998), Russia (1998), and Mongolia (2001).

20. Satoshi Oyane argues that the Japanese government had internalized the trade multilateralism through GATT/WTO as the principal policy idea and hence it was dismissive of FTA proliferation. See Oyane, *Kokusai rejīmu to Nichibei no gaikō kōsō: WTO, APEC, FTA no tenkan kyokumen* (International regimes and Japan-U.S. diplomatic initiatives: Turning point of WTO, APEC, FTA) (Tokyo: Yuhikaku, 2011), 202.

21. Donald K. Crone, "Does Hegemony Matter? The Reorganization of the Pacific Political Economy," *World Politics* 45, no. 4 (1993): 501–25.

22. Walter Hatch and Kozo Yamamura, *Asia in Japan's Embrace: Building a Regional Production Alliance* (Cambridge: Cambridge University Press, 1996); Peter J. Katzenstein and Takashi Shiraishi, *Network Power: Japan and Asia* (Ithaca, N.Y.: Cornell University Press, 1997).

23. Terada notes that the idea of "open regionalism" has its lineage in PBEC, PAFTAD, and PECC. In contrast, Oyane argues that there was a limited connection between these earlier regional efforts and APEC. See Terada, "The Origins of Japan's APEC Policy"; Oyane, *Kokusai rejīmu to Nichibei no gaikō kōsō*.

24. Kuniko Ashizawa, *Japan, the US, and Regional Institution-Building in the New Asia: When Identity Matters* (New York: Palgrave Macmillan, 2013).

25. Until then, MITI's Trade Policy Bureau had two functions: one to deal with bilateral trade issues and the other responsible for international economic institutions. No

office was overseeing regional trade matters. See Ashizawa, *Japan, the US, and Regional Institution-Building*, 41.

26. Yoichi Funabashi, *Asia Pacific Fusion: Japan's Role in APEC* (Washington, D.C.: Institute for International Economics, 1995), 105.

27. The eighth GATT Round started its negotiation in 1986 with ambitious goals, but negotiations hit a deadlock from 1988 to 1993, mostly over the differences on agricultural trade. After the breakthrough in 1993 the negotiation concluded with 123 members' signatures in April 1994, ushering in the World Trade Organization, the successor to the GATT, in January 1995. Another element of geoeconomics behind APEC came in the form of the Malaysian proposal of the East Asian Economic Caucus within APEC in 1990. Although Japan was attracted by the idea of creating an Asian caucus within APEC to push for Asia's preferred mode of liberalization, the Japanese government found it impossible to support it given the vocal opposition by Secretary of State James Baker of the United States. See Takashi Terada, "Constructing an 'East Asian' Concept and Growing Regional Identity: From EAEC to ASEAN+3," *Pacific Review* 16, no. 2 (2003): 251–77; Richard Higgott and Richard Stubbs, "Competing Conceptions of Economic Regionalism: APEC Versus EAEC in the Asia Pacific," *Review of International Political Economy* 2, no. 3 (1995): 516–35.

28. John Ravenhill, *APEC and the Construction of Pacific Rim Regionalism* (Cambridge: Cambridge University Press, 2001).

29. Oyane, *Kokusai rejīmu to Nichibei no gaikō kōsō*.

30. David P. Rapkin, "The United States, Japan, and the Power to Block: The APEC and AMF Cases," *Pacific Review* 14, no. 3 (2001): 373–410; Funabashi, *Asia Pacific Fusion*.

31. The nine sectors considered in the EVSL discussion were environmental goods, energy-related products, chemicals, toys, gemstones and jewelry, medical equipment, telecommunications, fish and fish products, and forestry products. The choice of these sectors was derived from the balance between the demands of advanced and developing countries, but the Japanese government was unwilling to accept the inclusion of fishery and forestry products. See Rapkin, "The United States, Japan, and the Power to Block"; Ellis S. Krauss, "The United States and Japan in APEC's EVSL Negotiations: Regional Multilateralism and Trade," in *Beyond Bilateralism: US-Japan Relations in the New Asia-Pacific*, ed. Ellis S. Krauss and T. J. Pempel (Stanford, Calif.: Stanford University Press, 2004); Oyane, *Kokusai rejīmu to Nichibei no gaikō kōsō*.

32. Rapkin, "The United States, Japan, and the Power to Block," 386–89.

33. It is worth noting, however, that APEC has been quite active in the trade facilitation and technical cooperation that would underpin economic integration among the member countries for the past twenty years (author's interview at APEC headquarters in Singapore, June 2015).

34. Japan's joining of the Comprehensive and Progressive Agreement of the Transpacific Partnership (TPP-11) and Japan-EU EPA as of early 2019 has expanded the coverage significantly.

35. Mireya Solís, "Japan's New Regionalism: The Politics of Free Trade Talks with Mexico," *Journal of East Asian Studies* 3, no. 3 (2003): 377–404; Naoko Munakata, "Whither

East Asian Economic Integration?," *Working Papers by CEAP Visiting Fellows* (2002), https://www.brookings.edu/wp-content/uploads/2016/06/2002_munakata.pdf. METI calls Japan's approach a *mamori no* (defensive) FTA, and Munakata calls it "defensive regionalism." See Munakata, "Has Politics Caught Up with Markets? In Search of East Asian Economic Regionalism," in *Beyond Japan: The Dynamics of East Asian Regionalism*, ed. Peter J. Katzenstein and Takashi Shiraishi (Ithaca, N.Y.: Cornell University Press, 2006).

36. Katada, *Banking on Stability*.

37. The Mexican government was about to conclude an FTA with the European Union and was keen to diversify its FTA partners even further as its trade dependence on the United States since NAFTA had come into effect was very concerning to it.

38. Noboru Hatakeyama, *Keizai tōgō no shinseiki: Moto tsūshōkōshō toppu no kaisou to teigen* (Economic integration in the new century: Memoir and recommendations by a former top trade negotiator) (Tokyo: Toyo Keizai Shipo, 2015).

39. Takumi Sakuyama, *Nihon no TPP kōshō sanka no shinjitsu: Sono seisaku katei no kaimei* (The truth of Japan's participation in the TPP negotiation: Investigation on the policy-making process) (Tokyo: Bunshin-do, 2015), 61–62.

40. Inkyo Cheong and Jungran Cho, "The Impact of Free Trade Agreements (FTAs) on Business in the Republic of Korea," *ADBI Working Paper Series* 156 (2009), https://www.econstor.eu/handle/10419/53663.

41. Richard E. Baldwin, "Managing the Noodle Bowl: The Fragility of East Asian Regionalism," *Singapore Economic Review* 53, no. 3 (2008): 449–78; Christopher M. Dent, "Networking the Region? The Emergence and Impact of Asia-Pacific Bilateral Free Trade Agreement Projects," *Pacific Review* 16, no. 1 (2003): 1–28. Dent used the term "lattice regionalism." In a way, it is misleading to call the bilateral FTA boom in the region "regionalism" as it refers to the proliferation of bilateral arrangements.

42. The WTO definition of "rules of origin" states: "rules of origin are the criteria needed to determine the national source of a product. Their importance is derived from the fact that duties and restrictions in several cases depend upon the source of imports." See WTO, https://www.wto.org/english/tratop_e/roi_e/roi_info_e.htm.

43. Gregory Corning notes, however, that one finds more complex and in many cases more stringent rules of origin included in the ASEAN-Japan Comprehensive Economic Partnership than in the bilateral FTAs between Japan and the ASEAN countries. See Corning, "Between Bilateralism and Regionalism in East Asia: The ASEAN–Japan Comprehensive Economic Partnership," *Pacific Review* 22, no. 5 (2009): 639–65.

44. Terada argues that the stagnating ASEAN integration efforts since the Asian financial crisis were accelerated as China came to propose its own FTA with ASEAN in 2000. See Takashi Terada, "Competitive Regionalism in Southeast Asia and Beyond: Role of Singapore and ASEAN," in *Competitive Regionalism: FTA Diffusion in the Pacific Rim*, ed. Mireya Solís, Barbara Stallings, and Saori N. Katada (Basingstoke, UK: Palgrave Macmillan, 2009), 175–76.

45. This demonstrates the fluidity of the "region" as a concept, which is a construct of "physical, psychological, and behavioral traits" that is defined and redefined. See

T. J. Pempel, *Remapping East Asia: The Construction of a Region* (Ithaca, N.Y.: Cornell University Press, 2005).

46. For the history of the EAFTA and CEPEA, see Hidetaka Yoshimatsu, "Diplomatic Objectives in Trade Politics: The Development of the China-Japan-Korea FTA," *Asia-Pacific Review* 22, no. 1 (2015): 100–23; Takashi Terada, "The Origins of ASEAN+6 and Japan's Initiatives: China's Rise and the Agent-Structure Analysis," *Pacific Review* 23, no. 1 (2010): 71–92; Gregory P. Corning, "Trade Regionalism in a Realist East Asia: Rival Visions and Competitive Bilateralism," *Asian Perspective* 35, no. 2 (2011): 259–86; Oyane, *Kokusai rejīmu to Nichibei no gaikō kōsō*, chap. 11. Oyane (232–33) argues that there were not many substantive differences between the EAFTA and CEPEA. Even though they were considered rival proposals, the respective main proponents, the Chinese and Japanese governments, made sure that neither of them would visibly progress more swiftly than the other.

47. TPP member countries were Chile, New Zealand, Singapore, and Brunei (original P-4 members); the United States, Australia, Peru, and Vietnam (joined negotiation in 2008); Malaysia (2010); Canada and Mexico (2011); and Japan (2013). Among these twelve, the United States and Japan are the largest economies and combined account for approximately 78 percent of the TPP GDP.

48. Mireya Solís and Saori N. Katada, "Unlikely Pivotal States in Competitive Free Trade Agreement Diffusion: The Effect of Japan's Trans-Pacific Partnership Participation on Asia-Pacific Regional Integration," *New Political Economy* 20, no. 2 (2015): 155–77.

49. Hank Lim, "The Way Forward for RCEP Negotiations," *East Asia Forum* (2012), https://www.eastasiaforum.org/2012/12/03/the-way-forward-for-rcep-negotiations/; Beginda Pakpahan, "Will RCEP Compete with the TPP?," *East Asia Forum* (2012), https://www.eastasiaforum.org/2012/11/28/will-rcep-compete-with-the-tpp/.

50. John Ravenhill, "The 'New East Asian Regionalism': A Political Domino Effect," *Review of International Political Economy* 17, no. 2 (2010): 178–208.

51. The lineage of this debate between top-down and bottom-up sources of regionalism goes back to the early phase of Western European integration in the 1960s between the intergovernmental perspective and the neofunctionalist perspective. See Stanley Hoffmann, "Obstinate or Obsolete? The Fate of the Nation-State and the Case of Western Europe," *Daedalus* 95, no. 3 (1966): 862–915; Ernst B. Haas and Philippe C. Schmitter, "Economics and Differential Patterns of Political Integration: Projections About Unity in Latin America," *International Organization* 18, no. 4 (1964): 705–37. For a discussion of the bottom-up dynamics in East Asia's regionalism, see Masahiro Kawai and Ganeshan Wignaraja, "The Asian 'Noodle Bowl': Is it Serious for Business?," *ADBI Working Paper Series* 136 (2009), https://www.adb.org/sites/default/files/publication/155991/adbi-wp136.pdf; Munakata, "Has Politics Caught Up with Markets?"; Mark S. Manger, *Investing in Protection: The Politics of Preferential Trade Agreements Between North and South* (Cambridge: Cambridge University Press, 2009).

52. Both India and Mongolia have applied to become APEC members, but APEC has frozen its membership expansion since 1997. After waiting twenty years to enter the organization, India was finally invited as an observer in 2011.

53. Vinod Aggarwal refers to this phenomenon of bilateral FTAs as being "nested" in larger trade liberalization and facilitation efforts. See Aggarwal, *Institutional Designs for a Complex World: Bargaining, Linkages, and Nesting* (Ithaca, N.Y.: Cornell University Press, 1998).

54. Aurelia George Mulgan, "Where Tradition Meets Change: Japan's Agricultural Politics in Transition," *Journal of Japanese Studies* 31, no. 2 (2005): 261–98; Davis, *Food Fights Over Free Trade*.

55. Saadia M. Pekkanen, Mireya Solís, and Saori N. Katada, "Trading Gains for Control: International Trade Forums and Japanese Economic Diplomacy," *International Studies Quarterly* 51, no. 4 (2007): 945–70.

56. Data from Shujiro Urata, "Japan's Trade Policy with Asia," *Public Policy Review* 10, no. 1 (2014): 1–31, as cited in Arata Kuno, "Revealing Tariff Structures Under the ASEAN+1 FTAs and ATIGA: Implications for a Possible ASEAN++ FTA," in *Comprehensive Mapping of FTAs in ASEAN and East Asia Phase II*, ed. Chang Jae Lee, Shujiro Urata, and Ikumo Isono (Jakarta: ERIA, 2012).

57. It is important to note that even small items, given opportune conditions, have been able to derail FTA agreements, such as in the case of seaweed in the Japan-Korea FTA. See Saori N. Katada and Mireya Solís, "Domestic Sources of Japanese Foreign Policy Activism: Loss Avoidance and Demand Coherence," *International Relations of the Asia-Pacific* 10, no. 1 (2010): 129–57.

58. Mireya Solís and Saori N. Katada, "The Japan-Mexico FTA: A Cross-Regional Step in the Path Towards Asian Regionalism," *Pacific Affairs* 80, no. 2 (2007): 279–301; Mulgan, "Where Tradition Meets Change." The relevant five Mexican agricultural products (the so-called five fingers) were pork, beef, chicken, oranges, and orange juice.

59. Sakuyama, *Nihon no TPP kōshō sanka no shinjitsu*.

60. Hidetaka Yoshimatsu and Patrick Ziltener, "Japan's FTA Strategy Toward Highly Developed Countries: Comparing Australia's and Switzerland's Experiences, 2000–09," *Asian Survey* 50, no. 6 (2010): 1058–81. Also see Takumi Sakuyama, "Seisaku Jōhō: Suisu no FTA senryaku kara Manabumono: Nichi-Suisu EPA kōshō no keiken kara" (Policy briefing: What we can learn from Japan-Swiss FTA strategy—from my experience as Japan-Swiss EPA negotiator)," *Primaff Review* 30 (2009): 36–41.

61. Megumi Naoi, *Building Legislative Coalitions for Free Trade in Asia: Globalization as Legislation* (New York: Cambridge University Press, 2015).

62. Hidetaka Yoshimatsu, "Japan's Quest for Free Trade Agreements: Constraints from Bureaucratic and Interest Group Politics," in *Japan's Future in East Asia and the Pacific*, ed. Mari Pangestu and Ligang Song (Canberra: ANU Press, 2007).

63. MAFF created an FTA Headquarters with five country-specific teams to formulate its FTA strategy in November 2003. MOFA expanded its FTA/EPA Office from thirty to forty staff to set up the Regional Economic Partnership Division in August 2004. METI established a new Economic Partnership Division with around eighty staff in July 2004. See Yoshimatsu, "Japan's Quest for Free Trade Agreements," 93.

64. Yoshimatsu, "Japan's Quest for Free Trade Agreements," 91.

65. The document is available at http://www.kantei.go.jp/jp/singi/keizairenkei/dai3/3gijisidai.html (accessed October 25, 2015).

66. Keidanren, under its strong chairman, Hiroshi Okuda, in 2004 started to grade the policy performance of major political parties as a way to determine its respective campaign contributions. The organization posed ten policy priorities, including "swift promotion of trade, investment and economic cooperation fit to respond to the intensifying global competition."

67. Mizuho reports the results of a survey conducted with 2,482 Japanese companies whose assets were above a certain size (capital stock over half a million dollars) in Japan in 2005. More than half of the companies responded that they wanted the Japanese government to negotiate an FTA with China either bilaterally or trilaterally with South Korea. The United States was the third most popular choice, but only about half of the companies chose it compared to those that chose China as their top choice. See Mizuho, "Nihon kigyō kara mita higashi ajia bijinesu to FTA: Takamaru kitai no ippoude Nihon nuki FTA e no genjitsuteki taio wo mosaku" (Business opportunities in East Asia and FTA for Japanese businesses: Rising expectations, as they search for pragmatic solutions for FTAs without Japan), *Mizuho Report* (2005).

68. Mizuho, "Nihon kigyō kara mita higashi ajia bijinesu to FTA."

69. See Mireya Solís, *Dilemmas of a Trading Nation: Japan and the United States in the Evolving Asia-Pacific Order* (Washington, D.C.: Brookings Institution Press, 2017), 134.

70. Katada and Solís, "Domestic Sources of Japanese Foreign Policy Activism"; Manger, *Investing in Protection*; Yorizumi Watanabe, *Kaisetsu FTA/EPA Kosho* (Ministry of Foreign Affairs Economic Affairs Bureau EPA negotiation team explains FTA and EPA negotiation), ed. Gaimusho Keizaikyoku EPA Kosho Team (Tokyo: Nihon Keizai Hyoronsha, 2007); Koichi Kitano, "Chiri: Eikyōryoku no ookii bumon betsu gyōkaidantai" (Chile: Influential trade groups sorted by industries), in *FTA no seiji keizai gaku: Ajia Raten Amerika nanakakoku no FTA kōshō* (Political economy of FTAs: Japan's FTA negotiations with seven countries from Asia and Latin America), ed. Shigeki Higashi (Tokyo: Institute of Developing Economies, 2007).

71. Solís and Katada, "The Japan-Mexico FTA."

72. Kitano, "Chiri."

73. Mulgan, "Where Tradition Meets Change." In addition to the "loss avoidance" that this group of industries pursued, the small number of active participants lobbying for Japan's FTA with Mexico permitted easier collective action. See Katada and Solís, "Domestic Sources of Japanese Foreign Policy Activism."

74. The rate has since then gradually increased up to 50 percent for Chile and 30 percent for the Philippines by 2018.

75. Kawai and Wignaraja, "The Asian 'Noodle Bowl': Is it Serious for Business?" METI, which promoted the Japan-ASEAN Comprehensive Economic Partnership agreement (in effect in 2008; basic service agreement in December 2013), likes to use the example of flat-screen TV production by a Japanese company in Southeast Asia: if Japan does not have a minilateral FTA with ASEAN collectively and also does not have an FTA with the countries where the company's parts manufacturers reside, the manufacturer has to pay the tariff on the goods made in an ASEAN country; for the parts that came from Japan and were exported to an ASEAN country without an FTA with Japan, the country would not accept the parts from Japan within the AFTA. Thus

the Japanese manufacturer would end up paying a 20–30 percent most-favored nation tariff to export to country X in ASEAN.

76. For all the policy recommendations put forward by the Keidanren regarding the economic partnership and trade/investment-related issues, see the Keidanren website, http://www.keidanren.or.jp/policy/index10.html.

77. From interviews in Tokyo with officials at Keidanren, METI, as well as FTA insiders at think tanks.

78. Yoichi Sekizawa, "FTA ni kansuru Nihon no pojishon no henka to sono haikei" (Changes of Japan's position toward FTA and their reasons), *Tokyo Daigaku Shakai kagaku Kenkyujo Discussion Paper Series*, Hikaku Chiiki Shugi Project No. 13 (2006), https://project.iss.u-tokyo.ac.jp/crep/pdf/rj/r13.pdf.

79. Hatch and Yamamura, *Asia in Japan's Embrace*.

80. Manger, *Investing in Protection*, chap. 7.

81. Mireya Solís, "Japan's Competitive FTA Strategy: Commercial Opportunity Versus Political Rivalry," in *Competitive Regionalism: FTA Diffusion in the Pacific Rim*, ed. Mireya Solís, Barbara Stallings, and Saori N. Katada (Basingstoke, UK: Palgrave Macmillan, 2009).

82. Yoshimatsu and Ziltener, "Japan's FTA Strategy Toward Highly Developed Countries," 1062.

83. I argue elsewhere that the Japanese government learned a lot from negotiating its FTA with Mexico. This includes some modalities such as a negative list for service liberalization and a chapter on business environment improvement. See Solís and Katada, "The Japan-Mexico FTA."

84. For the Kim government, the BIT with the United States and Japan was the cornerstone of its economic policy. See Andrew Kerner, "Why Should I Believe You? The Costs and Consequences of Bilateral Investment Treaties," *International Studies Quarterly* 53, no. 1 (2009): 73–102.

85. Katada and Solís, "Domestic Sources of Japanese Foreign Policy Activism."

86. Gregory P. Corning, "CJK Investment Agreements in East Asia: Building a Bifurcated Investment Regime," *Asian Politics & Policy* 6, no. 2 (2014): 285–306. Following the agreement with South Korea, Japan concluded this new generation of BITs with Vietnam (2003), Cambodia (2007), Laos (2008), Uzbekistan (2009), Papua New Guinea (2014), Kuwait (2014), Iraq (2014), Myanmar (2014), Mozambique (2014), Colombia (2011), Saudi Arabia (2013), Kazakhstan (2014), Uruguay (2015), Ukraine (2015), Oman (2015), and Iran (2016).

87. Akira Kotera argues that given the rise of emerging market countries such as China and India that do not agree on the desirable mode of investment liberalization, any multilateral investment treaties covering a large number of countries are extremely unlikely; hence the continued BIT and bilateral FTA proliferation in the world economy. See Kotera, "Kokusai tōshi: Gendai teki imi to mondaiten. Kazeijikō tono kankei wo fukumete" (Investment agreements: Contemporary significance and issues—including implication on taxation matters), *RIETI Policy Discussion Paper Series* 10-P-024 (2010).

88. Yoichiro Sato, "Substituting Multilateralism, Guiding Trilateralism: The Japan-ROK Investment Agreement in the Growing East Asian Regionalism," in *Changing Power Relations in Northeast Asia: Implications for Relations Between Japan and South Korea*, ed. Marie Söderberg (London: Routledge, 2011), 139.

89. Corning, "CJK Investment Agreements in East Asia"; Saadia M. Pekkanen, "Investment Regionalism in Asia: New Directions in Law and Policy?," *World Trade Review* 11, no. 1 (2012): 119–54; Sato, "Substituting Multilateralism."

90. Solís and Katada, "Unlikely Pivotal."

91. *Nihon keizai shimbun*, November 30, 2004.

92. The agreement came into effect in April 18, 2014, after the ratification by the three governments.

93. Corning, "CJK Investment Agreements in East Asia."

94. *Nihon keizai shimbun*, March 27, 2012. Jaemin Lee attributes the unclear and confusing investor-state dispute settlement (ISDS) mechanism set up for the CJK Trilateral Investment Treaty to various factors, including the three countries' litigation-averse cultures and lack of experience. See Lee, "An Important First Stride, but Beware of the Pitfalls: A Critical Analysis of the ISDS Mechanism of the 2012 Korea-China-Japan Trilateral Investment Treaty," *Chinese Journal of International Law* 12, no. 3 (2013): 509–41.

95. Megumi Naoi and Shujiro Urata, "Free Trade Agreements and Domestic Politics: The Case of the Trans-Pacific Partnership Agreement," *Asian Economic Policy Review* 8, no. 2 (2013): 326–49.

96. Peter A. Petri, Michael G. Plummer, and Fan Zhai, "The Trans-Pacific Partnership and Asia-Pacific Integration: A Quantitative Assessment," vol. 98, Peterson Institute for International Economics, 2012. Japan's Cabinet Office estimated in 2015 that the TPP would contribute an additional ¥14 trillion ($140 billion) in the next ten years.

97. Ian Bremmer, "State Capitalism Comes of Age," *Foreign Affairs* 88, no. 3 (2009): 40–55.

98. Michael D. Swaine, "Chinese Leadership and Elite Responses to the US Pacific Pivot," *China Leadership Monitor* 38 (2012): 1–26.

99. Christopher M. Dent, "Free Trade Agreements in the Asia-Pacific a Decade On: Evaluating the Past, Looking to the Future," *International Relations of the Asia-Pacific* 10, no. 2 (2010): 201–45.

100. Etel Solingen, "Of Dominoes and Firewalls: The Domestic, Regional, and Global Politics of International Diffusion," *International Studies Quarterly* 56, no. 4 (2012): 631–44; Leonardo Baccini and Andreas Dür, "The New Regionalism and Policy Interdependence," *British Journal of Political Science* 42, no. 1 (2012): 57–79.

101. Junichi Sugawara, "Nihon no TPP sanka mondai" (Study of Japan's participation in the TPP), in *Tsūshō seisaku no chōryū to Nihon: FTA senryaku to TPP* (Trend of commercial policy and Japan: FTA strategy and the TPP], ed. Ippei Yamazawa and Keiichi Umada (Tokyo: Keiso Shobo, 2012), 275.

102. Solís and Katada, "Unlikely Pivotal States."

103. The author's interview with a USTR official who participated in the TPP negotiations, Washington, D.C., December 18, 2015.

104. Japan also has the lowest overall tariff liberalization rate, 95 percent, while other members have 97 percent (Vietnam and Canada), 99 percent (Mexico, United States) and 100 percent (Chile, Peru, Malaysia, Australia, New Zealand, Brunei, and Singapore). See Caroline Freund, Tyler Moran, and Sarah Oliver, "Tariff Liberalization," in *Trans-Pacific Partnership: An Assessment*, ed. Cathleen Cimino-Isaacs and Jeffrey J. Schott, Policy Analyses in International Economics 104 (Washington, D.C.: Peterson Institute for International Economics, 2016).

105. Based on my own experience as a visiting scholar at RIETI in summer 2009.

106. Emphasis added. From policy speech by Prime Minister Naoto Kan at the 176th Extraordinary Session of the Diet, October 1, 2010, http://japan.kantei.go.jp /kan/statement/201010/01syosin_e.html.

107. Sugawara assesses that, in addition to the APEC agenda, Prime Minister Kan wanted (a) to improve the shaky U.S.-Japan relationship after the mishandling of the Futenma base issue by the DPJ, (b) to energize Japan's stagnant FTA strategy in East Asia, and (c) to provide "shock therapy" for the recessionary Japanese economy in the aftermath of the global financial crisis. See Sugawara, "Nihon no TPP sanka mondai."

108. See Naoi and Urata, "Free Trade Agreements and Domestic Politics," for an excellent analysis of how the agricultural opposition shapes the TPP discussion in Japan."

109. For the Medical Association, the technology-intensive medicine dominant in the U.S. medical sector would jeopardize the small independent medical facilities that predominate in Japan's health care. Meanwhile, the insurance industry feared that owing to Japan's relatively closed insurance market, particularly dominated by Postal Life Insurance, it would become the target of liberalization pressure.

110. Takashi Terada, "Higashi ajia FTA no domino ron to domino teishi ron" (Domino theory and firewall theory on East Asia's FTA), in *Henyō suru ajia to nichibei kankei* [Evolution of Asia and U.S.-Japan relations], ed. Yasuhiro Arikawa et al. (Tokyo: Toyo Keizai Shinposha, 2012).

111. All the statements are listed on the Keidanren website, https://www.keidanren.or.jp /policy/index10.html (accessed October 5, 2015).

112. Richard Baldwin argues that there has been a shift in the need for global governance of trade and investment since the 1990s, from a regime where "I will keep my market open if you keep yours open" to one of "I will offshore my factories and technologies if you assure my tangible and intangible assets are protected." See Baldwin, "WTO 2.0: Global Governance of Supply-Chain Trade," *Policy Insight* 64 (2012).

113. Junji Nakagawa, "Mega FTA no jidai: sono haikei to Nihon no tsūshō seisaku no kadai (Era of mega FTA: Its background and issues for Japan's trade policy)," *Kokusai mondai*, no. 632 (June 2014): 1–4.

114. Masayoshi Honma, "The TPP and Agricultural Reform in Japan," in *The Political Economy of Japanese Trade Policy*, ed. Aurelia George Mulgan and Masayoshi Honma (Hampshire, UK: Palgrave Macmillan, 2015), 111–12.

115. Shigeru Kanda and Yusuke Terabayashi, "TPP kosho no keii to kousho 21 bunya no gaiyo (tokushu tsuujo senkyo gono shuyo seisaku kadai 2)" (Details of TPP negotiation

and overview of 21 fields in the negotiation [special edition: major policy issues after the general election 2]), *Rippo to chosa* 346 (2013): 3–34.

116. The TPP required six countries with a total economic weight of over 85 percent of the TPP's GDP to ratify before the agreement could come into effect. In other words, both the United States and Japan had to ratify the agreement before there could be any hope of implementation.

117. These six are Mexico, Japan, Singapore, Canada, New Zealand, and Australia. The eleven TPP members represent nearly 500 million people and 13.5 percent of global GDP, or about $10 trillion, and CPTPP should generate an additional $147 billion in global income.

118. Takashi Terada, "Japan and TPP/TPP-11: Opening Black Box of Domestic Political Alignment for Proactive Economic Diplomacy in Face of 'Trump Shock,'" *Pacific Review* (2019): 1–29.

119. See Aurelia G. Mulgan, "CPTPP a Boost for Japan's Regional Trade Leadership," *East Asia Forum*, February 27, 2018, http://www.eastasiaforum.org/2018/02/27/cptpp -a-boost-for-japans-regional-trade-leadership/.

120. This proposal was presented and endorsed by APEC members in 2016 at the Lima leaders' meeting.

121. On how Prime Minister Abe and the LDP managed to do so at the time of the 2014 Lower House elections, see Saori N. Katada and Scott Wilbur, "Japan's Stealth Decision 2014: The Trans-Pacific Partnership," in *Japan Decides 2014: The Japanese General Election*, ed. Robert J. Pekkanen, Steven R. Reed, and Ethan Scheiner (London: Palgrave Macmillan, 2015).

6. Money and Finance

1. It is sometimes difficult to distinguish between monetary and financial issues. In this chapter I categorize macroeconomic issues, such as currency and foreign exchange related developments, as monetary and currency policies, while micro issues such as capital flows and capital market development are considered financial policies. Because these issues are closely connected, it is appropriate to discuss them as a set.

2. The three megabank groups are Mizuho Financial Group, Mitsubishi UFJ Financial Group, and Sumitomo Mitsui Baking Corporation.

3. Barry Eichengreen, *Exorbitant Privilege: The Rise and Fall of the Dollar and the Future of the International Monetary System* (New York: Oxford University Press, 2011); Jonathan Kirshner, *Currency and Coercion: The Political Economy of International Monetary Power* (Princeton, N.J.: Princeton University Press, 1997); Eswar S. Prasad, *The Dollar Trap: How the US Dollar Tightened Its Grip on Global Finance* (Princeton, N.J.: Princeton University Press, 2015).

4. Timothy J. Sinclair, *The New Masters of Capital: American Bond Rating Agencies and the Politics of Creditworthiness* (Ithaca, N.Y.: Cornell University Press, 2014).

5. The managing directors of the IMF have traditionally come from Europe.

6. Robert Wade, "Japan, the World Bank, and the Art of Paradigm Maintenance: The East Asian Miracle in Political Perspective," *New Left Review*, no. 217 (1996): 3–37; Jeffrey M. Chwieroth, "Testing and Measuring the Role of Ideas: The Case of Neoliberalism in the International Monetary Fund," *International Studies Quarterly* 51, no. 1 (2007): 5–30.

7. John Williamson, "What Washington Means by Policy Reform," in *Latin American Adjustment: How Much Has Happened*, ed. John Williamson (Washington, D.C.: Institute for International Economics, 1990).

8. Eric Helleiner, *States and the Reemergence of Global Finance: From Bretton Woods to the 1990s* (Ithaca, N.Y.: Cornell University Press, 1996), chap. 7.

9. The original concept of financial repression was introduced by Ronald McKinnon. See McKinnon, *Money and Capital in Economic Development* (Washington, D.C.: Brookings Institution Press, 2010 [1973]). Hugh Patrick defines financial repression as government policy where "low interest rate policies reduce the cost of funds to investors and the return to savers. . . . Credit rents—the difference between ceiling interest rates and market interest rates—are created and allocated among direct and indirect participants. The credit allocation process accordingly becomes distorted by political factors, personalistic considerations, rent-seeking behavior, and corruption. To maintain the system, entry has to be limited, competition among financial institutions and financial instruments constrained, and capital outflows to foreign countries restricted." See Patrick, *The Relevance of Japanese Finance and Its Main Bank System*, ed. Masahiko Aoki and Hugh Patrick (New York: Oxford University Press, 1994), 374–75. On bank dominance, see Robert Wade and Frank Veneroso, "The East Asian Crash and the Wall Street–IMF Complex," *New Left Review*, no. 228 (1998): 3–23.

10. Masaru Yoshitomi and Kenichi Ohno, "Capital-Account Crisis and Credit Contraction: The New Nature of Crisis Requires New Policy Responses," *ADBI Working Paper Series* No. 2 (1999), https://www.adb.org/sites/default/files/publication/157213/adbi-rp2.pdf; Robert Wade, "The Asian Debt-and-Development Crisis of 1997–?: Causes and Consequences," *World Development* 26, no. 8 (1998): 1535–53; Yong Wook Lee, "Japan and the Asian Monetary Fund: An Identity–Intention Approach," *International Studies Quarterly* 50, no. 2 (2006): 339–66.

11. Richard Higgott, "The Asian Economic Crisis: A Study in the Politics of Resentment," *New Political Economy* 3, no. 3 (1998): 333–56.

12. William W. Grimes, *Currency and Contest in East Asia: The Great Power Politics of Financial Regionalism*, Cornell Studies in Money (Ithaca, N.Y.: Cornell University Press, 2009); Douglas Webber, "Two Funerals and a Wedding? The Ups and Downs of Regionalism in East Asia and Asia-Pacific After the Asian Crisis," *Pacific Review* 14, no. 3 (2001): 339–72; Michael Wesley, "The Asian Crisis and the Adequacy of Regional Institutions," *Contemporary Southeast Asia* 21, no. 1 (1999): 54–73.

13. John Kirton, "Toward Multilateral Reform: The G20's Contribution," in *Reforming from the Top: A Leaders' 20 Summit*, ed. John English, Ramesh Thakur, and Andrew F. Cooper (Hong Kong: United Nations University Press, 2005); Saori N. Katada, "Balancing Act: Japan's Strategy in Global and Regional Financial Governance," in

A Leaders 20 Summit: Why, How, Who and When?, ed. John English, Ramesh Thakur, and Andrew F. Cooper (Tokyo: United Nations University Press, 2005).

14. The first proposal for establishing the New International Financial Architecture emerged in the aftermath of the Mexican peso crisis of 1994–1995. See Peter B. Kenen, *The International Financial Architecture: What's New? What's Missing?* (Washington, D.C.: Institute for International Economics, 2001). For the post–Asian financial crisis international architecture reform ideas, see Barry J. Eichengreen, *Toward a New International Financial Architecture: A Practical Post-Asia Agenda* (Washington, D.C.: Peterson Institute Press, 1999).

15. Saori N. Katada, *Banking on Stability: Japan and the Cross-Pacific Dynamics of International Financial Crisis Management* (Ann Arbor: University of Michigan Press, 2001).

16. Andrew Walter, *Governing Finance: East Asia's Adoption of International Standards* (Ithaca, N.Y.: Cornell University Press, 2008); Natasha Hamilton-Hart, "Monetary Politics in Southeast Asia: External Imbalances in Regional Context," *New Political Economy* 19, no. 6 (2014): 872–94; Joshua Aizenman and Jaewoo Lee, "Financial Versus Monetary Mercantilism: Long-Run View of Large International Reserves Hoarding," *World Economy* 31, no. 5 (2008): 593–611.

17. Edward Steinfeld, "The Capitalist Embrace: China Ten Years After the Asian Financial Crisis," in *Crisis as Catalyst: Asia's Dynamic Political Economy*, ed. Andrew MacIntyre, T. J. Pempel, and John Ravenhill (Ithaca, N.Y.: Cornell University Press, 2008).

18. Some (e.g., Ben Bernanke) argued that the savings glut on the part of many Asian exporting economies created the source of the financial crisis. See Ben S. Bernanke, "The Global Saving Glut and the US Current Account Deficit," remarks at the Sandridge Lecture, Virginia Association of Economists, Richmond, Virginia, 2005, http://www.federalreserve.gov/boardDocs/Speeches/2005/200503102/default.htm.

19. Analysis of the global financial crisis, or the great recession, is not within the scope of this study. There are many interesting books on the topic, for example, Barry Eichengreen, *Hall of Mirrors: The Great Depression, the Great Recession, and the Uses—and Misuses—of History* (New York: Oxford University Press, 2014); Martin Wolf, *The Shifts and the Shocks: What We've Learned—and Have Still to Learn—from the Financial Crisis* (London: Penguin, 2014).

20. Peter Knaack and Saori N. Katada, "Fault Lines and Issue Linkages at the G20: New Challenges for Global Economic Governance," *Global Policy* 4, no. 3 (2013): 236–46.

21. Cynthia A. Roberts, Leslie Elliott Armijo, and Saori N. Katada, *The BRICS and Collective Financial Statecraft* (New York: Oxford University Press, 2017).

22. Grimes, *Currency and Contest in East Asia*; Giancarlo Corsetti, Paolo Pesenti, and Nouriel Roubini, "What Caused the Asian Currency and Financial Crisis?," *Japan and the World Economy* 11, no. 3 (1999): 305–73.

23. William W. Grimes, "Internationalization of the Yen and the New Politics of Monetary Insulation," in *Monetary Orders: Ambiguous Economics, Ubiquitous Politics*, ed. Jonathan Kirshner (Ithaca, N.Y.: Cornell University Press, 2003); Barry Eichengreen, "The Parallel-Currency Approach to Asian Monetary Integration," *American Economic Review* 96, no. 2 (2006): 432–36; William W. Grimes, "East Asian Financial Regionalism in

Support of the Global Financial Architecture? The Political Economy of Regional Nesting," *Journal of East Asian Studies* 6, no. 3 (2006): 353–80; Saori N. Katada, "From a Supporter to a Challenger? Japan's Currency Leadership in Dollar-Dominated East Asia," *Review of International Political Economy* 15, no. 3 (2008): 399–417. A similar concern regarding Asia's overdependence on the dollar and the now shaky macro-economic foundation of this currency in the aftermath of the global financial crisis led the governor of the People's Bank of China, Zhou Xiaochuan, in March 2009 to call for a reform of international monetary system toward less reliance on the dollar and more on the synthetic global currency, such as the Special Drawing Rights (SDRs) of the IMF. The text of his famous speech is available at the BIS website, http://www.bis.org/review/r090402c.pdf.

24. Yongding Yu, "The Current RMB Exchange Rate Volatility and RMB Internationalization," *International Economic Review* 1 (2012): 18–26; Prasad, *The Dollar Trap*.

25. Robert Wade, "The First-World Debt Crisis of 2007–2010 in Global Perspective," *Challenge* 51, no. 4 (2008): 23–54.

26. Roberts, Armijo, and Katada, *The BRICS*.

27. Roberts, Armijo, and Katada, *The BRICS*, 86–87; Ilene Grabel, "Not Your Grandfather's IMF: Global Crisis, 'Productive Incoherence' and Developmental Policy Space," *Cambridge Journal of Economics* 35, no. 5 (2011): 805–30.

28. C. Randall Henning, *Tangled Governance: International Regime Complexity, the Troika, and the Euro Crisis* (New York: Oxford University Press, 2017).

29. Saori N. Katada, "Seeking a Place for East Asian Regionalism: Challenges and Opportunities Under the Global Financial Crisis," *Pacific Review* 24, no. 3 (2011): 273–90.

30. For example, R. Taggart Murphy, *The Weight of the Yen: How Denial Imperils America's Future and Ruins an Alliance* (New York: Norton, 1997); Daniel Burstein, *Yen! Japan's New Financial Empire and Its Threat to America* (New York: Fawcett Columbine, 1990).

31. Yoshiko Kojo, *Keizaiteki sōgo izon to kokka: Kokusai shūshi fukinkū zesei no seiji keizaigaku* (Economic interdependence and nations: Political economy of correcting the balance of payments imbalances) (Tokyo: Bokutaku Sha, 1996).

32. There are many excellent works on Japan's foreign exchange rate politics, for example, Paul Volcker and Toyoo Gyohten, *Changing Fortunes: The World's Money and the Threat to American Leadership* (New York: Crown, 1992); Yoichi Funabashi, *Managing the Dollar: From the Plaza to the Louvre* (Washington, D.C.: Institute for International Economics, 1989); Ronald I. McKinnon and Kenichi Ohno, *Dollar and Yen: Resolving Economic Conflict Between the United States and Japan* (Cambridge, Mass.: MIT Press, 1997); Kojo, *Keizaiteki sōgo izon to kokka*.

33. Gene Park et al., *Taming Japan's Deflation: The Debate Over Unconventional Monetary Policy* (Ithaca, N.Y.: Cornell University Press, 2018), chap. 4.

34. Katada, *Banking on Stability*.

35. Ming Wan called it Japan's "spending strategy." See Wan, "Spending Strategies in World Politics: How Japan Has Used Its Economic Power in the Past Decade," *International Studies Quarterly* 39, no. 1 (1995): 85–108.

36. Domestically, the Bank of Japan kept its loose monetary policy to induce depreciation of the yen in the latter half of the 1980s. This led to the expansion of Japan's
bubble economy. See Yoshiko Kojo, "Baburu keisei/hōkai no haikei to shiteno Nichibei keizai kankei" (Japan-U.S. economic relationship as a context of developing and
collapsing bubble economy), in *Heisei baburu no kenkyū gekan* (Study on heisei bubble
economy, vol. 2), ed. Michio Muramatsu and Masahiro Okuno (Tokyo: Toyo Keizai
Shinposha 2002).

37. *Banker* published a ranking of international banks based on bank assets. In 1985 Dai-
Ichi Kangyo Bank, Fuji Bank, Sumitomo Bank, Mitsubishi Bank, and Sanwa Bank
(Japan) made the top-ten list. In 1995 (at the height of the *yen-daka*), Japanese banks
occupied seven spots, with Sakura Bank and Norinchukin Bank added to the 1985
list. For a detailed analysis of the rise of Japan's financial power, see Masahiko Takeda
and Philip Turner, "The Liberalisation of Japan's Financial Markets: Some Major
Themes," *BIS Economic Papers No. 34* (1992), https://www.bis.org/publ/econ34.pdf.

38. See Jeffrey Frankel's prize-winning analysis of the topic, in which he argues that
although there was a slight uptick in the yen's influence in the region's invoicing due
to private-sector activities, there was no evidence of the Japanese government deliberately increasing use of the yen and creating a yen bloc in Asia. Frankel, "Is a Yen
Bloc Forming in Pacific Asia?," in *Finance and the International Economy: 5*, ed. Richard O'Brien (Oxford: Oxford University Press, 1991).

39. This increase reflects changes in Southeast Asian import items, often denominated
in U.S. dollars, from mostly natural resources to manufactured goods during this
period.

40. George S. Tavlas, "Currency Substitution and the International Demand for Yen,"
in *The Macroeconomics of International Currencies: Theory, Policy and Evidence*, ed. Paul
Mizen and Eric J. Pentecost (Cheltenham, UK: Edward Elgar, 1996).

41. Katada, "From a Supporter to a Challenger?"

42. Haruhiko Kuroda, *Tsūka gaikō: Zaimukan no 1300 nichi* (Currency diplomacy: 1,300
days of vice minister of financial affairs) (Tokyo: Toyo Keizai Shinposha, 2005).

43. C. Randall Henning and Saori N. Katada, "Cooperation Without Institutions: The
Case of East Asian Currency Arrangement," in *Asian Designs: Governance in the Contemporary World Order*, ed. Saadia M. Pekkanen (Ithaca, N.Y.: Cornell University Press,
2017).

44. The BOJ during this time had limited policy independence from the Ministry of
Finance. Every other BOJ governor (five-year terms) came from the MOF, and much
of its monetary policy was made in close coordination with the MOF. The BOJ
obtained more political independence in 1998 with the new BOJ law.

45. Shintaro Hamanaka, "Asian Financial Cooperation in the 1990s: The Politics of Membership," *Journal of East Asian Studies* 11, no. 1 (2011): 75–103. The original members
of the EMEAP were Japan, South Korea, Indonesia, Malaysia, Singapore, the Philippines, Thailand, Australia, and New Zealand. China (1992) and Hong Kong (1993)
joined later. Governor Fraser of the Australian Central Bank called in 1995 to elevate
the EMEAP as the BIS for Asia. Hamanaka argues that the reason this meeting started

out as very low profile and technical was to not make the noninclusion of the United States appear conspicuous.

46. Hamanaka, "Asian Financial Cooperation in the 1990s"; William W. Grimes, "The Rise of Financial Cooperation in Asia," in *The Oxford Handbook of the International Relations of Asia*, ed. Saadia M. Pekkanen, John Ravenhill, and Rosemary Foot (New York: Oxford University Press, 2014). Masuyuki Tadokoro argues that until the Asian financial crisis, Japan's financial authority focused on global forums such as the G7, IMF, and BIS as the center of activities and thus did not pay much attention to Asia's financial matters. See Tadokoro, "Ajia ni okeru chiiki tsūka kyōryoku no tenkai" (Development of regional currency cooperation in Asia), in *Nihon no Higashi Ajia kousou* (Japan's East Asia framework), ed. Yoshihide Soeya and Masayuki Tadokoro (Tokyo: Keio Gijuku Shuppankai, 2004), 116. My interviews with the MOF and MOFA at the time of the crisis also suggested that these officials did not even know who their counterparts in the finance ministries and central banks in East Asian governments were, and thus they did not know whom to call to discuss the matter.

47. Walter Hatch and Kozo Yamamura, *Asia in Japan's Embrace: Building a Regional Production Alliance* (Cambridge: Cambridge University Press, 1996).

48. In 1988 close to 45 percent of all initial foreign direct investment by Japanese companies was funded by Japanese banks. See MITI, *Kigyō jigyō katsudō kihon chōsa* (https://www.meti.go.jp/statistics/tyo/kaigaizi/index.html.

49. Unlike the "roadmap" laid out by Balassa on European regional integration, the progress of regional financial cooperation seems to have been more coherent and faster than trade and investment integration, as discussed in chapter 5. See Heribert Dieter and Richard Higgott, "Exploring Alternative Theories of Economic Regionalism: From Trade to Finance in Asian Co-operation?," *Review of International Political Economy* 10, no. 3 (2003): 430–54.

50. Grimes, *Currency and Contest in East Asia*, 69.

51. Takashi Terada argues that shock of the Asian financial crisis and antagonism against the IMF and global financial "mafia" helped Japan to spearhead financial regionalism efforts during this decade. See Terada, "Constructing an 'East Asian' Concept and Growing Regional Identity: From EAEC to ASEAN+3," *Pacific Review* 16, no. 2 (2003): 251–77.

52. Yoshitomi and Ohno, "Capital-Account Crisis and Credit Contraction"; Takatoshi Ito, "Growth, Crisis, and the Future of Economic Recovery in East Asia," *Rethinking the East Asian Miracle* (2001); Grimes, *Currency and Contest in East Asia*.

53. Anthony Rowley, "Asian Bond Market Plan Faces Hurdles," *Business Times*, Singapore, January 20, 2003.

54. Stephan Haggard, *The Political Economy of the Asian Financial Crisis* (Washington, D.C.: Institute for International Economics, 2000); Graciela L. Kaminsky and Carmen M. Reinhart, "The Twin Crises: The Causes of Banking and Balance-of-Payments Problems," *American Economic Review* 89, no. 3 (1999): 473–500.

55. Grimes, *Currency and Contest in East Asia*, 177.

56. Some argue that there was a dynamics of competitive devaluation among the economies facing the crisis, where once a competitor country devalues its currency, a

country also has to devalue in order to match its foreign exchange advantage. See Reuven Glick and Andrew K. Rose, "Contagion and Trade: Why Are Currency Crises Regional?," *Journal of International Money and Finance* 18, no. 4 (1999): 603–17.

57. Haruhiko Kuroda and Masahiro Kawai, "Strengthening Regional Financial Cooperation in East Asia," in *Financial Governance in East Asia: Policy Dialogue, Surveillance and Cooperation*, ed. Gordon De Brouwer and Yunjong Wang (London: Routledge Curzon, 2004), 21.

58. Grimes argues that the most important reason for the Japanese government's interest in internationalizing its currency at this juncture was to install insulation from such volatility. See Grimes, "Internationalization of the Yen."

59. C. H. Kwan, *En to gen kara miru Ajia no tsūka kiki* (The Asian currency crisis seen from the yen and the yuan) (Tokyo: Iwanami Shoten, 1997).

60. Shinji Takagi, *Conquering the Fear of Freedom: Japanese Exchange Rate Policy Since 1945* (Oxford: Oxford University Press, 2015), chap. 5.

61. Wesley, "The Asian Crisis." An MOF official mentioned in an interview that during the crisis it took some time for MOF officials to figure out whom to call to discuss the situation.

62. The Clinton administration did not think at the time that the Thai crisis was that serious, and it was constrained by having lost access to emergency funds as the result of the financial rescue it conducted for the Mexican peso crisis (1994–1995).

63. For Thailand, the Japanese government provided $4 billion bilaterally out of a $15.2 billion rescue package, while for Indonesia, it provided $10 billion out of more than $34.2 billion. South Korea's package (more than $58 billion) included a $21 billion contribution from Japan. See Masayuki Tadokoro, "Ajia ni okeru chiiki tsūka kyōryoku no tenkai" (Development of regional currency cooperation in Asia), in *Nihon no Higashi Ajia kousou* (Japan's East Asia framework), ed. Yoshihide Soeya and Masayuki Tadokoro (Tokyo: Keio Gijuku Shuppankai, 2004), 118.

64. In October 1998 the government extended larger financial support through the "New Miyazawa Initiative," with a total of $30 billion dollars in both short- and medium-term lending and credit guarantees to the six crisis-affected Asian countries of Thailand, Malaysia, Indonesia, the Philippines, South Korea, and Vietnam. See Katada, *Banking on Stability*; Jennifer A. Amyx, "Moving Beyond Bilateralism? Japan and the Asian Monetary Fund," *Pacific Economic Papers* 331 (2002), https://openresearch -repository.anu.edu.au/bitstream/1885/40431/3/pep-331.pdf.

65. Rodney Bruce Hall, "The Discursive Demolition of the Asian Development Model," *International Studies Quarterly* 47, no. 1 (2003): 71–99; Lee, "Japan and the Asian Monetary Fund."

66. Wade, "Japan, the World Bank, and the Art of Paradigm Maintenance."

67. Jennifer Amyx argues that the reason behind the Chinese reluctance was not so much China's rivalry with Japan as that the Japanese MOF approached China through the Hong Kong Monetary Authority, a misstep that antagonized the Chinese financial authorities. See Amyx, "What Motivates Regional Financial Cooperation in East Asia Today?," *AsiaPacific Issues* 76 (2005): 1–8.

68. Hatch and Yamamura, *Asia in Japan's Embrace*.

69. Gregory W. Noble and John Ravenhill, *The Asian Financial Crisis and the Architecture of Global Finance* (Cambridge: Cambridge University Press, 2000); T. J. Pempel, *The Politics of the Asian Economic Crisis*, Cornell Studies in Political Economy (Ithaca, N.Y.: Cornell University Press, 1999); Haggard, *The Political Economy of the Asian Financial Crisis.*

70. Jennifer A. Amyx, *Japan's Financial Crisis: Institutional Rigidity and Reluctant Change* (Princeton, N.J.: Princeton University Press, 2004); William W. Grimes, *Unmaking the Japanese Miracle: Macroeconomic Politics, 1985–2000* (Ithaca, N.Y.: Cornell University Press, 2002); Edward J. Lincoln, *Arthritic Japan: The Slow Pace of Economic Reform* (Washington, D.C.: Brookings Institution Press, 2004). For the entire list of 171 bank failures from 1991 through 2001, see the Deposit Insurance Corporation of Japan's website, https://www.dic.go.jp/katsudo/chosa/yohokenkyu/200509-4/4-9-1.html.

71. Tetsuro Toya and Jennifer A. Amyx, *The Political Economy of the Japanese Financial Big Bang: Institutional Change in Finance and Public Policymaking* (Oxford: Oxford University Press, 2006); Takagi, *Conquering the Fear of Freedom.*

72. Takatoshi Ito and Michael Melvin, "Japan's Big Bang and the Transformation of Financial Markets," *National Bureau of Economic Research Working Paper* No. 7247 (1999), https://www.nber.org/papers/w7247.

73. Council on Foreign Exchange and Other Transactions, "Internationalization of the Yen for the 21st Century: Japan's Response to Changes in Global Economic and Financial Environments," 1999, 1–2, http://www.mof.go.jp/english/if/elb064a.htm. This council and its subcouncil on the internationalization of the yen were given a mandate by the MOF to provide recommendations regarding the issue.

74. Park et al., *Taming Japan's Deflation.*

75. This is discussed further in chapter 7. The JBIC succeeded the Japan Export Import Bank, which was established in 1950. It changed its name to JBIC as it absorbed the Overseas Economic Cooperation Fund in 1999, but this OECF function was once again separated from it in 2008 when the JBIC was absorbed under the Japan Finance Corporation (JFC). (OECF, "Issues Related to the World Bank's Approach to Structural Adjustment: Proposal from a Major Partner," *OECF Occasional Paper* No. 1.) In 2012 the JBIC separated from the JFC as a joint stock company under the JBIC Law. NEXI was established under MITI as a system of trade insurance in 1950, but it became an incorporated administrative agency separate from MITI in 2001. The original JICA was established in 1974 as an agency to implement technical assistance as a part of Japan's economic cooperation. After absorbing the OECF function in 2008, the New JICA has become the largest foreign aid agency in the world, implementing economic cooperation in both loans and grants as well as technical cooperation.

76. Terada, "Constructing an 'East Asian' Concept."

77. Mitsuru Yaguchi, Ayako Yamaguchi, and Koji Sakuma, "Integration of Financial Markets in Japan and Asia—Financial Deepening in Asia Due to Japanese Banks' Entry," *Public Policy Review* 14, no. 5 (2018): 835–70.

78. Masahiro Kawai and Shinji Takagi, "Why Was Japan Hit So Hard by the Global Financial Crisis?," *ADBI Working Paper Series* No. 153 (2009), https://www.adb.org/sites/default/files/publication/156008/adbi-wp153.pdf.; Saori N. Katada, "Financial

Crisis Fatigue? Politics Behind Japan's Post–Global Financial Crisis Economic Contraction," *Japanese Journal of Political Science* 14, no. 2 (2013): 223–42.

79. Park et al., *Taming Japan's Deflation*, chap. 7. A $1 trillion carry-trade reversal also contributed to the yen appreciation.

80. Carol Wise, Leslie Elliott Armijo, and Saori N. Katada, *Unexpected Outcomes: How Emerging Economies Survived the Global Financial Crisis* (Washington, D.C.: Brookings Institution Press, 2015); Roberts, Armijo, and Katada, *The BRICS*.

81. William W. Grimes, "East Asian Financial Regionalism: Why Economic Enhancements Undermine Political Sustainability," *Contemporary Politics* 21, no. 2 (2015): 145–60.

82. In 2012 the CMIM agreed to double its available funding from $120 billion to $240 billion (effective in 2014).

83. The overall amount of the early phase of CMI was close to the original AMF proposal. But a country like the Philippines actually has access to only $9.5 billion in bilateral swaps. See Grimes, *Currency and Contest in East Asia*, 85–87.

84. Point 6 of the Joint Ministerial Statement of the Tenth ASEAN+3 Finance Ministers Meeting, http://www.mof.go.jp/english/if/as3_070505.htm, accessed November 15, 2007.

85. William W. Grimes, "The Future of Regional Liquidity Arrangements in East Asia: Lessons from the Global Financial Crisis," *Pacific Review* 24, no. 3 (2011): 291–310; Daniel McDowell, "The US as 'Sovereign International Last-Resort Lender': The Fed's Currency Swap Programme During the Great Panic of 2007–09," *New Political Economy* 17, no. 2 (2012): 157–78. Takatoshi Ito suggests that South Korea and other Asian preferred the currency swaps by the Federal Reserve because they were "quick, unlimited safety net without policy reform conditions," unlike the IMF or IMF-linked CMI. The power of Fed swaps was very impressive as they immediately stopped a sharp depreciation of their currencies. See Ito, "A New Financial Order in Asia: Will a RMB Bloc Emerge?," *Journal of International Money and Finance* 74 (2017): 232–57.

86. Kaewkamol Pitakdumrongkit, "Co-chairing International Negotiations: The Case of the Chiang Mai Initiative Multilateralization," *Pacific Review* 28, no. 4 (2015): 577–605. The Chinese contribution included the Hong Kong portion.

87. John D. Ciorciari, "Chiang Mai Initiative Multilateralization," *Asian Survey* 51, no. 5 (2011): 926–52.

88. See point 9 from the summary of the statement at the Twelfth ASEAN+3 Finance Ministers Meeting, Bali, Indonesia, May 3, 2009.

89. Masahiro Kawai and Cindy Houser, "Evolving ASEAN+3 ERPD: Towards Peer Reviews or Due Diligence?," *ADBI Discussion Paper* No. 79 (2007), https://www.adb.org/sites/default/files/publication/156718/adbi-dp79.pdf.

90. Chalongphob Sussangkarn, "Chiang Mai Initiative Multilateralization: Origin, Development, and Outlook," *Asian Economic Policy Review* 6, no. 2 (2011): 203–20.

91. For a thorough history of AMRO from its establishment to international organization, see Akkharaphol Chabchitrchaidol, Satoshi Nakagawa, and Yoichi Nemoto, "Quest for Financial Stability in East Asia: Establishment of an Independent

Surveillance Unit 'AMRO' and Its Future Challenges," *Public Policy Review* 14, no. 5 (2018): 1001–24.

92. A Japanese official close to AMRO noted that it and the IMF share the same objective of sound monetary and financial health of the Asian economies. The only difference is the way in which such an objective is achieved: the IMF through condemnation and public humiliation, and AMRO through quiet consultation and peer pressure (interview June 2015).

93. Steven Liao and Daniel McDowell, "Redback Rising: China's Bilateral Swap Agreements and Renminbi Internationalization," *International Studies Quarterly* 59, no. 3 (2015): 401–22; Grimes, "East Asian Financial Regionalism"; Yang Jiang, "The Limits of China's Monetary Diplomacy," in *The Great Wall of Money: Power and Politics in China's International Monetary Relations*, ed. Eric Helleiner and Jonathan Kirshner (Ithaca, N.Y.: Cornell University Press, 2014). Since 2013 the People's Bank of China added nine more countries to the list of bilateral currency swap agreements to bring the total to thirty-four by the end of 2015.

94. These are in addition to the agreements that Japan developed with China and South Korea in the context of the previous CMI. These currency swap agreements concluded by the Japanese government have gone through major ups and downs. With South Korea, after expanding the swap ceiling to the U.S. dollar equivalent of $70 billion in the aftermath of the global financial crisis in 2011, the agreement was phased out in 2015 following the diplomatic cooling between the two countries. With China, the tension after Japan's nationalization of the Senkaku/Diaoyutai Islands triggered the suspension of the agreement in 2013. In 2015 discussions to restart the swap agreements with both governments resumed among the finance ministries and central banks (*Nihon keizai shimbun*, January 14, 2016).

95. Renewed interest between Japan and China led the two governments to conclude a $30 billion currency swap agreement in October 2018, while the one between Japan and South Korea has not been revived at the time of writing (late 2019).

96. *Asahi shimbun*, October 7, 2017.

97. See Satoshi Shimizu "Development of Asian Bond Markets and Challenges: Keys to Market Expansion," *Public Policy Review* 14, no. 5 (September 2018): 958. Robert McCauley adds that as many East Asian governments began to accumulate foreign exchange reserves in order to be better prepared for balance-of-payments challenges in the future, a government's bond issuance has become an apt way to sterilize the holding of these large foreign exchange reserves. See McCauley, "Unifying Government Bond Markets in East Asia," *BIS Quarterly Review* (December 2003), https://www.bis.org/publ/qtrpdf/r_qto312h.pdf.

98. In 2013 capital flow within Asia constituted 15 percent of bank debt, 25 percent of equity, and 50 percent of FDI (Asian Development Bank, 2014).

99. Eric Chan et al., "Local Currency Bond Markets and the Asian Bond Fund 2 Initiative," *BIS Paper*, no. 63f (2012). The ABF2 consisted of two parts: one was the Pan Asian Bond Index Fund (PAIF), created to promote the development of index bond funds in Asian markets. This single bond index fund started with $1 billion and targeted investment in local currency denominated bonds in the eight EMEAP

member economies. See Dilip K. Das, "Evolving Domestic Bond Markets and Financial Deepening in Asia," *Global Economy Journal* 14, no. 1 (2014): 89–112. The PAIF has been managed by a private firm, State Street Global Advisors, and has done quite well since its inception in 2005; by its ten-year anniversary in 2015, it had expanded to $3 billion. The second component was a country-specific subfund under which $1 billion was to be invested in local currency–denominated bonds that the eight EMEAP governments have issued. Das (96) argues that the ABF2 was successful for three reasons: maturity rates of bond issuance grew quickly; market-making activity developed; and entry barriers for nonresident investors lowered progressively for the eight Asian markets.

100. Grimes, "East Asian Financial Regionalism," 363–64.

101. The first local-currency JBIC bond (30 million baht) was issued in Thailand in August 2005. Several credit guarantees were extended, including to Tri Petch Isuzu Co. (2004; Thailand), ORIX Leasing Malaysia Berhad (2006; Malaysia), and P. T. Summit Oto Finance (2006; Indonesia). Fumio Hoshi, *Ajia no Saiken shijō Ikusei ni muketa kokusai kyōryoku ginkō no Torikumi* (JBIC efforts to nurture Asian bond market), ed. Nihon Keizai Chosa Kyogkai, Chochikuritsu no teika; IS balansu no henkato Nihonkeizai: Shikin no Koritsu unyo to Kinyu sābisugyō no Kokusai kyosoryoku, 2006. The first case of recertification of the CBO in 2004 was with South Korea to fund the CBO with 7.7 billion yen using the corporate bonds of forty-six small and medium enterprises as collateral. Both the Indonesian and the Philippine governments issued Samurai bonds using the fourth scheme, totaling 255 billion yen. See Chang Rong Lu, "Zaimushō shudō no Nihon seifu ni yoru ASEAN+3 chiiki kinyu kyōryoku seisaku ni kansuru kōsatsu" (A study of the Japanese government's policy on ASEAN+3 financial cooperation led by the Ministry of Finance) (Ph.D. dissertation, Waseda University, 2015).

102. Lu, "Zaimushō shudō," chap. 4.

103. Grimes, *Currency and Contest in East Asia*, 179.

104. See Asian Bonds Online, https://asianbondsonline.adb.org/index.php.

105. Das, "Evolving Domestic Bond Markets," 94.

106. China and Japan contributed the same amount ($200 million each), while all other ASEAN+3 members and the ADB provided the rest. See the CGIF website, http://www.cgif-abmi.org/about/contributors.

107. ASEAN+3 Bond Market Forum (ABMF) website, https://wpqr4.adb.org/LotusQuickr/asean3abmf/Main.nsf/h_Toc/6464E9705AC986D8482577A4001763BE/?OpenDocument.

108. Kengo Mizuno, "Ajia saiken shijō inishiachibu (ABMI) no shinten to kadai" (Progress and issues related to Asian Bond Markets Initiative), in *Ajia ikinai kinyū kyōryoku saikou: shinten to kadai* (Revisiting intra-Asian financial cooperation: Perspectives and issues], ed. Chie Kashiwagara (Tokyo: Institute of Development Economies, 2012).

109. The Samurai bond is a yen-denominated bond issued in Tokyo by nonresident (i.e., non-Japanese) entities. In February 2019 the Malaysian government successfully raised ¥200 billion ($1.85 billion) in such bonds in Tokyo toward the country's fiscal reconstruction.

110. Former prime minister Yasuhiro Nakasone (2009) argued strongly in support of Asian currency, as did the prime minister and DPJ leader at that time, Yukio Hatoyama. See Yasuhiro Nakasone, "Kyōtsū tsūka ga hiraku Nihon to Ajia no mirai" (The future of Japan and Asia with a common currency), *Chuo koron* 124, no. 4 (2009): 182–93; Yukio Hatoyama, "My Political Philosophy," *Voice* (September 2009).

111. Xinhua Net, November 16, 2008.

112. SDR is a unit of account maintained by the IMF that uses the weighted average of the U.S. dollar, euro, pound sterling, and yen. For the political motives of Governor Zhou's announcement on the day preceding the G20 London Summit, see Gregory Chin and Yong Wang, "Debating the International Currency System: What's in a Speech," *China Security* 6, no. 1 (2010): 3–20.

113. The use of the yen as a foreign exchange reserve currency declined from 5.3 percent in 1996 to 4.1 percent in 2001 and 2.6 percent in 2005 (IMF). The invoice currency for Japanese trade with Southeast Asia remained flat between 1998 and 2005 at around 48 percent for Japanese exports to the region and 27 percent for Japanese imports (Japanese Ministry of Finance).

114. Katada, "From a Supporter to a Challenger?"

115. Companies in Japan have tended to invoice in the currency of the final destination of their export products. See Toru Iwami, "The Internationalization of Yen and Key Currency Questions," *IMF Working Paper* WP/94/41 (1994), https://www.imf.org/en/Publications/WP/Issues/2016/12/30/The-Internationalization-of-Yen-and-Key-Currency-Questions-1130.

116. Saori N. Katada, "Can China Internationalize the RMB? Lessons from Japan," *Foreign Affairs*, Snapshot, January 1, 2018.

117. Robert A. Mundell, "A Theory of Optimum Currency Areas," *American Economic Review* 51, no. 4 (1961): 657–65. East Asia compared reasonably favorably to Europe on the OCA criteria, based on economic indicators such as degree of economic diversification, openness, intraregional trade, labor and capital mobility, and response to common shocks. Even before the interest in post-AFC monetary integration heightened, Tamim Bayoumi and Barry Eichengreen had concluded that nine East Asian countries would meet the economic criteria for an OCA. A more recent review of the literature analyzing the feasibility of East Asian monetary integration by Shingo Watanabe and Masanobu Ogura notes that the majority (twelve out of fourteen) of those studies identified some groups of countries within East Asia as meeting the conditions. The major economic obstacles to the OCA, as often argued, are the different levels of economic development and lack of convergence in income per capita. See Bayoumi and Eichengreen, "Exchange Rate Volatility and Intervention: Implications of the Theory of Optimum Currency Areas," *Journal of International Economics* 45, no. 2 (1998): 191–209; Watanabe and Ogura, "How Far Apart Are Two ACUs from Each Other? Asian Currency Unit and Asian Currency Union," *Bank of Japan Working Paper Series* 06-E-20 (2006), https://www.boj.or.jp/en/research/wps_rev/wps_2006/data/wp06e20.pdf.

118. Benjamin Cohen notes that one way for a region to overcome the weight of the dollar is to "hang together." See Cohen, *The Future of Money* (Princeton, N.J.: Princeton University Press, 2004), chap. 5.

119. Institute for International Monetary Affairs (IIMA), "Report Summary of Studies on Towards a Regional Financial Architecture for East Asia" (2004), http://www.mof.go.jp/jouhou/kokkin/ASEAN+3research-1-1.pdf.

120. Henning and Katada, "Cooperation Without Institutions."

121. As of 2014 it is reported that China's foreign exchange reserves had reached US$4 trillion, though there has been a significant drop in the latter half of 2015. Other Asian countries such as Japan (US$1.3 trillion) and South Korea (US$350 billion) also top the list of countries with large foreign exchange reserves.

122. Eiji Ogawa and Junko Shimizu, "Progress Toward a Common Currency Basket System in East Asia," *RIETI Discussion Paper Series* 07-E-002 (2007): 1–22; Eiji Ogawa, "Currency Basket Strategy for Asian Currency Cooperation," *Financial Review* 81 (2006): 154–76; Eiji Ogawa and Michiru Sakane Kosaka, "Japan's Monetary and Financial Cooperation in East Asia—from the Viewpoint of the Spillover Effects of Currency Misalignment," *Public Policy Review* 10, no. 1 (2014): 33–52; Masahiro Kawai, "Asian Monetary Integration: A Japanese Perspective," *ADBI Working Paper Series* 475 (2014), https://www.adb.org/sites/default/files/publication/156330/adbi-wp475.pdf. While academic promoters such as Eiji Ogawa and Masahiro Kawai are independent academics, their research is contracted by RIETI (a METI-affiliated think tank) or the Policy Research Institute (an MOF-affiliated think tank). In addition, the Asian Development Bank Institute (ADBI), established in Tokyo in the late 1990s, is financially supported by the MOF.

123. High network effect emerges when the marginal utility of joining an activity increases with the total number of participating actors, while barriers to entry represent hindrances to alternative forms of cooperation. See Phillip Y. Lipscy, *Renegotiating the World Order: Institutional Change in International Relations* (New York: Cambridge University Press, 2017), 28.

124. Benjamin J. Cohen, *Currency Power: Understanding Monetary Rivalry* (Princeton, N.J.: Princeton University Press, 2018).

125. Ming Zhang, "Internationalization of the Renminbi: Developments, Problems and Influences," in *Global Financial Governance Confronts the Rising Powers: Emerging Perspectives on the New G20*, ed. C. Randall Henning and Andrew Walter (Montreal: McGill-Queen's Press, 2016). A comprehensive discussion on RMB internationalization is beyond the scope of this book. For some useful discussion, see Eswar S. Prasad, *Gaining Currency: The Rise of the Renminbi* (New York: Oxford University Press, 2017).

126. It is worthwhile noting that the first round of Japan's support for RMB use came under the Democratic Party of Japan's rule from September 2009 through December 2012. In addition to the well-known "East Asian Community" idea promoted by the DPJ's first prime minister, Hatoyama, the party tried (not very successfully) to balance its U.S. dependence with improved relations in Northeast Asia. Such efforts ended with rising tensions over the Senkaku Island disputes since September 2012 and were perpetuated with the DPJ's loss against the LDP in December 2012 elections.

127. Barry Eichengreen and Masahiro Kawai, "Issues for Renminbi Internationalization: An Overview," *ADBI Working Paper Series* 454 (2014), https://think-asia.org/handle/11540/1216.

128. Prasad, *Gaining Currency*, 113.

129. *China Daily* reported the announcement by China's State Administration of Foreign Exchange on January 26, 2017, http://www.chinadaily.com.cn/business/2017-01/26 /content_28059625.htm.

130. Hyoung-kyu Chey, "The International Politics of Reactive Currency Statecraft: Japan's Reaction to the Rise of the Chinese Renminbi," *New Political Economy* 24, no. 4 (2019): 510–29. Japanese nonfinancial corporations, especially small and medium firms, are not using the RMB to settle their trade with China despite the high volume of trade between the two countries. SWIFT estimates that the use of the RMB in Japan's trade with both mainland China and Hong Kong fluctuated from 3.1 percent in 2013 to 3.9 percent in 2014. This low rate then improved, with China's push, RMB use in Japan's trade with China rose to 6.9 percent in 2015.

131. Asiamoney, "Offshore RMB Poll 2017: Results," https://www.euromoney.com /article/b13fh6lljxyjfd/asiamoney-offshore-rmb-poll-2017-results#overall.

132. Satoshi Shimizu, "Advancing RMB Internationalization and Its Prospect: In Relation to Liberalization of Capital Transaction," *RIM Pacific Rim Business Information* 15, no. 57 (2015): 106.

7. Development and Foreign Aid

1. This chapter generally follows the OECD convention in using the terms "foreign aid" and "ODA" with respect to the Development Assistance Committee definition: "flows of official financing administered with the promotion of the economic development and welfare of developing countries as the main objective, and which are concessional in character with a grant element of at least 25 percent (using a fixed 10 percent rate of discount). By convention, ODA flows comprise contributions of donor government agencies, at all levels, to developing countries ('bilateral ODA') and to multilateral institutions. ODA receipts comprise disbursements by bilateral donors and multilateral institutions" (http://www.oecd.org/dac/stats/officialdevelopmentassistancedefinitio nandcoverage.htm#Definition; also IMF, External Debt Statistics). Meanwhile, terms such as "economic cooperation," "development cooperation," and the finance term referred to as "Other Official Flows" (OOF) often cover broader activities in support of economic development that do not satisfy at least one of the ODA conditions. Some emerging donors, such as China, do not apply the OECD/DAC criteria to their economic cooperation activities.

2. Emma Mawdsley, Laura Savage, and Sung-Mi Kim, "A 'Post-Aid World'? Paradigm Shift in Foreign Aid and Development Cooperation at the 2011 Busan High Level Forum," *Geographical Journal* 180, no. 1 (2014): 27–38; Nilima Gulrajani, "Transcending the Great Foreign Aid Debate: Managerialism, Radicalism and the Search for Aid Effectiveness," *Third World Quarterly* 32, no. 2 (2011): 199–216. Mawdsley et al. call this consensus in the 2000s the "Paris Agenda" or "aid effectiveness paradigm" led by

the OECD. Such an emphasis demonstrates the donors' struggle with their own legitimacy crisis and the influence of civil society organizations.

3. Ngaire Woods, "The Shifting Politics of Foreign Aid," *International Affairs* 81, no. 2 (2005): 393–409; Julie Gilson, "Building Peace or Following the Leader? Japan's Peace Consolidation Diplomacy," *Pacific Affairs* 80, no. 1 (2007): 27–47.

4. Gregory Chin and Yong Wang, "Debating the International Currency System: What's in a Speech," *China Security* 6, no. 1 (2010): 3–20.

5. World Bank, *World Development Report 1994: Infrastructure for Development* (New York: Oxford University Press, 1994).

6. Moisés Naím, "Rogue Aid," *Foreign Policy*, no. 159 (2007): 96–97.

7. The BRI is the updated English version of the name. In Chinese and Japanese, it still referred to as "One-belt-one-road."

8. Carol Lancaster, *Foreign Aid: Diplomacy, Development, Domestic Politics* (Chicago: University of Chicago Press, 2007), chap. 2.

9. Jean-Philippe Thérien, "Debating Foreign Aid: Right Versus Left," *Third World Quarterly* 23, no. 3 (2002): 449–66; Martha Finnemore, *National Interests in International Society*, Cornell Studies in Political Economy (Ithaca, N.Y.: Cornell University Press, 1996); Gregory T. Chin, "China as a 'Net Donor': Tracking Dollars and Sense," *Cambridge Review of International Affairs* 25, no. 4 (2012): 579–603.

10. Christopher Humphrey, "Developmental Revolution or Bretton Woods Revisited? The Prospects of the BRICS New Development Bank and the Asian Infrastructure Investment Bank," *ODI Working Paper* 418 (2015): 1–35.

11. John Williamson, "What Washington Means by Policy Reform," in *Latin American Adjustment: How Much Has Happened*, ed. John Williamson (Washington, D.C.: Institute for International Economics, 1990); Lancaster, *Foreign Aid*.

12. The UN MDGs comprise eight specific goals: (1) eradicate extreme poverty and hunger; (2) achieve universal primary education; (3) promote gender equality and empower women; (4) reduce child mortality; (5) improve maternal health; (6) combat HIV/AIDS, malaria, and other diseases; (7) ensure environmental sustainability; and (8) develop a global partnership for development. UN Millennium Goals, http://www.un.org/millenniumgoals/.

13. Remarks by George W. Bush at the International Conference on Financing for Development, Monterrey, Mexico, March 22, 2002, http://www.un.org/ffd/statements/usaE.htm.

14. Barbara Stallings and Eun Mee Kim, *Promoting Development: The Political Economy of East Asian Foreign Aid* (Singapore: Palgrave Macmillan, 2017), 119–22.

15. Because China is not an OECD/DAC member and its foreign aid definitions and numbers are not transparent, these estimates range widely. See Naohiro Kitano and Yukinori Harada, "Estimating China's Foreign Aid 2001–2013," *JICA Research Institute Working Paper Series* 78 (2014), https://www.jica.go.jp/jica-ri/publication/workingpaper/jrft3q00000025no-att/JICA-RI_WP_No.78_2014.pdf.

16. Deborah Bräutigam, "Aid 'with Chinese Characteristics': Chinese Foreign Aid and Development Finance Meet the OECD-DAC Aid Regime," *Journal of International*

Development 23, no. 5 (2011): 752–64; Jian-Ye Wang, "What Drives China's Growing Role in Africa?," *IMF Working Paper* No. 07/211 (2007), https://www.imf.org/en /Publications/WP/Issues/2016/12/31/What-Drives-Chinas-Growing-Role-in -Africa-21282; *Financial Times*, "China's Lending Hits New Heights," January 17, 2011. https://www.ft.com/content/488c60f4-2281-11e0-b6a2-00144feab49a.

17. Naím criticizes Beijing using "this cash to ensure its access to raw materials while also boosting international alliances that advanced China's growing global influence." Bräutigam, on the other hand, refers to China's turn-key based infrastructure aid and its modality as "aid with Chinese characteristics." See Naím, "Rogue Aid"; Bräutigam, "Aid 'with Chinese Characteristics.'"

18. Axel Dreher, Peter Nunnenkamp, and Rainer Thiele, "Are 'New' Donors Different? Comparing the Allocation of Bilateral Aid between Non-DAC and DAC Donor Countries," *World Development* 39, no. 11 (2011): 1950–68; Richard Manning, "Will 'Emerging Donors' Change the Face of International Co-operation?," *Development Policy Review* 24, no. 4 (2006): 371–85; Kangho Park, "New Development Partners and a Global Development Partnership," in *Catalyzing Development: A New Vision for Aid*, ed. Homi Kharas, Koji Makino, and Woojin Jung (Washington, D.C.: Brookings Institution Press, 2011).

19. Ngaire Woods, "Whose Aid? Whose Influence? China, Emerging Donors and the Silent Revolution in Development Assistance," *International Affairs* 84, no. 6 (2008): 1205–21.

20. Felix Zimmermann and Kimberly Smith, "More Actors, More Money, More Ideas for International Development Co-operation," *Journal of International Development* 23, no. 5 (2011): 722–38.

21. Mawdsley, Savage, and Kim, "A 'Post-Aid World'?," 30.

22. The entire list of goals and targets is available at the United Nations website, "Transforming Our World: The 2030 Agenda for Sustainable Development," https:// sustainabledevelopment.un.org/post2015/transformingourworld.

23. Homi Kharas and Julie Biau, "New Actors, New Instruments, New Priorities: Toward a Sustainable Development Transformation," in *Japan's Development Assistance: Foreign Aid and the Post-2015 Agenda*, ed. Hiroshi Kato, John Page, and Yasutani Shimomura (London: Palgrave Macmillan, 2016), 315.

24. Cynthia A. Roberts, Leslie Elliott Armijo, and Saori N. Katada, *The BRICS and Collective Financial Statecraft* (New York: Oxford University Press, 2017).

25. Yoshiaki Abe and Shigeo Katsu, "The World Bank and Japan," in *Japan's Development Assistance: Foreign Aid and the Post-2015 Agenda*, ed. Hiroshi Kato, John Page, and Yasutani Shimomura (London: Palgrave Macmillan, 2016), 255–59.

26. Asia here includes South, Central, Southeast, and Northeast Asia, as well as Oceania. The largest aid recipient countries historically were Indonesia and China (from the 1980s until 2008), while Vietnam and India have topped the list in recent years.

27. Sukehiro Hasegawa, *Japanese Foreign Aid: Policy and Practice* (New York: Praeger, 1975); Hiroshi Kato, "Japan's ODA 1954–2014: Changes and Continuities in a Central Instrument in Japan's Foreign Policy," in *Japan's Development Assistance: Foreign Aid and*

the Post-2015 Agenda, ed. Hiroshi Kato, John Page, and Yasutami Shimomura (London: Palgrave Macmillan, 2016); Saori N. Katada, "Japan's Foreign Aid after the San Francisco Peace Treaty," *Journal of American-East Asian Relations* 9, no. 3 (2000): 197–220; Yoko Yoshikawa, *Nippi baishō gaikō kōshō no kenkyū: 1949–1956* (A study of Japan-Philippines diplomatic negotiation on reparations between 1949 and 1956) (Tokyo: Keiso Shobo, 1991).

28. Sueo Sudo, *The Fukuda Doctrine and ASEAN: New Dimensions in Japanese Foreign Policy* (Singapore: Institute of Southeast Asian Studies, 1992); Shigeko Hayashi, *Japan and East Asian Monetary Regionalism: Towards a Proactive Leadership Role?* (London: Routledge, 2006).

29. Hayashi, *Japan and East Asian Monetary Regionalism*; Dennis T. Yasutomo, *Japan and the Asian Development Bank* (Santa Barbara, Calif.: Praeger, 1983). The Economic Commission for Asia and the Far East (currently the Economic and Social Commission for Asia and the Pacific) first proposed the ADB idea in 1960. See Kiyoshi Kodera, "Japan's Engagement with Multilateral Development Banks: Do Their Professional Paths Really Cross?," in *Japan's Development Assistance: Foreign Aid and the Post-2015 Agenda*, ed. Hiroshi Kato, John Page, and Yasutani Shimomura (London: Palgrave Macmillan, 2016), 21–22. Shintaro Hamanaka argues that the ADB has dual origins, proposed by both Japan and ECAFE. See Hamanaka, *Asian Regionalism and Japan: The Politics of Membership in Regional Diplomatic, Financial and Trade Groups* (London: Routledge, 2009).

30. Ming Wan, "Japan and the Asian Development Bank," *Pacific Affairs* 68, no. 4 (1995): 509–28. Most of the ADB loans were extended on a market-rate basis and hence are not counted toward ODA. The ADB, however, houses the Asian Development Fund, established in 1973, and has provided low-interest rate loans to the least developed countries in the region.

31. David Arase, *Buying Power: The Political Economy of Japan's Foreign Aid* (Boulder, Colo.: Lynne Rienner, 1995), 223.

32. Margee M. Ensign, *Doing Good or Doing Well? Japan's Foreign Aid Program* (New York: Columbia University Press, 1992); Arase, *Buying Power*.

33. OECD, *Development Co-Operation: Efforts and Policies of the Members of the Development Assistance Committee* (Paris: Organisation for Economic Co-operation and Development, 1988).

34. Historically the Japanese government allocated from one-fourth to one-third of its ODA to multilateral organizations (e.g., United Nations and MDBs), with the rest going to bilateral channels.

35. OECF, "Issues Related to the World Bank's Approach to Structural Adjustment: Proposal from a Major Partner," *OECF Occasional Paper* No. 1 (1991).

36. Robert Wade, "Japan, the World Bank, and the Art of Paradigm Maintenance: The East Asian Miracle in Political Perspective," *New Left Review*, no. 217 (1996): 3–37; World Bank, *The East Asian Miracle: Economic Growth and Public Policy* (New York: Oxford University Press, 1993).

37. Toshio Watanabe and Yuji Miura, *ODA (seifu kaihatsu enjo) Nihon ni naniga dekiruka* (ODA (official development assistance): What can Japan do?), vol. 1727 (Tokyo:

Chuo-shinsho, 2003); Akira Nishigaki, Yasutami Shimomura, and·Kazuto Tsuji, *Kaihasu enjo no keizaigaku—"kyōsei no sekai" to Nihon no ODA* (Economics of development assistance—"world of harmonious coexistence" and Japan's ODA) (Tokyo: Yuhikaku, 2011), 178–90.

38. Walter Hatch, *Asia's Flying Geese: How Regionalization Shapes Japan* (Ithaca, N.Y.: Cornell University Press, 2010), 211–14.

39. Yong Wook Lee, *The Japanese Challenge to the American Neoliberal World Order: Identity, Meaning, and Foreign Policy* (Stanford, Calif.: Stanford University Press, 2008); Kenichi Ohno, *Japanese Views on Economic Development: Diverse Paths to the Market* (Abingdon, UK: Routledge, 2012); Stallings and Kim, *Promoting Development.*

40. Steven Hall, "Managing Tied Aid Competition: Domestic Politics, Credible Threats, and the Helsinki Disciplines," *Review of International Political Economy* 18, no. 5 (2011): 646–72. Tied aid credits, as defined by the OECD, are "official or officially supported loans, credits, or associated financing packages where procurement of the goods or services involved is limited to the donor country or to a group of countries which does not include substantially all developing countries (or Central and Eastern European Countries (CEECs)/New Independent States (NIS) in transition)" (http://stats .oecd.org/glossary/detail.asp?ID=3089). It is widely known that tied aid increases the cost of a project by 15 to 30 percent, and that the lack of transparency has bred corruption and inefficiency. See Catrinus J. Jempa, *The Tying of Aid* (Paris: OECD Development Centre, 1991).

41. The UK aid agency became independent of its foreign ministry in 1997 and has pursued poverty eradication as its first priority by law since 2002.

42. Note that grant aid contracted to Japanese entities is not considered tied. See Sayuri Shirai, *Makuro kaihatsu keizaigaku—Taigai enjo no shinchōryū* (Macro development economics—recent trends in foreign aid) (Tokyo: Yuhikaku, 2005); Yuji Miura, *Keizai renkeika no enjo seisaku—ASEAN niokeru kyōsō to shien no baransu* (Foreign aid policy under economic cooperation—the balance of competition and aid in ASEAN), Gurobarizashon kano Ajia to Nihon no yakuwari (Tokyo: JICA Research Institute, 2006).

43. Lancaster, *Foreign Aid*, 139.

44. Tomoko Fujisaki et al., "Japan as Top Donor: The Challenge of Implementing Software Aid Policy," *Pacific Affairs* 69, no. 4 (1996): 519–39; Masahiro Kawai and Shinji Takagi, "Japan's Official Development Assistance: Recent Issues and Future Directions," *Journal of International Development* 16, no. 2 (2004): 255–80.

45. Kawai and Takagi, "Japan's Official Development Assistance."

46. John E. Ray, *Managing Official Export Credits: The Quest for a Global Regime* (Washington, D.C.: Institute for International Economics, 1995); Hall, "Managing Tied Aid Competition."

47. There are two major funding sources, one set up by MOFA in 1989 ("subsidy funds for NGO projects" and "grant assistance for grassroots projects" and, since 2001, additional funding assistance for NGO capacity building), and the other set up by the Ministry of Posts and Telecommunication in 1991 ("volunteer postal savings international aid"). The latter, however, has declined dramatically since the mid-1990s,

from ¥25 million in 1995 to merely ¥1 million in 2004. On the expansion of aid, see Kim Reimann, "The Outside In? Japanese International Development NGOs, the State, and International Norms," in *The State of Civil Society in Japan*, ed. Frank J. Schwartz and Susan J. Pharr (Cambridge: Cambridge University Press 2003), 303. Furthermore, between 2000 and 2004 the grassroots grants provided by MOFA doubled in size.

48. MOFA and NGOs emphasized the importance of transparency in these dialogue meetings. All minutes from the meetings are posted on the MOFA website, http://www.mofa.go.jp/mofaj/gaiko/oda/index/kaikaku/oda_ngo.html.

49. Lee, *The Japanese Challenge*; Lancaster, *Foreign Aid*, 122.

50. Yasunobu Okabe, "Japan Overseas Cooperation Volunteers: Its Genesis and Development," in *Japan's Development Assistance: Foreign Aid and the Post-2015 Agenda*, ed. Hiroshi Kato, John Page, and Yasutani Shimomura (London: Palgrave Macmillan, 2016), 233.

51. Makoto Imada and Robert Pekkanen discuss how the Kobe earthquake of 1995 enhanced the public appeal of civil society organizations overall. See Imada, "The Voluntary Response to the Hanshin Awaji Earthquake: A Trigger for the Development of the Voluntary and Non-Profit Sector in Japan," in *The Voluntary and Non-Profit Sector in Japan: The Challenge of Change*, ed. Stephen P. Osborne, Nissan Institute/RoutledgeCurzon Japanese Studies Series (New York: Routledge, 2003); Pekkanen, "Japan's New Politics: The Case of the NPO Law," *Journal of Japanese Studies* 26, no. 1 (2000): 111–48. See also Keiko Hirata, *Civil Society in Japan: The Growing Role of NGOs in Tokyo's Aid and Development Policy* (London: Palgrave Macmillan, 2002).

52. Steven W. Hook and Guang Zhang, "Japan's Aid Policy Since the Cold War," *Asian Survey* 38, no. 1 (1998): 1051–66; Saori N. Katada, "Japan's Two-Track Aid Approach: The Forces Behind Competing Triads," *Asian Survey* 42, no. 2 (2002): 320–42. See also Alan Rix's seminal institutional analysis of Japan's foreign aid, *Japan's Aid Program: A New Global Agenda* (Sydney: Australian Government Publishing Service, 1990).

53. Almost half of the funds for Japanese foreign aid originated from FILP, with the remaining half coming from the general accounting budget of the central government. Following the FILP reforms of 2000, postal savings no longer flow directly into government coffers to replenish the MOF trust fund, as these savings are now invested directly in the market. At the same time, the new Post Savings Bank is obligated by law to absorb the bulk of FILP bonds, which is the current source of yen loans. See Nishigaki, Shimomura, and Tsuji, *Kaihasu enjo no keizaigaku*, 191.

54. Kawai and Takagi argue that these ministries have uncoordinated views and different aid motives. See Kawai and Takagi, "Japan's Official Development Assistance," 262.

55. For details on how Japan's ODA contributed to building a regional production alliance between Japan and Asia, see Walter Hatch and Kozo Yamamura, *Asia in Japan's Embrace: Building a Regional Production Alliance* (Cambridge: Cambridge University Press, 1996), 115–29.

56. MITI's Economic Cooperation Committee in February 1996.

57. See Daniel Okimoto on the importance of various ministries in their impacts on Japan's trade policy formation. He discusses how MOFA did not have a domestic support base. There has been a continual discussion, though not a very realistic one, on abolishing MOFA because most of Japan's foreign economic policies have been conducted by MOF and MITI, not MOFA. Daniel I. Okimoto, "Political Inclusivity: The Domestic Structure of Trade," in *The Political Economy of Japan*, ed. Takashi Inoguchi and Daniel Okimoto (Stanford, Calif.: Stanford University Press, 1988).

58. According to Ming Wan, despite Japan's massive contribution to the ADB, Japan "talked" less, "received" less, and "weighted" less, especially relative to its power that grew in the 1980s. See Wan, "Spending Strategies in World Politics: How Japan has Used its Economic Power in the Past Decade," *International Studies Quarterly* 39, no. 1 (1995): 85–108.

59. MOF press release, March 23, 1999, https://www.mof.go.jp/english/international_policy/mdbs/adb/19990323.htm.

60. Kuroda was the International Finance Bureau chief during the time of the Asian financial crisis and became MOF vice minister of finance for international affairs (*zaimukan*) in July 1999 (following Eisuke Sakakibara). Kuroda retired from the MOF in early 2003. He stepped down from the position of ADB president in March 2013 to take the position of governor of the Bank of Japan.

61. Christopher M. Dent, "The Asian Development Bank and Developmental Regionalism in East Asia," *Third World Quarterly* 29, no. 4 (2008): 767–86.

62. Masahiro Kawai and Ganeshan Wignaraja, "ASEAN+3 or ASEAN+6: Which Way Forward?," *ADBI Discussion Paper* No. 77 (2007), https://www.adb.org/sites/default/files/publication/156716/adbi-dp77.pdf.

63. James Lynch, Alfredo Perdiguero, and Jason Rush, "The Role of ADB in ASEAN Integration," in *Economic Integration and Regional Development: The ASEAN Economic Community*, ed. Kiyoshi Kobayashi et al. (London: Routledge, 2017).

64. Dent, "The Asian Development Bank," 781.

65. Takashi Terada, "The Origins of ASEAN+6 and Japan's Initiatives: China's Rise and the Agent-Structure Analysis," *Pacific Review* 23, no. 1 (2010): 71–92.

66. Mie Oba, "The New Japan-ASEAN Partnership: Challenges in the Transformation of the Regional Context in East Asia," in *ASEAN-Japan Relations*, ed. Takashi Shiraishi and Takaaki Kojima (Singapore: ISEAS, 2014), 63.

67. Hidetaka Yoshimatsu, *Comparing Institution-Building in East Asia: Power Politics, Governance, and Critical Junctures* (Hampshire, UK: Palgrave Macmillan, 2014), 60.

68. Edward Lincoln argues that the new aid portion of the New Miyazawa Initiative was only $16 billion, and that the plan postponed the imminent decline of Japanese foreign aid. See Lincoln, "Japan: Using Power Narrowly," *Washington Quarterly* 27, no. 1 (2003): 111–27.

69. Part of Japan's declining net ODA number comes from increasing repayments of past yen loans. The MOF reported that in 2008 loan repayments from Asian countries were $1 billion more than that year's yen loan disbursements. With a gross disbursement of almost $20 billion in ODA in 2011, Japan would be ranked as the

second largest foreign aid donor in the world in gross ODA, after the United States.

70. One of the causes of the sagging domestic popularity of Japanese foreign aid emerged from a major scandal associated with LDP politician Muneo Suzuki in the early 2000s.

71. ODA Charter (Kyū seifu kaihatsu enjo taikō), 1992, available at http://www.mofa .go.jp/mofaj/gaiko/oda/seisaku/taikou/sei_1_1.html.

72. Lancaster, *Foreign Aid*, 130–131.

73. Kazuo Sunaga, "The Reshaping of Japan's Official Development Assistance (ODA) Charter," *FASID (Foundation for Advanced Studies on International Development) Discussion Paper on Development Assistance* 3 (2004): 1–31.

74. Stallings and Kim, *Promoting Development*, 39.

75. Sue Ellen Charlton, "Little Progress, Small Niches: The WID Mandate in Japanese Foreign Aid," in *Feminists Doing Development: A Practical Critique*, ed. Marilyn Porter and Ellen Judd (London: Zed Books, 1997).

76. Sadako Ogata and Johan Cels define the concept as "protecting people from severe and pervasive threats, both natural and societal, and empowering individuals and communities to develop the capacities for making informed choices and acting on their own behalf." See Ogata and Cels, "Human Security—Protecting and Empowering the People," *Global Governance* 9, no. 3 (2003): 273–82.

77. Caroline Thomas, "Global Governance, Development and Human Security: Exploring the Links," *Third World Quarterly* 22, no. 2 (2001): 159–75.

78. See Ministry of Foreign Affairs, "Chair's Summary, Friends of Human Security Meeting" (2006), https://www.mofa.go.jp/policy/human_secu/friends/summary0610 .html.

79. Peng Er Lam, *Japan's Peace-Building Diplomacy in Asia: Seeking a More Active Political Role* (London: Routledge, 2009); Gilson, "Building Peace or Following the Leader?"

80. The ODA Review (June 2010) is available at the MOFA website, https://www.mofa .go.jp/policy/oda/reform/index.html.

81. Development Cooperation Charter (February 2015), available at https://www.mofa .go.jp/policy/oda/page_000138.html.

82. Keidanren also called for the creation of an International Cooperation Agency in April 1997. Keiko Hirata argues that the Administrative Reform Council did not pursue the idea of an aid agency further because (a) it wanted to reduce the number of ministries and agencies, not add to them; (b) ODA involves too many ministries to achieve easy consolidation; and (c) the idea never became a priority in the council's deliberations. See Hirata, "New Challenges to Japan's Aid: An Analysis of Aid Policy-Making," *Pacific Affairs* 71, no. 3 (1998): 311–34.

83. The joint committee is headed by the cabinet secretary and includes the ministers of the three ministries included in the council plus three others: the minister of land, infrastructure, transport, and tourism; the minister for public management, home affairs, posts, and telecommunications; and the minster in charge of economic revitalization. See the organization chart on the MOFA site on ODA strategy, http:// www.mofa.go.jp/mofaj/gaiko/oda/about/keitai/taisei.html.

84. OECD, "OECD Development Assistance Peer Reviews: Japan 2010" (2011), https://www.oecd-ilibrary.org/development/oecd-development-assistance-peer-reviews-japan-2010_9789264098305-en.

85. Lee Poh Ping, "The Asian Financial Crisis: Understanding Japanese Assistance to Southeast Asia," *Kajian Malaysia* 20, no. 1 (2002): 33–55. Lancaster notes that this pressure applied by Japanese businesses to "retie" Japan's ODA proves the rule that there had indeed been untying of foreign aid in the 1990s, otherwise the business community would not have needed to exert such obvious pressure toward tying in this particular package. See Lancaster, *Foreign Aid*, 120.

86. Wade, "Japan, the World Bank, and the Art of Paradigm Maintenance"; Saori N. Katada, "Seeking a Place for East Asian Regionalism: Challenges and Opportunities Under the Global Financial Crisis," *Pacific Review* 24, no. 3 (2011): 273–90; Watanabe and Miura, *ODA (seifu kaihatsu enjo)*, 1727.

87. See the MOFA website, http://www.mofa.go.jp/region/asia-paci/idea0208-4.html.

88. OECD, "OECD Development Co-operation Peer Reviews: Japan 2014" (2014), http://www.oecd.org/dac/peer-reviews/Japan-peer-review-2014.pdf.

89. Yukiko Kuramoto, "Nihon no kaihatsu kyōryoku to kan min pātonā shippu" (Japan's development cooperation and its government-private sector partnership), *Chuo daigaku shakai kagaku kenkyujo nenpo* 21 (2017): 165–78.

90. The World Bank (2014) defines PPP as a "long-term contract between a private party and a government entity, for providing a public asset or service, in which the private party bears significant risk and management responsibility, and remuneration is linked to performance." See https://ppp.worldbank.org/public-private-partnership/overview/what-are-public-private-partnerships/.

91. Sunaga, "The Reshaping of Japan's Official Development Assistance (ODA) Charter," 7. For details and the list of projects that utilized STEP, see the JICA website, www.jica.go.jp/activities/schemes/finance_co/about/about.html.

92. Report from the Study Group on Asian PPP, April 2005, METI, 17 (translation by the author).

93. Ajia Infura Kenkyukai, *Ajia Infura Kenkyūkai Teigen: Infura PPP jigyō no suishin nimukete* (Proposal of Asia Infrastructure Study Group: How to promote infrastructure PPP projects) (Tokyo: Ministry of Land, Infrastructure, Transport, and Tourism, 2006).

94. JICA website (2013).

95. *Nihon keizai shimbun*, July 28, 2015.

96. METI, "PPP Tasukufosu Hokokusho" (PPP Task Force Report), 2010.

97. Megumi Muto and Koki Hirota, "Tonan Ajia niokeru Nihon no ODA no hensen to kadai: senpatsu ASEAN wo chūshin nishite" (Changes and challenges of Japan's ODA in Southeast Asia: Focused on forerunner ASEAN), in *Korekarano Nihon no kokusai kyōryoku: biggu dōnā kara sumāto dōnā he* (Future of Japan's international cooperation: From a big donor to a smart donor), ed. Takashi Kurosaki and Keijiro Otsuka (Tokyo: Nippon Hyoron sha, 2015), 45; Akira Ogiwara, "Kokusai kyosoryoku noaru pakkeiji gata infura jigyo no tenkai wo mezashite: PPP ni okeru kadai no kosatsu" (Developing the international competitiveness in the "Package of Overseas Infrastructure

Development"), *Collected Papers of the Research Center for PPP in Toyo University* 3 (2013): 80–101.

98. Toshiro Nishizawa, "Infrastructure Investment and Finance in Asia," *Public Policy Review* 14, no. 5 (2018): 925–53. Note explaining the concept on the World Bank website, "Public-Private Partnership in Infrastructure Resource Center" (https://ppp .worldbank.org/public-private-partnership/agreements/concessions-bots-dbos).

99. Yasuhiro Ezaki, "Ajia shinkōkoku infura bijinesu to Nihon kigyō no gurobaru risuku maneijimento taisei" (Infrastructure building business in Asia's emerging economies and the system of Japanese firms' global risk management), *Higashi Ajia hyouron* 8 (2016): 19–34.

100. Author interview with a former JICA expert, Tokyo, July 2016.

101. Muto and Hirota, "Tonan Ajia niokeru Nihon no ODA."

102. Hiroto Arakawa, "Ajia no infura gigyō: seisaku/seido zukuri no shien kagi" (Infrastructure projects in Asia: Policy and establishment of the system is the key), *Nihon keizai shimbun*, August 27, 2010.

103. For the full survey results, see *JBIC waga kuni seizō gyō no Kaigai jigyō tenkai ni kansuru chōsa hōkoku* (Survey report regarding the overseas business operations among Japan's manufacturing companies), https://www.jbic.go.jp/ja/information/press/press-2015 /1203-44372.html.

104. Hidemi Kimura and Yasuyuki Todo specifically note that the possible reasons for this vanguard effect are that foreign aid (a) provides information on the local business environment of the recipient countries that then gets transmitted to the donor country; (b) reduces the recipient country's investment risk as perceived by the firms; and (c) may introduce donor country-specific business practices, rules, and institutions into recipient countries. See Kimura and Todo, "Is Foreign Aid a Vanguard of Foreign Direct Investment? A Gravity-Equation Approach," *World Development* 38, no. 4 (2010): 482–97.

105. Yasuyuki Todo, "ODA to Nihon kigyō no kokusaika: Nihon to hienjo koku no aid-ani uin-uin no kankei wo kizuku" (ODA and internationalization of Japanese businesses: How to create a win-win relationship between Japan and aid recipients), *Kokusai mondai* 616 (2012): 44–54.

106. Kozo Kagawa and Yuka Kaneko, *Houseibi Shien ron: Seidokouchiku no kokusai kyōryoku nyūmon* (Theory of legislation assistance: Introductory book of institution building in international cooperation) (Kyoto: Minerva Shobo, 2007).

107. China hosts an annual seminar on civil law matters with the ICCLC but does not participate in training programs. Following phase 1, phases 2 and 3 have expanded legal institutions in the counterpart countries while also regularizing seminars and legal training sessions. See Tsuyoshi Murayama, "Hōmushō hōmu sōgō kenkyūsho ni yoru hoseibi shien he no torikumi" (Efforts of Research and Training Institute of the Ministry of Justice to support legislation), *Keio hogaku* 5 (2006): 351–63.

108. Prospectus for the Establishment of ICCLC, http://www.icclc.or.jp/english /prospectus/.

109. With the country's democratic transition, Myanmar became an active participant in legal system development support after 2012.

110. Mitsubishi Research Institute, *Heisei 26 nendo Gaimusho ODA hyoka. Hoseido seibi shien no hyoka. (Daisansha hyoka) Hokokusho* (Appraisal of 2014 Japan's ODA. Appraisal report of legal institutional building assistance [by the third party]) (Tokyo: Mitsubishi Research Institute, 2015). However, the budget allocated to legal and judicial development among Asian countries has not been large. According to an evaluation report by the institute, a total of $58 million was spent on such activities among Asian countries. Meanwhile, based on Afghanistan reconstruction data, the Japanese government spent $508.92 million in that country alone on legal and judicial development.

111. Houseido Seibishien ni Kansuru Kihon Houshin (*kaiteiban*), May 2013, http://www.mofa.go.jp/mofaj/gaiko/oda/bunya/governance/hoshin_1305.html. Translated by the author.

112. Saori N. Katada and Jessica Liao, "China and Japan in Pursuit of Infrastructure Development Leadership: Competition or Convergence?," *Global Governance* 26, no. 3 (forthcoming September 2020); Marie Soderberg, *The Business of Japanese Foreign Aid: Five Cases from Asia* (New York: Routledge, 2012).

113. Tatsufumi Yamagata, "Sustainable Development Goals and Japan: Sustainability Overshadows Poverty Education," *Asia-Pacific Development Journal* 23, no. 2 (2016): 1–17.

114. Keiichi Tsunekawa, "Kaihatsu enjo" (Development assistance), in *Nihon no gaikō daigokan* (Fifth volume on Japanese diplomacy), ed. Toshikazu Inoue et al. (Tokyo: Iwanami Shoten, 2013).

115. Foreign aid from China and Japan also clashed in Africa, but that topic is beyond the scope of this book. See Bertha Z. Osei-Hwedie, "China-Japan Rivalry in Africa," in *Africa in the Age of Globalisation: Perceptions, Misperceptions and Realities*, ed. Edward Shizha and Lamine Diallo (Abingdon, UK: Routledge, 2016).

116. Yiping Huang, "Understanding China's Belt & Road Initiative: Motivation, Framework and Assessment," *China Economic Review* 40 (2016): 314–21.

117. In 2017 the ADB revised this estimate upward to $26 trillion dollars in the next fifteen years, or $1.7 trillion per year. Asian Development Bank, "Meeting Asia's Infrastructure Needs," https://www.adb.org/publications/asia-infrastructure-needs.

118. A $40-billion Silk Road Fund was also established in 2014 to support the BRI.

119. It is widely reported that the United States, which showed concern over the AIIB's challenge to the existing development finance structure dominated by the World Bank and Asian Development Bank, in which the United States has predominant influence, put pressure on Australia, South Korea, and Indonesia not to join the AIIB (*New York Times*, October 9, 2014).

120. Hidetaka Yoshimatsu, "Japan's Export of Infrastructure Systems: Pursuing Twin Goals Through Developmental Means," *Pacific Review* 30, no. 4 (2017): 494–512.

121. The four pillars are (a) expansion and acceleration of assistance through the full mobilization of Japan's economic cooperation tools; (b) collaboration between Japan and the ADB; (c) doubling the supply of funding for projects with relatively high-risk profiles through JBIC; and (d) promoting quality infrastructure investment as an international standard. See METI website, http://www.meti.go.jp/english/press/2015/0521_01.html.

122. "Follow-up Measures of 'the Partnership for Quality Infrastructure,'" announcement by Japanese government, November 2015, http://www.mofa.go.jp/mofaj/gaiko/oda/about/doukou/page23_000754.html

123. *Nihon keizai shimbun*, July 5, 2015.

124. Part of the reason, some argue, is the lack of capacity among the recipient governments to identify needs and provide logical support. *Nihon keizai shimbun*, August 24, 2015.

125. Interview with a foreign aid specialist in Japan, January 2016.

126. Hidetaka Yoshimatsu, "New Dynamics in Sino-Japanese Rivalry: Sustaining Infrastructure Development in Asia," *Journal of Contemporary China* 27, no. 113 (2018): 719–34.

127. The document on these five principles is available the MOFA website, https://www.mofa.go.jp/files/000196472.pdf.

128. *Japan Times*, June 25, 2019.

129. Peng Er Lam, "China's Asian Infrastructure Investment Bank: East Asian Responses," *East Asian Policy* 6, no. 4 (2014): 127–35.

130. The concerns focused especially on the AIIB's decision not to have a resident board. See, for example, Masahiro Kawai, "Asian Infrastructure Investment Bank in the Evolving International Financial Order," in *Asian Infrastructure Investment Bank: China as Responsible Stakeholder?*, ed. Daniel Bob (Washington, D.C.: Sasakawa Peace Foundation, 2015).

131. Katsuya Okada, the DPJ president, quoted in the *Asahi shimbun*, April 2, 2015.

132. Even so, experts from the World Bank and the United States have had a major impact in the formation of the AIIB governance structure, as many of them became AIIB advisors while China and the participating members shaped the bank's structure and agreements during this time. In addition, the Obama administration acquired a stronger incentive to lead the TPP negotiation to success, given the popularity of the AIIB.

133. Many of these reforms both at the ADB and in Japan were already put in place as early as 2013 (and hence not stimulated by the AIIB issue). But the speed at which they came about and the heightened interest in them since spring 2015 are undeniable.

134. Statement by President Jim Yong Kim of the World Bank Group on the establishment of AIIB, June 28, 2015, http://www.worldbank.org/en/news/press-release/2015/06/28/statement-by-world-bank-group-president-jim-yong-kim-on-the-establishment-of-aiib.

135. The AIIB uses a formula based on each member's relative economic share in terms of GDP to calculate the capital stock allocation, with 75 percent of capital stock allocated to regional countries while the remaining 25 percent goes to extraregional countries. If Japan were to participate (without the United States) with its capital subscription remaining the same ($100 billion) in total, its capital subscription would rise to about $10.6 billion, which would get Japan about 9.8 percent of voting share. Calculation based on the estimation made by Kawai recalculated with the total subscription kept at $100 billion. See Kawai, "Asian Infrastructure Investment Bank," 16.

136. Masato Kanda, "Infura shien ni tsuite" (About infrastructure aid), *Finance: Zaimusho kohoshi* 51, no. 4 (2015): 2–13.

137. It was reported that the U.S. government put pressure on Australia and South Korea in 2014 not to join the AIIB. See *New York Times*, October 9, 2014, https://www.nytimes.com/2014/10/10/world/asia/chinas-plan-for-regional-development-bank-runs-into-us-opposition.html.

138. Several interviews and MOFA website.

139. *Nihon keizai shimbun*, April 2, 2015.

140. This is mostly due to the fact that the Japanese companies' bids are too high.

141. Reported in *Nihon keizai shimbun*, May 11, 2015.

142. Presentation by Tetsuji Mukuda, managing director of Keidanren, at the LDP joint committee hearing on the AIIB, May 20, 2015.

143. Presentation by Keisuke Yokoo, managing director of the Japan Committee for Economic Development (Keizai Dōyū Kai), at the LDP joint committee hearing on the AIIB, May 20, 2015.

144. According to *Nihon keizai shimbun*, April 2, 2018, there has been a major delay in the construction of the Jakarta-Bandung Rail; as of 2018 only 10 percent of construction was completed.

145. Yoshimatsu, "New Dynamics in Sino-Japanese Rivalry."

146. Yoshimatsu, "Japan's Export of Infrastructure Systems," 499–500.

Conclusion

1. Michio Muramatsu and Ikuo Kume, *Nihon seiji hendō no 30 nen: Seijika/kanryō/dandaichosa nimiru kōzō henyō* (Thirty years of political changes in Japan: Structural transformation of politicians, bureaucrats, and organizational survey) (Tokyo: Toyo Keizai Shinposha, 2006).

2. Kent E. Calder and Min Ye, "Regionalism and Critical Junctures: Explaining the 'Organization Gap' in Northeast Asia," *Journal of East Asian Studies* 4, no. 2 (2004): 191–226.

3. Phillip Y. Lipscy, *Renegotiating the World Order: Institutional Change in International Relations* (New York: Cambridge University Press, 2017).

4. Karl Polanyi, *The Great Transformation* (Boston: Beacon Press, 1944).

5. Steven K. Vogel, *Marketcraft: How Governments Make Markets Work* (New York: Oxford University Press, 2018).

6. World Bank, *The East Asian Miracle: Economic Growth and Public Policy* (New York: Oxford University Press, 1993). See the debates in John Page, "The East Asian Miracle: Four Lessons for Development Policy," *NBER Macroeconomics Annual* 9 (1994): 219–69; Alice H. Amsden, "Why Isn't the Whole World Experimenting with the East Asian Model to Develop?: Review of the East Asian Miracle," *World Development* 22, no. 4 (1994): 627–33; Robert Wade, "Introduction to the 2003 Paperback Edition," in

Governing the Market: Economic Theory and the Role of Government in East Asian Industrialization (Princeton, N.J.: Princeton University Press, 2004).

7. Singapore is another, but given its very small size and very open economy, the nature of the transition is not the same as with other developmentalist economies.

8. Vogel, *Marketcraft*.

9. Interview with a METI official in charge of the division rule strategy office (*rurusenryaku-shitsu*) in June 2015.

10. Mark Beeson, "Developmental States in East Asia: A Comparison of the Japanese and Chinese Experiences," *Asian Perspective* 33, no. 2 (2009): 5–39; Seung-Wook Baek, "Does China Follow "the East Asian Development Model?," *Journal of Contemporary Asia* 35, no. 4 (2005): 485–98; Edith Terry, *How Asia Got Rich: Japan, China and the Asian Miracle* (Armonk, N.Y.: M. E. Sharpe, 2002).

11. In Japan, critics of the Abe administration's strategy call this phenomenon Sinicization (*chūgoku-ka*) of Japanese foreign economic policy. According to Peter Katzenstein, however, Sinicization means a much broader phenomenon of civilizational processes beyond changes in the style of foreign economic strategy. See Katzenstein, ed., *Sinicization and the Rise of China: Civilizational Processes Beyond East and West* (New York: Routledge, 2012), 9.

12. At the time of this writing (fall 2019), the Japanese government is in the middle of a trade war with South Korea as Japan restricted its exports of specific chemicals important for producing semiconductors to South Korea. This bilateral tension came about from one of the history disputes in relation to compensation for forced labor taken from Korea to Japan during the colonization. Some (e.g., Mieczysław Boduszynski and Gene Park) argue that this move could discredit Japan's credibility as a champion of free trade, while Japan's trade experts (e.g., Masahiko Hosokawa) argue that this trade measure was taken to address the lax management over South Korea's exports to the North of technology subject to security concerns guided by the WTO. See Boduszynski and Park, "Trade Tensions: Why Shinzo Abe Has a Critical Role to Play," *National Interest* (2019), https://nationalinterest.org/blog/korea-watch/trade-tensions-why-shinzo-abe-has-critical-role-play-67407; Hosokawa, "Zusan kanri taisho ha kokusai gimu" (Lax management: It is our international obligation to address it), *Nihon keizai shimbun*, 2019.

13. Although there were some prominent works published prior to 1997, the boom to examine regionalism in East Asia started with the Asian financial crisis. See, for example, Peter J. Katzenstein and Takashi Shiraishi, *Network Power: Japan and Asia* (Ithaca, N.Y.: Cornell University Press, 1997).

14. For example, Gilbert Rozman, *Northeast Asia's Stunted Regionalism: Bilateral Distrust in the Shadow of Globalization* (Cambridge: Cambridge University Press, 2004); Evelyn Goh, *The Struggle for Order: Hegemony, Hierarchy, and Transition in Post-Cold War East Asia* (Oxford: Oxford University Press, 2013); Kuniko Ashizawa, "Japan's Approach Toward Asian Regional Security: From 'Hub-and-Spoke' Bilateralism to 'Multi-tiered,'" *Pacific Review* 16, no. 3 (2003): 361–82; Saori N. Katada, "Seeking a Place for East Asian Regionalism: Challenges and Opportunities Under the Global

Financial Crisis," *Pacific Review* 24, no. 3 (2011): 273–90; Yul Sohn, "Japan's New Regionalism: China Shock, Values, and the East Asian Community," *Asian Survey* 50, no. 3 (2010): 497–519.

15. For example, Peter J. Katzenstein and Takashi Shiraishi, *Beyond Japan: The Dynamics of East Asian Regionalism* (Ithaca, N.Y.: Cornell University Press, 2006); Saadia Pekkanen, ed., *Asian Designs: Governance in the Contemporary World Order* (Ithaca, NY.: Cornell University Press, 2016); Vinod K. Aggarwal, *Institutional Designs for a Complex World: Bargaining, Linkages, and Nesting* (Ithaca, N.Y.: Cornell University Press, 1998); Gregory P. Corning, "Between Bilateralism and Regionalism in East Asia: The ASEAN–Japan Comprehensive Economic Partnership," *Pacific Review* 22, no. 5 (2009): 639–65; Shintaro Hamanaka, *Asian Regionalism and Japan: The Politics of Membership in Regional Diplomatic, Financial and Trade Groups* (London: Routledge, 2009); Richard Higgott and Richard Stubbs, "Competing Conceptions of Economic Regionalism: APEC Versus EAEC in the Asia Pacific," *Review of International Political Economy* 2, no. 3 (1995): 516–35; Keiichi Tsunekawa, "Why So Many Maps There? Japan and Regional Cooperation," in *Remapping East Asia: The Construction of a Region*, ed. T. J. Pempel (Ithaca, N.Y.: Cornell University Press, 2004); Amitav Acharya, *Whose Ideas Matter? Agency and Power in Asian Regionalism* (Ithaca, N.Y.: Cornell University Press, 2009).

16. For example, William W. Grimes, *Currency and Contest in East Asia: The Great Power Politics of Financial Regionalism*, Cornell Studies in Money (Ithaca, N.Y.: Cornell University Press, 2009); Christopher M. Dent, *New Free Trade Agreements in the Asia-Pacific* (New York: Palgrave Macmillan, 2006); Richard E. Baldwin, "Managing the Noodle Bowl: The Fragility of East Asian Regionalism," *Singapore Economic Review* 53, no. 3 (2008): 449–78; John D. Ciorciari, "Chiang Mai Initiative Multilateralization," *Asian Survey* 51, no. 5 (2011): 926–52; Natasha Hamilton-Hart, "Asia's New Regionalism: Government Capacity and Cooperation in the Western Pacific," *Review of International Political Economy* 10, no. 2 (2003): 222–45; Shigeko Hayashi, *Japan and East Asian Monetary Regionalism: Towards a Proactive Leadership Role?* (London: Routledge, 2006); John Ravenhill, "The 'New East Asian Regionalism': A Political Domino Effect," *Review of International Political Economy* 17, no. 2 (2010): 178–208; Chalongphob Sussangkarn, "Chiang Mai Initiative Multilateralization: Origin, Development, and Outlook," *Asian Economic Policy Review* 6, no. 2 (2011): 203–20.

17. For example, Miles Kahler and Andrew MacIntyre, *Integrating Regions: Asia in Comparative Context* (Stanford, Calif.: Stanford University Press, 2013); Mark Beeson and Kanishka Jayasuriya, "The Political Rationalities of Regionalism: APEC and the EU in Comparative Perspective," *Pacific Review* 11, no. 3 (1998): 311–36.

18. In criticizing the theorization of European integration, Donald Puchala told the story of the blind men and the elephant. Several blind men approached an elephant and each touched the animal in an effort to discover what the beast looked like. Each man, however, touched a different part of the large animal, and thus each concluded that the elephant had the appearance of the part that he had touched. See Puchala, "Of Blind Men, Elephants and International Integration," *Journal of Common Market Studies* 10, no. 3 (1971): 267–84.

19. William W. Grimes, "East Asian Financial Regionalism in Support of the Global Financial Architecture? The Political Economy of Regional Nesting," *Journal of East Asian Studies* 6, no. 3 (2006): 353–80.

20. Ha-Joon Chang, *Kicking Away the Ladder: Development Strategy in Historical Perspective* (London: Anthem Press, 2002).

Bibliography

Abbott, Kenneth W., and Duncan Snidal. "Hard Law and Soft Law in International Governance." *International Organization* 54, no. 3 (2000): 420–33.

Abe, Yoshiaki, and Shigeo Katsu. "The World Bank and Japan." In *Japan's Development Assistance: Foreign Aid and the Post-2015 Agenda*, ed. Hiroshi Kato, John Page, and Yasutani Shimomura, 255–75. London: Palgrave Macmillan, 2016.

Abegglen, James C. *The Strategy of Japanese Business*. Cambridge, Mass.: Ballinger, 1984.

Acharya, Amitav. "Realism, Institutionalism, and the Asian Economic Crisis." *Contemporary Southeast Asia* 21, no. 1 (1999): 1–29.

———. *Whose Ideas Matter? Agency and Power in Asian Regionalism*. Ithaca, N.Y.: Cornell University Press, 2009.

Aggarwal, Vinod K. *Institutional Designs for a Complex World: Bargaining, Linkages, and Nesting*. Ithaca, N.Y.: Cornell University Press, 1998.

Aizenman, Joshua, and Jaewoo Lee. "Financial Versus Monetary Mercantilism: Long-Run View of Large International Reserves Hoarding." *World Economy* 31, no. 5 (2008): 593–611.

Ajia Infura Kenkyūkai. *Ajia Infura Kenkyūkai Teigen: Infura PPP Jigyō no Suishin nimukete* (Proposal of Asia Infrastructure Study Group: How to promote infrastructure PPP projects). Tokyo: Ministry of Land, Infrastructure, Transport, and Tourism, 2006.

Alter, Karen J. *The New Terrain of International Law: Courts, Politics, Rights*. Princeton, N.J.: Princeton University Press, 2014.

Amsden, Alice H. *Asia's Next Giant: South Korea and Late Industrialization*. New York: Oxford University Press, 1992.

———. "Diffusion of Development: The Late-Industrializing Model and Greater East Asia." *American Economic Review* 81, no. 2 (1991): 282–86.

——. "Why Isn't the Whole World Experimenting with the East Asian Model to Develop? Review of the East Asian Miracle." *World Development* 22, no. 4 (1994): 627–33.

Amyx, Jennifer A. *Japan's Financial Crisis: Institutional Rigidity and Reluctant Change.* Princeton, N.J.: Princeton University Press, 2004.

——. "Moving Beyond Bilateralism? Japan and the Asian Monetary Fund." *Pacific Economic Papers* 331 (2002). https://openresearch-repository.anu.edu.au/bitstream/1885/40431/3/pep-331.pdf.

——. "Regional Financial Cooperation in East Asia Since the Asian Financial Crisis." In *Crisis as Catalyst: Asia's Dynamic Political Economy,* ed. Andrew MacIntyre, T. J. Pempel, and John Ravenhill, 117–39. Cornell Studies in Political Economy. Ithaca, N.Y.: Cornell University Press, 2008.

——. "What Motivates Regional Financial Cooperation in East Asia Today?" *AsiaPacific Issues* 76 (2005): 1–8.

Andrews, David M. "Capital Mobility and State Autonomy: Toward a Structural Theory of International Monetary Relations." *International Studies Quarterly* 38, no. 2 (1994): 193–218.

Antkiewicz, Agata, and John Whalley. "China's New Regional Trade Agreements." *World Economy* 28, no. 10 (2005): 1539–57.

Arakawa, Hiroto. "Ajia no infura gigyō: Seisaku/seido zukuri no shien kagi" (Infrastructure projects in Asia: Policy and establishment of the system is the key). *Nihon keizai shimbun,* August 27, 2010.

Araki, Mitsuya. "Japan's Official Development Assistance: The Japan ODA Model That Began Life in Southeast Asia." *Asia-Pacific Review* 14, no. 2 (2007): 17–29.

Arase, David. *Buying Power: The Political Economy of Japan's Foreign Aid.* Boulder, Colo.: Lynne Rienner, 1995.

——. "Japan, the Active State? Security Policy After 9/11." *Asian Survey* 47, no. 4 (2007): 560–83.

Armijo, Leslie Elliott, and Saori N. Katada. "Theorizing the Financial Statecraft of Emerging Powers." *New Political Economy* 20, no. 1 (2015): 42–62.

Ashizawa, Kuniko. *Japan, the US, and Regional Institution-Building in the New Asia: When Identity Matters.* New York: Palgrave Macmillan, 2013.

——. "Japan's Approach Toward Asian Regional Security: From 'Hub-and-Spoke' Bilateralism to 'Multi-tiered.'" *Pacific Review* 16, no. 3 (2003): 361–82.

Asian Development Bank. *Infrastructure for a Seamless Asia.* Joint Study of the Asian Development Bank and the Asian Development Bank Institute. Manila: ADB, 2009.

Baccini, Leonardo, and Andreas Dür. "The New Regionalism and Policy Interdependence." *British Journal of Political Science* 42, no. 1 (2012): 57–79.

Baek, Seung-Wook. "Does China Follow 'the East Asian Development Model'?" *Journal of Contemporary Asia* 35, no. 4 (2005): 485–98.

Balassa, Bela. *The Theory of Economic Integration.* Homewood, Ill.: Routledge, 1961.

Baldwin, David A. *Economic Statecraft.* Princeton, N.J.: Princeton University Press, 1985.

Baldwin, Richard E. "The Causes of Regionalism." *World Economy* 20, no. 7 (1997): 865–88.

——. "Managing the Noodle Bowl: The Fragility of East Asian Regionalism." *Singapore Economic Review* 53, no. 3 (2008): 449–78.

——. "Multilateralising Regionalism: Spaghetti Bowls as Building Blocs on the Path to Global Free Trade." *World Economy* 29, no. 11 (2006): 1451–518.

——. Baldwin, Richard. "WTO 2.0: Global Governance of Supply-Chain Trade." *Policy Insight* 64 (2012).

Bayoumi, Tamim, and Barry Eichengreen. "Exchange Rate Volatility and Intervention: Implications of the Theory of Optimum Currency Areas." *Journal of International Economics* 45, no. 2 (1998): 191–209.

Beeson, Mark. "Developmental States in East Asia: A Comparison of the Japanese and Chinese Experiences." *Asian Perspective* 33, no. 2 (2009): 5–39.

——. "Japan's Reluctant Reformers and the Legacy of the Developmental State." In *Governance and Public Sector Reform in Asia: Paradigm Shifts or Business as Usual?*, ed. Anthony B. L. Cheung and Ian Scott, 67–88. New York: RoutledgeCurzon, 2003.

——. "Politics and Markets in East Asia: Is the Developmental State Compatible with Globalisation?" In *Political Economy and the Changing Global Order*, ed. Richard Stubbs and Geoffrey R. D. Underhill, 443–53. Oxford: Oxford University Press, 2005.

——. "What Does China's Rise Mean for the Developmental State Paradigm?" In *Asia After the Developmental State: Disembedding Autonomy*, ed. Toby Carroll and Darryl S. L. Jarvis, 174–97. Cambridge: Cambridge University Press, 2017.

Beeson, Mark, and Kanishka Jayasuriya. "The Political Rationalities of Regionalism: APEC and the EU in Comparative Perspective." *Pacific Review* 11, no. 3 (1998): 311–36.

Belderbos, René, Giovanni Capannelli, and Kyoji Fukao. "Local Procurement by Japanese Manufacturing Affiliates Abroad." In *Multinational Firms and Impacts on Employment, Trade and Technology: New Perspectives for a New Century*, ed. Robert E. Lipsey and Jean-Louis Mucchielli, 154–73. London: Routledge, 2002.

Belderbos, René, and Leo Sleuwaegen. "Japanese Firms and the Decision to Invest Abroad: Business Groups and Regional Core Networks." *Review of Economics and Statistics* 78, no. 2 (1996): 214–20.

Berger, Thomas U. *Cultures of Antimilitarism: National Security in Germany and Japan*. Baltimore: Johns Hopkins University Press, 1998.

——. "From Sword to Chrysanthemum: Japan's Culture of Anti-militarism." *International Security* 17, no. 4 (1993): 119–50.

——. "The Pragmatic Liberalism of an Adaptive State." In *Japan in International Politics: The Foreign Policies of an Adaptive State*, ed. Thomas U. Berger, Mike Mochizuki, and Jitsuo Tsuchiyama, 259–99. Boulder, Colo.: Lynne Rienner, 2007.

Berger, Thomas U., Mike Mochizuki, and Jitsuo Tsuchiyama, eds. *Japan in International Politics: The Foreign Policies of an Adaptive State*. Boulder, CO: Lynne Rienner, 2007.

Bergsten, C. Fred, and Marcus Noland. *Reconcilable Differences? United States-Japan Economic Conflict*. Washington, D.C.: Institute for International Economics, 1993.

Bernanke, Ben S. "The Global Saving Glut and the US Current Account Deficit." Remarks at the Sandridge Lecture, Virginia Association of Economists, Richmond, Virginia." 2005. http://www.federalreserve.gov/boardDocs/Speeches/2005/200503102/default.htm.

Bernard, Mitchell, and John Ravenhill. "Beyond Product Cycles and Flying Geese: Regionalization, Hierarchy, and the Industrialization of East Asia." *World Politics* 47, no. 2 (1995): 171–209.

Birdsall, Nancy, and Francis Fukuyama. "The Post-Washington Consensus: Development After the Crisis." *Foreign Affairs* 90, no. 2 (2011): 45–53.

Blackwill, Robert D., and Jennifer M. Harris. *War by Other Means: Geoeconomics and Statecraft.* Cambridge, Mass.: Harvard University Press, 2016.

Blinder, Alan S. *After the Music Stopped: The Financial Crisis, the Response, and the Work Ahead.* New York: Penguin, 2013.

Boduszynski, Mieczysław, and Gene Park. "Trade Tensions: Why Shinzo Abe Has a Critical Role to Play." *National Interest* (2019). https://nationalinterest.org/blog/korea-watch/trade-tensions-why-shinzo-abe-has-critical-role-play-67407.

Borden, William S. *The Pacific Alliance: United States Foreign Economic Policy and Japanese Trade Recovery, 1947–1955.* Madison: University of Wisconsin Press, 1984.

Bowles, Paul. "Asia's Post-Crisis Regionalism: Bringing the State Back In, Keeping the (United) States Out." *Review of International Political Economy* 9, no. 2 (2002): 244–70.

Bräutigam, Deborah. "Aid 'with Chinese Characteristics': Chinese Foreign Aid and Development Finance Meet the OECD-DAC Aid Regime." *Journal of International Development* 23, no. 5 (2011): 752–64.

——. *The Dragon's Gift: The Real Story of China in Africa.* New York: Oxford University Press, 2009.

Bremmer, Ian. *Every Nation for Itself: Winners and Losers in a G-Zero World.* New York: Penguin, 2012.

——. "State Capitalism Comes of Age." *Foreign Affairs* 88, no. 3 (2009): 40–55.

Breslin, Shaun. "Chinese Financial Statecraft and the Response to the Global Financial Crisis." In *Unexpected Outcomes: How Emerging Economies Survived the Global Financial Crisis,* ed. Carol Wise, Leslie E. Armijo, and Saori N. Katada, 25–47. Washington, D.C.: Brookings Institution Press, 2015.

Burstein, Daniel. *Yen! Japan's New Financial Empire and Its Threat to America.* New York: Fawcett Columbine, 1990.

Cabinet Office. *Japan Revitalization Strategy: Japan Is Back.* Tokyo: Kantei, 2013.

Cai, Kevin G. "The ASEAN-China Free Trade Agreement and East Asian Regional Grouping." *Contemporary Southeast Asia* 25, no. 3 (2003): 387–404.

——. *The Political Economy of East Asia: Regional and National Dimensions.* International Political Economy Series. Hampshire, UK: Palgrave Macmillan, 2008.

Calder, Kent E. *Circles of Compensation: Economic Growth and the Globalization of Japan.* Stanford, Calif.: Stanford University Press, 2017.

——. "Japanese Foreign Economic Policy Formation: Explaining the Reactive State." *World Politics* 40, no. 4 (1988): 517–41.

——. "Japan's Changing Political Economy." In *Japan's Emerging Global Role,* ed. Daniel Unger and Paul Blackburn, 121–31. Boulder, Colo.: Lynne Rienner, 1993.

Calder, Kent E., and Min Ye. "Regionalism and Critical Junctures: Explaining the 'Organization Gap' in Northeast Asia." *Journal of East Asian Studies* 4, no. 2 (2004): 191–226.

Callon, Scott. *Divided Sun: MITI and the Breakdown of Japanese High-tech Industrial Policy, 1975–1993*. Stanford, Calif.: Stanford University Press, 1997.

Campbell, Kurt. *The Pivot: The Future of American Statecraft in Asia*. New York: Hachette, 2016.

Capling, Ann, and John Ravenhill. "Multilateralising Regionalism: What Role for the Trans-Pacific Partnership Agreement?" *Pacific Review* 24, no. 5 (2011): 553–75.

Cargill, Thomas F., Michael M. Hutchison, and Takatoshi Ito. *The Political Economy of Japanese Monetary Policy*. Cambridge, Mass.: MIT Press, 2003.

Carpenter, Susan. *Why Japan Can't Reform*. London: Palgrave Macmillan, 2008.

Carroll, Toby, and Darryl S. L. Jarvis. *Asia After the Developmental State: Disembedding Autonomy*. Cambridge: Cambridge University Press, 2017.

Catalinac, Amy. *Electoral Reform and National Security in Japan: From Pork to Foreign Policy*. New York: Cambridge University Press, 2016.

Cerny, Philip G. *The Changing Architecture of Politics: Structure, Agency and the Future of the State*. London: Sage, 1990.

Chabchitrchaidol, Akkharaphol, Satoshi Nakagawa, and Yoichi Nemoto. "Quest for Financial Stability in East Asia: Establishment of an Independent Surveillance Unit 'AMRO' and Its Future Challenges." *Public Policy Review* 14, no. 5 (2018 2018): 1001–24.

Chan, Eric, Michael K. F. Chui, Frank Packer, and Eli M. Remolona. "Local Currency Bond Markets and the Asian Bond Fund 2 Initiative." *BIS Paper*, no. 63f (2012).

Chang, Ha-Joon. *Kicking Away the Ladder: Development Strategy in Historical Perspective*. London: Anthem Press, 2002.

Charlton, Sue Ellen. "Little Progress, Small Niches: The WID Mandate in Japanese Foreign Aid." In *Feminists Doing Development: A Practical Critique*, ed. Marilyn Porter and Ellen Judd, 42–56. London: Zed Books, 1997.

Chase, Robert S., Emily B. Hill, and Paul Kennedy. "Pivotal States and U.S. Strategy." *Foreign Affairs* 75 (1996): 33–51.

Chaudoin, Stephen, Helen V. Milner, and Xun Pang. "International Systems and Domestic Politics: Linking Complex Interactions with Empirical Models in International Relations." *International Organization* 69, no. 2 (2015): 275–309.

Cheong, Inkyo, and Jungran Cho. "The Impact of Free Trade Agreements (FTAs) on Business in the Republic of Korea." *ADBI Working Paper Series* 156 (2009). https://www.econstor.eu/handle/10419/53663.

Chey, Hyoung-kyu. "The International Politics of Reactive Currency Statecraft: Japan's Reaction to the Rise of the Chinese Renminbi." *New Political Economy* 24, no. 4 (2019): 510–29.

Chin, Gregory T. "The BRICS-led Development Bank: Purpose and Politics Beyond the G20." *Global Policy* 5, no. 3 (2014): 366–73.

——. "China as a 'Net Donor': Tracking Dollars and Sense." *Cambridge Review of International Affairs* 25, no. 4 (2012): 579–603.

Chin, Gregory, and Richard Stubbs. "China, Regional Institution-Building and the China–ASEAN Free Trade Area." *Review of International Political Economy* 18, no. 3 (2011): 277–98.

Chin, Gregory, and Yong Wang. "Debating the International Currency System: What's in a Speech." *China Security* 6, no. 1 (2010): 3–20.

Chwieroth, Jeffrey M. "Testing and Measuring the Role of Ideas: The Case of Neoliberalism in the International Monetary Fund." *International Studies Quarterly* 51, no. 1 (2007): 5–30.

Ciorciari, John D. "Chiang Mai Initiative Multilateralization." *Asian Survey* 51, no. 5 (2011): 926–52.

Clinton, Hillary. "America's Pacific Century." *Foreign Policy*, no. 189 (2011): 56–63.

Cohen, Benjamin J. *Currency Power: Understanding Monetary Rivalry*. Princeton, N.J.: Princeton University Press, 2018.

——. *The Future of Money*. Princeton, N.J.: Princeton University Press, 2004.

Corning, Gregory P. "Between Bilateralism and Regionalism in East Asia: The ASEAN–Japan Comprehensive Economic Partnership." *Pacific Review* 22, no. 5 (2009): 639–65.

——. "CJK Investment Agreements in East Asia: Building a Bifurcated Investment Regime." *Asian Politics & Policy* 6, no. 2 (2014): 285–306.

——. "Trade Regionalism in a Realist East Asia: Rival Visions and Competitive Bilateralism." *Asian Perspective* 35, no. 2 (2011): 259–86.

Corsetti, Giancarlo, Paolo Pesenti, and Nouriel Roubini. "What Caused the Asian Currency and Financial Crisis?" *Japan and the World Economy* 11, no. 3 (1999): 305–73.

Council on Foreign Exchange and Other Transactions. "Internationalization of the Yen for the 21st Century: Japan's Response to Changes in Global Economic and Financial Environments." 1999, 1–2. www.mof.go.jp/english/if/elb064a.htm.

Cowhey, Peter. "Pacific Trade Relations After the Cold War: GATT, NAFTA, ASEAN and APEC." In *United States–Japan Relations and International Institutions After the Cold War*, ed. Peter A. Gourevitch, Takashi Inoguchi, and Courtney Purrington, 183–226. La Jolla: Graduate School of International Relations and Pacific Studies, University of California, San Diego, 1995.

Cox, Robert W. "Middlepowermanship, Japan, and Future World Order." *International Journal* 44, no. 4 (1989 1989): 823–62.

Crone, Donald K. "Does Hegemony Matter? The Reorganization of the Pacific Political Economy." *World Politics* 45, no. 4 (1993): 501–25.

Curtis, Gerald L. *The Logic of Japanese Politics: Leaders, Institutions, and the Limits of Change.* New York: Columbia University Press, 2000.

——. "U.S. Relations with Japan." In *The Golden Age of the U.S.-China-Japan Triangle, 1972–1989*, ed. Ezra F. Vogel, Ming Yuan, and Akihiko Tanaka, 135–63. Cambridge, Mass.: Harvard University Press, 2002.

Das, Dilip K. "Evolving Domestic Bond Markets and Financial Deepening in Asia." *Global Economy Journal* 14, no. 1 (2014): 89–112.

Davis, Christina L. *Food Fights Over Free Trade: How International Institutions Promote Agricultural Trade Liberalization.* Princeton, N.J.: Princeton University Press, 2003.

Deeg, Richard, and Gregory Jackson. "Towards a More Dynamic Theory of Capitalist Variety." *Socio-Economic Review* 5, no. 1 (2007): 149–79.

Dent, Christopher M. "The Asian Development Bank and Developmental Regionalism in East Asia." *Third World Quarterly* 29, no. 4 (2008): 767–86.

------. "East Asia's New Developmentalism: State Capacity, Climate Change and Low-Carbon Development." *Third World Quarterly* 39, no. 6 (2018): 1191–210.

------. "Free Trade Agreements in the Asia-Pacific a Decade On: Evaluating the Past, Looking to the Future." *International Relations of the Asia-Pacific* 10, no. 2 (2010): 201–45.

------. "Networking the Region? The Emergence and Impact of Asia-Pacific Bilateral Free Trade Agreement Projects." *Pacific Review* 16, no. 1 (2003): 1–28.

------. *New Free Trade Agreements in the Asia-Pacific.* New York: Palgrave Macmillan, 2006.

Destler, Irving M., Haruhiro Fukui, and Hideo Sato. *The Textile Wrangle: Conflict in Japanese-American Relations, 1969–1971.* Ithaca, N.Y.: Cornell University Press, 1979.

Devlin, Robert, and Graciela Moguillansky. *Breeding Latin American Tigers: Operational Principles for Rehabilitating Industrial Policies.* Washington, D.C.: United Nations Economic Commission for Latin America and the Caribbean and the World Bank, 2011.

Dieter, Heribert, and Richard Higgott. "Exploring Alternative Theories of Economic Regionalism: From Trade to Finance in Asian Co-operation?" *Review of International Political Economy* 10, no. 3 (2003): 430–54.

Dirlik, Arif. "Beijing Consensus: Beijing 'Gongshi.' Who Recognizes Whom and to What End?" *Globalization and Autonomy Online Compendium* (2006): 9.

Dreher, Axel, Peter Nunnenkamp, and Rainer Thiele. "Are 'New' Donors Different? Comparing the Allocation of Bilateral Aid between nonDAC and DAC Donor Countries." *World Development* 39, no. 11 (2011): 1950–68.

Drezner, Daniel W. *The Sanctions Paradox: Economic Statecraft and International Relations.* New York: Cambridge University Press, 1999.

Economy, Elizabeth. "The AIIB Debacle: What Washington Should Do Now." In *Asia Unbound.* New York: Council on Foreign Relations, 2015.

Eichengreen, Barry. *Exorbitant Privilege: The Rise and Fall of the Dollar and the Future of the International Monetary System.* New York: Oxford University Press, 2011.

------. *Hall of Mirrors: The Great Depression, the Great Recession, and the Uses—and Misuses—of History.* New York: Oxford University Press, 2014.

------. "The Parallel-Currency Approach to Asian Monetary Integration." *American Economic Review* 96, no. 2 (2006): 432–36.

------. *Toward a New International Financial Architecture: A Practical Post-Asia Agenda.* Washington, D.C.: Peterson Institute Press, 1999.

Eichengreen, Barry, and Masahiro Kawai. "Issues for Renminbi Internationalization: An Overview." *ADBI Working Paper Series* 454 (2014). https://think-asia.org/handle/11540/1216.

Elkins, Zachary, Andrew T. Guzman, and Beth A. Simmons. "Competing for Capital: The Diffusion of Bilateral Investment Treaties, 1960–2000." *International Organization* 60, no. 4 (2006): 811–46.

Ensign, Margee M. *Doing Good or Doing Well? Japan's Foreign Aid Program.* New York: Columbia University Press, 1992.

Evans, Paul. "Between Regionalism and Regionalization: Policy Networks and the Nascent East Asian Institutional Identity." In *Remapping East Asia: The Construction of a Region*, ed. T. J. Pempel, 195–215. Ithaca, N.Y.: Cornell University Press, 2005.

Evans, Peter B. *Embedded Autonomy: States and Industrial Transformation.* Princeton, N.J.: Princeton University Press, 1995.

——. "The State as Problem and Solution: Predation, Embedded Autonomy, and Structural Change." In *The Politics of Economic Adjustment,* ed. Stephan Haggard and Robert R. Kaufman, 139–81. Princeton, N.J.: Princeton University Press, 1992.

Ezaki, Yasuhiro. "Ajia shinkōkoku infura bijinesu to Nihon kigyō no gurōbaru risuku maneijimento taisei" (Infrastructure building business in Asia's emerging economies and the system of Japanese firms' global risk management). *Higashi Ajia hyōron* 8 (2016): 19–34.

Fallows, James. *Looking at the Sun: The Rise of the New East Asian Economic and Political System.* New York: Vintage, 1994.

Fergusson, Ian F., and Bruce Vaughn. "The Trans-Pacific Strategic Economic Partnership Agreement." *CRS Report for Congress* (2009). https://apps.dtic.mil/dtic/tr/fulltext/u2/a512782.pdf.

Finnemore, Martha. *National Interests in International Society.* Cornell Studies in Political Economy. Ithaca, N.Y.: Cornell University Press, 1996.

Frankel, Jeffrey A. "Is a Yen Bloc Forming in Pacific Asia?" In *Finance and the International Economy: 5,* ed. Richard O'Brien, 5–20. Oxford: Oxford University Press, 1991.

——. *The Yen-Dollar Agreement: Liberalizing Japanese Capital Markets.* Cambridge, Mass.: MIT Press, 1984.

Freund, Caroline, Tyler Moran, and Sarah Oliver. "Tariff Liberalization." In *Trans-Pacific Partnership: An Assessment,* ed. Cathleen Cimino-Isaacs and Jeffrey J. Schott, 87–99. Policy Analyses in International Economics 104. Washington, D.C.: Peterson Institute for International Economics, 2016.

Friedman, David Bennett. *The Misunderstood Miracle: Industrial Development and Political Change in Japan.* Ithaca, N.Y.: Cornell University Press, 1988.

Fujisaki, Tomoko, Forrest Briscoe, James Maxwell, Misa Kishi, and Tatsujiro Suzuki. "Japan as Top Donor: The Challenge of Implementing Software Aid Policy." *Pacific Affairs* 69, no. 4 (1996): 519–39.

Funabashi, Yoichi. *Asia Pacific Fusion: Japan's Role in APEC.* Washington, D.C.: Institute for International Economics, 1995.

——. *Managing the Dollar: From the Plaza to the Louvre.* Washington, D.C.: Institute for International Economics, 1989.

——. *Nihon no taigai kōsō: Reisen go no bijon wo kaku* (Japan's foreign strategy: Drafting the post–Cold War vision). Tokyo: Iwanami Shoten, 1993.

Gallagher, Kevin. *Ruling Capital: Emerging Markets and the Reregulation of Cross-Border Finance.* Cornell Studies in Money. Ithaca, N.Y.: Cornell University Press, 2015.

Gallagher, Kevin, and Roberto Porzecanski. *The Dragon in the Room: China and the Future of Latin American Industrialization.* Stanford, Calif.: Stanford University Press, 2010.

Gerlach, Michael L. *Alliance Capitalism: The Social Organization of Japanese Business.* Berkeley: University of California Press, 1992.

Gerschenkron, Alexander. *Economic Backwardness in Historical Perspective: A Book of Essays.* Cambridge, Mass.: Harvard University Press 1962.

Giddens, Anthony. *The Third Way: The Renewal of Social Democracy.* Cambridge: Polity Press, 1999.

Gill, Indermit, and Homi Kharas. *An East Asian Renaissance: Ideas for Economic Growth*. Washington, D.C.: World Bank, 2007.

——. "The Middle-Income Trap Turns Ten." *Policy Research Working Paper* 7403 (2015): 27. https://elibrary.worldbank.org/doi/abs/10.1596/1813-9450-7403.

Gilson, Julie. "Building Peace or Following the Leader? Japan's Peace Consolidation Diplomacy." *Pacific Affairs* 80, no. 1 (2007): 27–47.

Glaser, Bonnie S. "Pivot to Asia: Prepare for Unintended Consequences." *Center for Strategic and International Studies: 2012 Global Forecast* (2012): 22–24. https://www.csis.org/analysis/pivot-asia-prepare-unintended-consequences.

Glick, Reuven, and Andrew K. Rose. "Contagion and Trade: Why Are Currency Crises Regional?" *Journal of International Money and Finance* 18, no. 4 (1999): 603–17.

Goh, Evelyn. *The Struggle for Order: Hegemony, Hierarchy, and Transition in Post–Cold War East Asia*. Oxford: Oxford University Press, 2013.

Gourevitch, Peter. *Politics in Hard Times: Comparative Responses to International Economic Crises*. Ithaca, N.Y.: Cornell University Press, 1986.

——. "The Second Image Reversed: The International Sources of Domestic Politics." *International Organization* 32, no. 4 (1978): 881–912.

Grabel, Ilene. "Not Your Grandfather's IMF: Global Crisis, 'Productive Incoherence' and Developmental Policy Space." *Cambridge Journal of Economics* 35, no. 5 (2011): 805–30.

Grieco, Joseph M. "Systemic Sources of Variation in Regional Institutionalization in Western Europe, East Asia, and the Americas." In *The Political Economy of Regionalism*, ed. Edward D. Mansfield and Helen V. Milner, 164–87. New York: Columbia University Press, 1997.

Griffith, Melissa K., Richard H. Steinberg, and John Zysman. "From Great Power Politics to a Strategic Vacuum: Origins and Consequences of the TPP and TTIP." *Business and Politics* 19, no. 4 (2017): 573–92.

Grimes, William W. *Currency and Contest in East Asia: The Great Power Politics of Financial Regionalism*. Cornell Studies in Money. Ithaca, N.Y.: Cornell University Press, 2009.

——. "East Asian Financial Regionalism: Why Economic Enhancements Undermine Political Sustainability." *Contemporary Politics* 21, no. 2 (2015): 145–60.

——. "East Asian Financial Regionalism in Support of the Global Financial Architecture? The Political Economy of Regional Nesting." *Journal of East Asian Studies* 6, no. 3 (2006): 353–80.

——. "The Future of Regional Liquidity Arrangements in East Asia: Lessons from the Global Financial Crisis." *Pacific Review* 24, no. 3 (July 2011): 291–310.

——. "Internationalization of the Yen and the New Politics of Monetary Insulation." In *Monetary Orders: Ambiguous Economics, Ubiquitous Politics*, ed. Jonathan Kirshner, 172–94. Ithaca, N.Y.: Cornell University Press, 2003.

——. "The Rise of Financial Cooperation in Asia." In *The Oxford Handbook of the International Relations of Asia*, ed. Saadia M. Pekkanen, John Ravenhill, and Rosemary Foot, 285–305. New York: Oxford University Press, 2014.

——. *Unmaking the Japanese Miracle: Macroeconomic Politics, 1985–2000*. Ithaca, N.Y.: Cornell University Press, 2002.

Gulrajani, Nilima. "Transcending the Great Foreign Aid Debate: Managerialism, Radicalism and the Search for Aid Effectiveness." *Third World Quarterly* 32, no. 2 (2011): 199–216.

Haas, Ernst B., and Philippe C. Schmitter. "Economics and Differential Patterns of Political Integration: Projections About Unity in Latin America." *International Organization* 18, no. 4 (1964): 705–37.

Haggard, Stephan. *Developmental States*. Cambridge Elements: Politics of Development. New York: Cambridge University Press, 2018.

——. "The Liberal View of the International Relations of Asia." In *The Oxford Handbook of the International Relations of Asia*, ed. Saadia M. Pekkanen, John Ravenhill, and Rosemary Foot, 45–64. New York: Oxford University Press, 2014.

——. *The Political Economy of the Asian Financial Crisis*. Washington, D.C.: Institute for International Economics, 2000.

Hall, Rodney Bruce. "The Discursive Demolition of the Asian Development Model." *International Studies Quarterly* 47, no. 1 (2003): 71–99.

Hall, Steven. "Managing Tied Aid Competition: Domestic Politics, Credible Threats, and the Helsinki Disciplines." *Review of International Political Economy* 18, no. 5 (2011): 646–72.

Hamanaka, Shintaro. "Asian Financial Cooperation in the 1990s: The Politics of Membership." *Journal of East Asian Studies* 11, no. 1 (2011): 75–103.

——. *Asian Regionalism and Japan: The Politics of Membership in Regional Diplomatic, Financial and Trade Groups*. London: Routledge, 2009.

Hamilton-Hart, Natasha. "Asia's New Regionalism: Government Capacity and Cooperation in the Western Pacific." *Review of International Political Economy* 10, no. 2 (2003): 222–45.

——. "Monetary Politics in Southeast Asia: External Imbalances in Regional Context." *New Political Economy* 19, no. 6 (2014): 872–94.

Hasegawa, Sukehiro. *Japanese Foreign Aid: Policy and Practice*. New York: Praeger, 1975.

Hatakeyama, Noboru. *Keizai tōgō no shinseiki: Moto tsūshōkōshō toppu no kaisou to teigen* (Economic integration in the new century: Memoir and recommendations by a former top trade negotiator). Tokyo: Toyo Keizai Shinpo, 2015.

Hatch, Walter. *Asia's Flying Geese: How Regionalization Shapes Japan*. Ithaca, N.Y.: Cornell University Press, 2010.

Hatch, Walter, and Kozo Yamamura. *Asia in Japan's Embrace: Building a Regional Production Alliance*. Cambridge: Cambridge University Press, 1996.

Hatoyama, Yukio. "My Political Philosophy." *Voice*, September (2009).

Hayashi, Shigeko. "The Developmental State in the Era of Globalization: Beyond the Northeast Asian Model of Political Economy." *Pacific Review* 23, no. 1 (2010): 45–69.

——. *Japan and East Asian Monetary Regionalism: Towards a Proactive Leadership Role?* London: Routledge, 2006.

Heginbotham, Eric, and Richard J. Samuels. "Mercantile Realism and Japanese Foreign Policy." *International Security* 22, no. 4 (1998): 171–203.

Helleiner, Eric. *States and the Reemergence of Global Finance: From Bretton Woods to the 1990s*. Ithaca, N.Y.: Cornell University Press, 1996.

——. *The Status Quo Crisis: Global Financial Governance After the 2008 Meltdown*. New York: Oxford University Press, 2014.

Hemmer, Christopher, and Peter J. Katzenstein. "Why Is There No NATO in Asia? Collective Identity, Regionalism, and the Origins of Multilateralism." *International Organization* 56, no. 3 (2002): 575–607.

Henning, C. Randall. *Tangled Governance: International Regime Complexity, the Troika, and the Euro Crisis*. New York: Oxford University Press, 2017.

Henning, C. Randall, and Saori N. Katada. "Cooperation Without Institutions: The Case of East Asian Currency Arrangement." In *Asian Designs: Governance in the Contemporary World Order*, ed. Saadia M. Pekkanen, 59–74. Ithaca, N.Y.: Cornell University Press, 2017.

Higgott, Richard. "The Asian Economic Crisis: A Study in the Politics of Resentment." *New Political Economy* 3, no. 3 (1998): 333–56.

Higgott, Richard, and Richard Stubbs. "Competing Conceptions of Economic Regionalism: APEC Versus EAEC in the Asia Pacific." *Review of International Political Economy* 2, no. 3 (1995): 516–35.

Higo, Masahiro. "Zaiseitōyūshi no genjō to kadai: 2001 nendo kaikaku ga zaitō no kinō ni ataeru eikyō" (Current state and challenges of fiscal investment and loan program: How 2001 reform affects the function of fiscal investment and loan program). *Bank of Japan Working Paper Series* WP01.1 (2001).

Hirata, Keiko. *Civil Society in Japan: The Growing Role of NGOs in Tokyo's Aid and Development Policy*. London: Palgrave Macmillan, 2002.

——. "New Challenges to Japan's Aid: An Analysis of Aid Policy-Making." *Pacific Affairs* 71, no. 3 (1998): 311–34.

Hirschman, Albert. *National Power and the Structure of International Trade*. Berkeley: University of California Press, 1945.

Hirsh, Michael. "How Japan Became the Adult at the Trade Table." *Foreign Policy*, April 10, 2019.

Hoffmann, Stanley. "Obstinate or Obsolete? The Fate of the Nation-State and the Case of Western Europe." *Daedalus* 95, no. 3 (1966): 862–915.

Honma, Masayoshi. "The TPP and Agricultural Reform in Japan." In *The Political Economy of Japanese Trade Policy*, ed. Aurelia George Mulgan and Masayoshi Honma, 94–122. New York: Palgrave Macmillan, 2015.

Hook, Steven W., and Guang Zhang. "Japan's Aid Policy Since the Cold War." *Asian Survey* 38, no. 1 (1998): 1051–66.

Hoshi, Fumio. "Ajia no saiken shijō ikusei ni muketa kokusaikyōryoku ginkō no torikumi: (JBIC efforts to nurture the Asian bond market). In *Chochikuritu no teika, IS baransu no henka to nihon keizai: Shikin no koritsu unyō to kinyū sābisugyō no kokusaikyōsōryoku*, ed. Nihon Keizai Chōsa Kyōgikai, 218–330. Tokyo: Nihon Keizai Chōsa Kyōgikai, 2006.

Hosokawa, Masahiko. "Zusan kanri taisho wa kokusai gimu" (Lax management: It is our international obligation to address it). *Nihon keizai shimbun* 2019, 29.

Hsueh, Roselyn. *China's Regulatory State: A New Strategy for Globalization*. Ithaca, N.Y.: Cornell University Press, 2011.

Hu, Dan. "The Relevance of Japanese Horizontal Keiretsu Affiliated Firms from the Perspective of Disclosure Quality." *SSRN Working Paper* 31 (2014).

Huang, Yiping. "Understanding China's Belt & Road Initiative: Motivation, Framework and Assessment." *China Economic Review* 40 (2016): 314–21.

Humphrey, Christopher. "Developmental Revolution or Bretton Woods Revisited? The Prospects of the BRICS New Development Bank and the Asian Infrastructure Investment Bank." *ODI Working Paper* 418 (2015): 1–35.

Hurrell, Andrew. *Regionalism in World Politics: Regional Organization and International Order.* New York: Oxford University Press, 1995.

Ikenberry, G. John. *After Victory: Institutions, Strategic Restraint, and the Rebuilding of Order After Major Wars.* Princeton Studies in International History and Politics. Princeton, N.J.: Princeton University Press, 2001.

——. "Conclusion: An Institutional Approach to American Foreign Economic Policy." *International Organization* 42, no. 1 (1988): 219–43.

——. "The Future of the Liberal World Order." *Foreign Affairs* 90, no. 3 (2011): 56–68.

Ikenberry, G. John, David A. Lake, and Michael Mastanduno. "Introduction: Approaches to Explaining American Foreign Economic Policy." *International Organization* 42, no. 1 (1988): 1–14.

Ikeo, Kazuhito. *Kaihatsu shugi no bōsō to hoshin: Kinyū sisutemu to heisei keizai* (Runaway state and self-preservation of developmentalism). Tokyo: NTT, 2006.

Imada, Makoto. "The Voluntary Response to the Hanshin Awaji Earthquake: A Trigger for the Development of the Voluntary and Non-Profit Sector in Japan." In *The Voluntary and Non-Profit Sector in Japan: The Challenge of Change*, ed. Stephen P. Osborne. Nissan Institute/RoutledgeCurzon Japanese Studies Series, 40–50. New York: Routledge, 2003.

Institute for International Monetary Affairs (IIMA). "Report Summary of Studies on Towards a Regional Financial Architecture for East Asia." (2004): 1–15. http://www.mof.go.jp/jouhou/kokkin/ASEAN+3research-1-1.pdf.

Ito, Mitsutoshi. "Kokkai 'shūgō zai' moderu" (Collective goods model of parliament). In *Nihon seiji hendō no 30 nen: Seijika/kanryō/dantaichosa ni miru kōzō henyō* (Thirty years of political changes in Japan: Structural transformation of politicians, bureaucrats, and organizational surveys), ed. Michio Muramatsu and Ikuo Kume, 25–48. Tokyo: Toyo Keizai Shinposha, 2006.

Ito, Takatoshi. "Growth, Crisis, and the Future of Economic Recovery in East Asia." *Rethinking the East Asian Miracle* (2001): 55–94.

——. "A New Financial Order in Asia: Will a RMB Bloc Emerge?" *Journal of International Money and Finance* 74 (2017): 232–57.

Ito, Takatoshi, and Michael Melvin. "Japan's Big Bang and the Transformation of Financial Markets." *National Bureau of Economic Research Working Paper* No. 7247 (1999). https://www.nber.org/papers/w7247.

Iwami, Toru. "The Internationalization of Yen and Key Currency Questions." *IMF Working Paper* WP/94/41(1994). https://www.imf.org/en/Publications/WP/Issues/2016/12/30/The-Internationalization-of-Yen-and-Key-Currency-Questions-1130.

Jayasuriya, Kanishka. "Embedded Mercantilism and Open Regionalism: The Crisis of a Regional Political Project." *Third World Quarterly* 24, no. 2 (2003): 339–55.

Jempa, Catrinus J. *The Tying of Aid.* Paris: OECD Development Centre, 1991.

Jetschke, Anja, and Saori Katada. "Asia." In *The Oxford Handbook of Comparative Regionalism,* ed. Tanja Borzel and Thomas Risse, 225–48. Oxford: Oxford University Press, 2016.

Jiang, Yang. "The Limits of China's Monetary Diplomacy." In *The Great Wall of Money: Power and Politics in China's International Monetary Relations,* ed. Eric Helleiner and Jonathan Kirshner, 156–83. Ithaca, N.Y.: Cornell University Press, 2014.

Johnson, Chalmers A. *Japan: Who Governs? The Rise of the Developmental State.* New York: Norton, 1995.

——. *MITI and the Japanese Miracle: The Growth of Industrial Policy: 1925–1975.* Stanford, Calif.: Stanford University Press, 1982.

Johnson, O. Thomas, and Jonathan Gimblett. "From Gunboats to BITs: The Evolution of Modern International Investment Law." In *Yearbook on International Investment Law & Policy 2010–2011,* ed. Karl P. Sauvant, 649–92. New York: Oxford University Press, 2010.

Kabashima, Ikuo, and Gill Steel. "The Koizumi Revolution." *PS: Political Science & Politics* 40, no. 1 (2007): 79–84.

Kagawa, Kozo, and Yuka Kaneko. *Hōseibi shien ron: Seidokōchiku no kokusai kyōryoku nyūmon* (Theory of legislation assistance: Introductory book of institution building in international cooperation). Kyoto: Minerva Shobo, 2007.

Kahler, Miles. "Legalization as Strategy: The Asia-Pacific Case." *International Organization* 54, no. 3 (2000): 549–71.

Kahler, Miles, and Andrew MacIntyre. *Integrating Regions: Asia in Comparative Context.* Stanford, Calif.: Stanford University Press, 2013.

Kalinowski, Thomas. "Korea's Recovery Since the 1997/98 Financial Crisis: The Last Stage of the Developmental State." *New Political Economy* 13, no. 4 (2008): 447–62.

Kaminsky, Graciela L., and Carmen M. Reinhart. "The Twin Crises: The Causes of Banking and Balance-of-Payments Problems." *American Economic Review* 89, no. 3 (1999): 473–500.

Kanda, Masato. "Infura shien ni tsuite" (About infrastructure aid). *Finance: Zaimushō Kōhōshi* 51, no. 4 (2015): 2–13.

Kanda, Shigeru, and Yusuke Terabayashi. "TPP kōsho no keii to kōsho 21 bunya no gaiyō (tokushu: tsūjō senkyo gono shuyō seisaku kadai 2)" (Details of TPP negotiation and overview of 21 fields in the negotiation [special edition: Major policy issues after the general election 2]). *Rippo to chosa* 346 (2013): 3–34.

Katada, Saori N. "Balancing Act: Japan's Strategy in Global and Regional Financial Governance." In *A Leaders 20 Summit: Why, How, Who and When?,* ed. John English, Ramesh Thakur, and Andrew F. Cooper, 97–120. Tokyo: United Nations University Press, 2005.

——. *Banking on Stability: Japan and the Cross-Pacific Dynamics of International Financial Crisis Management.* Ann Arbor: University of Michigan Press, 2001.

——. "Can China Internationalize the RMB? Lessons from Japan." *Foreign Affairs,* Snapshot, January 1, 2018.

———. "Financial Crisis Fatigue? Politics Behind Japan's Post-Global Financial Crisis Economic Contraction." *Japanese Journal of Political Science* 14, no. 2 (2013): 223–42.

———. "From a Supporter to a Challenger? Japan's Currency Leadership in Dollar-Dominated East Asia." *Review of International Political Economy* 15, no. 3 (2008): 399–417.

———. "Japan's Foreign Aid After the San Francisco Peace Treaty." *Journal of American-East Asian Relations* 9, no. 3 (2000): 197–220.

———. "Japan's Two-Track Aid Approach: The Forces Behind Competing Triads." *Asian Survey* 42, no. 2 (2002): 320–42.

———. "Mission Accomplished, or a Sisyphean Task? Japan's Regulatory Response to the Global Financial Crisis." In *Global Finance in Crisis: The Politics of International Regulatory Change*, ed. Eric Helleiner, Stefano Pagliari, and Hubert Zimmermann, 137–52. New York: Routledge, 2009.

———. "Seeking a Place for East Asian Regionalism: Challenges and Opportunities Under the Global Financial Crisis." *Pacific Review* 24, no. 3 (2011): 273–90.

———. "Two Aid Hegemons: Japanese-US Interaction and Aid Allocation to Latin America and the Caribbean." *World Development* 25, no. 6 (1997): 931–45.

———. "U.S. and Japanese Economic Statecraft Toward China: The Reshaping of the Asia-Pacific Economic Order." *NBR Special Report* 75 (2019): 1–9. https://www.nbr.org/publication/u-s-and-japanese-economic-statecraft-toward-china-the-reshaping-of-the-asia-pacific-economic-order/.

———. "Why Did Japan Suspend Foreign Aid to China? Japan's Foreign Aid Decision-Making and Sources of Aid Sanction." *Social Science Japan Journal* 4, no. 1 (2001): 39–58.

Katada, Saori N., and C. Randall Henning. "Currency and Exchange Rate Regime in Asia." In *The Oxford Handbook of the International Relations of Asia*, ed. Saadia M. Pekkanen, John Ravenhill, and Rosemary Foot, 306–26. New York: Oxford University Press, 2014.

Katada, Saori N., and Jessica Liao. "China and Japan in Pursuit of Infrastructure Development Leadership: Competition or Convergence?" *Global Governance* 26, no. 3 (forthcoming September 2020).

Katada, Saori N., and Mireya Solís. "Domestic Sources of Japanese Foreign Policy Activism: Loss Avoidance and Demand Coherence." *International Relations of the Asia-Pacific* 10, no. 1 (2010): 129–57.

Katada, Saori N., and Scott Wilbur. "Japan's Stealth Decision 2014: The Trans-Pacific Partnership." In *Japan Decides 2014: The Japanese General Election*, ed. Robert J. Pekkanen, Steven R. Reed, and Ethan Scheiner, 247–61. London: Palgrave Macmillan, 2015.

Kato, Hiroshi. "Japan's ODA 1954–2014: Changes and Continuities in a Central Instrument in Japan's Foreign Policy." In *Japan's Development Assistance: Foreign Aid and the Post-2015 Agenda*, ed. Hiroshi Kato, John Page, and Yasutami Shimomura, 1–18. London: Palgrave Macmillan, 2016.

Katz, Richard. *Japan: The System That Soured: The Rise and Fall of the Japanese Economic Miracle*. Armonk, N.Y.: M. E. Sharpe, 1998.

Katzenstein, Peter J. *Between Power and Plenty: Foreign Economic Policies of Advanced Industrial States*. Madison: University of Wisconsin Press, 1978.

———. "East Asia—Beyond Japan." In *Beyond Japan: The Dynamics of East Asian Regionalism*, ed. Peter J. Katzenstein and Takashi Shiraishi, 1–33. Ithaca, N.Y.: Cornell University Press, 2006.

———. "Introduction: Asian Regionalism in Comparative Perspective." In *Network Power: Japan and Asia*, ed. Peter J. Katzenstein and Takashi Shiraishi, 1–44. Ithaca, N.Y.: Cornell University Press, 1997.

———, ed. *Sinicization and the Rise of China: Civilizational Processes Beyond East and West.* New York: Routledge, 2012.

———. *A World of Regions: Asia and Europe in the American Imperium.* Ithaca, N.Y.: Cornell University Press, 2005.

Katzenstein, Peter J., and Takashi Shiraishi. *Beyond Japan: The Dynamics of East Asian Regionalism.* Ithaca, N.Y.: Cornell University Press, 2006.

———. *Network Power: Japan and Asia.* Ithaca, N.Y.: Cornell University Press, 1997.

Kawai, Masahiro. "Asian Infrastructure Investment Bank in the Evolving International Financial Order." In *Asian Infrastructure Investment Bank: China as Responsible Stakeholder?* ed. Daniel Bob, 5–26. Washington, D.C.: Sasakawa Peace Foundation, 2015.

———. "Asian Monetary Integration: A Japanese Perspective." *ADBI Working Paper Series* 475 (2014): 1–34. https://www.adb.org/sites/default/files/publication/156330/adbi-wp475 .pdf.

———. "Chūgoku ga shudō suru 'Ajia Infura Tōshi Ginkō' bijon mo gabanansu mo naki jittai" (China-led "Asian Infrastructure Investment Bank": There is no vision and no governance). *Wedge Infinity Report*, January 6, 2015. http://wedge.ismedia.jp/articles /-/4566?page=3.

Kawai, Masahiro, and Cindy Houser. "Evolving ASEAN+3 ERPD: Towards Peer Reviews or Due Diligence?" *ADBI Discussion Paper*, no. 79 (2007): 1–24. https://www.adb.org /sites/default/files/publication/156718/adbi-dp79.pdf.

Kawai, Masahiro, and Shinji Takagi. "Japan's Official Development Assistance: Recent Issues and Future Directions." *Journal of International Development* 16, no. 2 (2004): 255–80.

———. "Why Was Japan Hit So Hard by the Global Financial Crisis?" *ADBI Working Paper Series* 153 (2009): 1–15. https://www.adb.org/sites/default/files/publication/156008/adbi -wp153.pdf.

Kawai, Masahiro, and Ganeshan Wignaraja. "ASEAN+3 or ASEAN+6: Which Way Forward?" *ADBI Discussion Paper*, no. 77 (2007): 1–48. https://www.adb.org/sites/default /files/publication/156716/adbi-dp77.pdf.

———. "The Asian 'Noodle Bowl': Is It Serious for Business?" *ADBI Working Paper Series* 136 (2009): 1–33. https://www.adb.org/sites/default/files/publication/155991/adbi-wp136 .pdf.

Keidanren. "Keidanren: ODA kaikaku ni kansuru teigen" (Japan Business Federation's proposals for ODA reform). October 16, 2001. https://www.keidanren.or.jp/japanese /policy/2001/049.html.

Kenen, Peter B. *The International Financial Architecture: What's New? What's Missing?* Washington, D.C.: Institute for International Economics, 2001.

Kennedy, Scott. "The Myth of the Beijing Consensus." *Journal of Contemporary China* 19, no. 65 (2010): 461–77.

Keohane, Robert O. *After Hegemony: Cooperation and Discord in the World Political Economy.* Princeton, N.J.: Princeton University Press, 1984.

Keohane, Robert O., and Joseph S. Nye. *Power and Interdependence: World Politics in Transition.* Boston: Little, Brown, 1977.

Kerner, Andrew. "Why Should I Believe You? The Costs and Consequences of Bilateral Investment Treaties." *International Studies Quarterly* 53, no. 1 (2009): 73–102.

Kharas, Homi, and Julie Biau. "New Actors, New Instruments, New Priorities: Toward a Sustainable Development Transformation." In *Japan's Development Assistance: Foreign Aid and the Post-2015 Agenda,* ed. Hiroshi Kato, John Page, and Yasutani Shimomura, 310–26. London: Palgrave Macmillan, 2016.

Kimura, Hidemi, and Yasuyuki Todo. "Is Foreign Aid a Vanguard of Foreign Direct Investment? A Gravity-Equation Approach." *World Development* 38, no. 4 (2010): 482–97.

Kimura, Seishi. "Changing Context of Firm-based Late Industrialization in the Global Business Transformation." In *The Challenges of Late Industrialization: The Global Economy and the Japanese Commercial Aircraft Industry,* ed. Seishi Kimura, 33–78. New York: Palgrave Macmillan, 2007.

Kirshner, Jonathan. *Currency and Coercion: The Political Economy of International Monetary Power.* Princeton, N.J.: Princeton University Press, 1997.

Kirton, John. "Toward Multilateral Reform: The G20's Contribution." In *Reforming from the Top: A Leaders' 20 Summit,* ed. John English, Ramesh Thakur, and Andrew F. Cooper, 141–68. Hong Kong: United Nations University Press, 2005.

Kitano, Koichi. "Chiri: Eikyōryoku no ōkii bumon betsu gyōkaidantai" (Chile: Influential trade groups sorted by industries). In *FTA no seiji keizai gaku: Ajia raten Amerika nanakakoku no FTA kōshō* (Political economy of FTAs: Japan's FTA negotiations with seven countries from Asia and Latin America), ed. Shigeki Higashi, 223–49. Tokyo: Institute of Developing Economies, 2007.

Kitano, Naohiro, and Yukinori Harada. "Estimating China's Foreign Aid 2001–2013." *JICA Research Institute Working Paper Series* 78 (2014): 1–24. https://www.jica.go.jp/jica-ri /publication/workingpaper/jrft3q00000025no-att/JICA-RI_WP_No.78_2014.pdf.

Kitano, Shigeto. "Capital Controls, Public Debt and Currency Crises." *Journal of Economics* 90, no. 2 (2007): 117–42.

Klingler-Vidra, Robyn, and Ramon Pacheco Pardo. "Legitimate Social Purpose and South Korea's Support for Entrepreneurial Finance Since the Asian Financial Crisis." *New Political Economy,* January 8, 2019: 1–17.

Knaack, Peter, and Saori N. Katada. "Fault Lines and Issue Linkages at the G20: New Challenges for Global Economic Governance." *Global Policy* 4, no. 3 (2013): 236–46.

Kobayashi, Hideo. *Sangyō kūdōka no kokufuku: Sangyō tenkanki no Nihon to Ajia* (Conquering hollowing-out: Japan at the time of industrial structure transition and Asia). Tokyo: Chuo Koron Shinsha, 2003.

Kobayashi, Kimio. "Kokka kōmuin no amakudari konzetsu ni muketa kinnen no torikumi" (Recent efforts to eliminate golden parachute deal for national government official). *Leviathan* 62, no. 8 (2012): 27–63.

Kodera, Kiyoshi. "Japan's Engagement with Multilateral Development Banks: Do Their Professional Paths Really Cross?" In *Japan's Development Assistance: Foreign Aid and the Post-2015 Agenda*, ed. Hiroshi Kato, John Page, and Yasutani Shimomura, 19–35. London: Palgrave Macmillan, 2016.

Kohli, Harinder S., and Ashok Sharma. *A Resilient Asia Amidst Global Financial Crisis: From Crisis Management to Global Leadership.* New Delhi: SAGE and Asian Development Bank, 2010.

Kojima, Kiyoshi. "The "Flying Geese" Model of Asian Economic Development: Origin, Theoretical Extensions, and Regional Policy Implications." *Journal of Asian Economics* 11, no. 4 (2000): 375–401.

Kojo, Yoshiko. "Baburu keisei/hōkai no haikei to shiteno Nichibei keizai kankei" (Japan-- U.S. economic relationship as a context of developing and collapsing bubble economy). In *Heisei baburu no kenkyū gekan* (Study on heisei bubble economy, vol. 2), ed. Michio Muramatsu and Masahiro Okuno. Tokyo: Toyo Keizai Shinposha 2002.

——. *Keizaiteki sōgo izon to kokka: Kokusai shūshi fukinkō zesei no seiji keizaigaku* (Economic interdependence and nations: political economy of correcting the balance of payments imbalances). Tokyo: Bokutaku Sha, 1996.

Kotera, Akira. "Kokusai tōshi: Gendai teki imi to mondaiten. Kazeijikō tono kankei wo fukumete" (Investment agreements: Contemporary significance and issues—including implication on taxation matters). *RIETI Policy Discussion Paper Series* 10-P-024 (2010).

Krauss, Ellis S. "The United States and Japan in APEC's EVSL Negotiations: Regional Multilateralism and Trade." In *Beyond Bilateralism: US-Japan Relations in the New Asia-Pacific*, ed. Ellis S. Krauss and T. J. Pempel, 272–95. Stanford, Calif.: Stanford University Press, 2004.

Kuisma, Mikko. "Social Democratic Internationalism and the Welfare State After the 'Golden Age.'" *Cooperation and Conflict* 42, no. 1 (2007): 9–26.

Kumakura, Masanaga. "Enyasu taibōron no seiji keizaigaku" (Political economy of eager-waiting theory of weak yen). *Kokusai kinyū* (International finance), no. 2148 (2013): 22–29.

Kume, Ikuo. "Rieki dantai seiji no henyō" (Changes in the politics of interest groups). In *Nihon seiji hendō no 30 nen: Seijika/kanryō/dantaichōsa nimiru kōzō henyō* (Thirty years of political changes in Japan: Structural transformation of politicians, bureaucrats, and organizational surveys), ed. Michio Muramatsu and Ikuo Kume, 259–76. Tokyo: Toyo Keizai Shinposha, 2006.

Kuno, Arata. "Revealing Tariff Structures Under the ASEAN+1 FTAs and ATIGA: Implications for a Possible ASEAN++ FTA." In *Comprehensive Mapping of FTAs in ASEAN and East Asia Phase II*, ed. Chang Jae Lee, Shujiro Urata, and Ikumo Isono. Jakarta: ERIA, 2012.

Kuramoto, Yukiko. "Nihon no kaihatsu kyōroku to kan min pātona shippu" (Japan's development cooperation and its government-private sector partnership). *Chuo daigaku shakai kagaku kenkyūjo nenpō* 21 (2017): 165–78.

Kurihara, Fumiko. *Nihon no taibei taika chokusetsu tōshi no shin tenkai* (Japanese direct foreign investment in the United States and Canada: New developments since 1985), vol. 31. Tokyo: *Ochanomizu Chiri*, 1990, 43–54

Kuroda, Haruhiko. *Tsūka gaikō: Zaimukan no 1300 nichi* (Currency diplomacy: 1,300 days of vice minister of financial affairs). Tokyo: Toyo Keizai Shinposha, 2005.

Kuroda, Haruhiko, and Masahiro Kawai. "Strengthening Regional Financial Cooperation in East Asia." In *Financial Governance in East Asia: Policy Dialogue, Surveillance and Cooperation*, ed. Gordon De Brouwer and Yunjong Wang, 136–66. London: Routledge-Curzon, 2004.

Kusano, Atsushi. "Tettei kenshō: Shingikai wa kakuremino dearu" (Thorough investigation: Commissions are used as a cover). *Shokun* 27, no. 7 (1995): 98–110.

Kushida, Kenji E., and Phillip Y. Lipscy. *Japan Under the DPJ: The Politics of Transition and Governance*. Stanford, Calif.: Walter H. Shorenstein Asia-Pacific Research Center, 2013.

Kwan, C. H. *En to gen kara miru Ajia no tsūka kiki* (The Asian currency crisis seen from the yen and the yuan). Tokyo: Iwanami Shoten, 1997.

Kwei, Elaine. "Chinese Trade Bilateralism: Politics Still in Command." In *Bilateral Trade Agreements in the Asia-Pacific: Origins, Evolution, and Implication*, ed. Vinod K. Aggarwal and Shujiro Urata, 117–39. Abingdon-on-Thames, UK: Routledge, 2006.

Lake, David A. "Delegating Divisible Sovereignty: Sweeping a Conceptual Minefield." *Review of International Organizations* 2, no. 3 (2007): 219–37.

——. "Open Economy Politics: A Critical Review." *Review of International Organizations* 4, no. 3 (2009): 219–44.

——. "The State and American Trade Strategy in the Pre-Hegemonic Era." *International Organization* 42, no. 1 (1988): 33–58.

Lam, Peng Er. "China's Asian Infrastructure Investment Bank: East Asian Responses." *East Asian Policy* 6, no. 4 (2014): 127–35.

——. *Japan's Peace-Building Diplomacy in Asia: Seeking a More Active Political Role*. London: Routledge, 2009.

Lancaster, Carol. *Foreign Aid: Diplomacy, Development, Domestic Politics*. Chicago: University of Chicago Press, 2007.

Lee, Jaemin. "An Important First Stride, but Beware of the Pitfalls: A Critical Analysis of the ISDS Mechanism of the 2012 Korea–China–Japan Trilateral Investment Treaty." *Chinese Journal of International Law* 12, no. 3 (2013): 509–41.

Lee, Yong Wook. "Japan and the Asian Monetary Fund: An Identity–Intention Approach." *International Studies Quarterly* 50, no. 2 (2006): 339–66.

——. *The Japanese Challenge to the American Neoliberal World Order: Identity, Meaning, and Foreign Policy*. Stanford, Calif.: Stanford University Press, 2008.

Lee, Yong Wook, and Sun Young Kwak. "Neo-liberal Korea and Still Developmentalist Japan: Myth or Reality?" *Global Economic Review* 38, no. 3 (2009): 277–95.

Lewis, Meredith Kolsky. "The Trans-Pacific Partnership Agreement and Development." In *Trade Liberalisation and International Co-operation: A Legal Analysis of the Trans-Pacific Partnership Agreement*, ed. Tania Voon, 28–49. Cheltenham, UK: Edward Elgar, 2009.

Liao, Steven, and Daniel McDowell. "Redback Rising: China's Bilateral Swap Agreements and Renminbi Internationalization." *International Studies Quarterly* 59, no. 3 (2015): 401–22.

Lim, Hank. "The Way Forward for RCEP Negotiations." *East Asia Forum* (2012). https://www.eastasiaforum.org/2012/12/03/the-way-forward-for-rcep-negotiations/.

Lincoln, Edward J. *Arthritic Japan: The Slow Pace of Economic Reform*. Washington, D.C.: Brookings Institution Press, 2004.

——. "Japan: Using Power Narrowly." *Washington Quarterly* 27, no. 1 (2003): 111–27.

——. "Japan's Financial Mess." *Foreign Affairs* 77 (1998): 57–66.

——. *Japan's New Global Role*. Piscataway, N.J.: Transaction, 1993.

Lind, Jennifer. *Sorry States: Apologies in International Politics*. Ithaca, N.Y.: Cornell University Press, 2008.

Lipscy, Phillip Y. "Japan's Asian Monetary Fund Proposal." *Stanford Journal of East Asian Affairs* 3, no. 1 (2003): 93–103.

——. *Renegotiating the World Order: Institutional Change in International Relations*. New York: Cambridge University Press, 2017.

Lu, Chang Rong. "Zaimushō shudō no nihon seifu ni yoru ASEAN+3 chiiki kinyū kyōryoku seisaku ni kansuru kōsatsu" (A study of the Japanese government's policy on ASEAN+3 financial cooperation led by the Ministry of Finance). Ph.D. dissertation, Waseda University, 2015.

Lukauskas, Arvid. "Financial Restriction and the Developmental State in East Asia Toward a More Complex Political Economy." *Comparative Political Studies* 35, no. 4 (2002): 379–412.

Luttrell, David, Tyler Atkinson, and Harvey Rosenblum. "Assessing the Costs and Consequences of the 2007–09 Financial Crisis and Its Aftermath." *Economic Letter* 8, no. 7 (2013): 1–4.

Lynch, James, Alfredo Perdiguero, and Jason Rush. "The Role of ADB in ASEAN Integration." In *Economic Integration and Regional Development: The ASEAN Economic Community*, ed. Kiyoshi Kobayashi, Khairuddin Abdul Rashid, Masahiko Furuichi, and William P. Anderson, 34–44. London: Routledge, 2017.

Mabuchi, Masaru. "Kanryōsei no henyō; ishuku suru kanryō (Changes of the bureaucratic system; cowering bureaucrats)." In *Nihon seiji hendō no 30 nen: Seijika/kanryō/dantaichosa nimiru kōzō henyō* (Thirty years of political changes in Japan: Structural transformation of politicians, bureaucrats, and organizational surveys), ed. Michio Muramatsu and Ikuo Kume, 137–58. Tokyo: Toyo Keizai Shinposha, 2006.

MacIntyre, Andrew J., T. J. Pempel, and John Ravenhill. *Crisis as Catalyst: Asia's Dynamic Political Economy*. Ithaca, N.Y.: Cornell University Press, 2008.

Mahbubani, Kishore. *The New Asian Hemisphere: The Irresistible Shift of Global Power to the East*. New York: PublicAffairs, 2008.

Manger, Mark S. *Investing in Protection: The Politics of Preferential Trade Agreements Between North and South*. Cambridge: Cambridge University Press, 2009.

Manning, Richard. "Will 'Emerging Donors' Change the Face of International Cooperation?" *Development Policy Review* 24, no. 4 (2006): 371–85.

Mansfield, Edward D., and Helen V. Milner. "The New Wave of Regionalism." *International Organization* 53, no. 3 (1999): 589–627.

Mattlin, Mikael, and Mikael Wigell. "Geoeconomics in the Context of Restive Regional Powers." *Asia Europe Journal* 14, no. 2 (2015): 125–34.

Maull, Hanns W. "Germany and Japan: The New Civilian Powers." *Foreign Affairs* 69 (1989): 91–106.

Mawdsley, Emma, Laura Savage, and Sung-Mi Kim. "A 'Post-Aid World'? Paradigm Shift in Foreign Aid and Development Cooperation at the 2011 Busan High Level Forum." *Geographical Journal* 180, no. 1 (2014): 27–38.

McCauley, Robert N. "Unifying Government Bond Markets in East Asia." *BIS Quarterly Review* (December 2003): 89–98. https://www.bis.org/publ/qtrpdf/r_qt0312h.pdf.

McDowell, Daniel. "The US as 'Sovereign International Last-Resort Lender': The Fed's Currency Swap Programme During the Great Panic of 2007–09." *New Political Economy* 17, no. 2 (April 2012): 157–78.

McGray, Douglas. "Japan's Gross National Cool." *Foreign Policy* 130, no. 1 (2002): 44–54.

McKinnon, Ronald I. *Money and Capital in Economic Development.* Washington, D.C.: Brookings Institution Press, 2010 [1973].

McKinnon, Ronald I., and Kenichi Ohno. *Dollar and Yen: Resolving Economic Conflict Between the United States and Japan.* Cambridge, Mass.: MIT Press, 1997.

Ministry of Economy, Trade, and Industry. "PPP Tasukufosu hokokusho" (PPP Task Force report). 2010.

Mishima, Ko. "The Changing Relationship Between Japan's LDP and the Bureaucracy: Hashimoto's Administrative Reform Effort and Its Politics." *Asian Survey* 38, no. 10 (1998): 968–85.

——. "Grading Japanese Prime Minister Koizumi's Revolution: How Far Has the LDP's Policymaking Changed?" *Asian Survey* 47, no. 5 (2007): 727–48.

——. "A Missing Piece in Japan's Political Reform." *Asian Survey* 53, no. 4 (2013): 703–27.

Mitsubishi Research Institute. "Heisei 26 nendo Gaimushō ODA hyōka. Hōseido seibi shien no hyōka. (Daisansha hyōka) Hōkokusho" (Appraisal of 2014 Japan's ODA. Appraisal report of legal institutional building assistance [by the third party]). Tokyo: Mitsubishi Research Institute, 2015.

Miura, Yuji. *Keizai renkeika no enjo seisaku—ASEAN niokeru kyōso to shien no baransu* (Foreign aid policy under economic cooperation—the balance of competition and aid in ASEAN). Gurōbarizēshon kano Ajia to nihon no yakuwari. Tokyo: JICA Research Institute, 2006.

Miyashita, Akitoshi. "Gaiatsu and Japan's Foreign Aid: Rethinking the Reactive-Proactive Debate." *International Studies Quarterly* 43, no. 4 (1999): 695–731.

Mizuho. "Nihon kigyō kara mita higashi ajia bijinesu to FTA: Takamaru kitai no ippōde Nihon nuki FTA e no genjitsuteki taiō wo mosaku" (Business opportunities in East Asia and FTA for Japanese businesses: Rising expectations, as they search for pragmatic solutions for FTAs without Japan). *Mizuho Report* (2005).

Mizuno, Kengo. "Ajia saiken shijō inishiachibu (ABMI) no shinten to kadai" (Progress and issues related to Asian bond markets initiative). In *Ajia ikinai kinyū kyōryoku saikō: shinten to kadai* (Revisiting intra-Asian financial cooperation: Perspectives and issues), ed. Chie Kashiwagara. Tokyo: Institute of Development Economies, 2012.

Moravcsik, Andrew. "Taking Preferences Seriously: A Liberal Theory of International Politics." *International Organization* 51, no. 4 (1997): 513–53.

Mosley, Layna. "Room to Move: International Financial Markets and National Welfare States." *International Organization* 54, no. 4 (2000): 737–73.

Mulgan, Aurelia George. *Japan's Failed Revolution: Koizumi and the Politics of Economic Reform*. Canberra: Asia Pacific Press, 2002.

——. "Japan's Political Leadership Deficit." *Australian Journal of Political Science* 35, no. 2 (2000): 183–202.

——. "Japan's 'Un-Westminster' System: Impediments to Reform in a Crisis Economy." *Government and Opposition* 38, no. 1 (2003): 73–91.

——. "Where Tradition Meets Change: Japan's Agricultural Politics in Transition." *Journal of Japanese Studies* 31, no. 2 (2005): 261–98.

Munakata, Naoko. "Has Politics Caught Up with Markets? In Search of East Asian Economic Regionalism." In *Beyond Japan: The Dynamics of East Asian Regionalism*, ed. Peter J. Katzenstein and Takashi Shiraishi, 130–57. Ithaca, N.Y.: Cornell University Press, 2006.

——. "Whither East Asian Economic Integration?" *Working Papers by CEAP Visiting Fellows* (2002): 1–40. https://www.brookings.edu/wp-content/uploads/2016/06/2002_munakata.pdf.

Mundell, Robert A. "A Theory of Optimum Currency Areas." *American Economic Review* 51, no. 4 (1961): 657–65.

Muramatsu, Michio. *Seikan sukuramu gata rīdāshippu no hōkai* (Collapse of leadership created by a unified front of politicians and bureaucrats). Tokyo: Toyo Keizai Shinposha, 2010.

Muramatsu, Michio, and Ikuo Kume. *Nihon seiji hendō no 30 nen: Seijika/kanryō/dantaichosa nimiru kōzō henyō* (Thirty years of political changes in Japan: Structural transformation of politicians, bureaucrats, and organizational surveys). Tokyo: Toyo Keizai Shinposha, 2006.

Murayama, Tsuyoshi. "Hōmushō hōmu sōgō kenkyūshō ni yoru hōseibi shien e no torikumi" (Efforts of Research and Training Institute of the Ministry of Justice to support legislation). *Keio hōgaku* 5 (2006): 351–63.

Murphy, R. Taggart. *The Weight of the Yen: How Denial Imperils America's Future and Ruins an Alliance*. New York: Norton, 1997.

Muto, Megumi, and Koki Hirota. "Tōnan ajia niokeru nihon no ODA no hensen to kadai: senpatsu asean wo chūshin nishite" (Changes and challenges of Japan's ODA in Southeast Asia: Focused on forerunner ASEAN). In *Korekarano Nihon no kokusai kyōryoku: biggu dōnā kara sumāto dōnā e* (Future of Japan's international cooperation: From a big donor to a smart donor), ed. Takashi Kurosaki and Keijiro Ootsuka, 35–60. Tokyo: Nippon Hyōron sha, 2015.

Naím, Moisés. "Rogue Aid." *Foreign Policy*, no. 159 (2007): 96–97.

Nakagawa, Junji. "Competitive Regionalism Through Bilateral and Regional Rule-Making: Standard Setting and Locking-In." In *Competitive Regionalism: FTA Diffusion in the Pacific Rim*, ed. Mireya Solís, Barbara Stallings, and Saori N. Katada, 74–93. International Political Economy Series. Basingstoke, UK: Palgrave Macmillan, 2009.

——. "Mega FTA no jidai: sono haikei to nihon no tsūshō seisaku no kadai" (The era of mega FTA: Its background and issues for Japan's trade policy)." *Kokusai mondai*, no. 632 (June 2014): 1–4.

Nakasone, Yasuhiro. "Kyōtsū tsūka ga hiraku Nihon to Ajia no mirai" (The future of Japan and Asia with a common currency). *Chuo koron* 124, no. 4 (2009): 182–93.

Naoi, Megumi. *Building Legislative Coalitions for Free Trade in Asia: Globalization as Legislation*. New York: Cambridge University Press, 2015.

Naoi, Megumi, and Ellis Krauss. "Who Lobbies Whom? Special Interest Politics Under Alternative Electoral Systems." *American Journal of Political Science* 53, no. 4 (2009): 874–92.

Naoi, Megumi, and Shujiro Urata. "Free Trade Agreements and Domestic Politics: The Case of the Trans-Pacific Partnership Agreement." *Asian Economic Policy Review* 8, no. 2 (2013): 326–49.

Narlikar, Amrita, Martin Daunton, and Robert M. Stern, eds. *The Oxford Handbook on the World Trade Organization*. Oxford: Oxford University Press, 2012.

Nishigaki, Akira, Yasutami Shimomura, and Kazuto Tsuji. *Kaihasu enjo no keizaigaku—"Kyōsei no sekai" to Nihon no ODA* (Economics of development assistance—"world of harmonious coexistence" and Japan's ODA). Tokyo: Yuhikaku, 2011.

Nishikawa, Akiko. "Shingikai nado shiteki shimonkikan no genjō to ronten" (Current status and issues of advisory bodies of the central government). *National Diet Library Research and Legislative Reference* 57, no. 5 (2007): 59–73.

Nishizawa, Toshiro. "Infrastructure Investment and Finance in Asia." *Public Policy Review* 14, no. 5 (2018): 925–53.

Noble, Gregory W., and John Ravenhill. *The Asian Financial Crisis and the Architecture of Global Finance*. Cambridge: Cambridge University Press, 2000.

Oatley, Thomas. "The Reductionist Gamble: Open Economy Politics in the Global Economy." *International Organization* 65, no. 2 (2011): 311–41.

Oba, Mie. *Ajia taiheiyō chiiki keisei e no dōtei: Kyōkai kokka Nichigō no aidentiti mosaku to chiiki-shugi* (Road to the creation of Asia-Pacific region: Japan's and Australia's search for their identity as a boundary nation and the regionalism). Kyoto: Minerva Shobo, 2004.

——. *Jūsōteki chiiki toshiteno Ajia: Tairitsu to kyōzon no kōzu* (Asia as a multilayered region: Framed by conflicts and coexistence). Tokyo: Yuhikaku, 2014.

——. "The New Japan-ASEAN Partnership: Challenges in the Transformation of the Regional Context in East Asia." In *ASEAN-Japan Relations*, ed. Takashi Shiraishi and Takaaki Kojima, 55–72. Singapore: ISEAS, 2014.

Ogata, Sadako, and Johan Cels. "Human Security—Protecting and Empowering the People." *Global Governance* 9, no. 3 (2003): 273–82.

Ogawa, Eiji. "Currency Basket Strategy for Asian Currency Cooperation." *Financial Review* 81 (2006): 154–76.

Ogawa, Eiji, and Michiru Sakane Kosaka. "Japan's Monetary and Financial Cooperation in East Asia—from the Viewpoint of the Spillover Effects of Currency Misalignment." *Public Policy Review* 10, no. 1 (2014): 33–52.

Ogawa, Eiji, and Junko Shimizu. "Progress Toward a Common Currency Basket System in East Asia." *RIETI Discussion Paper Series* 07-E-002 (2007): 1–22.

Ogiwara, Akira. "Kokusai kyōsōryoku noaru pakkeiji gata infura jigyō no tenkai wo mezashite: PPP ni okeru kadai no kōsatsu" (Developing the international competitiveness in the "Package of Overseas Infrastructure Development"). *Collected Papers of the Research Center for PPP in Toyo University* 3 (2013): 80–101.

Ohno, Kenichi. *Japanese Views on Economic Development: Diverse Paths to the Market*. Abingdon, UK: Routledge, 2012.

———. *Tojōkoku Nippon no ayumi: Edo kara Heisei madeno keizai hatten* (The path traveled by Japan as a developing country: Economic growth from Edo to Heisei). Tokyo: Yuhikaku, 2005.

Okabe, Yasunobu. "Japan Overseas Cooperation Volunteers: Its Genesis and Development." In *Japan's Development Assistance: Foreign Aid and the Post-2015 Agenda*, ed. Hiroshi Kato, John Page, and Yasutani Shimomura, 222–36. London: Palgrave Macmillan, 2016.

Okawara, Nobuo, and Peter J. Katzenstein. "Japan and Asian-Pacific Security: Regionalization, Entrenched Bilateralism and Incipient Multilateralism." *Pacific Review* 14, no. 2 (2001): 165–94.

Okimoto, Daniel I. "Political Inclusivity: The Domestic Structure of Trade." In *The Political Economy of Japan*, ed. Takashi Inoguchi and Daniel Okimoto, 305–44. Stanford, Calif.: Stanford University Press, 1988.

Organisation for Economic Co-operation and Development (OECD). *Development Co-Operation: Efforts and Policies of the Members of the Development Assistance Committee*. Paris: OECD, 1988.

———. "OECD Development Assistance Peer Reviews: Japan 2010." (2011): 1–126. https://www.oecd-ilibrary.org/development/oecd-development-assistance-peer-reviews-japan-2010_9789264098305-en.

———. "OECD Development Co-operation Peer Reviews: Japan 2014." (2014): 1–110. http://www.oecd.org/dac/peer-reviews/Japan-peer-review-2014.pdf.

Osei-Hwedie, Bertha Z. "China-Japan Rivalry in Africa." In *Africa in the Age of Globalisation: Perceptions, Misperceptions and Realities*, ed. Edward Shizha and Lamine Diallo, 133–47. Abingdon, UK: Routledge, 2016.

Ostry, Jonathan D., Atish R. Ghosh, Marcos Chamon, and Mahvash S. Qureshi. "Tools for Managing Financial-Stability Risks from Capital Inflows." *Journal of International Economics* 88, no. 2 (2012): 407–21.

Overseas Economic Cooperation Fund (OECF). "Issues Related to the World Bank's Approach to Structural Adjustment: Proposal from a Major Partner." *OECF Occasional Paper* No. 1 (1991).

Oyane, Satoshi. *Kokusai rejīmu to Nichibei no gaikō kōsō: WTO, APEC, FTA no tenkan kyokumen* (International regimes and Japan-U.S. diplomatic initiatives: Turning point of WTO, APEC, FTA). Tokyo: Yuhikaku, 2011.

Ozawa, Ichiro. *Nihon kaizō keikaku* (A plan to transform Japan). Tokyo: Kodansha, 1993.

Ozawa, Terutomo. "Foreign Direct Investment and Economic Development." *Transnational Corporations* 1, no. 1 (1992): 27–54.

Page, John. "The East Asian Miracle: Four Lessons for Development Policy." *NBER Macroeconomics Annual* 9 (1994): 219–69.

Pakpahan, Beginda. "Will RCEP Compete with the TPP?" *East Asia Forum* (November 28, 2012). https://www.eastasiaforum.org/2012/11/28/will-rcep-compete-with-the-tpp/.

Park, Gene. *Spending Without Taxation: FILP and the Politics of Public Finance in Japan*. Stanford, Calif.: Stanford University Press, 2011.

Park, Gene, Saori N. Katada, Giacomo Chiozza, and Yoshiko Kojo. *Taming Japan's Deflation: The Debate Over Unconventional Monetary Policy.* Ithaca, N.Y.: Cornell University Press, 2018.

Park, Kangho. "New Development Partners and a Global Development Partnership." In *Catalyzing Development: A New Vision for Aid,* ed. Homi Kharas, Koji Makino, and Woojin Jung, 38–60. Washington, D.C.: Brookings Institution Press, 2011.

Park, Yung Ho. "The Governmental Advisory Commission System in Japan." *Administration & Society* 3, no. 4 (1972): 435–67.

Patrick, Hugh. "The Relevance of Japanese Finance and Its Main Bank System." In *The Japanese Main Bank System: Its Relevance for Developing and Transforming Economies* ed. Masahiko Aoki and Hugh Patrick. New York: Oxford University Press, 1994.

Pekkanen, Robert. "Japan's New Politics: The Case of the NPO Law." *Journal of Japanese Studies* 26, no. 1 (2000): 111–48.

Pekkanen, Saadia, ed. *Asian Designs: Governance in the Contemporary World Order.* Ithaca, N.Y.: Cornell University Press, 2016.

——. "Investment Regionalism in Asia: New Directions in Law and Policy?" *World Trade Review* 11, no. 1 (2012): 119–54.

——. *Japan's Aggressive Legalism: Law and Foreign Trade Politics Beyond the WTO.* Stanford, Calif.: Stanford University Press, 2008.

Pekkanen, Saadia M., Mireya Solís, and Saori N. Katada. "Trading Gains for Control: International Trade Forums and Japanese Economic Diplomacy." *International Studies Quarterly* 51, no. 4 (2007): 945–70.

Pekkanen, Saadia, and Kellee Tsai. *Japan and China in the World Political Economy.* New York: Routledge, 2006.

Pempel, T. J. "Challenges to Bilateralism: Changing Foes, Capital Flows, and Complex Forums." In *Beyond Bilateralism: US–Japan Relations in the New Asia Pacific,* ed. Ellis S. Krauss and T. J. Pempel, 1–36. Stanford, Calif.: Stanford University Press, 2004.

——. "How Bush Bungled Asia: Militarism, Economic Indifference and Unilateralism Have Weakened the United States Across Asia." *Pacific Review* 21, no. 5 (2008): 547–81.

——. *The Politics of the Asian Economic Crisis.* Cornell Studies in Political Economy. Ithaca, N.Y.: Cornell University Press, 1999.

——. *Regime Shift: Comparative Dynamics of the Japanese Political Economy.* Ithaca, N.Y.: Cornell University Press, 1998.

——. "Regime Shift: Japanese Politics in a Changing World Economy." *Journal of Japanese Studies* 23, no. 2 (1997): 333–61.

——. *Remapping East Asia: The Construction of a Region.* Ithaca, N.Y.: Cornell University Press, 2005.

——. "Structural Gaiatsu: International Finance and Political Change in Japan." *Comparative Political Studies* 32, no. 8 (1999): 907–32.

Perroni, Carlo, and John Whalley. "The New Regionalism: Trade Liberalization or Insurance?" *Canadian Journal of Economics* 33, no. 1 (2000): 1–24.

Petri, Peter A., Michael G. Plummer, and Fan Zhai. *The Trans-Pacific Partnership and Asia-Pacific Integration: A Quantitative Assessment,* vol. 98, Washington, D.C.: Peterson Institute for International Economics, 2012.

Phillips, Nicola. "Bridging the Comparative/International Divide in the Study of States." *New Political Economy* 10, no. 3 (2005): 335–43.

Ping, Lee Poh. "The Asian Financial Crisis: Understanding Japanese Assistance to Southeast Asia." *Kajian Malaysia* 20, no. 1 (2002): 33–55.

Pirie, Iain. "Korea and Taiwan: The Crisis of Investment-led Growth and the End of the Developmental State." *Journal of Contemporary Asia* 48, no. 1 (2018): 133–58.

Pitakdumrongkit, Kaewkamol. "Co-chairing International Negotiations: The Case of the Chiang Mai Initiative Multilateralization." *Pacific Review* 28, no. 4 (2015): 577–605.

Polanyi, Karl. *The Great Transformation.* Boston: Beacon Press, 1944.

Porzecanski, Arturo C. *Latin America: The Missing Financial Crisis*, vol. 6. New York: United Nations, 2010.

Prasad, Eswar S. *The Dollar Trap: How the US Dollar Tightened Its Grip on Global Finance.* Princeton, N.J.: Princeton University Press, 2015.

——. *Gaining Currency: The Rise of the Renminbi.* New York: Oxford University Press, 2017.

Prestowitz, Clyde. *Trading Places: How We Are Giving Our Future to Japan & How to Reclaim It.* New York: Basic Books, 1990.

Puchala, Donald J. "Of Blind Men, Elephants and International Integration." *Journal of Common Market Studies* 10, no. 3 (1971): 267–84.

Purrington, Courtney. "Tokyo's Policy Responses During the Gulf War and the Impact of the 'Iraqi Shock' on Japan." *Pacific Affairs* 65, no. 2 (1992): 161–81.

Putnam, Robert D. "Diplomacy and Domestic Politics: The Logic of Two-level Games." *International Organization* 42, no. 3 (1988): 427–60.

Pyle, Kenneth B. *The Japanese Question: Power and Purpose in a New Era.* Washington, D.C.: American Enterprise Institute, 1996.

Rajan, Raghuram. *Fault Lines.* New York: HarperCollins, 2012.

Ramo, Joshua Cooper. *The Beijing Consensus: Notes on the New Physics of Chinese Power.* London: Foreign Policy Centre, 2004.

Ramseyer, J. Mark, and Frances McCall Rosenbluth. *Japan's Political Marketplace.* Cambridge, Mass.: Harvard University Press, 1993.

Rapkin, David P. "The United States, Japan, and the Power to Block: The APEC and AMF Cases." *Pacific Review* 14, no. 3 (2001): 373–410.

Ravenhill, John. *APEC and the Construction of Pacific Rim Regionalism.* Cambridge: Cambridge University Press, 2001.

——. "The 'New East Asian Regionalism': A Political Domino Effect." *Review of International Political Economy* 17, no. 2 (2010): 178–208.

Ray, John E. *Managing Official Export Credits: The Quest for a Global Regime.* Washington, D.C.: Institute for International Economics, 1995.

Reed, Steven R. "Is Japanese Government Really Centralized?" *Journal of Japanese Studies* 8, no. 1 (1982): 133–64.

Reed, Steven R., Ethan Scheiner, Daniel M. Smith, and Michael F. Thies. "The 2012 Election Results: The LDP Wins Big by Default." In *Japan Decides 2012: The Japanese General Election*, ed. Robert J. Pekkanen, Steven R. Reed, and Ethan Scheiner, 34–46. New York: Springer, 2013.

Reimann, Kim. "The Outside In? Japanese International Development NGOs, the State, and International Norms." In *The State of Civil Society in Japan*, ed. Frank J. Schwartz and Susan J. Pharr, 298–315. Cambridge: Cambridge University Press, 2003.

Rix, Alan. *Japan's Aid Program: A New Global Agenda*. Sydney: Australian Government Publishing Service, 1990.

Roberts, Cynthia, Leslie Elliott Armijo, and Saori N. Katada. "The BRICS and Collective Financial Statecraft: Hanging Together, but Why and How?" Paper presented to ISA Annual Convention, New Orleans, 2015.

Roberts, Cynthia A., Leslie Elliott Armijo, and Saori N. Katada. *The BRICS and Collective Financial Statecraft*. New York: Oxford University Press, 2017.

Rosenbluth, Frances McCall. *Financial Politics in Contemporary Japan*. Ithaca, N.Y.: Cornell University Press, 1989.

Rosenbluth, Frances McCall, and Michael F. Thies. *Japan Transformed: Political Change and Economic Restructuring*. Princeton, N.J.: Princeton University Press, 2010.

Rosendorff, B. Peter, and Helen V. Milner. "The Optimal Design of International Trade Institutions: Uncertainty and Escape." *International Organization* 55, no. 4 (2001): 829–57.

Roubini, Nouriel, and Stephen Mihm. *Crisis Economics: A Crash Course in the Future of Finance*. London: Penguin Group, 2010.

Routley, Laura. "Developmental States in Africa? A Review of Ongoing Debates and Buzzwords." *Development Policy Review* 32, no. 2 (2014): 159–77.

Rozman, Gilbert. *Northeast Asia's Stunted Regionalism: Bilateral Distrust in the Shadow of Globalization*. Cambridge: Cambridge University Press, 2004.

Ruggie, John Gerard. "International Regimes, Transactions, and Change: Embedded Liberalism in the Postwar Economic Order." *International Organization* 36, no. 2 (1982): 379–415.

Sakuyama, Takumi. *Nihon no TPP kōshō sanka no shinjitsu: Sono seisaku katei no kaimei* (The truth of Japan's participation in the TPP negotiation: Investigation on the policy making process). Tokyo: Bunshin-do, 2015.

——. "Seisaku jōhō: Suisu no FTA senryaku kara manabumono: Nichi-Suisu EPA kōshō no keiken kara" (Policy briefing: What we can learn from Japan-Swiss FTA strategy—from my experience as Japan-Swiss EPA negotiator). *Primaff Review* 30 (2009): 36–41.

Samuels, Richard J. *Securing Japan: Tokyo's Grand Strategy and the Future of East Asia*. Ithaca, N.Y.: Cornell University Press, 2007.

Sato, Yoichiro. "Substituting Multilateralism, Guiding Trilateralism: The Japan-ROK Investment Agreement in the Growing East Asian Regionalism." In *Changing Power Relations in Northeast Asia: Implications for Relations Between Japan and South Korea*, ed. Marie Söderberg, 138–53. London: Routledge, 2011.

Sawada, Yasuyuki, and Yasuyuki Todo. "Tojōkoku no hinkon sakugen ni okeru seifu kaihatsu enjo no yakuwari" (The role of official development assistance in reducing poverty among developing countries). *RIETI Policy Discussion Paper Series* 10-P-021 (2010): 1–17. http://www.dl.ndl.go.jp/view/download/digidepo_8703930_po_10p021.pdf ?contentNo=1&alternativeNo=.

Schaede, Ulrike. *Choose and Focus: Japanese Business Strategies for the 21st Century*. Ithaca, N.Y.: Cornell University Press, 2008.

Scheiner, Ethan, Robert Pekkanen, Michio Muramatsu, and Ellis Krauss. "When Do Interest Groups Contact Bureaucrats Rather than Politicians? Evidence on Fire Alarms and Smoke Detectors from Japan." *Japanese Journal of Political Science* 14, no. 3 (2013): 283–304.

Schmiegelow, Henrik, and Michele Schmiegelow. "How Japan Affects the International System." *International Organization* 44, no. 4 (1990): 553–88.

Schoppa, Leonard J. *Bargaining with Japan: What American Pressure Can and Cannot Do*. New York: Columbia University Press, 1997.

——. *Race for the Exits: The Unraveling of Japan's System of Social Protection*. Ithaca, N.Y.: Cornell University Press, 2008.

——. "Two-Level Games and Bargaining Outcomes: Why Gaiatsu Succeeds in Japan in Some Cases but Not Others." *International Organization* 47, no. 3 (1993): 353–86.

Schwartz, Frank J. *Advice and Consent: The Politics of Consultation in Japan*. Cambridge: Cambridge University Press, 2001.

Sekizawa, Yoichi. "FTA ni kansuru Nihon no pojishon no henka to sono haikei" (Changes of Japan's position toward FTA and their reasons). *Tokyo Daigaku Shakai kagaku Kenkyujo Discussion Paper Series* Hikaku Chiiki Shugi Project No. 13 (2006): 1–16. https://project.iss.u-tokyo.ac.jp/crep/pdf/rj/r13.pdf.

Shambaugh, David. *China Goes Global: The Partial Power*. New York: Oxford University Press, 2013.

Sheng, Andrew. *From Asian to Global Financial Crisis: An Asian Regulator's View of Unfettered Finance in the 1990s and 2000s*. New York: Cambridge University Press, 2009.

Shimizu, Junko, and Kiyotaka Sato. "Abenomics, Yen Depreciation, Trade Deficit, and Export Competitiveness." *RIETI Discussion Paper Series* 15-E-020 (2015): 1–31.

Shimizu, Satoshi. "Advancing RMB Internationalization and Its Prospect: In Relation to Liberalization of Capital Transaction." *RIM Pacific Rim Business Information* 15, no. 57 (2015): 106.

——. "Development of Asian Bond Markets and Challenges: Keys to Market Expansion." *Public Policy Review* 14, no. 5 (September 2018): 955–1000.

Shinoda, Tomohito. *Contemporary Japanese Politics: Institutional Changes and Power Shifts*. New York: Columbia University Press, 2013.

——. "Japan's Failed Experiment: The DPJ and Institutional Change for Political Leadership." *Asian Survey* 52, no. 5 (2012): 799–821.

——. *Kantei Gaikō: Seiji rīdāshippu no yukue* (Diplomacy by Prime Minister's Office: Whither political leadership?) Tokyo: Asahi Shimbun Shuppan, 2004.

Shirai, Sayuri. *Makuro kaihatsu keizaigaku—Taigai enjo no shinchōryū* (Macro development economics—recent trends in foreign aid). Tokyo: Yuhikaku, 2005.

Shiraishi, Takashi. "Japan and Southeast Asia." In *Network Power: Japan and Asia*, ed. Peter J. Katzenstein and Takashi Shiraishi, 169–94. Ithaca, N.Y.: Cornell University Press, 1997.

——. "The Third Wave: Southeast Asia and Middle-Class Formation in the Making of a Region." In *Beyond Japan: The Dynamics of East Asian Regionalism*, ed. Peter J. Katzenstein and Takashi Shiraishi, 237–71. Ithaca, N.Y.: Cornell University Press, 2006.

Sinclair, Timothy J. *The New Masters of Capital: American Bond Rating Agencies and the Politics of Creditworthiness*. Ithaca, N.Y.: Cornell University Press, 2014.

Soderberg, Marie. *The Business of Japanese Foreign Aid: Five Cases from Asia*. New York: Routledge, 2012.

Soeya, Yoshihide. *Japan's "Middle Power" Diplomacy: Post-War Japan's Choice and Strategy*. Tokyo: Chikuma Shobo, 2005.

Sohn, Yul. "Japan's New Regionalism: China Shock, Values, and the East Asian Community." *Asian Survey* 50, no. 3 (2010): 497–519.

Solingen, Etel. "Of Dominoes and Firewalls: The Domestic, Regional, and Global Politics of International Diffusion." *International Studies Quarterly* 56, no. 4 (2012): 631–44.

Solís, Mireya. *Banking on Multinationals: Public Credit and the Export of Japanese Sunset Industries*. Stanford, Calif.: Stanford University Press, 2004.

——. *Dilemmas of a Trading Nation: Japan and the United States in the Evolving Asia-Pacific Order*. Washington, D.C.: Brookings Institution Press, 2017.

——. "Japan's Competitive FTA Strategy: Commercial Opportunity Versus Political Rivalry." In *Competitive Regionalism: FTA Diffusion in the Pacific Rim*, ed. Mireya Solís, Barbara Stallings, and Saori N. Katada, 198–215. Basingstoke, UK: Palgrave Macmillan, 2009.

——. "Japan's New Regionalism: The Politics of Free Trade Talks with Mexico." *Journal of East Asian Studies* 3, no. 3 (2003): 377–404.

——. "The Trans-Pacific Partnership: Can the United States Lead the Way in Asia-Pacific Integration?" *Pacific Focus* 27, no. 3 (2012): 319–41.

Solís, Mireya, and Saori N. Katada. "Explaining FTA Proliferation: A Policy Diffusion Framework." In *Competitive Regionalism: FTA Diffusion in the Pacific Rim*, ed. Mireya Solís, Barbara Stallings, and Saori N. Katada, 1–24. Basingstoke, UK: Palgrave Macmillan, 2009.

——. "The Japan-Mexico FTA: A Cross-regional Step in the Path Towards Asian Regionalism." *Pacific Affairs* 80, no. 2 (2007): 279–301.

——. "Unlikely Pivotal States in Competitive Free Trade Agreement Diffusion: The Effect of Japan's Trans-Pacific Partnership Participation on Asia-Pacific Regional Integration." *New Political Economy* 20, no. 2 (2015): 155–77.

Solís, Mireya, Barbara Stallings, and Saori N. Katada. *Competitive Regionalism: FTA Diffusion in the Pacific Rim*. International Political Economy Series. Basingstoke, UK: Palgrave Macmillan, 2009.

Soskice, David W., and Peter A. Hall. *Varieties of Capitalism: The Institutional Foundations of Comparative Advantage*. New York: Oxford University Press, 2001.

Stallings, Barbara. "Korea's Victory Over the Global Financial Crisis of 2008–09." In *Unexpected Outcomes: How Emerging Economies Survived the Global Financial Crisis*, ed. Carol Wise, Leslie E. Armijo, and Saori N. Katada, 48–73. Washington, D.C.: Brookings Institution Press, 2015.

Stallings, Barbara, and Eun Mee Kim. "Japan, Korea, and China: Styles of ODA in East Asia." In *Japan's Development Assistance: Foreign Aid and the Post-2015 Agenda*, ed. Hiroshi Kato, John Page, and Yasutani Shimomura, 120–34. London: Palgrave Macmillan, 2016.

——. *Promoting Development: The Political Economy of East Asian Foreign Aid*. Singapore: Palgrave Macmillan, 2017.

Staples, Andrew. *Responses to Regionalism in East Asia: Japanese Production Networks in the Automotive Sector.* New York: Palgrave Macmillan, 2008.

Steinfeld, Edward. "The Capitalist Embrace: China Ten Years After the Asian Financial Crisis." In *Crisis as Catalyst: Asia's Dynamic Political Economy*, ed. Andrew MacIntyre, T. J. Pempel, and John Ravenhill, 183–205. Ithaca, N.Y.: Cornell University Press, 2008.

Stone, Randall W. *Controlling Institutions: International Organizations and the Global Economy.* Cambridge: Cambridge University Press, 2011.

Strange, Susan. *The Retreat of the State: The Diffusion of Power in the World Economy.* New York: Cambridge University Press, 1996.

Streeck, Wolfgang. "Introduction: Explorations into the Origins of Nonliberal Capitalism in Germany and Japan." In *The Origins of Nonliberal Capitalism: Germany and Japan in Comparison*, ed. Wolfgang Streeck and Kozo Yamamura, 1–38. Ithaca, N.Y.: Cornell University Press, 2005.

Streeck, Wolfgang, and Kozo Yamamura, eds. *The Origins of Nonliberal Capitalism: Germany and Japan in Comparison.* Ithaca, N.Y.: Cornell University Press, 2005.

Stubbs, Richard. "What Ever Happened to the East Asian Developmental State? The Unfolding Debate." *Pacific Review* 22, no. 1 (2009): 1–22.

Subramanian, Arvind. *Eclipse: Living in the Shadow of China's Economic Dominance.* Washington, D.C.: Peterson Institute for International Economics, 2011.

Sudo, Sueo. *The Fukuda Doctrine and ASEAN: New Dimensions in Japanese Foreign Policy.* Singapore: Institute of Southeast Asian Studies, 1992.

Sugawara, Junichi. "Nihon no TPP sanka mondai" (Study of Japan's participation in the TPP). In *Tsūshō seisaku no chōryū to Nihon; FTA senryaku to TPP* (The trend of commercial policy and Japan: FTA strategy and the TPP), ed. Ippei Yamazawa and Keiichi Umada, 270–86. Tokyo: Keiso Shobo, 2012.

Suginohara, Masako. "The Politics of Economic Nationalism in Japan: Backlash Against Inward Foreign Direct Investment?" *Asian Survey* 48, no. 5 (2008): 839–59.

Sunaga, Kazuo. "The Reshaping of Japan's Official Development Assistance (ODA) Charter." *FASID (Foundation for Advanced Studies on International Development) Discussion Paper on Development Assistance* 3 (2004): 1–31.

Sussangkarn, Chalongphob. "Chiang Mai Initiative Multilateralization: Origin, Development, and Outlook." *Asian Economic Policy Review* 6, no. 2 (2011): 203–20.

Swaine, Michael D. "Chinese Leadership and Elite Responses to the US Pacific Pivot." *China Leadership Monitor* 38 (2012): 1–26.

Sweijs, Tim, Willem Theo Oosterveld, Emily Knowles, and Menno Schellekens. "Why Are Pivot States So Pivotal? The Role of Pivot States in Regional and Global Security." In *Strategic Monitor 2014: Four Strategic Challenges*. Netherlands: Hague Centre for Strategic Studies, 2014.

Tachiki, Dennis. "Between Foreign Direct Investment and Regionalism: The Role of Japanese Production Networks." In *Remapping East Asia: The Construction of a Region*, ed. T. J. Pempel, 149–69. Ithaca, N.Y.: Cornell University Press, 2005.

Tadokoro, Masayuki. "Ajia ni okeru chiiki tsūka kyōryoku no tenkai" (Development of regional currency cooperation in Asia). In *Nihon no higashi ajia kōsō* (Japan's East Asia framework), ed. Yoshihide Soeya and Masayuki Tadokoro, 113–38. Tokyo: Keio Gijuku Shuppankai, 2004.

Takagi, Shinji. *Conquering the Fear of Freedom: Japanese Exchange Rate Policy Since 1945.* Oxford: Oxford University Press, 2015.

Takeda, Masahiko, and Philip Turner. "The Liberalisation of Japan's Financial Markets: Some Major Themes." *BIS Economic Papers* No. 34 (1992): 1–134. https://www.bis.org /publ/econ34.pdf.

Takenaka, Harukata. *Shushō shihai: nihon seiji no henbō* (Dominance of the prime minister: Transfiguration of Japanese politics). Tokyo: Chuo koron shinsha, 2006.

Tatebayashi, Masahiko. "Seitō naibu soshiki to seitō kan kōshō katei no henyō" (Transformation of inside organizations of political parties and the process of intra-party negotiation). In *Nihon seiji hendō no 30 nen: Seijika/kanryō/dantaichosa nimiru kōzō henyō* (Thirty years of political changes in Japan: Structural transformation of politicians, bureaucrats, and organizational surveys), ed. Michio Muramatsu and Ikuo Kume, 67–94. Tokyo: Toyo Keizai Shinposha, 2006.

Tavlas, George S. "Currency Substitution and the International Demand for Yen." In *The Macroeconomics of International Currencies: Theory, Policy and Evidence*, ed. Paul Mizen and Eric J. Pentecost, 178–92. Cheltenham, UK: Edward Elgar, 1996.

Terada, Takashi. "Competitive Regionalism in Southeast Asia and Beyond: Role of Singapore and ASEAN." In *Competitive Regionalism: FTA Diffusion in the Pacific Rim*, ed. Mireya Solís, Barbara Stallings, and Saori N. Katada, 161–80. Basingstoke, UK: Palgrave Macmillan, 2009.

——. "Constructing an 'East Asian' Concept and Growing Regional Identity: From EAEC to ASEAN+3." *Pacific Review* 16, no. 2 (2003): 251–77.

——. "Higashi ajia FTA no domino ron to domino teishi ron" (Domino theory and firewall theory on East Asia's FTA). In *Henyō suru ajia to nichibei kankei* (Evolution of Asia and U.S.-Japan relations), ed. Yasuhiro Arikawa, Shujiro Urata, Takashi Yoshino, Shotaro Yachi, and Shunji Yanai, 43–72. Tokyo: Toyo Keizai Shinposha, 2012.

——. "Japan and TPP/TPP-11: Opening Black Box of Domestic Political Alignment for Proactive Economic Diplomacy in Face of 'Trump Shock.'" *Pacific Review* (2019): 1–29.

——. "The Origins of ASEAN+6 and Japan's Initiatives: China's Rise and the Agent-Structure Analysis." *Pacific Review* 23, no. 1 (2010): 71–92.

——. "The Origins of Japan's APEC Policy: Foreign Minister Takeo Miki's Asia-Pacific Policy and Current Implications." *Pacific Review* 11, no. 3 (1998): 337–63.

Terry, Edith. *How Asia Got Rich: Japan, China and the Asian Miracle.* Armonk, N.Y.: M. E. Sharpe, 2002.

Thérien, Jean-Philippe. "Debating Foreign Aid: Right Versus Left." *Third World Quarterly* 23, no. 3 (2002): 449–66.

Thomas, Caroline. "Global Governance, Development and Human Security: Exploring the Links." *Third World Quarterly* 22, no. 2 (2001): 159–75.

Thurbon, Elizabeth. *Developmental Mindset: The Revival of Financial Activism in South Korea.* Ithaca, N.Y.: Cornell University Press, 2016.

Thurbon, Elizabeth, and Linda Weiss. "The Developmental State in the Late Twentieth Century." In *Handbook of Alternative Theories of Economic Development*, ed. Erik S. Reinert, Jayati Ghosh, and Rainer Kattel, 637–50. Cheltenham, UK: Edward Elgar, 2016.

Todo, Yasuyuki. "ODA to Nihon kigyō no kokusaika: Nihon to hienjokoku no aidani uin-uin no kankei wo kizuku" (ODA and internationalization of Japanese businesses: How to create a win-win relationship between Japan and aid recipients). *Kokusai Mondai* 616 (2012): 44–54.

Tokunaga, Shojiro. *Japan's Foreign Investment and Asian Economic Interdependence: Production, Trade, and Financial Systems*. Tokyo: University of Tokyo Press, 1992.

Toya, Tetsuro, and Jennifer A. Amyx. *The Political Economy of the Japanese Financial Big Bang: Institutional Change in Finance and Public Policymaking*. Oxford: Oxford University Press, 2006.

Tsunekawa, Keiichi. "Kaihatsu enjo" (Development assistance). In *Nihon no gaikō daigokan* (Fifth volume on Japanese diplomacy), ed. Toshikazu Inoue, Sumio Hatano, Tetsuya Sakai, Ryosei Kokubun, and Ryo Oshiba, 173–98. Tokyo: Iwanami Shoten, 2013.

——. "Why So Many Maps There? Japan and Regional Cooperation." In *Remapping East Asia: The Construction of a Region*, ed. T. J. Pempel, 101–48. Ithaca, N.Y.: Cornell University Press, 2004.

Ueda, Kazuo. "Solving Japan's Economic Puzzle." *Far Eastern Economic Review* (2009): 49–51.

Upham, Frank K. *Law and Social Change in Postwar Japan*. Cambridge, Mass.: Harvard University Press, 2009.

Urata, Shujiro. "Japan's Trade Policy with Asia." *Public Policy Review* 10, no. 1 (2014): 1–31.

Van Wolferen, Karel. *The Enigma of Japanese Power: People and Politics in a Stateless Nation*. New York: Vintage, 1989.

Vogel, Ezra F. *Japan as Number One: Lessons for America*. Cambridge, Mass.: Harvard University Press, 1979.

Vogel, Steven K. *Freer Markets, More Rules: Regulatory Reform in Advanced Industrial Countries*. Ithaca, N.Y.: Cornell University Press, 1996.

——. *Japan Remodeled: How Government and Industry Are Reforming Japanese Capitalism*. Ithaca, N.Y.: Cornell University Press, 2006.

——. *Marketcraft: How Governments Make Markets Work*. New York: Oxford University Press, 2018.

Volcker, Paul, and Toyoo Gyohten. *Changing Fortunes: The World's Money and the Threat to American Leadership*. New York: Crown, 1992.

Wade, Robert. "The Asian Debt-and-Development Crisis of 1997–? Causes and Consequences." *World Development* 26, no. 8 (1998): 1535–53.

——. "The Developmental State: Dead or Alive?" *Development and Change* 49, no. 2 (2018): 518–46.

——. "The First-World Debt Crisis of 2007–2010 in Global Perspective." *Challenge* 51, no. 4 (2008): 23–54.

——. *Governing the Market: Economic Theory and the Role of Government in East Asian Industrialization*. Princeton, N.J.: Princeton University Press, 1990.

———. "Introduction to the 2003 Paperback Edition." In *Governing the Market: Economic Theory and the Role of Government in East Asian Industrialization*. Princeton, N.J.: Princeton University Press, 2004.

———. "Japan, the World Bank, and the Art of Paradigm Maintenance: The East Asian Miracle in Political Perspective." *New Left Review*, no. 217 (1996): 3–37.

Wade, Robert, and Frank Veneroso. "The East Asian Crash and the Wall Street-IMF Complex." *New Left Review*, no. 228 (1998): 3–23.

Wallace, William. "Political Cooperation: Integration Through Intergovernmentalism." In *Policy-Making in the European Community*, ed. Helen S. Wallace, William Wallace, and Carole Webb. New York: Wiley, 1983.

Walter, Andre. "NGOs, Business, and International Investment: The Multilateral Agreement on Investment, Seattle, and Beyond." *Global Governance* 7, no. 1 (2001): 51–73.

Walter, Andrew. *Governing Finance: East Asia's Adoption of International Standards*. Ithaca, N.Y.: Cornell University Press, 2008.

Wan, Ming. "Japan and the Asian Development Bank." *Pacific Affairs* 68, no. 4 (1995): 509–28.

———. "Spending Strategies in World Politics: How Japan Has Used Its Economic Power in the Past Decade." *International Studies Quarterly* 39, no. 1 (1995): 85–108.

Wang, Jian-Ye. "What Drives China's Growing Role in Africa?" *IMF Working Paper* No. 07/211 (2007): 1–30. https://www.imf.org/en/Publications/WP/Issues/2016/12/31/What-Drives-Chinas-Growing-Role-in-Africa-21282.

Watanabe, Shingo, and Masanobu Ogura. "How Far Apart Are Two ACUs from Each Other? Asian Currency Unit and Asian Currency Union." *Bank of Japan Working Paper Series* 06-E-20 (2006): 1–32. https://www.boj.or.jp/en/research/wps_rev/wps_2006/data/wp06e20.pdf.

Watanabe, Toshio, and Yuji Miura. *ODA (seifu kaihatsu enjo) Nihon ni naniga dekiruka* (ODA [official development assistance]: What can Japan do?), vol. 1727. Tokyo: Chuo-shinsho, 2003.

Watanabe, Yorizumi. *Kaisetsu FTA/EPA kōshō* (Ministry of Foreign Affairs Economic Affairs Bureau EPA negotiation team explains FTA and EPA negotiation). Ed. Gaimushō Keizaikyoku EPA Kōshō Team. Tokyo: Nihon Keizai Hyoronsha, 2007.

Webber, Douglas. "Two Funerals and a Wedding? The Ups and Downs of Regionalism in East Asia and Asia-Pacific After the Asian Crisis." *Pacific Review* 14, no. 3 (2001): 339–72.

Weiss, Linda. "Governed Interdependence: Rethinking the Government-Business Relationship in East Asia." *Pacific Review* 8, no. 4 (1995): 589–616.

Wesley, Michael. "The Asian Crisis and the Adequacy of Regional Institutions." *Contemporary Southeast Asia* 21, no. 1 (1999): 54–73.

Williamson, John. "What Washington Means by Policy Reform." In *Latin American Adjustment: How Much Has Happened*, ed. John Williamson, 7–20. Washington, D.C.: Institute for International Economics, 1990.

Wise, Carol, Leslie Elliott Armijo, and Saori N. Katada. *Unexpected Outcomes: How Emerging Economies Survived the Global Financial Crisis*. Washington, D.C.: Brookings Institution Press, 2015.

Witt, Michael A. *Changing Japanese Capitalism: Societal Coordination and Institutional Adjustment*. Cambridge: Cambridge University Press, 2006.

Wolf, Martin. *Fixing Global Finance*. Baltimore: Johns Hopkins University Press, 2010.

——. *The Shifts and the Shocks: What We've Learned—and Have Still to Learn—from the Financial Crisis*. London: Penguin, 2014.

Wong, Joseph. *Betting on Biotech: Innovation and the Limits of Asia's Developmental State*. Ithaca, N.Y.: Cornell University Press, 2011.

Woo-Cumings, Meredith. *The Developmental State*. Ithaca, N.Y.: Cornell University Press, 1999.

Woodall, Brian. *Japan Under Construction: Corruption, Politics, and Public Works*. Berkeley: University of California Press, 1996.

Woods, Ngaire. "The Shifting Politics of Foreign Aid." *International Affairs* 81, no. 2 (2005): 393–409.

——. "Whose Aid? Whose Influence? China, Emerging Donors and the Silent Revolution in Development Assistance." *International Affairs* 84, no. 6 (2008): 1205–21.

World Bank. *The East Asian Miracle: Economic Growth and Public Policy*. New York: Oxford University Press, 1993.

——. *World Development Report 1994: Infrastructure for Development*. New York: Oxford University Press, 1994.

Yaguchi, Mitsuru, Ayako Yamaguchi, and Koji Sakuma. "Integration of Financial Markets in Japan and Asia—Financial Deepening in Asia Due to Japanese Banks' Entry." *Public Policy Review* 14, no. 5 (2018): 835–70.

Yamagata, Tatsufumi. "Sustainable Development Goals and Japan: Sustainability Overshadows Poverty Eeduction." *Asia-Pacific Development Journal* 23, no. 2 (2016): 1–17.

Yasutomo, Dennis T. *Japan and the Asian Development Bank*. Santa Barbara, Calif.: Praeger, 1983.

Yeung, Henry Wai-chung. "Governing the Market in a Globalizing Era: Eevelopmental States, Global Production Networks and Inter-firm Dynamics in East Asia." *Review of International Political Economy* 21, no. 1 (2014): 70–101.

——. *Strategic Coupling: East Asian Industrial Transformation in the New Global Economy*. Ithaca, N.Y.: Cornell University Press, 2016.

Yoshikawa, Yoko. *Nippi baishō gaikō kōshō no kenkyū: 1949–1956* (A study of Japan-Philippines diplomatic negotiation on reparation between 1949 and 1956). Tokyo: Keiso Shobo, 1991.

Yoshimatsu, Hidetaka. *Comparing Institution-Building in East Asia: Power Politics, Governance, and Critical Junctures*. Hampshire, UK: Palgrave Macmillan, 2014.

——. "Diplomatic Objectives in Trade Politics: The Development of the China-Japan-Korea FTA." *Asia-Pacific Review* 22, no. 1 (2015): 100–23.

——. *Japan and East Asia in Transition: Trade Policy, Crisis and Evolution, and Regionalism*. New York: Palgrave Macmillan, 2003.

——. "Japan's Export of Infrastructure Systems: Pursuing Twin Goals Through Developmental Means." *Pacific Review* 30, no. 4 (2017): 494–512.

——. "Japan's Quest for Free Trade Agreements: Constraints from Bureaucratic and Interest Group Politics." In *Japan's Future in East Asia and the Pacific*, ed. Mari Pangestu and Ligang Song, 80–102. Canberra: ANU Press, 2007.

——. "New Dynamics in Sino-Japanese Rivalry: Sustaining Infrastructure Development in Asia." *Journal of Contemporary China* 27, no. 113 (2018): 719–34.

——. "Regional Cooperation in Northeast Asia: Searching for the Mode of Governance." *International Relations of the Asia-Pacific* 10, no. 2 (2010): 247–74.

Yoshimatsu, Hidetaka, and Patrick Ziltener. "Japan's FTA Strategy Toward Highly Developed Countries: Comparing Australia's and Switzerland's Experiences, 2000–09." *Asian Survey* 50, no. 6 (2010): 1058–81.

Yoshitomi, Masaru, and Kenichi Ohno. "Capital-Account Crisis and Credit Contraction: The New Nature of Crisis Requires New Policy Responses." *ADBI Working Paper Series* No. 2 (1999): 1–32. https://www.adb.org/sites/default/files/publication/157213/adbi-rp2 .pdf.

Yu, Yongding. "The Current RMB Exchange Rate Volatility and RMB Internationalization." *International Economic Review* 1 (2012): 18–26.

Zhang, Ming. "Internationalization of the Renminbi: Developments, Problems and Influences." In *Global Financial Governance Confronts the Rising Powers: Emerging Perspectives on the New G20*, ed. C. Randall Henning and Andrew Walter, 151–76. Montreal: McGill-Queen's Press, 2016.

Zhao, Quansheng. "Japan's Aid Diplomacy with China." In *Japan's Foreign Aid: Power and Policy in a New Era*, ed. Bruce Koppel and Robert Orr, 163–87. Boulder, Colo.: Westview Press, 1993.

Zhu, Yuchao. " 'Performance Legitimacy' and China's Political Adaptation Strategy." *Journal of Chinese Political Science* 16, no. 2 (2011): 123–40.

Zimmermann, Felix, and Kimberly Smith. "More Actors, More Money, More Ideas for International Development Co-operation." *Journal of International Development* 23, no. 5 (2011): 722–38.

Zoellick, Robert. "The United States, Europe, and the World Trading System." Remarks Before the Kangaroo Group, Strasbourg, May 15, 2001: 1–9. https://ustr.gov/archive /assets/Document_Library/USTR_Speeches/2001/asset_upload_file206_4282.pdf.

Zysman, John. *Governments, Markets, and Growth: Financial Systems and the Politics of Industrial Change*. Ithaca, N.Y.: Cornell University Press, 1984.

Index

Figures and tables are indicated by "*f*" and "*t*" after page numbers.

2030 Agenda (UN), 155

Abe, Shinzō: on active Japan, 1; on AIIB membership, 179; bilateral currency swap agreements under, 140; BRI, response to, 177–78, 181; China, competition with, 193; foreign aid under, 151, 177; infrastructure exports, team supporting, 181–82; LDP under, 70; ministerial power and, 42; ODA implementation under, 169; on regional geoeconomic strategy, weaknesses in, 192; rise of, 63; stability under, 192; TPP, actions on, 43, 98, 103, 110, 114, 115, 116
Abenomics, 3, 83, 115, 177, 180
actors, impact on strategy implementation, 26–27
Administrative Reform Council, 253n82
advisory council (*shingi-kai*) system, 73–74, 185, 218n28

Afghanistan, legal and judicial development in, 256n110
Aggarwal, Vinod, 228n53
Agreement on Trade-Related Aspects of Intellectual Property Rights (TRIPs), 88
Agreement on Trade-Related Investment Measures (TRIMs), 88
agricultural industry: agricultural products, Japan-U.S. trade in, 90–91; five sacred areas of, 112, 114; MAFF protection of, 102; TPP, opposition to, 113–14, 115; trade liberalization, stance on, 93, 99, 100–101, 106
aid effectiveness paradigm, 246–47n2
alliance capitalism (iron triangle) system, 66, 74, 85
amakudari (descending from heaven) practice, 74–75, 180, 185
Amari, Akira, 115
Amyx, Jennifer, 239n67

antitrust law, revision of (1997), 220n51

Arase, David, 14, 157

ASEAN+1 FTAs, 97

ASEAN+3: Bond Market Forum, 142; Chiang Mai Initiative and, 130; China's preference for, 97, 111; establishment of, 8; Macroeconomic Research Office (AMRO), 129, 139, 186, 196, 242n92; tripartite economic dialogue and, 108–9

ASEAN+6, 4f, 97, 98

ASEAN++ formula, 98

Asia: dollar, overdependence on, 236n23; economic growth in, 3–4, 4f; financial integration of, 140–43, 143f; future of regionalism and regional governance in, 194–96; hub-and-spoke alliance system, 15; infrastructure investment gap, 176; intraregional trade in, 60, 61f; Japan's bilateral foreign aid in, 156–57; Japan's decreasing importance to, 184; legal development, budgets for, 256n110; outward FDI flows to, 81, 81f; regionalism in, 203n60; U.S. pivot toward, 63; U.S. presence in, 3. *See also* Asia-Pacific, geoeconomics of; East Asia

Asia Bonds Online (ABO) website, 142

Asiamoney (magazine), on RMB banks, 149

Asian Bond Fund (ABF), 8, 141, 242n99

Asian Bond Initiatives, 130, 149

Asian Bond Market Initiative (ABMI), 119, 120, 129, 131, 141–42, 145, 186

Asian Bond Monitor (ADB), 142

Asian Currency Crisis Support Facility, 164

Asian currency unit (ACU), 123, 132, 145

Asian Development Bank (ADB): ABO website, 142; BRI size versus, 177;

importance, 151, 157; on infrastructure investment gap, 176; Japan's engagement with, 8, 164, 165, 186; loan rates, 249n30; Office of Regional Economic Integration, 132; proposal for, 249n29; reforms to, 179–80; Regional Cooperation and Integration (RCI) strategy, 165

Asian Development Bank Institute (ADBI), 151, 245n122

Asian Development Fund, 249n30

Asian Infrastructure Investment Bank (AIIB): businesses' lack of support for, 187; capital stock allocation, 257n135; China and, 64; establishment of, 62, 152, 155, 177; governance structure, influences on, 257n132; impact of, 179–81; proposal for, 8–9, 176; U.S. concerns over, 256n119

Asian Lomé Convention, 91

Asian Monetary Fund (AMF), 8, 122, 129, 132–33

Asian Recovery Information Center, 164

Asia-Pacific, geoeconomics of, 45–65; China, impact of rise of, 53–58, 54t; conclusions on, 65; economic cooperation, 91–93; FTA frenzy in, 89; geoeconomic environment, 62–65, 187–88; introduction to, 2–4, 4f, 6–7, 45, 46–51t, 51; Japan, in shifting Asia-Pacific balance, 52–53; Japan, regional economic dynamics and, 58–62, 59f, 60f, 61t; TPP and Japan's strategic advantage in, 109–12

Asia-Pacific Economic Cooperation (APEC), 7, 18, 63, 91–93, 99–100, 225n27, 225n33, 227n52

Asia-Pacific geoeconomic strategy: Asia-Pacific, geoeconomics of,

45–65; conclusions on, 183–96; development and foreign aid, 150–82; foreign economic policy, domestic institutions, and regional governance, 30–44; introduction to, 1–9; Japan, economic transformation, 66–85; Japan, regional geoeconomic strategy, 10–29; money and finance, 119–49; trade and investment, 86–118. See also *detailed entries for these topics*

Asō, Tarō, 149, 177–79

Association of Southeast Asian Nations (ASEAN): ASEAN-China Free Trade Area, 89; ASEAN-Japan Comprehensive Economic Partnership, 97, 226n43; Early Harvest Program, 223n10; integration efforts, 226n44; Japan, bilateral agreements with, 96, 97; Japan's participation in, 202n48; Master Plan on Connectivity, 165; public projects, direct bond funding of, 173; Swap Agreement, 130; TPP versus, 193. See also *entries beginning "ASEAN"*

Australia: ASEAN+1 FTA with, 97; as EMEAP member, 237–38n45; Japan, bilateral agreements with, 96, 101; as Japan exports destination, 60f; Japan's GDP, influence on, 103; as liberal market economy, 38; as part of Asia-Pacific region, 192–93; RMB and, 148; tariff liberalization, 232n104; U.S. bilateral trade agreements with, 55, 89

auto manufacturing firms, 84

Baker, James, 225n27

Balassa, Bela, 28

Baldwin, Richard, 232n112

Bangladesh: Japan's BIT with, 224n19; legal systems, foreign aid support for, 175

Banker (magazine), ranking of international banks, 237n37

Bank for International Settlements (BIS), 122

Bank of Japan (BOJ): domestic monetary policy, 237n36; institutional reforms, 72, 120; International Bureau, 135; Ministry of Finance, policy independence from, 237n44; monetary policy of, 125; RMB support and, 148; yen appreciation and, 136

Bank of Japan Law (rev. 1997), 72

Bank of Tokyo-Mitsubishi (later Mitsubishi UFJ), 148–49

banks, megabanks, 78, 120, 136, 148, 220n51, 233n2. See also *names of specific banks*

Basic Policy for Legal System Development Support (Cabinet Office), 175

"Basic Policy for the Promotion of Future Economic Partnership Agreements" (Council of Ministers on the Promotion of Economic Partnership), 102–3

Bayoumi, Tamim, 244n117

Belt-and-Road Initiative (BRI, China): discussion of, 175–79, 181; emergence of, 62, 152; goals of, 64; impact of, 6, 8; Japan's response to, 177–79; RMB internationalization and, 124

Berger, Thomas, 14

Bernanke, Ben, 235n18

Big Bang financial reform, 120, 133–34

big businesses. *See* businesses

bilateral currency swap agreements, 139–40

bilateral investment treaties (BITs), 88, 108,
    222n2, 224n19, 230n84, 230n86, 230n87
bilateralism, 17–18, 20, 66, 90, 117
Blanco, Herminio, 94
blind men, elephants and, 260n18
Bogor Declaration, 92
bond markets, expansions of, 140–43,
    143f
Bräutigam, Deborah, 248n17
Brazil: government-business
    collaborations, 203n57; impact of
    global financial crisis on, 137
Bremmer, Ian, 55
Bretton Woods institutions, 58, 65
BRIC(S), 58, 64, 124, 155, 213n22
BRICS Development Bank (New
    Development Bank, NDB), 64, 124,
    155
Britain (United Kingdom): foreign aid
    levels, 166; gunboat diplomacy,
    204n74; inward FDI, 221n68; as
    liberal market economy, 38; RMB
    and, 148; tied aid, 160; UK aid
    agency, 250n41
Brunei: Japan, bilateral agreements
    with, 96, 100; P-4 and, 89; tariff
    liberalization, 232n104
bureaucratic fragmentation
    (sectionalism): conclusions on, 189;
    foreign aid and, 162, 163; FTA
    negotiations and, 99, 101–3; impact
    of, 5, 14, 42–43; under Koizumi, 73;
    TPP negotiations and, 115
bureaucrats, politicians and big business
    and, changing relationship among,
    68–69
Busan High-Level Forum on Aid
    Effectiveness, 155
Bush, George W., 63, 89, 154
business conglomerates (*keiretsu*) system,
    78, 79

businesses (corporations, big businesses):
    BRI and AIIB, responses to, 181;
    bureaucrats and politicians and,
    changing relationship among, 68–69;
    corporate profits, 76f; disembedding
    of, 5, 11, 39–42, 101–3; economic
    ministries, distance between, 73–75;
    foreign direct investment by, funding
    for, 238n48; foreign ownership of,
    220n53; FTAs, influences on, 103–6,
    105t, 229n67; globalization of, 2, 33;
    governmental funding for, 218n34;
    influences on trade strategy, 103–6,
    105t; invoice currencies of, 244n115;
    as leaders of economic expansion,
    125; overseas investments, 40; TPP's
    impact on, 110. *See also* government-
    business relations; Keidanren

Cabinet Office, 72, 102, 115, 166, 175
Calder, Kent E., 14
Cambodia: BIT with, 230n86; legal
    systems, foreign aid support for, 174,
    175
Canada: Japan, bilateral agreements
    with, 101; RMB and, 148; tariff
    liberalization, 232n104
capitalism: capitalism debates, 34–39;
    varieties of, 38
Catalinac, Amy, 32–33
catch-up strategies, of late industrializer
    states, 35
Cels, Johan, 253n76
Center for Asian Financial Cooperation
    (BOJ), 135
checkbook diplomacy, 13
Chiang Mai Initiative (CMI): Asian
    financial crisis and, 129; conclusions
    on, 189; defensive nature of, 34;
    establishment of, 119, 130, 138;
    impact of global financial crisis on,

138; institution building for, 145; Japan's support for, 8; objectives, 130; origins of, 22; success of, 28, 120, 149

Chiang Mai Initiative Multilateralization (CMIM), 137–40, 186, 196, 241n82

Chile: Japan, bilateral agreements with, 96, 99–100, 104; P-4 and, 89; South Korea, FTA with, 104; tariff liberalization, 232n104

China: AIIB and, 257n132; ASEAN+1 FTA with, 97; bond market, 140; as challenge to development cooperation paradigm, 175–77; civil law, seminar on, 255n104; CJK Trilateral Investment Treaty, 107–9, 231n94; CMIM and, 138; currency swap agreements, 139, 242n93, 242n94, 242n95; development cooperation paradigm, challenge to, 175–77; economic growth, 3–4, 4f, 26, 42, 61, 214n28; economy, size of, 212n9; EHP, 223n10; foreign exchange reserves, 245n121; foreign investments, 152, 215n49; GDP, 4f, 54–55, 54f, 58, 59f; going global strategy, 53; impact of Asian financial crisis on, 122; Indonesia, relationship with, 181; as late industrializer state, 35; OECD/DAC criteria, lack of use of, 246n1; regional and global economy, challenges to, 53–58, 54f; regional and global economy, engagement with, 52; regional strategy, 89; rise of, 37, 53–58, 54t, 65, 184; shift from foreign aid recipient to donor, 154; socialist market economy model, 55; state capitalism, 55; U.S., conflict with, 1, 5, 6–7, 34, 53. *See also* Belt-and-Road Initiative

China, Japan and: bilateral agreements, 101, 108, 224n19; changing relationship of, 188; China as Japan exports destination, 60f; foreign aid competition with Japan, 150–51; Japanese businesses' desire for FTA with China, 103; relationship between, 52–53, 147–49, 193–94

China, trade: China-Japan-Korea Free Trade Agreement, 86, 112, 185; FTA negotiations, 89–90; TPP and, 98, 111, 215n47; U.S., trade war with, 65, 192, 194; U.S., trade with, 224n17; WTO, accession to, 3

China Development Bank, 154, 176

China International Payment System (Cross-Border Inter-Bank Payment System, CIPS), 148

China-Japan Finance Dialogue communiqué, 149

China-Japan-Korea (CJK) Trilateral Investment Treaty, 107–9, 231n94

civil service scandals, 73

civil society, foreign aid engagement with, 161–62

Clinton, Bill, and Clinton administration, 53, 92, 239n62

Clinton, Hillary, 63, 213–14n27

Cohen, Benjamin, 244n118

Cold War: economic competition during, versus post–Cold War era, 198n6; influence of, on Europe versus Asia, 15

collateralized bond obligations (CBOs), 243n101

Colombia, BIT with, 230n86

companies. *See* businesses

comparative political economy (CPE), 31–34, 38

competition, policy diffusion and, 34

competitive devaluation, 238–39n56

Comprehensive and Progressive
Agreement for the Trans-Pacific
Partnership (CPTPP, TPP-11), 98,
116–17, 194, 233n117
Comprehensive Economic Partnership
Agreement, 111
comprehensive economic partnership
(CEP) agreements, 222n1
Comprehensive Economic Partnership
for East Asia (CEPEA, ASEAN+6),
97, 111, 165
concerted unilateralism, 92, 93
convoy system (*gosō sendan hōshiki*), 67,
78, 85, 185, 190, 219–20n49
coordinated market economy (CME)
model, 38
Corning, Gregory P., 109, 226n43
corporations. *See* businesses
Council of Ministers on the Promotion
of Economic Partnership, 102–3
Council on Economic and Fiscal Policy
(CEFP), 72
Cowhey, Peter, 16–17
Credit Guarantee Investment Facility
(CGIF, ABMI), 142
credit rating agencies, 121
credit rents, 234n9
Cross-Border Inter-Bank Payment
System (China International Payment
System, CIPS), 148
cross-shareholding, 220n52
currencies: currency swaps and currency
swap agreements, 241n85, 242n93,
242n94, 242n95; exchange rates,
Japan's obsession with, 124–26;
stability of, 145; volatility of, 131.
See also renminbi; yen

Daiwa Bank, 219n46
Das, Dilip K., 243n99
deleveraging, 56, 136

Democratic Party of Japan/Democratic
Party (DPJ): on AIIB, 179; electoral
campaign manifesto, 217n11; electoral
success (2009), 70; Keidanren
contributions to, 79, 80f; ODA
policies, 169; renminbi, support for,
245n126; TPP, concern over, 113
Dent, Christopher M., 165, 226n41
deposit protection (payoff system), 77
descending from heaven (*amakudari*)
practice, 74–75, 185
developmentalism and developmental
state: capitalism debates and, 34–39;
conflict with liberal economic
strategy, 191; influence of, 41; Japan
as developmental state, 39–40, 112
development and foreign aid, 150–82;
AIIB, 179–81; bifurcated tracks of,
170; concessional loan-based aid, 160,
162–63; conclusions on, 182, 186–87;
definition of, 246n1; development
cooperation, 150, 151, 155, 175–77,
182; development trinity (*sanmi ittai*)
approach, 39, 67, 150, 189;
government-business relationships
and, 170–75; introduction to, 8–9,
150–51; Japan's rise to foreign aid
superpower, 156–58, 159t, 160–65,
161f; MDBs, development funding
by, 64–65; norm building and pursuit
of national economic interest
through, 166, 167f, 168–70, 182; path
to, 23, 24t; quality infrastructure
investments, 177, 178, 181–82;
request-base foreign aid, 66–67;
shifting ground for, 152–56, 153f;
vanguard effects of, 174–75. *See also*
Belt-and-Road Initiative; official
development assistance
Development Assistance Committee
(DAC, OECD), 151, 153f, 158, 162, 166

Development Cooperation Charter, 169

Doha Development Round, 25, 88, 108

Doha Round negotiations (WTO), 57

Dollar-Yen Agreement, 125

domestic politics (domestic economic dynamics): domestic market reform, 39; domestic regulatory capacities, 214n32; foreign aid and, 163–64; influence of, 13, 14, 15–16, 25, 66, 99, 112–14; international systems, interaction with, 31–32

dominance of administrative guidance (gyōsei shidō), 67

double mismatch problem, 123, 130–31, 143

double movement thesis, 189

Early Harvest Program (EHP) agreement, 89, 223n10

Early Voluntary Sectoral Liberalization (EVSL), 92–93, 225n31

East Asia: East Asia Free Trade Area, 111; East Asian Miracle, 190, 191; East Asian Summit, 165; economic balance in, 59, 59f; FTA frenzy in, 89; interdependence of, 16; as optimum currency area, 244n117; regional institutions, 21, 202n49

East Asian Miracle, The (World Bank), 160

economic ministries, distance between big businesses and, 73–75

economic partnership agreements (EPAs): conclusions on, 185; event chronology, 46–51t; FTAs as, 222n1; investment chapters in, 86; Japan's use of, 90, 94, 95t, 96–99. See also free trade agreements

Economic Partnership Division (METI), 228n63

Economic Planning Agency, 71, 162

Economic Research Institute for ASEAN and East Asia (ERIA), 151, 165

Economic Review and Policy Dialogue (ERPD), 139

economy: at early stages of industrial catch-up, 207n26; economic cooperation (keizai kyōryoku), 150, 157; economic reforms, 78–79; economic regionalism, rise of, 33–34; economic statecraft, 11–12; mature economies, 36–37; middle-income traps, 208n38. See also economic partnership agreements; GDP; geoeconomics; global economic governance

Egypt, Japan's BIT with, 224n19

Eichengreen, Barry, 244n117

electoral reform (1994), 32, 71–73, 185

elephants, blind men and, 260n18

embedded autonomy, 35–36

embedded liberalism, 13, 19

embedded mercantilism: conclusions on, 185; description of, 13; discussion of, 19; fading of, 182; influence of, 100, 103; of old-style regional strategy, 17, 93, 125, 128–29; as strategy, 14; trinity economic development approach and, 150. See also convoy system

emergency liquidity mechanisms, 130

emulation, forces of, 27

engineering, procurement, and construction (EPC) projects, 172, 173

EPAs, bilateral to regional, 94–95, 96t, 97–99

ethics laws, 73

European currency unit (ECU), 132

Europe and Eurozone: GDP, 4f; outward FDI flows to, 81, 81f; regional trade, 87–88; sovereign debt crisis (2009–2014), 124

European Single Market, 87

European Union: Japan, FTA negotiations with, 112, 117; Mexico and, 226n37; South Korea, FTA with, 96

Evans, Peter B., 35–36

events, chronology of, 46–51t

exchange rates, Japan's obsession with, 124–26

executive branch, focus on, 12

Executives' Meeting of East Asia-Pacific Central Banks (EMEAP), 8, 128, 141, 237n45, 242–43n99

Export-Import Bank of China, 154, 176

external pressure. *See* foreign (external) pressure (*gaiatsu*)

factional (*habatsu*) politics, 71

finance. *See* money and finance

Financial Stability Board, 123

Financial Stability Forum (FSF), 122

Financial Supervisory Agency (later Financial Services Agency, FSA), 72, 74

Fiscal Investment Loan Program (FILP, Zaisei Tōyushi), 74, 162, 166, 251n53

flying geese pattern, 16, 79

foreign aid. *See* development and foreign aid

foreign direct investments (FDI): funding for, 238n48; inward, 83–84; outward, growth of, 18, 79–82, 81f; outward and inward, 221n66, 221n68; in Thailand and Malaysia, 106

foreign economic policy, domestic institutions, and regional governance, 30–44; comparative and international political economy divide, bridging of, 31–34; conclusions on, 43–44; developmental state and capitalism debates, 34–39; introduction to, 6, 30–31; state-led liberal strategy, sources of, 39–43

foreign (external) pressure (*gaiatsu*), 13, 27, 115

foreign policy: comparative perspective on, 14–16; foreign economic policy making, approaches to, 205n2; reactivism of, 13–14. *See also* development and foreign aid

four-ministry system (*yonshō-taisei*), 102, 163

France: as coordinated market economy, 38; foreign aid levels, 166; inward FDI, 221n68; tied aid, 160

Frankel, Jeffrey, 237n37

Fraser, Bernie, 237n45

Free and Open Indo-Pacific (FOIP), 65, 152, 177, 178

free trade agreements (FTAs): in Asia-Pacific region (2008), 215n42; bilateral, prevalence of, 230n87; bilateral and regional, growth of, 88f; conclusions on, 189; domino effect of, 33–34; growing preference for, 7; Japan's use of, 94, 95t, 96–99, 118; new strategy on, 86–87; numbers of, 224n19; as PTAs, 222n1; WTO rules and, 106–7. *See also* economic partnership agreements

Free Trade Area of the Asia Pacific (FTAAP), 97–98, 111, 117

Friends of Human Security, 169

Friends of Thailand, 132

FTA Headquarters (MAFF), 228n63

Fukuda Doctrine, 157, 202n48

functional determinants, 28

G7, 52, 57, 122–23, 177–78, 223n15, 238n46

G10, 101

G20, 57, 122, 123, 137, 144, 154–55, 177–79, 212–13n18, 213n22

gang-of-four Japan revisionists, 207n25
GDP: China's, 54–55, 54f, 58, 59f;
  Japan's, 54–55, 54f, 58, 59f, 103, 110;
  of major regions and countries, 4f;
  United States, 4f, 54–55
General Agreement on Tariffs and Trade
  (GATT): GATT Round
  negotiations, 225n27; GATT/WTO
  rules, article 24, 100; impact of, 25;
  Japan's support for, 22, 91; Uruguay
  Round, 88, 90, 92. See also World
  Trade Organization
General Agreement on Trade in
  Services (GATS), 88
geoeconomics: definition of,
  197n1(intro.); description of, 2;
  domestic institutions and, 184–85;
  geoeconomic environment (since
  2013), 62–65
Germany: as coordinated market
  economy, 38; foreign aid levels, 166;
  inward FDI, 221n68; Japan's
  comparison with, 14–15; RMB and,
  148; tied aid, 160
global economic governance: challenges
  of, Japan's response to, 33–34;
  financial and monetary governance,
  121–24; global and regional economic
  orders, China's impact on, 53–58;
  multilateralism in, 33–34; trade and
  investment governance, 87–90, 88f
globalization: global and regional
  events, chronology of, 46–51t; global
  standards, promotion of, 22–23;
  global value chains, 40–41, 81;
  impact of, 27, 33; of Japan's economy,
  190
gosō sendan hōshiki (convoy system), 67,
  78, 85, 185, 190, 219–20n49
governance, foreign aid and
  development governance, 152,

155–56. See also foreign economic
  policy, domestic institutions, and
  regional governance; global
  economic governance
government-business relations: changes
  to, 67–69, 73–75; conclusions on,
  84–85, 184–85, 188–89, 193–94;
  conflicts in, 191; foreign aid and, 163,
  170–75, 187; government–big
  business power balance, 75–84, 76f,
  80f, 81f, 82–83f; government
  revenues versus corporate profits, 75,
  76f; under iron triangle system, 66;
  in late industrializer states, 35–36;
  role of, in trade and investments, 16;
  strategic coupling, 210n61
Greater Co-Prosperity Sphere, 17
Grieco, Joseph M., 26, 202n49
Grimes, William W., 195, 239n58
Group of 7, 57
Gulf Cooperation Council (GCC), 96
gunboat diplomacy (Britain), 204n74
gyōsei shidō (dominance of administrative
  guidance), 67

habatsu (factional) politics, 71
Hamanaka, Shintaro, 237–38n45,
  249n29
Hambantota International Port (Sri
  Lanka), 215n49
Hashimoto, Ryūtaro, 42, 69, 71, 74, 133,
  166
Hatakeyama, Noboru, 94
Hatoyama, Yukio, 113, 244n110,
  245n126
Hawke, Robert, 92
health care, differing styles of, 232n109
Helsinki Disciplines, 160
high network effect, emergence of,
  245n123
Higo, Masahiro, 218n34

Hirata, Keiko, 253n82

Hokkaido Takushoku Bank, 77, 133

holding companies, 77

hollowing out (*kūdōka*), 83, 221n64, 221n67

Hong Kong, bilateral agreements, 139, 224n19

House of Councillors (Upper House, Japan), electoral reform, 217n13

House of Representatives (Lower House), impact of electoral reform on, 71

housing loan companies (Jūsen), 77

Hu, Dan, 220n52

hub-and-spoke alliance system, 15, 17

Hu Jintao, 144

humanitarianism, in ODA goals, 168

human security, 8, 168–69, 182, 253n76

Human Security Network, 169

Ikenberry, G. John, 31, 204n72, 205n2

Imada, Makoto, 251n51

IMF-link (of CMI), 138–39, 140

India: as aid donor, 154; APEC membership, 227n52; ASEAN+1 FTA with, 97; GDP, 4*f*; impact of global financial crisis on, 137; Japan, bilateral agreements with, 96, 99; as Japan exports destination, 60*f*; as part of Asia-Pacific region, 192–93

Indonesia: bilateral agreements, 96, 100, 139, 140; economic outlook for, 214n28; as EMEAP member, 237–38n45; external pressures on, 36; Japan's support during financial crisis, 132, 239n63, 239n64; legal systems, foreign aid support for, 175; Samurai bonds, issuance of, 243n101

industrialization, late industrializer states, 35–36

informal diplomacy, 17

infrastructure: economic infrastructure development, 171; importance of, 174; infrastructure-building, Japan's foreign aid and, 150; infrastructure development programs, 152, 176, 189; mercantilist behaviors toward, 23; privately funded infrastructure projects, 172–73; quality infrastructure investments, 177, 178, 181–82; regional infrastructure initiative, 179–81; yen loans for, 158. *See also* Belt-and-Road Initiative

Initiative for Development in East Asia (IDEA), 171

institutions: Bretton Woods institutions, criticisms of, 58; in developmental states, 35; domestic foreign aid institutions, 162–64; geoeconomics and domestic institutions, 184–85; impact on strategy implementation, 26; informal rules, 204n71; infrastructure investments and, 181–82; institutionalization, 19, 26; institution building, in new regional geoeconomic strategy, 21–22; political institutions, changes in, 69–75; politics and governance institutions, changes in, 67–75; quality infrastructure investments, 181–82; regional, East Asia's lack of, 202n49; regional institution building, 129, 137–40, 164–65, 198n4; sticky institutions, 41. *See also* foreign economic policy, domestic institutions, and regional governance; *names of specific institutions*

insurance industry, 113, 232n109

Inter-American Development Bank, 153

international banks, rankings of, 237n37

International Bureau (BOJ), 135

International Bureau (formerly International Finance Bureau, MOF), 72

International Civil and Commercial Law Center (ICCLC), 174–75

International Conference on Financing for Development (UN), 153–54

International Cooperation Agency, 253n82

International Cooperation Bureau, 169–70

International Development Association (World Bank), 154

International Finance Bureau (IFB, Kokusai Kinyū Kyoku, Kokkinkyoku, International Bureau), 134

international investment agreements (IIAs), 88–89

International Monetary Fund (IMF): AMRO and, 139, 242n92; Asian financial crisis, actions on, 122, 133; Asian perceptions of, 25; critiques of, 58, 213n26; global financial crisis, responses to, 137; increased funding for, 213n22; influence of, 3; Japan's support for, 22; managing directors of, 233n5; RMB and, 124; Special Drawing Rights, 124, 144, 236n23, 244n112; U.S. voting shares in, 121

international political economy (IPE), bridging of divide with comparative political economy, 31–34

international relations, levels of analysis in, 30

international systems, interaction with domestic politics, 31–32

Intra-Regional Trade Promotion Talks, 91

Invest Japan Office, 83

investment. See trade and investment

investor-state dispute settlement (ISDS) mechanism, 231n94

Iran, BIT with, 230n86

Iraq, BIT with, 230n86

iron triangle (alliance capitalism) system, 66, 74, 85

Ishikawa Project, 174

Ito, Takatoshi, 241n85

JA (Japan Agricultural Cooperatives), 113

Jakarta-Bandung High-Speed Rail, 181

Japan: as advanced capitalist economy, 40; Asia-Pacific economy, strategic advantage in, 109–12; Asia's increasing importance to, 184; BITs, 224n19; BRI, response to, 177–79; capital outflows, 126; China, relationship with, 52–53, 147–49, 188, 193, 194; CJK Trilateral Investment Treaty, 107–9, 231n94; CMIM and, 138; corporations, power balance with, 75–85, 76f, 80f, 81f, 82–83f; electoral reform, 217n13; elements of transformation of, 1–2; as EMEAP member, 237–38n45; EPA partners, domestic politics and choice of, 99–101; event chronology, 46–51t; on EVSL discussion sectors, 225n31; exchange rate obsession, 124–26; FDI, outward and inward, 221n66, 221n68; financial and monetary strategy, 124–26, 126f, 127t, 128–29; financial crisis, responses to, 219n47; foreign exchange reserves, 245n121; government revenues, 76f; influence of, 65, 195; legal measures, aversion to, 202n47; market role of, 189–92; as pivotal state, 15, 34; as reactive state, 13–14, 32; regional economic

Japan (*continued*)
dynamics and, 58–62, 59*f*, 60*f*, 61*t*;
regional financial and monetary
environment and, 135–47, 136*f*, 143*f*;
in shifting Asia-Pacific balance,
52–53; strategic ambivalence, 193; in
TPP negotiations, 98, 215n48; U.S.,
relationship with, 14, 18, 21, 52; zero
sum game of leadership of, 216n8.
See also bureaucratic fragmentation

Japan, economic transformation, 66–85;
government–big business power
balance, 75–85, 76*f*, 80*f*, 81*f*, 82–83*f*;
introduction to, 7, 66–67; politics
and governance institutions, changes
in, 67–75

Japan, economy: as coordinated market
economy, 38; dual economy of, 22;
economic "miracle," debate over
source of, 207n25; economic
stagnation, 3; GDP, 4*f*; regional
GDP, share of, 58, 59*f*; world GDP,
share of, 54–55, 54*f*

Japan, foreign aid: as aid superpower,
158, 159*t*, 160–62, 161*f*; domestic
foreign aid institutions, 162–64;
foreign aid recipients, 248n26;
foreign aid superpower, rise to,
156–58, 159*t*, 160–65, 161*f*; funding
sources for, 251n53

Japan, regional geoeconomic strategy,
10–29; alternative explanations of,
27–29; conclusions on, 184–89;
defining of, 11–13; early stage of,
99–106; emergence of, 93–94, 95*t*,
96–99; foreign policy, comparative
perspective on, 14–16; foreign policy
since 1945, characterization of,
13–14; general characteristics, 20–23;
geoeconomics and domestic
institutions and, 184–85;

implementation paths, diversity of,
185–89; introduction to, 5–6, 10–11;
in late 2010s, 192–94; old-style
regional geoeconomic strategy,
16–20; policy implementation,
varying paths of, 23–24, 24*t*; regional
geoeconomic strategy, defining,
11–13; research questions on, 24–27;
shifts in, 29, 30, 33, 129; sources of,
39–43; start of, 129–35; summary
of, 24*t*. *See also* Asia-Pacific,
geoeconomics of; development and
foreign aid; money and finance;
state-led regional strategy; trade and
investment

Japan, trade: ASEAN+1 FTA with, 97;
China-Japan-Korea Free Trade
Agreement, 86, 112, 185; currency
denominations of foreign trade, by
region, 127*t*; export destinations, 60,
60*f*; FTAs and, 222n1, 228n57;
Japan-ASEAN Preferential Trade
Arrangements, 91; trade
multilateralism, belief in, 224n20;
trade strategy (prior to late 1990s),
90–91; U.S., trade with, 211n2

Japan Agricultural Cooperatives (JA), 113

Japan-ASEAN Comprehensive
Economic Partnership Agreement
(JACEAP), 22, 229–30n75

Japan Bank for International
Cooperation (JBIC): businesses'
reliance on, 181; changes to, under
Abe, 178; establishment of, 240n75;
functions of, 141; Jakarta-Bandung
High-Speed Rail and, 181; JBIC
Law, changes to, 178; local-currency
bonds, 141, 243n101; non-ODA
lending by, 170; role of, 135

Japan Business Federation. *See*
Keidanren

Japan Development Bank, 74
Japanese Agricultural Cooperatives, 115
Japanese Government Bonds, 79, 134
Japan Export Import Bank, 74, 240n75
Japan External Trade Organization
  (JETRO), 83, 94, 104
Japan Finance Corporation (JFC), 240n75
Japan International Cooperation Agency
  (JICA), 12, 135, 141, 163, 170–71,
  173, 181, 240n75
Japan Investment Council, 83
Japan Medical Association, 113
Japan Overseas Cooperation Volunteers
  (JOCV), 162
Japan Premium (risk premium), 77,
  219n46
Japan-Singapore Economic Partnership
  Agreement, 96
Japan-Southeast Asia PTA, 91
Jiang, Zemin, 53
Jin Liqun, 155, 180
Joint Committee on Economic
  Cooperation and Infrastructure, 169
Joko Widodo (Jokowi), 181
Jūsen (housing loan companies), 77

Kabashima, Ikuo, 217–18n23
Kalinowski, Thomas, 36
Kamath, K. V., 155
Kan, Naoto, 112–13, 232n107
Katzenstein, Peter J., 31, 259n11
Kawai, Masahiro, 132, 164, 251n54,
  257n135
Kazakhstan, BIT with, 230n86
Keidanren (Japan Business Federation):
  on AIIB, 181; FTA strategy, support
  for, 105; industry associations,
  support for, 220n56; influence of,
  103; on International Cooperation
  Agency, 253n82; ODA policy,
  recommendations on, 168; policy

performance grading by, 229n66;
  political contributions, 79, 80f; role
  of, 85; TPP, support for, 114. See also
  businesses
keiretsu (business conglomerates) system,
  78, 79
keizai kyōryoku (economic cooperation),
  150, 157
Kim Dae-Jung, 108, 230n84
Kim Jim Yong, 180
Kimura, Hidemi, 174, 255n104
Kobe earthquake, 251n51
Kobe Research Group, 145
Koizumi, Junichirō: economic
  ministries and, 42; foreign aid under,
  171; FTAs, actions on, 104; inward
  investments, concern with, 83;
  popularity, 217–18n23; reforms
  under, 69, 70, 71, 72–73, 102
kokka kōmuin rinri hō (National Ethics
  Law for Central Government Public
  Servants, 2000), 73
Korea. See South Korea
Korea-U.S. FTA (KORUS), 96, 215n42
Kotera, Akira, 230n87
kūdōka (hollowing out), 83, 221n64,
  221n67
Kume, Ikuo, 68, 185
Kuroda, Haruhiko, 128, 132, 164, 252n60
Kuwait, BIT with, 230n86

Labor Standards Laws, 78
Lake, David A., 31, 206n12
Lancaster, Carol, 254n85
Laos: BIT with, 230n86; legal systems,
  foreign aid support for, 175
lattice regionalism, 226n41
lattice regionalism, 226n41
Lee, Jaemin, 231n94
legal systems, foreign aid support for, 174
legislators. See politics

Lehman Brothers, 56, 123, 135–36
Liberal Democratic Party (LDP): agricultural sector and, 100; on AIIB membership, 179; changes in power of, 70; declining influence over bureaucrats, 68–69; instability of, 69–70; Keidanren contributions to, 79, 80f, 220n56; as majority party in the Diet, 113–14; ODA Reform Working Group, 168
liberal institutionalism, 204n72. *See also* state-led regional strategy
liberal market economy (LME) model, 38
Lincoln, Edward, 252n68
Lipscy, Phillip Y., 28, 145, 187
Liu Kun, 149
Long-Term Credit Bank of Japan, 219n45
Long-Term Trust Bank, 133
Lower House (House of Representatives), impact of electoral reform on, 71

Macroeconomic Research Office (AMRO, ASEAN), 129, 139, 186, 196, 242n92
Mahathir bin Mohamed, 97
Malaysia: bilateral currency swap agreements, 139; economy, 61, 214n28; as EMEAP member, 237–38n45; investment protection in, 106; Japan, bilateral agreements with, 96; Japan's support during financial crisis, 239n64; proposal for APEC East Asian Economic Caucus, 225n27; RMB and, 148; Samurai bonds, issuance of, 243n109; tariff liberalization, 232n104
Manila Framework Group, 133
manufacturing sector, 79–81, 81f, 82–83f, 83–84, 114

maritime disputes, 4
markets, Japan's role in, 189–92
Mastanduno, Michael, 31
Master Plan on Connectivity (ASEAN), 165
McKinnon, Ronald, 234n9
Medical Association, 232n109
megabanks, 78, 120, 136, 148, 220n51, 233n2
mercantilism, 1, 11, 14, 84. *See also* embedded mercantilism
Mexico: FTAs, 96, 189, 226n37, 229n73, 230n83; Japan, bilateral agreements with, 99–100, 101, 104; tariff liberalization, 232n104
middle-income traps, 208n38
Millennium Development Goals (MDGs), 152, 153–54, 155, 247n12
Minister Conference for the Economic Development of Southeast Asia, 17
Ministry of Agriculture, Forestry, and Fisheries (MAFF), 72, 74, 100, 101, 102, 228n63
Ministry of Economy, Trade, and Industry (METI): advisory councils, 74; on AIIB, 180; CEPEA and, 97; Economic Partnership Division, 228n63; EPA negotiations, involvement in, 102; foreign aid management by, 162; "Global Economic Strategy," 165; hollowing out, survey on, 221n67; Japan–ASEAN Comprehensive Economic Partnership agreement, promotion of, 229–30n75; PPP modality and, 172; on TPP, 111. *See also* Ministry of International Trade and Industry
Ministry of the Environment, 72
Ministry of Finance (MOF): advisory councils, 74; on AIIB, 180; Bank of Japan's policy independence from,

237n44; dominance of, 43; embedded mercantilism of policies of, 128; EPA negotiations, involvement in, 102; as foreign aid coordinator, 162, 169–70; on loan repayments, 252n69; MOFA versus, 252n57; new geoeconomic strategy, impact on, 188; New Miyazawa Initiative, 141; regional financial strategy and, 134–35; restructuring of, 72, 120; World Bank, challenges to, 132

Ministry of Foreign Affairs (MOFA): on AIIB, 180; bilateralist diplomacy of, 18; dominance of, 43; EPA negotiations, involvement in, 102; foreign aid management, 162; FTA/EPA Office, 228n63; as funding source, 250n47, 251n48; lack of reforms to, 71; lack of support base, 252n57; new geoeconomic strategy, impact on, 188; NGOs, funding for, 161–62

Ministry of International Trade and Industry (MITI): APEC and, 92, 117; on hollowing out, 221n64; MOFA versus, 252n57; Nippon Export and Investment Insurance, 240n75; reforms to, 71; Trade Policy Bureau, 224–25n25. *See also* Ministry of Economy, Trade, and Industry

Ministry of Justice, International Cooperation Department, 175

Ministry of Posts and Telecommunication, 250–51n47

Ministry of Trade (South Korea), 94

Mitsubishi UFJ (previously Bank of Tokyo-Mitsubishi), 148–49

mixed-member majoritarian (MMM) electoral system, 71

Mizuho Bank, 148–49

Mizuho Financial Group, 229n67

Mochizuki, Mike, 14

modularization in supply chains, 222n72

money and finance, 119–49; conclusions on, 186; financial reforms, 76–78; financial repression, concept of, 234n9; global financial and monetary governance, evolution of, 121–24; global financial crisis (2008–2009), impact of, 3, 45–46, 56–58, 62, 63, 122–24, 135–37; introduction to, 7–8, 119–21; Japan-led regional financial and monetary environment, 135–47, 136*f*, 143*f*; Japan's internal financial crises, 119–20, 133, 219n45; Japan's old-style strategy, 124–26, 126*f*, 127*t*, 128–29; path to, 23–24, 24*t*; regional financial and monetary cooperation, 129–32, 238n49; regional financial and monetary strategy, sudden shift in, 132–35; RMB, internationalization of, 147–49; state-led liberal strategy, start of, 129–35; U.S. as dominant power in, 121

money and finance, Asian financial crisis (1997–1998): impact of, 7–8, 21, 36, 45, 60–61, 94, 186; influence on Japan's foreign aid, 164; Japan's response to, 132; trigger for, 131

Mongolia: APEC membership, 227n52; bilateral agreements, 99, 224n19; legal systems, foreign aid support for, 175

Monterrey Consensus, 154

Moravcsik, Andrew, 13

Mori, Yoshirō, 72

Mozambique, BIT with, 230n86

Multilateral Agreement on Investment (MAI), 88, 108

multilateral development banks (MDBs), 64, 153, 155. *See also* Asian Development Bank multilateral investment treaties, 230n87

Muramatsu, Michio, 68, 69, 185, 216n8

Myanmar: BIT with, 230n86; Japan's foreign aid to, 172; legal system development support, 255n109

Naím, Moisés, 248n17

Nakao, Takehiko, 180

Nakasone, Yasuhiro, 244n110

Naoi, Megumi, 32, 101

narrow economic interests, 28–29

National Administration Organization Act, 73–74

National Ethics Law for Central Government Public Servants (*kokka kōmuin rinri hō*, 2000), 73

National Public Service Act (rev. 2007), 74

Nemoto, Yōichi, 139

neoliberalism, 2, 57, 71

neomercantilism, 1, 16

New Development Bank (NDB, BRICS Development Bank), 64, 124, 155

New International Financial Architecture, 122, 235n14

New Japan International Cooperation Agency (New JICA), 170, 240n75

New Miyazawa Initiative, 141, 166, 170, 239n64, 252n68

New ODA Charter, 168

"New Roadmap" and "New Roadmap Plus" (ABMI), 142

New Zealand: ASEAN+1 FTA with, 97; as EMEAP member, 237–38n45; Japan, bilateral agreements with, 101; as liberal market economy, 38; P-4 and, 89; as part of Asia-Pacific region, 192–93; tariff liberalization, 232n104

NGO Assistance Division (MOFA), 162

Nihon keizai shimbun (newspaper), editorial on CJK treaty, 109

Nikai, Toshihiro, 165

Nippon Credit Bank, 219n45

Nippon Export and Investment Insurance (NEXI), 72, 135, 141, 240n75

Nomura Group, 135–36

nongovernmental organizations (NGOs), foreign aid projects and, 161–62

nonliberal capitalism, 38

nonperforming loan (NPL) problem, 72, 77, 84, 133

nonregular workers, 220n54

noodle bowl phenomenon, 96, 104, 165

Nordic countries, as coordinated market economy, 38

norm building and pursuit of national economic interest, 166, 167*f*, 168–70

North America, outward FDI flows to, 81, 81*f*

North American Free Trade Agreement (NAFTA), 25, 87, 89, 226n37

Nye-Armitage Report, 53

Oatley, Thomas, 32

Obama administration: AIIB and, 152; Asia, efforts in, 51; rebalancing strategy, 3, 53; TPP and, 63–64, 98, 110, 116, 257n132

Obuchi, Keizō, 96, 168–69

Oceania, outward FDI flows to, 81*f*

ODA Taikō, 68

Office of Regional Economic Integration (OREI, ADB), 132, 164

official development assistance (ODA): definition of, 246n1; levels of, 153, 153*f*, 161, 166, 170, 252–53n69; policies on, 168–70; pressures to retie, 254n85; purposes of, 157;

successes of, 158; as tied aid, 157–58; top donors, 158, 159*t*
Ogata, Sadako, 168, 253n76
Ogura, Masanobu, 244n117
Okimoto, Daniel, 252n57
Okuda, Hiroshi, 229n66
old-style foreign aid strategy, 156–58, 159*t*, 160–65, 161*f*, 183
old-style monetary and financial strategy, 125
old-style regional geoeconomic strategy, 16–20, 39
old-style regional trade and investment strategy, 90–93
Oman, BIT with, 230n86
Open Door Policy (China), 55
open economy politics (OEP), 206n12
open regionalism, 19
optimum currency areas (OCAs), 145, 244n117
Organisation for Economic Co-operation and Development (OECD), 88, 151, 160
Organization for Asian Economic Cooperation, 91
ORIX Leasing Malaysia Berhad, 243n101
Other Official Flows (OOF), 246n1
Overseas Economic Cooperation Council, 169
Overseas Economic Cooperation Fund (OECF), 160, 163, 240n75
overseas production, 81, 82–83*f*, 83
Oyane, Satoshi, 224n20, 224n23, 227n46
Ozawa, Ichirō, 70

P. T. Summit Oto Finance company, 243n101
Pacific Basin Economic Council (PBEC), 91
Pacific Economic Cooperation Council (PECC), 91

Pacific Trade and Development Conference (PAFTAD), 91
Pakistan, Japan's BIT with, 224n19
Pan Asian Bond Index Fund (PAIF), 242–43n99
Papua New Guinea, BIT with, 230n86
Paris Agenda, 246–47n2
Partnership for Quality Infrastructure (PQI), 178
Patrick, Hugh, 234n9
payoff system (deposit protection), 77
Pekkanen, Robert, 251n51
Pempel, T. J., 17, 19
People's Bank of China, 139, 147, 242n93
Peru: Japan, bilateral agreements with, 99–100; tariff liberalization, 232n104
P-4 (Trans-Pacific Strategic Economic Partnership Agreement), 89, 112
Philippines: bilateral agreements, 96, 107, 140; as EMEAP member, 237–38n45; Japan's foreign aid to, 172, 239n64; Samurai bonds, issuance of, 243n101
Phillips, Nicola, 31
Ping, Lee Poh, 170
pivotal states, 15, 34, 110, 111, 200n25
Plaza Accord, 18, 52, 79, 119, 125, 223n15
Polanyi, Karl, 189
policy diffusion, 9, 15, 34, 195
policy implementation, varying paths of, 23–24
Policy Research Institute, 145, 245n122
politics: comparative and international political economies, 31–34; Keidanren's political contributions, 79, 80*f*; political versus bureaucratic power, 42–43; politician-bureaucratic scrummage leadership, 216n8; politicians, changing power balance with bureaucrats, 68–69, 190; politics

politics (*continued*)

    and governance institutions, changes
        in, 67–75. *See also* Democratic Party
        of Japan/Democratic Party; Liberal
        Democratic Party; *names of individual
        politicians*
populism, rise of, 65
Postal Life Insurance, 74, 232n109
Postal Savings, 74
Post Savings Bank, 251n53
preferential trade agreements (PTAs), 25,
    222n1
private–public sector balance, 76f
production networks, 40–41, 81, 82–83f,
    83, 84, 184, 188
public opinion, on foreign aid, 166,
    167f
public-private partnership (PPP)
    arrangements, 8, 151–52, 171–73,
    181–82, 191, 254n90
Puchala, Donald, 260n18
Putnam, Robert D., 31

Ravenhill, John, 21
region, fluidity of concept of, 226n45
Regional Comprehensive Economic
    Partnership (RCEP, formerly
    CEPEA), 86, 111, 117, 185
Regional Cooperation and Integration
    (RCI) strategy (ADB), 165
Regional Economic Monitoring Unit
    (REMU), 164
regional economic orders. *See* global
    economic governance
Regional Economic Partnership
    Division (MOFA), 228n63
Regional Financial Cooperation
    Division (MOF), 135
regional geoeconomic strategies, 2, 12,
    23, 24t, 28. *See also* Japan, regional
    geoeconomic strategy

regionalism: debate over sources of,
    227n51; factors influencing, 28; in
    new regional geoeconomic strategy,
    20–21, 137; regional currency
    initiatives, 145–46; regional
    economic governance, Japan's focus
    on, 2; regional economic strategy, 23,
    24t; regional governance and, future
    of, 194–96; regionalization, 20;
    regional monetary union, 131–32,
    145; regional players, impact of
    interests of, 28; regional production
    networks, 84; regional trade
    agreements (RTAs), 34; trend toward
    (during 1990s), 27
Regional Settlement Intermediary
    (RSI), 142
relational foreign pressures, 32
renminbi (RMB): expansion of use of,
    8; internationalization of, 55, 123–24,
    130, 139, 147–49; Japan's support for,
    245n126; use in trade, 246n130
request-base foreign aid, 66–67
Research Institute of Economic,
    Trade, and Industry (RIETI), 145,
    245n122
research questions, 24–27
Revised National Public Service Act,
    218–19n36
RMB Qualified Foreign Institutional
    Investor (RQFII) status, 148
Rosenbluth, Frances McCall, 32, 71
Rozman, Gilbert, 202n49
Ruggie, John Gerard, 19
rule making: CMIM and, 138–39;
    conclusions on, 186; formal rules, in
    new regional geoeconomic strategy,
    21–22, 26; informal rules and
    relations, 17, 18–19; in investment,
    107–9; limited nature of, 43; regional
    geoeconomic strategy and, 194; TPP

negotiations and, 117; as trade and investment strategy, 106–9

rules of origin, 97, 104, 115, 226n42, 226n43

Russia: impact of global financial crisis on, 137; Japan's BIT with, 224n19

Sakakibara, Eisuke, 132

Samurai bonds, 141, 143, 143*f*, 243n101, 243n109

sanmi ittai (development trinity) approach, 39, 67, 150, 189

Saudi Arabia, BIT with, 230n86

Schaede, Ulrike, 222n72

Schoppa, Leonard J., 219–20n49

seaweed, 96, 228n57

second image reversed approach, 32

sectionalism. *See* bureaucratic fragmentation

security: development, connection with, 152; human security, 168–69

Sen, Amartya, 168

Senkaku/Diaoyutai Islands dispute, 242n94, 245n126

Seoul Development Consensus for Shared Growth, 154–55

shingi-kai (advisory council) system, 73–74, 185, 218n28

Silk Road Fund, 256n118

Singapore: bilateral agreements, 55, 89, 96, 100, 107, 139, 140; as EMEAP member, 237–38n45; financial sector, liberalization in, 62; P-4 and, 89; tariff liberalization, 232n104

Singapore issues, 22, 88, 106, 204n73, 223n6

Single European Act, 92

single nontransferable vote (SNTV) electoral system, 71

Sinicization (*chūgoku-ka*), of Japanese foreign economic policy, 259n11

social compensation, 41

socialist market economy model (China), 55

Socialist Party, 70

social sector, as ODA target, 171

society-centered approaches to foreign economic policy, 205n2

Southeast Asia, as Japan exports destination, 60*f*

South Korea: as aid donor, 154; ASEAN+1 FTA with, 97; bilateral currency swap agreements, 140; BIT with, 230n86; Chile, FTA with, 104; China-Japan-Korea Free Trade Agreement, 86, 112, 185; CJK Trilateral Investment Treaty, 107–9, 231n94; CMIM and, 138; currency swap agreement with, 242n94, 242n95; developmental mindset of, 37; as EMEAP member, 237–38n45; external pressures on, 36; foreign aid levels, 166; foreign exchange reserves, 245n121; GDP, 4*f*; Japan, bilateral agreements with, 96, 108, 228n57; Japan, trade war with, 259n12; as Japan exports destination, 60*f*; Japan's support during financial crisis, 132, 239n63, 239n64; Korea--U.S. FTA, 215n42; as late industrializer state, 35; U.S., FTA with, 55, 89, 215n42

Special Drawing Rights (SDRs), 124, 144, 236n23, 244n112

special-interest policy tribe (*zoku*) politics, 71

Special Terms of Economic Partnership (STEP), 171, 173

Sri Lanka: Chinese investments in, 215n49; Japan's BIT with, 224n19 state-led regional strategy: conclusions on, 43–44, 190–91; general characteristics of, 20–23; implementation, 5–6, 23–24, 24t; shift to, 30; sources of, 39–43; start of, 129–35; in trade and investment, early stage of, 99–106; in trade and investment, emergence of, 93–94, 95t, 96–99

state-owned enterprises (SOEs), 38, 55, 61, 98, 111, 215n47

states: regional order, support for, 12; retreat of, under globalization, 36; role in political economy, 31; state-centered approaches to foreign economic policy, 205n2. *See also* government-business relations

State Street Global Advisors, 243n99

Steel, Gill, 217–18n23

Stone, Randall W., 204n71

strategic coupling, definition of, 210n61

structural foreign pressures, 32

Structural Impediment Initiative (SII) talks, 52, 77, 90

Stubbs, Richard, 37

Sugawara, Junichi, 232n107

supply chains: expansion of, 184; FTAs supporting, 97; global value chains, 40–41, 81; importance of, 84, 222n72; investment protection and, 106; TPP and, 114

sustainable development goals (SDGs), 155, 176

Suzuki, Muneo, 253n70

Swaine, Michael D., 110

Sweijs, Tim, 200n25

Switzerland, bilateral agreements, 96, 99, 101

system-centered approaches to foreign economic policy, 205n2

Tachiki, Dennis, 40

Tadokoro, Masayuki, 238n46

Taiwan: as aid donor, 154; foreign aid levels, 166; as late industrializer state, 35

Takagi, Shinji, 251n54

tariff liberalization, 100, 112, 232n104

tatewari gyōsei (vertical compartmentalization), 42

technology firms, 84

Terada, Takashi, 224n23, 226n44, 238n51

Thailand: as aid donor, 154; Asian bond market, idea for, 140; bilateral currency swap agreements, 139, 140; currency crisis (1997), 122, 131, 132, 239n62, 239n63, 239n64; as EMEAP member, 237–38n45; external pressures on, 36; investment protection in, 106; Japan, bilateral agreements with, 96, 107; Japan's GDP, influence on, 103; JBIC local-currency bonds, 243n101; RMB and, 148

Thaksin Shinawatra, 140

Thies, Michael F., 32, 71

three arrows (of Abenomics), 115

Tiananmen Square Incident, 52

tied aid, 150, 157–58, 160–61, 161f, 170, 172, 250n40

Todo, Yasuyuki, 174, 255n104

Tokyo, as financial center, 120, 128, 133–34

TPP. *See* Trans-Pacific Partnership

trade and investment, 86–118; Asia, intraregional trade in, 60, 61f; China-Japan, 53; conclusions on, 117–18, 185–86; currency denominations of foreign trade, by region, 127t; EPA investment protection, 106; FTA utilization for exports, 105*t*; global trade and investment governance, evolution of, 87–90, 88*f*; implementation paths, 185–89; introduction to, 7, 86–87; investment rules and tripartite investment treaty, 107–9; Japan, investment opportunities in, 40; Japan's export destinations, 60, 60*f*; Japan's trade surplus, 39, 124–25; liberalization of, 87, 92–93; multilateral investment agreements, push for, 88; old-style regional trade and investment strategy, 90–93; path to, 23, 24*t*; rule making as strategy for, 106–9; shift from multilateralism to regional and bilateral arrangements, 87; South Korea-Japan trade war, 259n12; state-led liberal strategy in, early stage of, 99–106; state-led liberal strategy in, emergence of, 93–94, 95*t*, 96–99; trade multilateralism, 222n3, 224n20; ultimate instrument of strategy for, 109–17; U.S.–China trade war, 56, 65; U.S.-Japan, 18, 52, 65, 90–91. *See also* Asia-Pacific Economic Cooperation; China, trade; Japan, trade; United States, trade

Trade Policy Bureau (MITI), 224–25n25

transformation of Japanese political economy. *See* Japan, economic transformation

Trans-Pacific Partnership (TPP): ASEAN versus, 193; China as shadow negotiator of, 215n47; Comprehensive and Progressive Agreement for, 98, 116–17, 186, 194, 233n117; emergence of, 25, 62–63, 112–15; Japan's pursuit of, 2, 23, 113, 184, 185, 188; Japan's strategic advantage and, 109–12; Kan's interest in, 112–13; member countries, 227n47; mentioned, 22, 86; negotiations for, 89, 98; perceptions of, 63–64; ratification of, 233n116; on SOEs, 55; tariff liberalization under, 112, 232n104; TPP-11, 7; TPP Task Force, 103; U.S. withdrawal from, 65, 98, 116, 186, 194

Trans-Pacific Strategic Economic Partnership Agreement (P-4), 89, 112

Trilateral Joint Research Project, 109

Tri Petch Isuzu Co., 243n101

Trump, Donald: America First policy, 192; China, impact of economic attack on, 149; on China's trade practices, 56; economic priorities of, 65; Free and Open Indo-Pacific (FOIP) initiatives, 152; TPP, withdrawal from, 65, 98, 116, 186, 194; TPP and, 3, 7; on U.S.-Japan trade, 211n2; U.S.'s international role under, 193

Tsuchiyama, Jitsuo, 14

Turkey, Japan's BIT with, 224n19

Ukraine, BIT with, 230n86

unilateralism, 201n43

United Kingdom. *See* Britain

United Nations: Development Program, 168; International Conference on Financing for Development, 153–54; Millennium Development Goals, 152, 153–54, 155, 247n12; 2030 Agenda, 155

United States: ADB and, 157; AIIB and, 152, 179, 256n119, 257n132, 258n137; Asia, presence in, 3, 45, 51; China, conflict with, 1, 5, 6–7, 34, 53; financial and monetary dominance, 121; foreign aid levels, 166; foreign economic policy making by, 205n2;

United States (*continued*)

Great Recession, 123; hegemony of, in Europe versus in Asia, 15; international role of, under Trump, 193; inward FDI, 221n68; Japan, bilateralism with, 18, 101; Japan, relationship with, 21, 52; liberalization pressure on Japan, softening of, 224n17; as liberal market economy, 38; as source of global financial crisis, 56; subprime mortgage crisis, 63; tariff liberalization, 232n104; tied aid, 160; in TPP negotiations, 215n48; world GDP, share of, 54–55, 54*f. See also* U.S. dollar

United States, trade: bilateral trade agreements, 55, 89, 96, 215n42; China, trade war with, 56, 65, 192, 194; China, trade with, 224n17; Japan, trade with, 18, 52, 65, 90–91, 103, 211n2; as Japan exports destination, 60*f*; regional trade, 87–88; U.S.-Canada Free Trade Agreement, 92

Upper House (House of Councillors, Japan), electoral reform, 217n13

Uruguay, BIT with, 230n86

Uruguay Round (GATT), 88, 90, 92

U.S. dollar: Asian dependence on, 119, 134, 143–44, 145–46, 149; dominance of, 119, 121, 123; yen-dollar exchange rate, 125, 126*f*

U.S.-Japan Textile Negotiations, 52

Uzbekistan: BIT with, 230n86; legal systems, foreign aid support for, 175

vanguard effect (of Japanese aid), 174–75

vertical compartmentalization (*tatewari gyōsei*), 42

Vietnam: bilateral EPA with, 222n2; BIT with, 230n86; economic growth,

sources of, 61; Japan, bilateral agreements with, 96; Japan's support during financial crisis, 239n64; legal systems, foreign aid support for, 174, 175, 187; tariff liberalization, 232n104

Vogel, Steven K., 38–39, 189–90

Voluntary Export Restraints measure, 90

Wade, Robert, 40

Wan, Ming, 252n58

War on Terror, 3, 14, 53, 154

war reparations, 156

Washington Consensus model, 37, 55, 57, 65, 121, 123

Watanabe, Shingo, 244n117

Wei Benhua, 139

West Germany, relationship with U.S., 15

White Paper on International Economy and Trade (METI), 83

Williamson, John, 121

Worker Dispatching Act, 78

World Bank: AIIB, influence on, 257n132; BRI size versus, 177; infrastructure investments by, 153; International Development Association, 154; Japan's support for, 22; MOF's challenges to, 132; PPP, definition of, 254n90; public-private partnership arrangements, 152; U.S. voting shares in, 121

World Trade Organization (WTO): China's accession to, 3; establishment of, 88, 225n27; on FTAs, 222n1; GATT/WTO rules, article 24, 100; impact of, 25; ineffectiveness of, 57; Japan, influence on, 224n17; Japan's support for, 22, 91; rules of origin, definition of, 226n42; Singapore issues, consideration of, 223n6;

WTO-Plus rules, 106–7. *See also* General Agreement on Tariffs and Trade

Xi Jinping, 63, 64, 152, 176, 192

Yamagata, Tatsufumi, 176
Yamaichi Securities, 77
yen: appreciation in value of, 52, 79, 119, 136; as foreign exchange reserve currency, 244n113; internationalization of, 123, 126, 128, 131, 134, 143–45, 191; rise of, 125–26, 126f, 128; RMB currency swap agreements, 148; *yen-daka* (yen appreciation, strong yen) episodes, 79, 83, 126, 184; yen-dollar exchange rate, 125, 126f

Yeung, Henry Wai-chung, 210n61
yonshō-taisei (four-ministry system), 102, 163
Yoshida Doctrine, 13
Yoshimatsu, Hidetaka, 84, 223n10
Yudhoyono (Indonesian president), 181

Zhou Xiaochuan, 144, 236n23
zoku (special-interest policy tribe) politics, 71

CONTEMPORARY ASIA IN THE WORLD
David C. Kang and Victor D. Cha, Editors

Beyond the Final Score: The Politics of Sport in Asia, Victor D. Cha, 2008

The Power of the Internet in China: Citizen Activism Online, Guobin Yang, 2009

China and India: Prospects for Peace, Jonathan Holslag, 2010

India, Pakistan, and the Bomb: Debating Nuclear Stability in South Asia, Šumit Ganguly and S. Paul Kapur, 2010

Living with the Dragon: How the American Public Views the Rise of China, Benjamin I. Page and Tao Xie, 2010

East Asia Before the West: Five Centuries of Trade and Tribute, David C. Kang, 2010

Harmony and War: Confucian Culture and Chinese Power Politics, Yuan-kang Wang, 2011

Strong Society, Smart State: The Rise of Public Opinion in China's Japan Policy, James Reilly, 2012

Asia's Space Race: National Motivations, Regional Rivalries, and International Risks, James Clay Moltz, 2012

Never Forget National Humiliation: Historical Memory in Chinese Politics and Foreign Relations, Zheng Wang, 2012

Green Innovation in China: China's Wind Power Industry and the Global Transition to a Low-Carbon Economy, Joanna I. Lewis, 2013

The Great Kantō Earthquake and the Chimera of National Reconstruction in Japan, J. Charles Schencking, 2013

Security and Profit in China's Energy Policy: Hedging Against Risk, Øystein Tunsjø, 2013

Return of the Dragon: Rising China and Regional Security, Denny Roy, 2013

Contemporary Japanese Politics: Institutional Changes and Power Shifts, Tomohito Shinoda, 2013

Contentious Activism and Inter-Korean Relations, Danielle L. Chubb, 2014

Dams and Development in China: The Moral Economy of Water and Power, Bryan Tilt, 2014

Marching Through Suffering: Loss and Survival in North Korea, Sandra Fahy, 2015

The Japan–South Korea Identity Clash: East Asian Security and the United States, Brad Glosserman and Scott A. Snyder, 2015

Nation at Play: A History of Sport in India, Ronojoy Sen, 2015

The China Boom: Why China Will Not Rule the World, Ho-fung Hung, 2015

Japan's Security Renaissance: New Policies and Politics for the Twenty-First Century, Andrew L. Oros, 2017

Japan, South Korea, and the United States Nuclear Umbrella: Deterrence After the Cold War, Terrence Roehrig, 2017

GMO China: How Global Debates Transformed China's Agricultural Biotechnology Policies, Cong Cao, 2018

Dying for Rights: Putting North Korea's Human Rights Abuses on the Record, Sandra Fahy, 2019